OTHER BOOKS BY DEE BROWN

The Year of the Century: 1876
The Galvanized Yankees
Action at Beecher Island
Grierson's Raid
The Girl from Fort Wicked
Pawnee, Blackfoot and Cheyenne;
    History and Folklore of the Plains,
    from the Writings of George Bird Grinnell
Fort Phil Kearny: an American Saga
The Gentle Tamers
The Bold Cavaliers
Yellowhorse
Creek Mary's Blood
Hear that Lonesome Whistle Blow
Killdeer Mountain
Conspiracy of Knaves
Dee Brown's Folktales of the Native American

BURY MY HEART AT WOUNDED KNEE

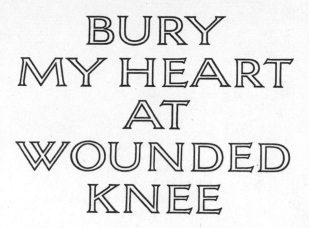

BURY MY HEART AT WOUNDED KNEE

An Indian History of the American West

by DEE BROWN

AN OWL BOOK
HENRY HOLT AND COMPANY
New York

Henry Holt and Company, LLC
Publishers since 1866
115 West 18th Street
New York, New York 10011

Henry Holt® is a registered trademark
of Henry Holt and Company, LLC.

Library of Congress Cataloging-in-Publication Data
Brown, Dee Alexander.
Bury my heart at Wounded Knee : an Indian history
of the American West / by Dee Brown.
p. cm.
Includes bibliographical references and index.
ISBN 0-8050-6634-9 (hb)—ISBN 0-8050-6669-1 (pb)
1. Indians of North America—Wars—West (U.S.)
2. Indians of North America—West (U.S.)—History.
3. West (U.S.)—History. I. Title.
E81.B75   2001
978'.00497—dc21   00-040958

Henry Holt books are available for special promotions and
premiums. For details contact: Director, Special Markets.

First published in hardcover in 1971 by
Holt, Rinehart and Winston

Thirtieth Anniversary Edition 2001

Designed by Winston Potter

Printed in the United States of America
7 9 10 8

Grateful acknowledgment is made to Holt, Rinehart and Winston, Inc.,
for permission to reprint the lines from "American Names" from
Ballads and Poems by Stephen Vincent Benét. Copyright © 1931 by
Stephen Vincent Benét. Copyright © 1959 by Rosemary Carr Benét.

For
Nicolas Brave Wolf

Contents

List of Illustrations

Chapter Eighteen

Chapter Nineteen

Preface

AN ancient tradition tells us that the interval between the birth of the parents and the arrival of their first offspring averages thirty years. We call that a generation. Thirty years ago, early in 1971, this book was born. And so now it is beginning its second generation.

As the first generation ends, it is almost a cliché to say that enormous changes have occurred during the time that has passed. Yet vast changes certainly have affected the present-day descendants of the old tribal prophets whose stories are told in these pages.

During the past generation, some tribal reservations have prospered, others have not. There are now, and probably always will be, disagreements within tribes as to the direction their people should take. In spite of the many personal frustrations and difficulties young seekers of knowledge experience, it is no longer unusual to meet American-Indian lawyers, physicians, college professors, computer specialists, artists, writers, or members of almost any other profession or trade. Yet on some reservations there is still a shortage of proper places in which to live. And the county with the deepest poverty in the United States is still a tribal reservation.

Judging from letters I have received through the years, the readers who have given life to this book come from almost all the hundred or so ethnic groups that comprise this unique and awesome place called America. Small though the comparative number of American Indians is, almost all other Americans seem to have an earnest fascination for their history, their arts and literature, their attitude toward the natural world, and their philosophy of human existence.

And this wide interest exists beyond the borders of America into the lands of other people and other cultures. Name a small nation, one whose people have a history of past injustices and oppression, and this book will likely be in print there.

We rarely know the full power of words, in print or spoken. It
is my hope that time has not dulled the words herein and that
they will continue through the coming generation to be as true
and direct as I originally meant them to be.

DEE BROWN
in the year 2000

Introduction

SINCE the exploratory journey of Lewis and Clark to the Pacific Coast early in the nineteenth century, the number of published accounts describing the "opening" of the American West has risen into the thousands. The greatest concentration of recorded experience and observation came out of the thirty-year span between 1860 and 1890—the period covered by this book. It was an incredible era of violence, greed, audacity, sentimentality, undirected exuberance, and an almost reverential attitude toward the ideal of personal freedom for those who already had it.

During that time the culture and civilization of the American Indian was destroyed, and out of that time came virtually all the great myths of the American West—tales of fur traders, mountain men, steamboat pilots, goldseekers, gamblers, gunmen, cavalrymen, cowboys, harlots, missionaries, schoolmarms, and homesteaders. Only occasionally was the voice of an Indian heard, and then more often than not it was recorded by the pen of a white man. The Indian was the dark menace of the myths, and even if he had known how to write in English, where would he have found a printer or a publisher?

Yet they are not all lost, those Indian voices of the past. A few authentic accounts of American western history were recorded by Indians either in pictographs or in translated English, and some managed to get published in obscure journals, pamphlets, or books of small circulation. In the late nineteenth century, when the white man's curiosity about Indian survivors of the wars reached a high point, enterprising newspaper reporters frequently interviewed warriors and chiefs and gave them an opportunity to express their opinions on what was happening in the West. The quality of these interviews varied greatly, depending upon the abilities of the interpreters, or upon the inclination of the Indians to speak freely. Some feared reprisals for telling the truth, while others delighted in hoaxing reporters with tall tales and shaggy-dog stories. Contemporary newspaper statements by Indians must therefore be read with skepticism, although some of them are masterpieces of irony and others burn with outbursts of poetic fury.

Among the richest sources of first-person statements by Indians are the records of treaty councils and other formal meetings with civilian and military representatives of the United States government. Isaac Pitman's new stenographic system was coming into vogue during the second half of the nineteenth century, and when Indians spoke in council a recording clerk sat beside the official interpreter.

Even when the meetings were in remote parts of the West, someone usually was available to write down the speeches, and because of the slowness of the translation process, much of what was said could be recorded in longhand. Interpreters quite often were half-bloods who knew spoken languages but seldom could read or write. Like most oral peoples they and the Indians depended upon imagery to express their thoughts, so that the English translations were filled with graphic similes and metaphors of the natural world. If an eloquent Indian had a poor interpreter, his words might be transformed to flat prose, but a good interpreter could make a poor speaker sound poetic.

Most Indian leaders spoke freely and candidly in councils with white officials, and as they became more sophisticated in such matters during the 1870's and 1880's, they demanded the right to choose their own interpreters and recorders. In this latter period, all members of the tribes were free to speak, and some of the older men chose such opportunities to recount events they had witnessed in the past, or to sum up the histories of their peoples. Although the Indians who lived through this doom period of their civilization have vanished from the earth, millions of their words are preserved in official records. Many of the more important council proceedings were published in government documents and reports.

Out of all these sources of almost forgotten oral history, I have tried to fashion a narrative of the conquest of the American West as the victims experienced it, using their own words whenever possible. Americans who have always looked westward when reading about this period should read this book facing eastward.

This is not a cheerful book, but history has a way of intruding upon the present, and perhaps those who read it will have a clearer understanding of what the American Indian is, by knowing what he was. They may be surprised to hear words of gentle reasonableness coming from the mouths of Indians stereotyped in the American myth as ruthless savages. They may learn something about their own relationship to the earth from a people who were true conservationists. The Indians knew that life was equated with the earth and its resources, that America was a paradise, and they could not comprehend why the intruders from the East were determined to destroy all that was Indian as well as America itself.

And if the readers of this book should ever chance to see the poverty, the hopelessness, and the squalor of a modern Indian reservation, they may find it possible to truly understand the reasons why.

Urbana, Illinois   DEE BROWN
April, 1970

I shall not be there. I shall rise and pass.
Bury my heart at Wounded Knee.

—STEPHEN VINCENT BENÉT

BURY MY HEART AT WOUNDED KNEE

ONE

"Their Manners Are Decorous and Praiseworthy"

Where today are the Pequot? Where are the Narragansett, the Mohican, the Pokanoket, and many other once powerful tribes of our people? They have vanished before the avarice and the oppression of the White Man, as snow before a summer sun.

Will we let ourselves be destroyed in our turn without a struggle, give up our homes, our country bequeathed to us by the Great Spirit, the graves of our dead and everything that is dear and sacred to us? I know you will cry with me, "Never! Never!"

—TECUMSEH OF THE SHAWNEES

IT BEGAN with Christopher Columbus, who gave the people the name *Indios.* Those Europeans, the white men, spoke in different dialects, and some pronounced the word *Indien,* or *Indianer,* or Indian. *Peaux-rouges,* or redskins, came later. As was the custom of the people when receiving strangers, the Tainos on the island of San Salvador generously presented Columbus and his men with gifts and treated them with honor.

"So tractable, so peaceable, are these people," Columbus wrote to the King and Queen of Spain, "that I swear to your Majesties there is not in the world a better nation. They love their neighbors as themselves, and their discourse is ever sweet and gentle, and accompanied with a smile; and though it is true that they are naked, yet their manners are decorous and praiseworthy."

All this, of course, was taken as a sign of weakness, if not heathenism, and Columbus being a righteous European was convinced the people should be "made to work, sow and do all that is necessary and to *adopt our ways.*" Over the next four

centuries (1492–1890) several million Europeans and their descendants undertook to enforce their ways upon the people of
the New World.

Columbus kidnapped ten of his friendly Taino hosts and carried them off to Spain, where they could be introduced to the
white man's ways. One of them died soon after arriving there,
but not before he was baptized a Christian. The Spaniards were
so pleased that they had made it possible for the first Indian
to enter heaven that they hastened to spread the good news
throughout the West Indies.

The Tainos and other Arawak people did not resist conversion
to the Europeans' religion, but they did resist strongly when
hordes of these bearded strangers began scouring their islands
in search of gold and precious stones. The Spaniards looted and
burned villages; they kidnapped hundreds of men, women, and
children and shipped them to Europe to be sold as slaves.
Arawak resistance brought on the use of guns and sabers, and
whole tribes were destroyed, hundreds of thousands of people
in less than a decade after Columbus set foot on the beach of
San Salvador, October 12, 1492.

Communications between the tribes of the New World were
slow, and news of the Europeans' barbarities rarely overtook the
rapid spread of new conquests and settlements. Long before the
English-speaking white men arrived in Virginia in 1607, however, the Powhatans had heard rumors about the civilizing tech-
niques of the Spaniards. The Englishmen used subtler methods.
To ensure peace long enough to establish a settlement at James-
town, they put a golden crown upon the head of Wahunsonacook,
dubbed him King Powhatan, and convinced him that he should
put his people to work supplying the white settlers with food.
Wahunsonacook vacillated between loyalty to his rebellious subjects and to the English, but after John Rolfe married his daughter, Pocahontas, he apparently decided that he was more English
than Indian. After Wahunsonacook died, the Powhatans rose
up in revenge to drive the Englishmen back into the sea from
which they had come, but the Indians underestimated the power
of English weapons. In a short time the eight thousand Powhatans were reduced to less than a thousand.

In Massachusetts the story began somewhat differently but

ended virtually the same as in Virginia. After the Englishmen landed at Plymouth in 1620, most of them probably would have starved to death but for aid received from friendly natives of the New World. A Pemaquid named Samoset and three Wampanoags named Massasoit, Squanto, and Hobomah became self-appointed missionaries to the Pilgrims. All spoke some English, learned from explorers who had touched ashore in previous years. Squanto had been kidnapped by an English seaman who sold him into slavery in Spain, but he escaped through the aid of another Englishman and finally managed to return home. He and the other Indians regarded the Plymouth colonists as helpless children; they shared corn with them from the tribal stores, showed them where and how to catch fish, and got them through the first winter. When spring came they gave the white men some seed corn and showed them how to plant and cultivate it.

For several years these Englishmen and their Indian neighbors lived in peace, but many more shiploads of white people continued coming ashore. The ring of axes and the crash of falling trees echoed up and down the coasts of the land which the white men now called New England. Settlements began crowding in upon each other. In 1625 some of the colonists asked Samoset to give them 12,000 additional acres of Pemaquid land. Samoset knew that land came from the Great Spirit, was as endless as the sky, and belonged to no man. To humor these strangers in their strange ways, however, he went through a ceremony of transferring the land and made his mark on a paper for them. It was the first deed of Indian land to English colonists.

Most of the other settlers, coming in by thousands now, did not bother to go through such a ceremony. By the time Massasoit, great chief of the Wampanoags, died in 1662 his people were being pushed back into the wilderness. His son Metacom foresaw doom for all Indians unless they united to resist the invaders. Although the New Englanders flattered Metacom by crowning him King Philip of Pokanoket, he devoted most of his time to forming alliances with the Narragansetts and other tribes in the region.

In 1675, after a series of arrogant actions by the colonists, King Philip led his Indian confederacy into a war meant to save

the tribes from extinction. The Indians attacked fifty-two settlements, completely destroying twelve of them, but after
months of fighting, the firepower of the colonists virtually exterminated the Wampanoags and Narragansetts. King Philip
was killed and his head publicly exhibited at Plymouth for
twenty years. Along with other captured Indian women and
children, his wife and young son were sold into slavery in the
West Indies.

When the Dutch came to Manhattan Island, Peter Minuit
purchased it for sixty guilders in fishhooks and glass beads, but
encouraged the Indians to remain and continue exchanging
their valuable peltries for such trinkets. In 1641, Willem Kieft
levied tribute upon the Mahicans and sent soldiers to Staten
Island to punish the Raritans for offenses which had been committed not by them but by white settlers. The Raritans resisted
arrest, and the soldiers killed four of them. When the Indians
retaliated by killing four Dutchmen, Kieft ordered the massacre
of two entire villages while the inhabitants slept. The Dutch
soldiers ran their bayonets through men, women, and children,
hacked their bodies to pieces, and then leveled the villages with
fire.

For two more centuries these events were repeated again and
again as the European colonists moved inland through the passes
of the Alleghenies and down the westward-flowing rivers to the
Great Waters (the Mississippi) and then up the Great Muddy
(the Missouri).

The Five Nations of the Iroquois, mightiest and most advanced of all the eastern tribes, strove in vain for peace. After
years of bloodshed to save their political independence, they
finally went down to defeat. Some escaped to Canada, some fled
westward, some lived out their lives in reservation confinement.

During the 1760's Pontiac of the Ottawas united tribes in the
Great Lakes country in hopes of driving the British back across
the Alleghenies, but he failed. His major error was an alliance
with French-speaking white men who withdrew aid from the
peaux-rouges during the crucial siege of Detroit.

A generation later, Tecumseh of the Shawnees formed a great
confederacy of midwestern and southern tribes to protect their

lands from invasion. The dream ended with Tecumseh's death in battle during the War of 1812.

Between 1795 and 1840 the Miamis fought battle after battle, and signed treaty after treaty, ceding their rich Ohio Valley lands until there was none left to cede.

When white settlers began streaming into the Illinois country after the War of 1812, the Sauks and Foxes fled across the Mississippi. A subordinate chief, Black Hawk, refused to retreat. He created an alliance with the Winnebagos, Pottawotamies, and Kickapoos, and declared war against the new settlements. A band of Winnebagos, who accepted a white soldier chief's bribe of twenty horses and a hundred dollars, betrayed Black Hawk, and he was captured in 1832. He was taken East for imprisonment and display to the curious. After he died in 1838, the governor of the recently created Iowa Territory obtained Black Hawk's skeleton and kept it on view in his office.

In 1829, Andrew Jackson, who was called Sharp Knife by the Indians, took office as President of the United States. During his frontier career, Sharp Knife and his soldiers had slain thousands of Cherokees, Chickasaws, Choctaws, Creeks, and Seminoles, but these southern Indians were still numerous and clung stubbornly to their tribal lands, which had been assigned them forever by white men's treaties. In Sharp Knife's first message to his Congress, he recommended that all these Indians be removed westward beyond the Mississippi. "I suggest the propriety of setting apart an ample district west of the Mississippi . . . to be guaranteed to the Indian tribes, as long as they shall occupy it."

Although enactment of such a law would only add to the long list of broken promises made to the eastern Indians, Sharp Knife was convinced that Indians and whites could not live together in peace and that his plan would make possible a final promise which never would be broken again. On May 28, 1830, Sharp Knife's recommendations became law.

Two years later he appointed a commissioner of Indian affairs to serve in the War Department and see that the new laws affecting Indians were properly carried out. And then on June 30, 1834, Congress passed *An Act to Regulate Trade and Inter-*

*course with the Indian Tribes and to Preserve Peace on the
Frontiers.* All that part of the United States west of the Mississippi "and not within the States of Missouri and Louisiana
or the Territory of Arkansas" would be Indian country. No white
persons would be permitted to trade in the Indian country without a license. No white traders of bad character would be permitted to reside in Indian country. No white persons would be permitted to settle in the Indian country. The military force of
the United States would be employed in the apprehension of
any white person who was found in violation of provisions of the
act.

Before these laws could be put into effect, a new wave of white
settlers swept westward and formed the territories of Wisconsin
and Iowa. This made it necessary for the policy makers in Washington to shift the "permanent Indian frontier" from the Mississippi River to the 95th meridian. (This line ran from Lake
of the Woods on what is now the Minnesota-Canada border,
slicing southward through what are now the states of Minnesota
and Iowa, and then along the western borders of Missouri,
Arkansas, and Louisiana, to Galveston Bay, Texas.) To keep the
Indians beyond the 95th meridian and to prevent unauthorized
white men from crossing it, soldiers were garrisoned in a series
of military posts that ran southward from Fort Snelling on the
Mississippi River to forts Atkinson and Leavenworth on the
Missouri, forts Gibson and Smith on the Arkansas, Fort Towson on the Red, and Fort Jesup in Louisiana.

More than three centuries had now passed since Christopher
Columbus landed on San Salvador, more than two centuries
since the English colonists came to Virginia and New England.
In that time the friendly Tainos who welcomed Columbus
ashore had been utterly obliterated. Long before the last of the
Tainos died, their simple agricultural and handicraft culture
was destroyed and replaced by cotton plantations worked by
slaves. The white colonists chopped down the tropical forests
to enlarge their fields; the cotton plants exhausted the soil;
winds unbroken by a forest shield covered the fields with sand.
When Columbus first saw the island he described it as "very
big and very level and the trees very green . . . the whole of
it so green that it is a pleasure to gaze upon." The Europeans

who followed him there destroyed its vegetation and its inhabitants—human, animal, bird, and fish—and after turning it into a wasteland, they abandoned it.

On the mainland of America, the Wampanoags of Massasoit and King Philip had vanished, along with the Chesapeakes, the Chickahominys, and the Potomacs of the great Powhatan confederacy. (Only Pocahontas was remembered.) Scattered or reduced to remnants were the Pequots, Montauks, Nanticokes, Machapungas, Catawbas, Cheraws, Miamis, Hurons, Eries, Mohawks, Senecas, and Mohegans. (Only Uncas was remembered.) Their musical names remained forever fixed on the American land, but their bones were forgotten in a thousand burned villages or lost in forests fast disappearing before the axes of twenty million invaders. Already the once sweet-watered streams, most of which bore Indian names, were clouded with silt and the wastes of man; the very earth was being ravaged and squandered. To the Indians it seemed that these Europeans hated everything in nature—the living forests and their birds and beasts, the grassy glades, the water, the soil, and the air itself.

The decade following establishment of the "permanent Indian frontier" was a bad time for the eastern tribes. The great Cherokee nation had survived more than a hundred years of the white man's wars, diseases, and whiskey, but now it was to be blotted out. Because the Cherokees numbered several thousands, their removal to the West was planned to be in gradual stages, but discovery of Appalachian gold within their territory brought on a clamor for their immediate wholesale exodus. During the autumn of 1838, General Winfield Scott's soldiers rounded them up and concentrated them into camps. (A few hundred escaped to the Smoky Mountains and many years later were given a small reservation in North Carolina.) From the prison camps they were started westward to Indian Territory. On the long winter trek, one of every four Cherokees died from cold, hunger, or disease. They called the march their "trail of tears." The Choctaws, Chickasaws, Creeks, and Seminoles also gave up their homelands in the South. In the North, surviving remnants of the Shawnees, Miamis, Ottawas, Hurons, Delawares, and many other once mighty tribes walked or traveled by horseback and

wagon beyond the Mississippi, carrying their shabby goods,
their rusty farming tools, and bags of seed corn. All of them
arrived as refugees, poor relations, in the country of the proud
and free Plains Indians.

Scarcely were the refugees settled behind the security of the
"permanent Indian frontier" when soldiers began marching
westward through the Indian country. The white men of the
United States—who talked so much of peace but rarely seemed
to practice it—were marching to war with the white men who
had conquered the Indians of Mexico. When the war with Mexico ended in 1847, the United States took possession of a vast
expanse of territory reaching from Texas to California. All of
it was west of the "permanent Indian frontier."

In 1848 gold was discovered in California. Within a few
months, fortune-seeking easterners by the thousands were crossing the Indian Territory. Indians who lived or hunted along the
Santa Fe and Oregon trails had grown accustomed to seeing an
occasional wagon train licensed for traders, trappers, or missionaries. Now suddenly the trails were filled with wagons, and
the wagons were filled with white people. Most of them were
bound for California gold, but some turned southwest for New
Mexico or northwest for the Oregon country.

To justify these breaches of the "permanent Indian frontier,"
the policy makers in Washington invented Manifest Destiny, a
term which lifted land hunger to a lofty plane. The Europeans
and their descendants were ordained by destiny to rule all of
America. They were the dominant race and therefore responsible
for the Indians—along with their lands, their forests, and their
mineral wealth. Only the New Englanders, who had destroyed
or driven out all their Indians, spoke against Manifest Destiny.

In 1850, although none of the Modocs, Mohaves, Paiutes,
Shastas, Yumas, or a hundred other lesser-known tribes along
the Pacific Coast were consulted on the matter, California became the thirty-first state of the Union. In the mountains of
Colorado gold was discovered, and new hordes of prospectors
swarmed across the Plains. Two vast new territories were organized, Kansas and Nebraska, encompassing virtually all the
country of the Plains tribes. In 1858 Minnesota became a state,

its boundaries being extended a hundred miles beyond the 95th meridian, the "permanent Indian frontier."

And so only a quarter of a century after enactment of Sharp Knife Andrew Jackson's Indian Trade and Intercourse Act, white settlers had driven in both the north and south flanks of the 95th meridian line, and advance elements of white miners and traders had penetrated the center.

It was then, at the beginning of the 1860's, that the white men of the United States went to war with one another—the Bluecoats against the Graycoats, the great Civil War. In 1860 there were probably 300,000 Indians in the United States and Territories, most of them living west of the Mississippi. According to varying estimates, their numbers had been reduced by one-half to two-thirds since the arrival of the first settlers in Virginia and New England. The survivors were now pressed between expanding white populations on the East and along the Pacific coasts—more than thirty million Europeans and their descendants. If the remaining free tribes believed that the white man's Civil War would bring any respite from his pressures for territory, they were soon disillusioned.

The most numerous and powerful western tribe was the Sioux, or Dakota, which was separated into several subdivisions. The Santee Sioux lived in the woodlands of Minnesota, and for some years had been retreating before the advance of settlements. Little Crow of the Mdewkanton Santee, after being taken on a tour of eastern cities, was convinced that the power of the United States could not be resisted. He was reluctantly attempting to lead his tribe down the white man's road. Wabasha, another Santee leader, also had accepted the inevitable, but both he and Little Crow were determined to oppose any further surrender of their lands.

Farther west on the Great Plains were the Teton Sioux, horse Indians all, and completely free. They were somewhat contemptuous of their woodland Santee cousins who had capitulated to the settlers. Most numerous and most confident of their ability to defend their territory were the Oglala Tetons. At the beginning of the white man's Civil War, their outstanding leader was Red Cloud, thirty-eight years old, a shrewd warrior chief. Still too young to be a warrior was Crazy Horse, an intelligent and fearless teen-aged Oglala.

Among the Hunkpapas, a smaller division of the Teton Sioux, a young man in his mid-twenties had already won a reputation as a hunter and warrior. In tribal councils he advocated unyielding opposition to any intrusion by white men. He was Tatanka Yotanka, the Sitting Bull. He was mentor to an orphaned boy named Gall. Together with Crazy Horse of the Oglalas, they would make history sixteen years later in 1876.

Although he was not yet forty, Spotted Tail was already the chief spokesman for the Brulé Tetons, who lived on the far western plains. Spotted Tail was a handsome, smiling Indian who loved fine feasts and compliant women. He enjoyed his way of life and the land he lived upon, but was willing to compromise to avoid war.

Closely associated with the Teton Sioux were the Cheyennes. In the old days the Cheyennes had lived in the Minnesota country of the Santee Sioux, but gradually moved westward and acquired horses. Now the Northern Cheyennes shared the Powder River and the Bighorn country with the Sioux, frequently camping near them. Dull Knife, in his forties, was an outstanding leader of the Northern branch of the tribe. (To his own people Dull Knife was known as Morning Star, but the Sioux called him Dull Knife, and most contemporary accounts use that name.)

The Southern Cheyennes had drifted below the Platte River, establishing villages on the Colorado and Kansas plains. Black Kettle of the Southern branch had been a great warrior in his youth. In his late middle age, he was the acknowledged chief, but the younger men and the Hotamitaneos (Dog Soldiers) of the Southern Cheyennes were more inclined to follow leaders such as Tall Bull and Roman Nose, who were in their prime.

The Arapahos were old associates of the Cheyennes and lived in the same areas. Some remained with the Northern Cheyennes, others followed the Southern branch. Little Raven, in his forties, was at this time the best-known chief.

South of the Kansas-Nebraska buffalo ranges were the Kiowas. Some of the older Kiowas could remember the Black Hills, but the tribe had been pushed southward before the combined power of Sioux, Cheyenne, and Arapaho. By 1860 the Kiowas had made their peace with the northern plains tribes and had become allies of the Comanches, whose southern plains they had entered. The Kiowas had several great leaders—an aging chief, Satank; two vigorous fighting men in their thirties, Satanta and Lone Wolf; and an intelligent statesman, Kicking Bird.

The Comanches, constantly on the move and divided into many small bands, lacked the leadership of their allies. Ten Bears, very old, was more a poet than a warrior chief. In 1860, half-breed Quanah Parker, who would lead the Comanches in a last great struggle to save their buffalo range, was not yet twenty years old.

In the arid Southwest were the Apaches, veterans of 250 years of guerrilla warfare with the Spaniards, who taught them the finer arts of torture and mutilation but never subdued them. Although few in number—probably not more than six thousand divided into several bands—their reputation as tenacious defenders of their harsh and pitiless land was already well established. Mangas Colorado, in his late sixties, had signed a treaty of friendship with the United States, but was already disillusioned by the influx of miners and soldiers into his territory. Cochise, his son-in-law, still believed he could get along with the white Americans. Victorio and Delshay distrusted the white intruders and gave them a wide berth. Nana, in his fifties but tough as rawhide, considered the English-speaking white men no different from the Spanish-speaking Mexicans he had been fighting all his life. Geronimo, in his twenties, had not yet proved himself.

The Navahos were related to the Apaches, but most Navahos had taken the Spanish white man's road and were raising sheep and goats, cultivating grain and fruit. As stockmen and weavers, some bands of the tribe had grown wealthy. Other Navahos continued as nomads, raiding their old enemies the Pueblos, the white settlers, or prosperous members of their own tribe. Manuelito, a stalwart mustachioed stock raiser, was head chief—chosen by an election of the Navahos held in 1855. In 1859, when a few wild Navahos raided United States citizens in their territory, the U.S. Army retaliated not by hunting down the culprits but by destroying the hogans and shooting all the livestock belong-

ing to Manuelito and members of his band. By 1860, Manuelito
and some Navaho followers were engaged in an undeclared war
with the United States in northern New Mexico and Arizona.

In the Rockies north of the Apache and Navaho country were
the Utes, an aggressive mountain tribe inclined to raid their more
peaceful neighbors to the south. Ouray, their best-known leader,
favored peace with white men even to the point of soldiering
with them as mercenaries against other Indian tribes.

In the far West most of the tribes were too small, too divided,
or too weak to offer much resistance. The Modocs of northern
California and southern Oregon, numbering less than a thousand, fought guerrilla-fashion for their lands. Kintpuash, called
Captain Jack by the California settlers, was only a young man
in 1860; his ordeal as a leader would come a dozen years later.

Northwest of the Modocs, the Nez Percés had been living in
peace with white men since Lewis and Clark passed through
their territory in 1805. In 1855, one branch of the tribe ceded
Nez Percé lands to the United States for settlement, and agreed
to live within the confines of a large reservation. Other bands of
the tribe continued to roam between the Blue Mountains of
Oregon and the Bitterroots of Idaho. Because of the vastness of
the Northwest country, the Nez Percés believed there would always be land enough for both white men and Indians to use as
each saw fit. Heinmot Tooyalaket, later known as Chief Joseph,
would have to make a fateful decision in 1877 between peace
and war. In 1860 he was twenty years old, the son of a chief.

In the Nevada country of the Paiutes a future Messiah named
Wovoka, who later would have a brief but powerful influence
upon the Indians of the West, was only four years old in 1860.

During the following thirty years these leaders and many more
would enter into history and legend. Their names would become
as well known as those of the men who tried to destroy them.
Most of them, young and old, would be driven into the ground
long before the symbolic end of Indian freedom came at Wounded
Knee in December, 1890. Now, a century later, in an age without heroes, they are perhaps the most heroic of all Americans.

TWO

The Long Walk of the Navahos

1860—March 12, U.S. Congress passes Pre-emption Bill, providing
free land to settlers in western territories. April 3, first Pony
Express leaves St. Joseph, Missouri; delivers letters at
Sacramento, California, April 13. April 23, Democratic
National Convention at Charleston, South Carolina, divides on
the slavery issue. May 16–18, Republican National Convention
in Chicago nominates Abraham Lincoln for President. June,
population of U.S. reaches 31,443,321. July, Spencer
repeating rifle invented. November 6, Abraham Lincoln
receives only 40 percent of popular vote but wins Presidency.
December 20, South Carolina secedes from the Union.

1861—February 4, Confederate Congress organized at Montgomery,
Alabama. February 9, Jefferson Davis elected President of
Confederate States. February 11, Abraham Lincoln says
farewell to friends and neighbors at Springfield, Illinois, and
leaves by train for Washington. March, President Davis asks
for 100,000 soldiers to defend the Confederacy. April 12,
Confederates open fire on Fort Sumter. April 14, Fort Sumter
falls. April 15, President Lincoln calls for 75,000 volunteer
soldiers. July 21, First Battle of Bull Run; Union Army falls
back on Washington. October 6, rioting Russian students close
down University of St. Petersburg. October 25, Pacific
Telegraph line between St. Louis and San Francisco completed.
December 5, Gatling gun is patented. December 14, British
mourn death of Albert, Prince Consort of Queen Victoria.
December 30, U.S. banks suspend gold payments.

When our fathers lived they heard that the Americans were coming across the great river westward. . . . We heard of guns and powder and lead—first flintlocks, then percussion caps, and now repeating rifles. We first saw the Americans at Cottonwood Wash. We had wars with the Mexicans and the Pueblos. We captured mules from the Mexicans, and had many mules. The Americans came to trade with us. When the Americans first came we had a big dance, and they danced with our women. We also traded.

—MANUELITO OF THE NAVAHOS

MANUELITO and other Navaho leaders made treaties with the Americans. "Then the soldiers built the fort here," Manuelito remembered, "and gave us an agent who advised us to behave well. He told us to live peaceably with the whites; to keep our promises. They wrote down the promises, so that we would always remember them." [1]

Manuelito tried to keep the promises in the treaty, but after the soldiers came and burned his hogans and killed his livestock because of something a few wild young Navahos had done, he grew angry at the Americans. He and his band had been wealthy, but the soldiers had made them poor. To become *ricos* again they must raid the Mexicans to the south, and for this the Mexicans called them *ladrones,* or thieves. For as long as anyone could remember, the Mexicans had been raiding Navahos to steal their young children and make slaves of them, and for as long as anyone could remember the Navahos had been retaliating with raids against the Mexicans.

After the Americans came to Santa Fe and called the country New Mexico, they protected the Mexicans because they had become American citizens. The Navahos were not citizens because they were Indians, and when they raided the Mexicans, soldiers would come rushing into the Navaho country to punish

14

them as outlaws. This was all an angry puzzle to Manuelito and
his people, for they knew that many of the Mexicans had Indian
blood, and yet no soldiers ever went rushing after the Mexicans
to punish them for stealing Navaho children.

The first fort the Americans built in the Navaho country was
in a grassy valley at the mouth of Canyon Bonito. They called
it Fort Defiance, and put their horses out to graze on pastureland
long prized by Manuelito and his people. The soldier chief told
the Navahos that the pastures belonged to the fort, and ordered
them to keep their animals away. Because there was no fencing,
the Navahos could not prevent their livestock from straying to
the forbidden meadows. One morning a company of mounted
soldiers rode out of the fort and shot all the animals belonging
to the Navahos.

To replace their horses and mules, the Navahos raided the
soldiers' herds and supply trains. The soldiers in turn began attacking bands of Navahos. In February, 1860, Manuelito led
five hundred warriors against the Army's horse herd, which was
grazing a few miles north of Fort Defiance. The Navaho lances
and arrows were no match for the well-armed soldier guard.
They suffered more than thirty casualties but captured only a
few horses. During the following weeks, Manuelito and his ally
Barboncito built up a force of more than a thousand warriors,
and in the darkness of the early hours of April 30, they surrounded Fort Defiance. Two hours before dawn, the Navahos
attacked the fort from three sides. They were determined to wipe
it off the face of their land.

They came very near succeeding. With a rattle of fire from
their few old Spanish guns, the Navahos drove in the sentries
and overran several buildings. As startled soldiers poured from
their barracks, they met showers of arrows, but after several
minutes of confusion the soldiers formed files and soon commenced a steady musket fire. When daylight came, the Navahos
pulled back into the hills, satisfied that they had taught the
soldiers a good lesson.

The United States Army, however, considered the attack a
challenge of the flag flying over Fort Defiance, an act of war. A
few weeks later Colonel Edward Richard Sprigg Canby, at the
head of six companies of cavalry and nine of infantry, was scour-

ing the Chuska Mountains in search of Manuelito's hostiles. The troops marched through the redrock country until they wore out their horses and almost died of thirst. Although they seldom saw any Navahos, the Indians were there, harassing the column's flanks but making no direct attacks. By the end of the year, both sides grew weary of the foolish game. The soldiers were unable to punish the Navahos, and the Navahos were unable to attend to their crops and livestock.

In January, 1861, Manuelito, Barboncito, Herrero Grande, Armijo, Delgadito, and other _rico_ leaders agreed to meet Colonel Canby at a new fort the soldiers were building thirty-five miles southeast of Fort Defiance. The new fort was called Fort Fauntleroy in honor of a soldier chief. At the end of the parleys with Canby, the Navahos chose Herrero Grande as head chief (February 21, 1861). The leaders agreed that it was best to live in peace, and Herrero Grande promised to drive all _ladrones_ from the tribe. Manuelito was not sure that this promise could be carried out, but he signed his name to Canby's paper. A prosperous stockraiser again, he believed in the virtues of peace and honesty.

After the winter meeting at Fort Fauntleroy, there were several months of friendship between the soldiers and the Navahos. Rumors reached the Indians of a big war somewhere far to the east, a war between the white Americans of the North and South. They learned that some of Canby's soldiers had exchanged their bluecoats for graycoats and gone East to fight against the Bluecoat soldiers there. One of them was the Eagle Chief, Colonel Thomas Fauntleroy; his name was blotted out, and now they called the post Fort Wingate.

In this time of friendship, the Navahos went often to Fort Fauntleroy (Wingate) to trade and draw rations from their agent. Most of the soldiers made them welcome, and a custom grew up of having horse races between the Navahos and the soldiers. All the Navahos looked forward to these contests, and on racing days hundreds of men, women, and children would dress in their brightest costumes and ride their finest ponies to Fort Wingate. On a crisp sunny morning in September several races were run, but the special race of the day was scheduled at noon. It was to be between Pistol Bullet (a name given Man-

1. *Manuelito, chief of the Navahos, painted by Julian Scott for the United States Census Bureau in 1891.*

uelito by the soldiers) on a Navaho pony, and a lieutenant on a quarter horse. Many bets were made on this race—money, blankets, livestock, beads, whatever a man had to use for a bet. The horses jumped off together, but in a few seconds everyone could see that Pistol Bullet (Manuelito) was in trouble. He lost control of his pony, and it ran off the track. Soon everyone knew that Pistol Bullet's bridle rein had been slashed with a knife. The Navahos went to the judges—who were all soldiers—and demanded that the race be run again. The judges refused; they declared the lieutenant's quarter horse was the winner. Immediately the soldiers formed a victory parade for a march into the fort to collect their bets.

Infuriated by this trickery, the Navahos stormed after them, but the fort's gates were slammed shut in their faces. When a Navaho attempted to force an entrance, a sentinel shot him dead.

What happened next was written down by a white soldier chief, Captain Nicholas Hodt:

> The Navahos, squaws, and children ran in all directions and were shot and bayoneted. I succeeded in forming about twenty men. . . . I then marched out to the east side of the post; there I saw a soldier murdering two little children and a woman. I hallooed immediately to the soldier to stop. He looked up, but did not obey my order. I ran up as quick as I could, but could not get there soon enough to prevent him from killing the two innocent children and wounding severely the squaw. I ordered his belts to be taken off and taken prisoner to the post. . . . Meanwhile the colonel had given orders to the officer of the day to have the artillery [mountain howitzers] brought out to open upon the Indians. The sergeant in charge of the mountain howitzers pretended not to understand the order given, for he considered it as an unlawful order; but being cursed by the officer of the day, and threatened, he had to execute the order or else get himself in trouble. The Indians scattered all over the valley below the post, attacked the post herd, wounded the Mexican herder, but did not succeed in getting any stock; also attacked the expressman some ten miles from the post, took his horse and mail-bag and wounded him in the arm. After the massacre there were no more Indians to be seen about the post with the exception of a few squaws, favorites of the

2. *Juanita, wife of Manuelito, as a member of the Navaho delegation to Washington in 1874. Photo from the Smithsonian Institution.*

officers. The commanding officer endeavored to make peace
again with the Navahos by sending some of the favorite squaws
to talk with the chiefs; but the only satisfaction the squaws
received was a good flogging.[2]

After that day, September 22, 1861, it was a long time before
there was friendship again between white men and Navahos.

Meanwhile an army of Confederate Graycoats had marched
into New Mexico and fought big battles with the Bluecoats along
the Rio Grande. Kit Carson, the Rope Thrower, was a leader of
the Bluecoats. Most of the Navahos trusted Rope Thrower
Carson because he had always talked one way to the Indians
and they hoped to make peace with him when he was finished
with the Graycoats.

In the spring of 1862, however, many more Bluecoats came
marching into New Mexico from the west. They called themselves the California Column. Their General James Carleton
wore stars on his shoulders and was more powerful than the
Eagle Chief, Carson. These Californians camped along the Rio
Grande Valley, but they had nothing to do because the Graycoats had all fled into Texas.

The Navahos soon learned that Star Chief Carleton had a
great hunger for their land and whatever metal wealth might be
hidden under it. "A princely realm," he called it, "a magnificent
pastoral and mineral country." As he had many soldiers with
nothing to do but march around their parade grounds rattling
their guns, Carleton began looking about for Indians to fight. The
Navahos, he said, were "wolves that run through the mountains"
and must be subdued.

Carleton turned his attention first to the Mescalero Apaches,
who numbered less than a thousand and lived in scattered bands
between the Rio Grande and the Pecos. His plan was to kill or
capture all Mescaleros and then confine the survivors on a
worthless reservation along the Pecos. This would leave the rich
Rio Grande Valley open for land claims and settlement by
American citizens. In September, 1862, he sent out an order:

> There is to be no council held with the Indians, nor any talks.
> The men are to be slain whenever and wherever they can be
> found. The women and children may be taken as prisoners,
> but, of course, they are not to be killed.[3]

This was not Kit Carson's way of dealing with Indians, many of whom he counted as friends from his trading days. He sent his soldiers into the mountains, but he also opened up lines of communication with the Mescalero leaders. By late autumn he had arranged for five chiefs to visit Santa Fe and negotiate with General Carleton. While en route to Santa Fe, two of the chiefs and their escorts met a detachment of soldiers under command of a former saloonkeeper, Captain James (Paddy) Graydon. Graydon pretended great friendship for the Mescaleros, giving them flour and beef for their long journey. A short time later, near Gallina Springs, Graydon's scouting party came upon the Mescaleros again. What happened there is not clear, because no Mescalero survived the incident. A white soldier chief, Major Arthur Morrison, reported briefly: "The transaction was very strangely committed by Captain Graydon . . . and from what I can learn he deceived these Indians, going right into their camp and giving them liquor, afterwards shot them down, they of course thinking him to come with friendly purposes, as he had given them flour, beef, and provisions."

The other three chiefs, Cadette, Chato, and Estrella, reached Santa Fe and assured General Carleton that their people were at peace with the white men and wanted only to be left alone in their mountains. "You are stronger than we," Cadette said. "We have fought you so long as we had rifles and powder; but your arms are better than ours. Give us like weapons and turn us loose, we will fight you again; but we are worn-out; we have no more heart; we have no provisions, no means to live; your troops are everywhere; our springs and water holes are either occupied or overlooked by your young men. You have driven us from our last and best stronghold, and we have no more heart. Do with us as may seem good to you, but do not forget we are men and braves." [4]

Carleton haughtily informed them that the only way the Mescaleros could achieve peace would be to leave their country and go to the Bosque Redondo, the reservation he had prepared for them on the Pecos. There they would be kept in confinement by soldiers at a new military post called Fort Sumner.

Outnumbered by the soldiers, unable to protect their women and children, and trusting in the goodwill of Rope Thrower Car-

son, the Mescalero chiefs submitted to Carleton's demands and
took their people into imprisonment at Bosque Redondo.

With some uneasiness, the Navahos had been watching Carleton's quick and ruthless conquest of their cousins, the Mescalero
Apaches. In December, eighteen of the *rico* leaders—including
Delgadito and Barboncito, but not Manuelito—traveled to
Santa Fe to see the general. They told him they represented
peaceful Navaho herdsmen and farmers who wanted no war.
This was the first time they had looked upon Star Chief Carleton. His face was hairy, his eyes were fierce, and his mouth was
that of a man without humor. He did not smile when he told Delgadito and the others: "You can have no peace until you give
other guarantees than your word that the peace should be kept.
Go home and tell your people so. I have no faith in your promises." [5]

By the spring of 1863, most of the Mescaleros had either fled
to Mexico or been herded into the Bosque Redondo. In April
Carleton went to Fort Wingate "to gather information for a
campaign against the Navahos as soon as the grass starts sufficiently to support stock." He arranged a meeting with Delgadito
and Barboncito near Cubero, and bluntly informed the chiefs
that the only way they could prove their peaceful intentions
would be to take their people out of the Navaho country and
join the "contented" Mescaleros at Bosque Redondo. To this
Barboncito replied: "I will not go to the Bosque. I will never
leave my country, not even if it means that I will be killed."

On June 23 Carleton set a deadline for Navaho removal to the
Bosque Redondo. "Send for Delgadito and Barboncito again,"
he instructed the commanding officer at Fort Wingate, "and
repeat what I before told them, and tell them that I shall feel
very sorry if they refuse to come in. . . . Tell them they can
have until the twentieth day of July of this year to come in—
they and all those who belong to what they call the peace party;
*that after that day every Navaho that is seen will be considered
as hostile and treated accordingly;* that after that day the door
now open will be closed." [6] The twentieth of July came and
went, but no Navahos volunteered to surrender.

In the meantime, Carleton had ordered Kit Carson to march his troops from the Mescalero country to Fort Wingate and prepare for a war against the Navahos. Carson was reluctant; he complained that he had volunteered to fight Confederate soldiers, not Indians, and he sent Carleton a letter of resignation.

Kit Carson liked Indians. In the old days he had lived with them for months at a time without seeing another white man. He had fathered a child by an Arapaho woman and had lived for a time with a Cheyenne woman. But after he married Josefa, daughter of Don Francisco Jaramillo of Taos, Carson had taken new roads, grown prosperous, and claimed land for a ranch. He discovered that in New Mexico there was room at the top even for a rough, superstitious, illiterate mountain man. He learned to read and write a few words, and although he was only five feet six inches tall, his name touched the sky. Famous as he was, the Rope Thrower never overcame his awe of the well-dressed, smooth-talking men at the top. In 1863 in New Mexico the biggest man at the top was Star Chief Carleton. And so in the summer of that year Kit Carson withdrew his resignation from the Army and went to Fort Wingate to take the field against the Navahos. Before the campaign was over, his reports to Carleton were echoing the Manifest Destiny presumptions of the arrogant man from whom he took orders.

The Navahos respected Carson as a fighter, but they had no use for his soldiers—the New Mexico Volunteers. Many of them were Mexicans, and the Navahos had been chasing them out of their country as long as anyone could remember. There were ten times as many Navahos as Mescaleros, and they had the advantage of a vast and rugged country broken by deep canyons, steep-banked arroyos, and precipice-flanked mesas. Their stronghold was Canyon de Chelly, cutting westward for thirty miles from the Chuska Mountains. Narrowing in some places to fifty yards, the canyon's redrock walls rose a thousand feet or more, with overhanging ledges offering excellent defensive positions against invaders. At points where the canyon widened to several hundred yards, the Navahos grazed sheep and goats on pasturage, or raised corn, wheat, fruit, and melons on cultivated soil. They were especially proud of their peach orchards, carefully

tended since the days of the Spaniards. Water flowed plentifully
through the canyon for most of the year, and there were enough
cottonwood and box-elder trees to supply wood for fuel.

Even when they learned that Carson had marched a thousand
soldiers to Pueblo Colorado and had hired his old friends the
Utes to serve as trackers, the Navahos were still scornful. The
chiefs reminded their people of how in the old days they had
driven the Spaniards from their land. "If the Americans come
to take us, we will kill them," the chiefs promised, but they
took precautions to secure the safety of their women and children. They knew the mercenary Utes would try to make captives of them for sale to wealthy Mexicans.

Late in July Carson moved up to Fort Defiance, renamed
it for the Indians' old adversary Canby, and began sending out
reconnaissance detachments. He probably was not surprised that
few Navahos could be found. He knew that the only way to
conquer them was to destroy their crops and livestock—scorch
their earth—and on July 25 he sent Major Joseph Cummings
to bring in all livestock that could be found and to harvest or
burn all corn and wheat along the Bonito. As soon as the
Navahos discovered what Cummings was doing to their winter
food supply, he became a marked man. A short time later a
Navaho marksman shot him out of his saddle, killing him instantly. They also raided Carson's corral near Fort Canby, recaptured some sheep and goats, and stole the Rope Thrower's
favorite horse.

General Carleton was far more nettled by such incidents than
Carson, who had lived with Indians long enough to appreciate bold
retorts. On August 18 the general decided to "stimulate the
zeal" of his troops by posting prize money for captured Navaho
livestock. He offered to pay twenty dollars for "every sound,
serviceable horse or mule," and one dollar per head for sheep
brought in to the commissary at Fort Canby.

As the soldiers' pay was less than twenty dollars per month,
the bounty offer did stimulate them, and some of the men extended it to the few Navahos they were able to kill. To prove
their soldierly abilities, they began cutting off the knot of hair
fastened by a red string which the Navahos wore on their heads.
The Navahos could not believe that Kit Carson condoned

scalping, which they considered a barbaric custom introduced by the Spaniards. (The Europeans may or may not have introduced scalping to the New World, but the Spanish, French, Dutch, and English colonists made the custom popular by offering bounties for scalps of their respective enemies.)

Although Carson continued his steady destruction of grain fields, of bean and pumpkin patches, he was moving too slowly to suit General Carleton. In September Carleton ordered that thenceforth every Navaho male was to be killed or taken prisoner on sight. He wrote out for Carson the exact words he was to use to captured Navahos: "Say to them—'Go to the Bosque Redondo, or we will pursue and destroy you. We will not make peace with you on any other terms. . . . This war shall be pursued against you if it takes years, now that we have begun, until you cease to exist or move. There can be no other talk on the subject.' "

About this same time the general was writing War Department headquarters in Washington, demanding an additional regiment of cavalry. More soldiers were needed, he said, because of a new gold strike not far west of the Navaho country, troops sufficient "to whip the Indians and to protect the people going to and at the mines. . . . Providence has indeed blessed us . . . the gold lies here at our feet to be had by the mere picking of it up!" [7]

Under Carleton's obsessive prodding, Kit Carson accelerated his scorched-earth program, and by autumn had destroyed most of the herds and grain between Fort Canby and Canyon de Chelly. On October 17 two Navahos appeared under a truce flag at Fort Wingate. One of them was El Sordo, emissary for his brothers Delgadito and Barboncito and their five hundred followers. Their food supply was gone, El Sordo said; they were reduced to eating piñon nuts. They were almost naked of clothing and blankets, and were too fearful of soldiers' scouting parties to build fires for warmth. They did not wish to go far away to the Bosque, but would build hogans nearby Fort Wingate, where they would always be under the eyes of the soldiers as peaceful Indians. In nine days Delgadito and Barboncito would come with the five hundred. The chiefs would be willing to go to Santa Fe to see the Star Chief and sue for peace.

Captain Rafael Chacon, commanding Fort Wingate, posted the compromise offer to General Carleton, who replied: "The Navaho Indians have no choice in the matter; they must come in and go to the Bosque Redondo, or remain in their own country, at war." [8]

Having no choice in the matter, and burdened with women and children suffering from cold and starvation, Delgadito surrendered. Barboncito, El Sordo, and many of the warriors waited in the mountains to see what would happen to their people.

Those who had surrendered were sent to the Bosque Redondo, but Carleton arranged for the first captives to be given special treatment—the best rations, the best shelters—on the journey and upon arrival at the Bosque. Forbidding as was that barren plain on the Pecos, Delgadito was impressed by the kindness of his captors. When the Star Chief informed him that he could return to Fort Wingate with his family if he would persuade other Navaho leaders that life at the Bosque was better than starvation and freezing, Delgadito agreed to go. At the same time, the general ordered Kit Carson to invade Canyon de Chelly, destroy food and livestock, and kill or capture the Navahos in that last stronghold.

In preparation for the Chelly campaign, Carson assembled a pack herd to carry supplies, but on December 13 Barboncito and his warriors swooped down on the herd and ran the mules off to the canyon, where they could be used as a winter meat supply. Carson sent two detachments of soldiers in pursuit, but the Navahos divided into several small parties and escaped under cover of a heavy snowstorm. Lieutenant Donaciano Montoya's cavalrymen stumbled upon a small camp, charged it, drove the Navahos into a cedar brake, and captured thirteen women and children. The lieutenant reported: "Indian was shot through the right side but succeeded in escaping through the tangled underwood. His son, a little boy of ten years old and very intelligent for an Indian, was taken a short time afterwards, and reported that his father died amongst the rocks in a neighboring arroyo."

With no mules for packing supplies, Kit Carson now informed General Carleton that the Canyon de Chelly expedition would have to be delayed. The general promptly replied: "You will not delay the expedition on account of lack of transportation. You will have the men carry their blankets and, if necessary, three or four days' rations in haversacks." [9]

On January 6, 1864, the soldiers marched out of Fort Canby. Captain Albert Pfeiffer led a small force, which was to enter the east end of Canyon de Chelly. Kit Carson led a larger force, which was to enter the west end. Six inches of snow lay on the ground, temperature was below freezing, and the marching was slow.

A week later Pfeiffer entered the canyon. From rims and ledges hundreds of half-starved Navahos hurled stones, pieces of wood, and Spanish curses upon the heads of the soldiers. But they could not stop them. Pfeiffer's men destroyed hogans, food caches, and livestock; they killed three Navahos who came within range of their muskets, found two elderly Navahos frozen to death, and captured nineteen women and children.

Carson meanwhile had established a camp at the west end and was scouting the canyon from the rims. On January 12, one of his patrols encountered a band of Navahos, killing eleven of them. Two days later the two commands linked up. The entire canyon had been traversed without a major fight.

That evening three Navahos approached the soldiers' camp under a truce flag. Their people were starving and freezing, they told Carson. They chose to surrender rather than die. "You have until tomorrow morning," Carson replied. "After that time my soldiers will hunt you down." Next morning, sixty ragged and emaciated Navahos arrived at the camp and surrendered.

Before returning to Fort Canby, Carson ordered complete destruction of Navaho properties within the canyon—including their fine peach orchards, more than five thousand trees. The Navahos could forgive the Rope Thrower for fighting them as a soldier, for making prisoners of them, even for destroying their food supplies, but the one act they never forgave him for was cutting down their beloved peach trees.

During the next few weeks as news of the soldiers' entry into Canyon de Chelly spread through the hidden camps of the Navahos, the people lost heart. "We fought for that country because we did not want to lose it," Manuelito said afterward. "We lost nearly everything. . . . The American nation is too

powerful for us to fight. When we had to fight for a few days
we felt fresh, but in a short time we were worn out and the soldiers starved us out." [10]

On January 31 Delgadito with his reassurances of conditions
at Bosque Redondo persuaded 680 more Navahos to surrender
at Fort Wingate. Severe winter weather and lack of food forced
others to come into Fort Canby. By mid-February 1,200 were
there, hungry and destitute. The Army issued them scanty rations, and the very old and the very young began to die. On
February 21 Herrero Grande came in with his band, and the
numbers rose to 1,500. By early March three thousand had
surrendered at both forts, and the trails to the north were filled
with fearful Navahos approaching over the frozen snow. But
the *rico* chiefs, Manuelito, Barboncito, and Armijo, refused to
quit. With their people they stayed in the mountains, still determined not to surrender.

During March the Long Walk of the Navahos to Fort Sumner
and the Bosque Redondo was set in motion. The first contingent
of 1,430 reached Fort Sumner on March 13; ten died en route;
three children were kidnapped, probably by Mexicans among
the soldier escort.

Meanwhile a second group of 2,400 had left Fort Canby, their
numbers already reduced by 126 who had died at the fort. The
long caravan included 30 wagons, 3,000 sheep, and 473 horses.
The Navahos had the fortitude to bear freezing weather, hunger,
dysentery, jeers of the soldiers, and the hard three-hundred-mile
journey, but they could not bear the homesickness, the loss of
their land. They wept, and 197 of them died before they reached
their cruel destination.

On March 20 eight hundred more Navahos left Fort Canby,
most of them women, children, and old men. The Army supplied
them only twenty-three wagons. "On the second day's march,"
the officer in command reported, "a very severe snowstorm set
in which lasted for four days with unusual severity, and occa-
sioned great suffering amongst the Indians, many of whom were
nearly naked and of course unable to withstand such a storm."
When they reached Los Pinos, below Albuquerque, the Army
commandeered the wagons for other use, and the Navahos had

to camp in the open. By the time the journey could be resumed, several children had vanished. "At this place," a lieutenant commented, "officers who have Indians in charge will have to exercise extreme vigilance, or the Indians' children will be stolen from them and sold." This contingent reached the Bosque on May 11, 1864. "I left Fort Canby with 800 and received 146 en route to Fort Sumner, making about 946 in all. Of this number about 110 died."

Late in April one of the holdout chiefs, Armijo, appeared at Fort Canby and informed the post commander (Captain Asa Carey) that Manuelito would arrive in a few days with Navahos who had spent the winter far to the north along the Little Colorado and San Juan. Armijo's band of more than four hundred came in a few days later, but Manuelito halted his people a few miles away at a place called Quelitas and sent a messenger to inform the soldier chief that he would like to have a talk with him. During the parley which followed, Manuelito said that his people wished to stay near the fort, plant their grain crops, and graze their sheep as they had always done.

"There is but one place for you," Captain Carey replied, "and that is to go to the Bosque."

"Why must we go to the Bosque?" Manuelito asked. "We have never stolen or murdered, and have at all times kept the peace we promised General Canby." He added that his people feared they were being collected at the Bosque so the soldiers could shoot them down as they had at Fort Fauntleroy in 1861. Carey assured him that this was not so, but Manuelito said he would not surrender his people until he had talked with his old friend Herrero Grande or some of the other Navaho leaders who had been at the Bosque.

When General Carleton heard that there was a chance of Manuelito surrendering, he sent four carefully chosen Navahos from the Bosque (but not Herrero Grande) to use their influence on the reluctant war chief. They did not convince Manuelito. One June night after they had talked, Manuelito and his band vanished from Quelitas and went back to their hiding places along the Little Colorado.

In September he heard that his old ally Barboncito had been

captured in the Canyon de Chelly. Now he, Manuelito, was the
last of the *rico* holdouts, and he knew the soldiers would be looking everywhere for him.

During the autumn, Navahos who had escaped from the
Bosque Redondo began returning to their homeland with frightening accounts of what was happening to the people there. It
was a wretched land, they said. The soldiers prodded them with
bayonets and herded them into adobe-walled compounds where
the soldier chiefs were always counting them and putting numbers down in little books. The soldier chiefs promised them
clothing and blankets and better food, but their promises were
never kept. All the cottonwood and mesquite had been cut down,
so that only roots were left for firewood. To shelter themselves
from rain and sun they had to dig holes in the sandy ground,
and cover and line them with mats of woven grass. They lived
like prairie dogs in burrows. With a few tools the soldiers gave
them they broke the soil of the Pecos bottomlands and planted
grain, but floods and droughts and insects killed the crops, and
now everyone was on half-rations. Crowded together as they
were, disease had begun to take a toll of the weaker ones. It
was a bad place, and although escape was difficult and dangerous
under the watchful eyes of the soldiers, many were risking their
lives to get away.

Meanwhile, Star Chief Carleton had persuaded the Vicario
of Santa Fe to sing a Te Deum in celebration of the Army's
successful removal of the Navahos to the Bosque, and the general described the place to his superiors in Washington as "a
fine reservation . . . there is no reason why they [the Navahos]
will not be the most happy and prosperous and well-provided-for
Indians in the United States. . . . At all events . . . we can
feed them cheaper than we can fight them."

In the eyes of the Star Chief, his prisoners were only mouths
and bodies. "These six thousand mouths must eat, and these six
thousand bodies must be clothed. When it is considered what
a magnificent pastoral and mineral country they have surrendered to us—a country whose value can hardly be estimated
—the mere pittance, in comparison, which must at once be given
to support them, sinks into insignificance as a price for their
natural heritage."

And no advocate of Manifest Destiny ever phrased his support of that philosophy more unctuously than he: "The exodus of this whole people from the land of their fathers is not only an interesting but a touching sight. They have fought us gallantly for years on years; they have defended their mountains and their stupendous canyons with a heroism which any people might be proud to emulate; but when, at length, they found it was their destiny, too, as it had been that of their brethren, tribe after tribe, away back toward the rising of the sun, to give way to the insatiable progress of our race, they threw down their arms, and, as brave men entitled to our admiration and respect, have come to us with confidence in our magnanimity, and feeling that we are too powerful and too just a people to repay that confidence with meanness or neglect—feeling that having sacrificed to us their beautiful country, their homes, the associations of their lives, the scenes rendered classic in their traditions, we will not dole out to them a miser's pittance in return for what they know to be and what we know to be a princely realm." [11]

Manuelito had not thrown down his arms, however, and he was too important a chief for General Carleton to permit such incorrigibility to continue unchallenged. In February, 1865, Navaho runners from Fort Wingate brought Manuelito a message from the Star Chief, a warning that he and his band would be hunted down to the death unless they came in peaceably before spring. "I am doing no harm to anyone," Manuelito told the messengers. "I will not leave my country. I intend to die here." But he finally agreed to talk again with some of the chiefs who were at the Bosque Redondo.

In late February, Herrero Grande and five other Navaho leaders from the Bosque arranged to meet Manuelito near the Zuni trading post. The weather was cold, and the land was covered with deep snow. After embracing his old friends, Manuelito led them back into the hills where his people were hidden. Only about a hundred men, women, and children were left of Manuelito's band; they had a few horses and a few sheep. "Here is all I have in the world," Manuelito said. "See what a trifling amount. You see how poor they are. My children are eating palmilla roots." After a pause he added that his horses were in no condition for travel to the Bosque. Herrero replied that he had no authority to extend the time set for him to surrender, and he warned Manuelito in a friendly way that he would be risking the lives of his people if he did not come in and surrender. Manuelito wavered. He said he would surrender for the sake of the women and children; then he added that he would need three months to get his livestock in order. Finally he declared flatly that he could not leave his country.

"My God and my mother live in the West, and I will not leave them. It is a tradition of my people that we must never cross the three rivers—the Grande, the San Juan, the Colorado. Nor could I leave the Chuska Mountains. I was born there. I shall remain. I have nothing to lose but my life, and *that* they can come and take whenever they please, but I will not move. I have never done any wrong to the Americans or the Mexicans. I have never robbed. If I am killed, innocent blood will be shed."

Herrero said to him: "I have done all I could for your benefit; have given you the best advice; I now leave you as if your grave were already made." [12]

In Santa Fe a few days later Herrero Grande informed General Carleton of Manuelito's defiant stand. Carleton's response was a harsh order to the commander at Fort Wingate: "I understand if Manuelito . . . could be captured his band would doubtless come in; and that if you could make certain arrangements with the Indians at the Zuni village, where he frequently comes on a visit and to trade, they would cooperate with you in his capture. . . . Try hard to get Manuelito. Have him securely ironed and carefully guarded. It will be a mercy to others whom he controls to capture or kill him at once. I prefer he should be captured. If he attempts to escape . . . he will be shot down." [13]

But Manuelito was too clever to fall into Carleton's trap at Zuni, and he managed to avoid capture through the spring and summer of 1865. Late in the summer Barboncito and several of his warriors escaped from Bosque Redondo; they were said to be in the Apache country of Sierra del Escadello. So many Navahos were slipping away from the reservation that Carleton posted permanent guards for forty miles around Fort Sumner. In August the general ordered the post commander to kill every Navaho found off the reservation without a pass.

When the Bosque's grain crops failed again in the autumn of 1865, the Army issued the Navahos meal, flour, and bacon which had been condemned as unfit for soldiers to eat. Deaths began to rise again, and so did the number of attempted escapes.

Although General Carleton was being openly criticized now by New Mexicans for conditions at Bosque Redondo, he continued to hunt down Navahos. At last, on September 1, 1866, the chief he wanted most—Manuelito—limped into Fort Wingate with twenty-three beaten warriors and surrendered. They were all in rags, their bodies emaciated. They still wore leather bands on their wrists for protection from the slaps of bowstrings, but they had no war bows, no arrows. One of Manuelito's arms hung useless at his side from a wound. A short time later Barboncito came in with twenty-one followers and surrendered for the second time. Now there were no more war chiefs.

Ironically, only eighteen days after Manuelito surrendered, General Carleton was removed from command of the Army's Department of New Mexico. The Civil War, which had brought Star Chief Carleton to power, had been over for more than a year, and the New Mexicans had had enough of him and his pompous ways.

When Manuelito arrived at the Bosque a new superintendent was there, A. B. Norton. The superintendent examined the soil on the reservation and pronounced it unfit for cultivation of grain because of the presence of alkali. "The water is black and brackish, scarcely bearable to the taste, and said by the Indians to be unhealthy, because one-fourth of their population have been swept off by disease." The reservation, Norton added, had cost the government millions of dollars. "The sooner it is abandoned and the Indians removed, the better. I have heard it suggested that there was speculation at the bottom of it. . . . Do you expect an Indian to be satisfied and contented deprived of the common comforts of life, without which a white man would not be contented anywhere? Would any sensible man select a spot for a reservation for 8,000 Indians where the water is scarcely bearable, where the soil is poor and cold, and where the muskite [mesquite] roots 12 miles distant are the only wood for the Indians to use? . . . If they remain on this reservation

they must always be held there by force, and not from choice.
O! let them go back, or take them to where they can have good
cool water to drink, wood plenty to keep them from freezing to
death, and where the soil will produce something for them to
eat. . . ." [14]

For two years a steady stream of investigators and officials
from Washington paraded through the reservation. Some were
genuinely compassionate; some were mainly concerned with re-
ducing expenditures.

"We were there for a few years," Manuelito remembered.
"Many of our people died from the climate. . . . People from
Washington held a council with us. He explained how the whites
punished those who disobeyed the law. We promised to obey
the laws if we were permitted to get back to our own country.
We promised to keep the treaty. . . . We promised four times
to do so. We all said 'yes' to the treaty, and he gave us good
advice. He was General Sherman."

When the Navaho leaders first saw the Great Warrior Sherman
they were fearful of him because his face was the same as Star
Chief Carleton's—fierce and hairy with a cruel mouth—but his
eyes were different, the eyes of a man who had suffered and
knew the pain of it in others.

"We told him we would try to remember what he said," Manuelito recalled. "He said: 'I want all you people to look at me.'
He stood up for us to see him. He said if we would do right we
could look people in the face. Then he said: 'My children, I will
send you back to your homes.'"

Before they could leave, the chiefs had to sign the new treaty
(June 1, 1868), which began: "From this day forward all war
between the parties to this agreement shall forever cease." Barboncito signed first, then Armijo, Delgadito, Manuelito, Herrero
Grande, and seven others.

"The nights and days were long before it came time for us to
go to our homes," Manuelito said. "The day before we were
to start we went a little way towards home, because we were
so anxious to start. We came back and the Americans gave us
a little stock and we thanked them for that. We told the drivers
to whip the mules, we were in such a hurry. When we saw the
top of the mountain from Albuquerque we wondered if it was

3. *A Navaho warrior of the 1860's. Photographed by John Gaw Meem and reproduced by permission of the Denver Art Museum.*

our mountain, and we felt like talking to the ground, we loved
it so, and some of the old men and women cried with joy when
they reached their homes." [15]

And so the Navahos came home. When the new reservation
lines were surveyed, much of their best pastureland was taken
away for the white settlers. Life would not be easy. They would
have to struggle to endure. Bad as it was, the Navahos would
come to know that they were the least unfortunate of all the
western Indians. For the others, the ordeal had hardly begun.

IN A SACRED MANNER I LIVE

Courtesy of the Bureau of American Ethnology Collection

> In a sacred manner
> I live.
> To the heavens
> I gazed.
> In a sacred manner I live.
> My horses
> Are many.

THREE

Little Crow's War

1862—*April 6,* General Grant defeats Confederates in Battle of Shiloh. May 6, Henry D. Thoreau dies at age 45. May 20, Congress passes Homestead Act, granting 160 acres of western land to settlers at $1.25 per acre. July 2, Congress passes Morrill Act for creation of land-grant colleges. July 10, construction of Central Pacific Railroad begins. August 30, Union Army defeated in Second Battle of Bull Run. September 17, Confederate Army defeated at Antietam. September 22, Lincoln declares all slaves free from January 1, 1863. October 13, in Germany, Bismarck delivers "blood-and-iron" speech. December 13, Union Army suffers severe losses and defeat at Fredericksburg; nation plunged into gloom; some Army units near mutiny as they go into winter quarters. December 29, General Sherman defeated at Chickasaw Bayou. Victor Hugo's *Les Miserables* and Turgenev's *Fathers and Sons* published.

1863—*April 2,* bread riot in Richmond, Virginia. May 2–4, Confederates win victory at Chancellorsville. July 1–3, Union Army defeats Confederates at Gettysburg. July 4, Vicksburg falls to Grant's army. July 11, drafting of soldiers for Union Army begins. July 13–17, several hundred lives lost in New York City draft riots; other riots occur in many cities. July 15, President Davis orders first conscriptions for Confederate service. September 5, bread riots in Mobile; value of Confederate dollar drops to eight cents. October 1, five Russian war vessels enter port of New York and are warmly received. November 24–25, Confederates defeated at Chattanooga. December 8, President Lincoln offers amnesty to Confederates willing to return allegiance to the Union.

The whites were always trying to make the Indians give up their life and live like white men—go to farming, work hard and do as they did—and the Indians did not know how to do that, and did not want to anyway. . . . If the Indians had tried to make the whites live like them, the whites would have resisted, and it was the same way with many Indians.

—WAMDITANKA (BIG EAGLE) OF THE SANTEE SIOUX

ALMOST a thousand miles north of the Navaho country and at this same time of the white men's great Civil War, the Santee Sioux were losing their homeland forever. The Santees were of four divisions—the Mdewkantons, Wahpetons, Wahpekutes, and Sissetons. They were woodland Sioux but kept close ties and shared a strong tribal pride with their blood brothers of the prairies, the Yanktons and the Tetons. The Santees were the "people of the farther end," the frontier guardians of the Sioux domain.

During the ten years preceding the Civil War, more than 150,-000 white settlers pushed into Santee country, thus collapsing the left flank of the once "permanent Indian frontier." As the result of two deceptive treaties, the woodland Sioux surrendered nine-tenths of their land and were crowded into a narrow strip of territory along the Minnesota River. From the beginning, agents and traders had hovered around them like buzzards around the carcasses of slaughtered buffalo, systematically cheating them out of the greater part of the promised annuities for which they had been persuaded to give up their lands.

"Many of the white men often abused the Indians and treated them unkindly," Big Eagle said. "Perhaps they had excuse, but the Indians did not think so. Many of the whites always seemed to say by their manner when they saw an Indian, 'I am better than you,' and the Indians did not like this. There was excuse

38

for this, but the Dakotas [Sioux] did not believe there were better men in the world than they. Then some of the white men abused the Indian women in a certain way and disgraced them, and surely there was no excuse for that. All these things made many Indians dislike the whites." [1]

In the summer of 1862 everything seemed to go badly between the Santees and the white men. Most of the wild game was gone from the reservation land, and when the Indians crossed into their old hunting grounds now claimed by white settlers, there was often trouble. For the second year running, the Indians' crop yields were poor, and many of them had to go to the agency traders to obtain food on credit. The Santees had learned to hate the credit system because they had no control over the accounts. When their annuities came from Washington, the traders held first claim on the money, and whatever amount the traders claimed in their accounts, government agents would pay them. Some of the Santees had learned to keep accounts, and although their records might be less by many dollars than the traders' accounts, the government agents would not accept them.

Ta-oya-te-duta (Little Crow) became very angry with the traders during the summer of 1862. Little Crow was a chief of the Mdewkantons, as had been his father and grandfather before him. He was sixty years old and always wore long-sleeved garments to cover his lower arms and wrists, which were withered as the result of badly healed wounds received in battle during his youth. Little Crow had signed both the treaties that tricked his people out of their land and the money promised for the land. He had been to Washington to see the Great Father, President Buchanan; he had exchanged his breechclouts and blankets for trousers and brass-buttoned jackets; he had joined the Episcopal Church, built a house, and started a farm. But during the summer of 1862 Little Crow's disillusionment was turning to anger.

In July several thousand Santees assembled at the Upper Agency on Yellow Medicine River to collect their annuities, which were pledged by the treaties, so that they might exchange them for food. The money did not arrive, and there were rumors that the Great Council (Congress) in Washington had expended all their gold fighting the great Civil War and could not send any money to the Indians. Because their people were starving, Little Crow and some of the other chiefs went to their agent, Thomas Galbraith, and asked why they could not be issued food from the agency warehouse, which was filled with provisions. Galbraith replied that he could not do this until the money arrived, and he brought up a hundred soldiers to guard the warehouse. On August 4 five hundred Santees surrounded the soldiers while others broke into the warehouse and began carrying out sacks of flour. The white soldier chief, Timothy Sheehan, sympathized with the Santees. Instead of firing upon them he persuaded agent Galbraith to issue pork and flour to the Indians and await payment until the money arrived. After Galbraith did this, the Santees went away peacefully. Little Crow did not leave, however, until the agent promised to issue similar amounts of food to the Santees at the Lower Agency, thirty miles downriver at Redwood.

Although Little Crow's village was near the Lower Agency, Galbraith kept him waiting several days before arranging a council at Redwood for August 15. Early that morning Little Crow and several hundred hungry Mdewkantons assembled, but it was obvious from the beginning that Galbraith and the four traders at the Lower Agency had no intention of issuing food from their stores before arrival of the annuity funds.

Angered by yet another broken promise, Little Crow arose, faced Galbraith, and spoke for his people: "We have waited a long time. The money is ours, but we cannot get it. We have no food, but here are these stores, filled with food. We ask that you, the agent, make some arrangement by which we can get food from the stores, or else we may take our own way to keep ourselves from starving. When men are hungry they help themselves." [2]

Instead of replying, Galbraith turned to the traders and asked them what they would do. Trader Andrew Myrick declared contemptuously: "So far as I am concerned, if they are hungry let them eat grass or their own dung." [3]

For a moment the circle of Indians was silent. Then came an outburst of angry shouts, and as one man the Santees arose and left the council.

The words of Andrew Myrick angered all the Santees, but to

4. *Little Crow, or Tshe-ton Wa-ka-wa Ma-ni, the Hawk That Hunts Walking. From a photograph taken in 1858 by A. Zeno Shindler, courtesy of the Smithsonian Institution.*

Little Crow they were like hot blasts upon his already seared emotions. For years he had tried to keep the treaties, to follow the advice of the white men and lead his people on their road. It seemed now that he had lost everything. His own people were losing faith in him, blaming him for their misfortunes, and now the agents and traders had turned against him. Earlier that summer the Lower Agency Mdewkantons had accused Little Crow of betraying them when he signed away their lands by treaties. They had elected Traveling Hail to be their speaker in place of Little Crow. If Little Crow could have persuaded agent Galbraith and the traders to give his people food, they would have respected him again, but he had failed.

In the old days he could have regained leadership by going to war, but the treaties pledged him not to engage in hostilities with either the white men or other tribes. Why was it, he wondered, that the Americans talked so much of peace between themselves and the Indians, and between Indians and Indians, and yet they themselves waged such a savage war with the Graycoats that they had no money left to pay their small debts to the Santees? He knew that some of the young men in his band were talking openly of war with the white men, a war to drive them out of the Minnesota Valley. It was a good time to fight the whites, they said, because so many Bluecoat soldiers were away fighting the Graycoats. Little Crow considered such talk foolish; he had been to the East and seen the power of the Americans. They were everywhere like locusts and destroyed their enemies with great thundering cannon. War upon the white men was unthinkable.

On Sunday, August 17, Little Crow attended the Episcopal Church at the Lower Agency and listened to a sermon delivered by the Reverend Samuel Hinman. At the conclusion of services, he shook hands with the other worshipers and returned to his house, which was two miles upriver from the agency.

Late that night Little Crow was awakened by the sound of many voices and the noisy entry of several Santees into his sleeping room. He recognized the voice of Shakopee. Something very important, something very bad, had happened. Shakopee, Mankato, Medicine Bottle, and Big Eagle all had come, and they said Wabasha would soon arrive for a council.

Four young men of Shakopee's band who were hungry for food had crossed the river that sunny afternoon to hunt in the Big Woods, and something very bad had happened there. Big Eagle told about it: "They came to a settler's fence, and here they found a hen's nest with some eggs in it. One of them took the eggs, when another said: 'Don't take them, for they belong to a white man and we may get into trouble.' The other was angry, for he was very hungry and wanted to eat the eggs, and he dashed them to the ground and replied: 'You are a coward. You are afraid of the white man. You are afraid to take even an egg from him, though you are half-starved. Yes, you are a coward, and I will tell everybody so.' The other replied: 'I am not a coward. I am not afraid of the white man, and to show you that I am not I will go to the house and shoot him. Are you brave enough to go with me?' The one who had called him coward said: 'Yes, I will go with you, and we will see who is the braver of us two.' Their two companions then said: 'We will go with you, and we will be brave, too.' They all went to the house of the white man, but he got alarmed and went to another house where there were some other white men and women. The four Indians followed them and killed three men and two women. Then they hitched up a team belonging to another settler and drove to Shakopee's camp . . . and told what they had done." [4]

On hearing of the murders of the white people, Little Crow rebuked the four young men, and then sarcastically asked Shakopee and the others why they had come to him for advice when they had chosen Traveling Hail to be their spokesman. The leaders assured Little Crow that he was still their war chief. No Santee's life would be safe now after these killings, they said. It was the white man's way to punish all Indians for the crimes of one or a few; the Santees might as well strike first instead of waiting for the soldiers to come and kill them. It would be better to fight the white men now while they were fighting among themselves far to the south.

Little Crow rejected their arguments. The white men were too powerful, he said. Yet he admitted the settlers would exact bitter vengeance because women had been killed. Little Crow's son, who was present, said later that his father's face grew haggard and great beads of sweat stood out on his forehead.

At last one of the young braves cried out: "Ta-oya-te-duta [Little Crow] is a coward!"

"Coward" was the word that had started the killings, the challenge to the young boy who was afraid to take the white man's eggs even when he was starving. "Coward" was not a word that a Sioux chief could take lightly, even though he was halfway on the white man's road.

Little Crow's reply (as remembered by his young son): "Ta-oya-te-duta is not a coward, and he is not a fool! When did he run away from his enemies? When did he leave his braves behind him on the warpath and turn back to his tepee? When he ran away from your enemies, he walked behind on your trail with his face to the Ojibways and covered your backs as a she-bear covers her cubs! Is Ta-oya-te-duta without scalps? Look at his war feathers! Behold the scalp locks of your enemies hanging there on his lodgepoles! Do you call him a coward? Ta-oya-te-duta is not a coward, and he is not a fool. Braves, you are like little children; you know not what you are doing.

"You are full of the white man's devil water. You are like dogs in the Hot Moon when they run mad and snap at their own shadows. We are only little herds of buffalo left scattered; the great herds that once covered the prairies are no more. See!—the white men are like the locusts when they fly so thick that the whole sky is a snowstorm. You may kill one—two—ten; yes, as many as the leaves in the forest yonder, and their brothers will not miss them. Kill one—two—ten, and ten times ten will come to kill you. Count your fingers all day long and white men with guns in their hands will come faster than you can count.

"Yes; they fight among themselves—away off. Do you hear the thunder of their big guns? No; it would take you two moons to run down to where they are fighting, and all the way your path would be among white soldiers as thick as tamaracks in the swamps of the Ojibways. Yes; they fight among themselves, but if you strike at them they will all turn on you and devour you and your women and little children just as the locusts in their time fall on the trees and devour all the leaves in one day.

"You are fools. You cannot see the face of your chief; your eyes are full of smoke. You cannot hear his voice; your ears are full of roaring waters. Braves, you are little children—you are fools. You will die like the rabbits when the hungry wolves hunt them in the Hard Moon of January.

"Ta-oya-te-duta is not a coward; he will die with you." [5]

Big Eagle then spoke for peace, but he was shouted down. Ten years of abuse by white men—the broken treaties, the lost hunting grounds, the unkept promises, the undelivered annuities, their hunger for food while the agency warehouses overflowed with it, the insulting words of Andrew Myrick—all rose up to put the murders of the white settlers into the background.

Little Crow sent messengers upstream to summon the Wahpetons and Sissetons to join in the war. The women were awakened and began to run bullets while the warriors cleaned their guns.

"Little Crow gave orders to attack the agency early next morning and to kill all the traders," Big Eagle said afterward. "The next morning, when the force started to attack the agency, I went along. I did not lead my band, and I took no part in the killing. I went to save the lives of two particular friends if I could. I think others went for the same reason, for nearly every Indian had a friend he did not want killed; of course he did not care about anybody's else friend. The killing was nearly all done when I got there. Little Crow was on the ground directing operations. . . . Mr. Andrew Myrick, a trader, with an Indian wife, had refused some hungry Indians credit a short time before when they asked him for some provisions. He said to them: 'Go and eat grass.' Now he was lying on the ground dead, with his mouth stuffed full of grass, and the Indians were saying tauntingly: 'Myrick is eating grass himself.' " [6]

The Santees killed twenty men, captured ten women and children, emptied the warehouses of provisions, and set the other buildings afire. The remaining forty-seven inhabitants (some of whom were aided in their escapes by friendly Santees) fled across the river to Fort Ridgely, thirteen miles downstream.

On the way to Fort Ridgely the survivors met a company of forty-five soldiers marching to the aid of the agency. The Reverend Hinman, who the previous day had preached the last sermon ever heard by Little Crow, warned the soldiers to turn back. The soldier chief, John Marsh, refused to heed the warning and marched into a Santee ambush. Only twenty-four of his men escaped alive to make their way back to the fort.

Encouraged by his first successes, Little Crow decided to attack the Soldiers' House itself, Fort Ridgely. Wabasha and his band had arrived, Mankato's force had been increased by more warriors, fresh allies were reported on their way from the Upper Agency, and Big Eagle could no longer remain neutral while his people were at war.

During the night these chiefs and their several hundred warriors moved down the Minnesota Valley and early on the morning of August 19 began assembling on the prairie west of the fort. "The young men were all anxious to go," said Lightning Blanket, one of the participants, "and we dressed as warriors in war paint, breechclouts and leggings, with a large sash around us to keep our food and ammunition in." [7]

When some of the untried young men saw the sturdy stone buildings of the Soldiers' House and the armed Bluecoats waiting there, they had second thoughts about attacking the place. On the way down from the Lower Agency they had talked of how easy it would be to raid the village on the Cottonwood, New Ulm. The town across the river was filled with stores to be looted, and no soldiers were there. Why could they not do their fighting at New Ulm? Little Crow told them the Santees were at war, and to be victorious they must defeat the Bluecoat soldiers. If they could drive the soldiers from the valley, then all the white settlers would go away. The Santees could gain nothing by killing a few white people at New Ulm.

But in spite of Little Crow's scoldings and entreaties, the young men began to drift away toward the river. Little Crow consulted with the other chiefs, and they decided to delay the assault on Fort Ridgely until the next day.

That evening the young men returned from New Ulm. They had frightened the people there, they said, but the town was too strongly defended, and besides, a bad lightning storm came out of the sky in the afternoon. Big Eagle called them "marauding Indians" without a chief to lead them, and that night they all agreed to stay together and attack Fort Ridgely the following morning.

"We started at sunrise," Lightning Blanket said, "and crossed the river at the agency on the ferry, following the road to the top of the hill below Faribault's Creek, where we stopped for a short rest. There the plans for attacking the fort were given out by Little Crow. . . .

"After reaching the fort, the signal, three volleys, was to be given by Medicine Bottle's men to draw the attention and fire of the soldiers, so the men on the east (Big Eagle's) and those on the west and south (Little Crow's and Shakopee's) could rush in and take the fort.

"We reached the Three Mile Creek before noon and cooked something to eat. After eating we separated, I going with the footmen to the north, and after leaving Little Crow we paid no attention to the chiefs; everyone did as he pleased. Both parties reached the fort about the same time, as we could see them passing to the west, Little Crow on a black pony. The signal, three shots, was given by our side, Medicine Bottle's men. After the signal the men on the east, south, and west were slow in coming up. While shooting we ran up to the building near the big stone one. As we were running in we saw the man with the big guns, whom we all knew, and as we were the only ones in sight he shot into us, as he had gotten ready after hearing the shooting in our direction. Had Little Crow's men fired after we fired the signal, the soldiers who shot at us would have been killed. Two of our men were killed and three hurt, two dying afterward. We ran back into the creek and did not know whether the other men would come up close or not, but they did and the big guns drove them back from that direction. If we had known that they would come up close, we could have shot at the same time and killed all, as the soldiers were out in the big opening between the buildings. We did not fight like white men with one officer; we all shot as we pleased. The plan of rushing into the buildings was given up, and we shot at the windows, mostly at the big stone building, as we thought many of the whites were in there.

"We could not see them, so were not sure we were killing any. During the shooting we tried to set fire to the buildings with fire arrows, but the buildings would not burn, so we had to get more powder and bullets. The sun was about two hours high when we went around to the west of the fort, and decided to go back to Little Crow's village and come and keep up the fighting next day. . . .

"There were about four hundred Indians in this attack; no

women were along. They all stayed at Little Crow's village. The
cooking was done by boys ten to fifteen years of age, too young
to fight." [8]

That evening in the village, both Little Crow and Big Eagle
were low in spirits because they had not been able to take the
Soldiers' House. Big Eagle opposed another attack. The Santees
did not have enough warriors to storm the soldiers' big guns,
he said. They would lose too many men if they made another
attack. Little Crow said he would decide later what to do. Meanwhile everyone should go to work making as many bullets as
possible; there was plenty of gunpowder left from the agency
storehouse.

Later in the evening the situation changed. Four hundred
Wahpeton and Sisseton warriors came in from the Upper Agency
and offered to join the Mdewkantons in their war against the
white men. Little Crow was elated. The Santee Sioux were united
again, eight hundred strong, surely enough warriors to take Fort
Ridgely. He called a war council and issued strict orders for the
next day's fighting. This time they must not fail.

"Early on August 22 we started," Lightning Blanket said, "but
the grass was wet with dew, more than on the day of the first
attack, so the sun was quite high before we traveled very far
and it was just before the middle of the day when we reached
the fort. . . . We did not stop to eat this time, but each carried
something to eat in his legging sash and ate it in the middle of
the day, while fighting." [9]

Big Eagle said the second fight at Fort Ridgely was a grand
affair. "We went down determined to take the fort, for we knew
it was of the greatest importance to us to have it. If we could
take it we would soon have the whole Minnesota Valley."

This time, instead of approaching the fort boldly, the Santee
warriors fastened prairie grass and flowers to their headbands
as a means of concealment and then crept up the gullies and
crawled through the brush until they were close enough to fire
upon the defenders. A shower of blazing arrows set roofs afire;
then the Santees rushed the stables. "In this fight," said Wakonk-
dayamanne, "I came up on the south side to the stables and tried
to get a horse. As I was leading it out a shell burst in the stable
near me and the horse sprang over me and got away, knocking

5. *Big Eagle. Photo by Simons and Shepherd at Camp McClellan in Davenport, Iowa. Courtesy of Minnesota Historical Society.*

me down. When I got up I saw a mule running and I was so mad I shot it." [10] For a few minutes there was hand-to-hand fighting around the stables, but again the Santees had to give way before fierce blasts of the soldiers' artillery.

Little Crow was wounded, not seriously, but the loss of blood weakened him. When he withdrew from the field to regain his strength, Mankato led another assault. Double-charges of canister shot cut down the rushing warriors, and the attack failed.

"But for the cannon I think we would have taken the fort," Big Eagle said. "The soldiers fought us so bravely we thought there were more of them than there were." (About 150 soldiers and twenty-five armed civilians defended Fort Ridgely on August 22.) Big Eagle lost the most men in the fighting that day.

Late in the afternoon the Santee leaders called off the attack. "The sun was now setting low," Lightning Blanket said, "and after we saw the men on the south and west driven back by the big guns, and could see Little Crow and his men going to the northwest, we decided to join them and see what to do. . . . After joining them we supposed we were going back to Little Crow's village for more warriors. . . . Little Crow told us there were no more warriors, and a discussion followed. Some wanted to renew the attack on the fort the next morning and then go to New Ulm; others wanted to attack New Ulm early the next morning and then come back and take the fort. We were afraid the soldiers would get to New Ulm first." [11]

The soldiers that Lightning Blanket referred to were 1,400 men of the Sixth Minnesota Regiment approaching from St. Paul. They were led by a soldier chief quite well known to the Santee Sioux. He was the Long Trader, Colonel Henry H. Sibley. Of the $475,000 promised the Santees in their first treaty, Long Trader Sibley had claimed $145,000 for his American Fur Company as money due for overpayments to the Santees. The Santees believed the fur company had underpaid them, but their agent Alexander Ramsey had accepted Sibley's claim, as well as the claims of other traders, so that the Santees received practically nothing for their lands. (Ramsey was now the governor of Minnesota, and he had appointed the Long Trader to be the Eagle Chief of the Minnesota regiment.)

At midmorning of August 23, the Santees attacked New Ulm. They streamed out of the woods in bright sunlight, formed an arc across the prairie, and swept toward the town. The citizens of New Ulm were ready for them. After the abortive attack by the young braves on August 19, the townspeople had built barricades, brought in more weapons, and secured the help of militia from towns down the valley. When the Santees came within a mile and a half of the forward line of white defenders, the mass of warriors began spreading like a fan. At the same time, they increased their speed and began yelling war cries to frighten the white men. Mankato was the war leader on this day (Little Crow lay wounded in his village), and his plan of attack was to envelop the town.

The firing on both sides was sharp and rapid, but the onrush of Indians was slowed by the citizens, who used loopholed buildings for defensive positions. Early in the afternoon the Santees set fire to several structures on the windward side of New Ulm in expectation of advancing under a smoke screen. Sixty warriors, mounted and on foot, charged a barricade, but were driven back by heavy volleys. It was a long and bitter battle, fought in the streets, dwellings, outhouses, and store buildings. When darkness fell, the Santees departed without a victory, but they left behind them the smoldering ruins of 190 buildings and more than a hundred casualties among the stubborn defenders of New Ulm.

Three days later the advance column of Long Trader Sibley's regiment reached Fort Ridgely, and the Santees began withdrawing up the Minnesota Valley. They had with them more than two hundred prisoners, mostly white women and children and a considerable number of half-breeds known to be sympathetic toward the whites. After establishing a temporary village about forty miles above the Upper Agency, Little Crow began negotiating with other Sioux leaders in the area, hoping to gain their support. He had little success. One reason for their lack of enthusiasm was Little Crow's failure to drive the soldiers from Fort Ridgely. Another reason was the indiscriminate killing of white settlers on the north side of the Minnesota River, a bloody slaughter carried out by marauding bands of undisciplined young men while Little Crow was besieging Fort Ridgely. Several hundred settlers had been trapped in their cabins without warning. Many had been brutally slain. Others had fled to safety, some to the villages of the Sioux bands that Little Crow hoped would join his cause.

Although Little Crow was contemptuous of those who made war on defenseless settlers, he knew that his decision to begin the war had unleashed the raiders. But it was too late to turn back. The war against the soldiers would go on as long as he had warriors to fight them.

On September 1 he decided to make a scout downriver to test the strength of Long Trader Sibley's army. The Santees divided into two forces, Little Crow leading 110 warriors along the north side of the Minnesota, while Big Eagle and Mankato scouted the south bank with a larger force.

Little Crow's plan was to avoid a frontal meeting with the soldiers, and instead slip around to the rear of Sibley's lines and try to capture the army's supply train. To do this he made a wide swing to the north, bringing his warriors close to several settlements which had withstood attacks from marauders during the previous two weeks. The temptation to raid some of the smaller settlements brought on dissension among Little Crow's followers. On the second day of the reconnaissance, one of the subchiefs called a war council and proposed that they attack the settlements for plunder. Little Crow was opposed. Their enemies were the soldiers, he insisted; they must fight the soldiers. At the end of the council, seventy-five warriors joined the subchief for plundering. Only thirty-five loyal followers remained with Little Crow.

On the following morning Little Crow's small party unexpectedly met a company of seventy-five soldiers. During the running battle which followed, the sound of musketry brought the defecting Santees of the previous day rushing back to Little Crow's rescue. In bloody close-in fighting, the soldiers used their bayonets, but the Santees killed six and wounded fifteen of their enemy before the latter escaped in a hasty retreat to Hutchinson.

For the next two days the Santees reconnoitered around Hutchinson and Forest City, but the soldiers remained within stockades. On September 5 runners brought news of a battle a few miles to the southwest. Big Eagle and Mankato had trapped the Long Trader's soldiers at Birch Coulee.

During the night before the battle at Birch Coulee, Big Eagle and Mankato had quietly surrounded the soldiers' camp so they could not escape. "Just at dawn the fight began," Big Eagle said. "It continued all day and the following night until late the next morning. Both sides fought well. Owing to the white men's way of fighting they lost many men. Owing to the Indians' way of fighting they lost but few. . . . About the middle of the afternoon our men became much dissatisfied at the slowness of the fight, and the stubbornness of the whites, and the word was passed around the lines to get ready to charge the camp. The brave Mankato wanted to charge after the first hour. . . .

"Just as we were about to charge, word came that a large number of mounted soldiers were coming up from the east toward Fort Ridgely. This stopped the charge and created some excitement. Mankato at once took some men from the coulee and went out to meet them. . . . Mankato flourished his men around so, and all the Indians in the coulee kept up a noise, and at last the whites began to fall back, and they retreated about two miles and began to dig breastworks. Mankato followed them and left about thirty men to watch them, and returned to the fight at the coulee with the rest. The Indians were laughing when they came back at the way they had deceived the white men, and we were all glad that the whites had not pushed forward and driven us away. . . .

"The next morning General Sibley came with a very large force and drove us away from the field. We took our time getting away. Some of our men said they remained till Sibley got up and that they fired at some of his men as they were shaking hands with some of the men of the camp. Those of us who were on the prairie went back to the westward and on down the valley. . . . There was no pursuit. The whites fired their cannons at us as we were leaving the field, but they might as well have beaten a big drum for all the harm they did. They only made a noise. We went back across the river to our camps in the old village, and then on up the river to the Yellow Medicine and the mouth of the Chippewa, where Little Crow joined us. . . . At last the word came that Sibley with his army was again on the move against us. . . . He had left a letter for Little Crow in a split stick on the battlefield of Birch Coulee, and some of our men found it and brought it in. . . ." [12]

The message left by the Long Trader was brief and noncommittal:

> If Little Crow has any proposition to make, let him send a
> half-breed to me, and he shall be protected in and out of camp.
>   H. H. Sibley, Col. Com'd Mil. Ex'n.[13]

Little Crow of course did not trust this man who was sharp
enough to get away with so much of the Santees' treaty money.
But he decided to send a reply. He thought that perhaps the Long
Trader, who had been up at the White Rock (St. Paul), did not
know why the Santees had gone to war. Little Crow also wanted
Governor Ramsey to know the reasons for the war. Many of the
neutrals among the Santees were frightened at what Ramsey had
told the white Minnesotans: "The Sioux Indians must be exterminated or driven forever beyond the borders of the state." [14]

Little Crow's message of September 7 to General Sibley:

> For what reason we have commenced this war I will tell you.
> It is on account of Major Galbraith. We made a treaty with
> the government, and beg for what we do get, and can't get that
> till our children are dying with hunger. It is the traders who
> commenced it. Mr. A. J. Myrick told the Indians that they
> would eat grass or dirt. Then Mr. Forbes told the Lower Sioux
> that they were not men. Then Roberts was working with his
> friends to defraud us out of our moneys.* If the young braves
> have pushed the white men, I have done this myself. So I want
> you to let Governor Ramsey know this. I have a great many
> prisoners, women and children. . . . I want you to give me an
> answer to the bearer.

General Sibley's reply:

> LITTLE CROW—You have murdered many of our people without
> any sufficient cause. Return me the prisoners under a flag of
> truce, and I will talk with you then like a man.[15]

Little Crow had no intention of returning the prisoners before
the Long Trader gave some indication of whether he meant to
carry out Governor Ramsey's dictum of extermination or exile
for the Santees. He wanted to use the prisoners for bargaining. In

---

* Thomas J. Galbraith was the reservation agent. A. J. Myrick, William Forbes,
and Louis Roberts were post traders at the Lower Agency.

the councils of the various bands, however, there was much disagreement over what course the Santees should take before Sibley's army reached the Yellow Medicine. Paul Mazakootemane of the Upper Agency Sissetons condemned Little Crow for starting the war. "Give me all these white captives," he demanded. "I will deliver them up to their friends. . . . Stop fighting. No one who fights with the white people ever becomes rich, or remains two days in one place, but is always fleeing and starving." [16]

Wabasha, who had been in the battles at Fort Ridgely and New Ulm, was also in favor of opening a road to peace by freeing the prisoners, but his son-in-law Rda-in-yan-ka spoke for Little Crow and the majority of the warriors: "I am for continuing the war, and am opposed to the delivery of the prisoners. I have no confidence that the whites will stand by any agreement they make if we give them up. Ever since we treated with them, their agents and traders have robbed and cheated us. Some of our people have been shot, some hung; others placed upon floating ice and drowned; and many have been starved in their prisons. It was not the intention of the nation to kill any of the whites until after the four men returned from Acton and told what they had done. When they did this, all the young men became excited, and commenced the massacre. The older ones would have prevented it if they could, but since the treaties they have lost all their influence. We may regret what has happened, but the matter has gone too far to be remedied. We have got to die. Let us, then, kill as many of the whites as possible, and let the prisoners die with us." [17]

On September 12 Little Crow gave the Long Trader one last chance to end the war without further bloodshed. In his message he assured Sibley that the prisoners were being treated kindly. "I want to know from you as a friend," he added, "what way that I can make peace for my people."

Unknown to Little Crow, on that same day Wabasha sent Sibley a secret message, blaming Little Crow for starting the war and claiming that he (Wabasha) was a friend of the "good white people." He did not mention that he had fought them a few weeks earlier at Fort Ridgely and New Ulm. "I have been kept back by threats that I should be killed if I did anything to help the whites," he declared, "but if you will now appoint some place for me to meet you, myself and the few friends that I have will get

all the prisoners we can, and with our family go to whatever place
you will appoint for us to meet."

Sibley answered both messages immediately. He scolded Little
Crow for not giving up the prisoners, telling him that was not the
way to make peace, but he did not answer the war leader's plea
for a way to end the fighting. Instead Sibley wrote a long letter to
Little Crow's betrayer, Wabasha, giving him explicit instructions
for using a truce flag for delivery of the prisoners. "I shall be
glad to receive all true friends of the whites," Sibley promised,
"with as many prisoners as they can bring, and I am powerful
enough to crush all who attempt to oppose my march, and to
punish those who have washed their hands in innocent blood." [18]

After Little Crow received the Long Trader's cold reply to his
entreaty, he knew there was no hope for peace except abject surrender. If the soldiers could not be beaten, then it was either
death or exile for the Santee Sioux.

On September 22 scouts reported that Sibley's soldiers had gone
into camp at Wood Lake. Little Crow decided to give them battle
before they reached the Yellow Medicine.

"All our fighting chiefs were present and all our best fighting
Indians," Big Eagle said. "We felt that this would be the deciding
fight of the war." Again as they had done at Birch Coulee, the
Santees silently prepared an ambush for the soldiers. "We could
hear them laughing and singing. When all our preparations were
made Little Crow and I and some other chiefs went to the mound
or hill to the west so as to watch the fight better when it should
commence. . . .

"The morning came and an accident spoiled our plans. For some
reason Sibley did not move early as we expected he would. Our
men were lying hidden, waiting patiently. Some were very near
the camp lines in the ravine, but the whites did not see a man of
all our men. I do not think they would have discovered our am-
buscade. It seemed a considerable time after sun-up when some
four or five wagons with a number of soldiers started out from the
camp in the direction of the old Yellow Medicine agency. We
learned afterwards that they were going without orders to dig
potatoes over at the agency, five miles away. They came on over
the prairie, right where part of our line was. Some of the wagons
were not in the road, and if they had kept straight on would

have driven right over our men as they lay in the grass. At last they came so close that our men had to rise up and fire. This brought on the fight, of course, but not according to the way we had planned it. Little Crow saw it and felt very badly. . . .

"The Indians that were in the fight did well, but hundreds of our men did not get into it and did not fire a shot. They were out too far. The men in the ravine and the line connecting them with those on the road did most of the fighting. Those of us on the hill did our best, but we were soon driven off. Mankato was killed here, and we lost a very good and very brave war chief. He was killed by a cannon ball that was so nearly spent that he was not afraid of it, and it struck him in the back, as he lay on the ground, and killed him. The whites drove our men out of the ravine by a charge and that ended the battle. We retreated in some disorder, though the whites did not offer to pursue us. We crossed a wide prairie, but their horsemen did not follow us. We lost fourteen or fifteen men killed and quite a number wounded. Some of the wounded died afterwards, but I do not know how many. We carried off no dead bodies, but took away all our wounded. The whites scalped all our dead men—so I have heard." (After the soldiers mutilated the dead Santees, Sibley issued an order forbidding such action: "The bodies of the dead, even of a savage enemy shall not be subjected to indignities by civilized and Christian men.")[19]

That evening in the Santees' camp twelve miles above the Yellow Medicine, the chiefs held a last council. Most of them were now convinced that the Long Trader was too strong for them. The woodland Sioux must surrender or flee to join their cousins, the prairie Sioux of the Dakota country. Those who had taken no part in the fighting decided to stay and surrender, certain that the delivery of the white prisoners would win them the friendship of Long Trader Sibley forever. They were joined by Wabasha, who persuaded his son-in-law Rda-in-yan-ka to stay. At the last minute, Big Eagle also decided to stay. Some of the half-breeds assured him that if he surrendered he would only be held as a prisoner of war a short time. He would live to regret his decision.

Next morning, bitter with defeat and feeling the weight of his sixty years, Little Crow made a last speech to his followers. "I

am ashamed to call myself a Sioux," he said. "Seven hundred of
our best warriors were whipped yesterday by the whites. Now we
had better all run away and scatter out over the plains like buffalo and wolves. To be sure, the whites had wagon-guns and better
arms than we, and there were many more of them. But that is no
reason why we should not have whipped them, for we are brave
Sioux and whites are cowardly women. I cannot account for the
disgraceful defeat. It must be the work of traitors in our midst." [20]
He and Shakopee and Medicine Bottle then ordered their people
to dismantle their tepees. In a few wagons taken from the agency,
they loaded their goods and provisions, their women and children,
and started westward. The Moon of the Wild Rice (September)
was coming to an end, and the cold moons were near at hand.

On September 26, with the assistance of Wabasha and Paul
Mazakootemane, who displayed truce flags, Sibley marched into
the Santee camp and demanded immediate delivery of the captives; 107 whites and 162 half-breeds were released to the soldiers.
In a council which followed, Sibley announced that the Santees
should consider themselves prisoners of war until he could discover and hang the guilty ones among them. The peace leaders
protested with obsequious avowals of friendship, such as Paul
Mazakootemane's: "I have grown up like a child of yours. With
what is yours, you have caused me to grow, and now I take your
hand as a child takes the hand of his father. . . . I have regarded
all white people as my friends, and from them I understand this
blessing has come." [21]

Sibley replied by putting a cordon of artillery around the camp.
He then sent out half-breed messengers to warn all Santees in the
Minnesota Valley to come in to Camp Release (as he had named
the place). Those who refused to come in voluntarily would be
hunted down and captured or killed. While the Santees were being
rounded up and disarmed, the soldiers cut down trees and con-
structed a huge log building. Its purpose was soon made clear,
when most of the male Santees—about 600 of the camp's 2,000
Indians—were chained together in pairs and imprisoned there.

Meanwhile Sibley had chosen five of his officers to form a military court to try all Santees suspected of engaging in the uprising.
As the Indians had no legal rights, he saw no reason to appoint a
defense counsel for them.

The first suspect brought before the court was a mulatto named Godfrey who was married to a woman of Wabasha's band and had been living at the Lower Agency for four years. Witnesses were three white women who had been among the captives. None accused him of rape, none had seen him commit a murder, but they said they had heard Godfrey boast of killing seven white people at New Ulm. On this evidence the military court found Godfrey guilty of murder and sentenced him to be hanged.

When Godfrey learned later that the court would be willing to commute his death sentence if he would identify Santees guilty of participating in the attacks, he became a willing informant, and the trials proceeded smoothly, as many as forty Indians a day being sentenced to imprisonment or death. On November 5 the trials ended; 303 Santees had been sentenced to death, sixteen to long prison terms.

The responsibility for extinguishing so many human lives, even if they were "devils in human shape," was more than Long Trader Sibley wanted to bear alone. He shifted the burden to the commander of the Military Department of the Northwest, General John Pope. General Pope in turn passed the final decision to the President of the United States, Abraham Lincoln. "The Sioux prisoners will be executed unless the President forbids it," General Pope informed Governor Ramsey, "which I am sure he will not do."

Being a man of conscience, however, Abraham Lincoln asked for "the full and complete record of the convictions; if the record does not fully indicate the more guilty and influential of the culprits, please have a careful statement made on these points and forward to me." On receipt of the trial records, the President assigned two lawyers to examine them so as to differentiate between murderers and those who had engaged only in battle.

Lincoln's refusal to authorize immediate hanging of the 303 condemned Santees angered General Pope and Governor Ramsey. Pope protested that "the criminals condemned ought in every view to be at once executed without exception. . . . Humanity requires an immediate disposition of the case." Ramsey demanded authority from the President to order speedy executions of the 303 condemned men, and warned that the people of Minnesota would take "private revenge" on the prisoners if Lincoln did not act quickly.[22]

While President Lincoln was reviewing the trial records, Sibley moved the condemned Indians to a prison camp at South Bend on the Minnesota River. While they were being escorted past New Ulm, a mob of citizens that included many women attempted "private revenge" on the prisoners with pitchforks, scalding water, and hurled stones. Fifteen prisoners were injured, one with a broken jaw, before the soldiers could march them beyond the town. Again on the night of December 4 a mob of citizens stormed the prison camp intent upon lynching the Indians. The soldiers kept the mob at bay, and next day transferred the Indians to a stronger stockade near the town of Mankato.

In the meantime Sibley decided to keep the remaining 1,700 Santees—mostly women and children—as prisoners, although they were accused of no crime other than having been born Indians. He ordered them transferred overland to Fort Snelling, and along the way they too were assaulted by angry white citizens. Many were stoned and clubbed; a child was snatched from its mother's arms and beaten to death. At Fort Snelling the four-mile-long procession was shunted into a fenced enclosure on damp bottomland. There, under soldier guard, housed in dilapidated shelters and fed on scanty rations, the remnants of the once proud woodland Sioux awaited their fate.

On December 6 President Lincoln notified Sibley that he should "cause to be executed" thirty-nine of the 303 convicted Santees. "The other condemned prisoners you will hold subject to further orders, taking care that they neither escape nor are subjected to any unlawful violence." [23]

Execution date was the twenty-sixth day of December in the Moon When the Deer Shed Their Horns. That morning the town of Mankato was filled with vindictive and morbidly curious citizens. A regiment of soldiers marched in to keep order. At the last minute, one Indian was given a reprieve. About ten o'clock, the thirty-eight condemned men were marched from the prison to the scaffold. They sang the Sioux death song until soldiers pulled white caps over their heads and placed nooses around their necks. At a signal from an army officer, the control rope was cut and thirty-eight Santee Sioux dangled lifeless in the air. But for the intercession of Abraham Lincoln there would have been three hundred; even so, a spectator boasted that it was "America's greatest mass execution."

A few hours later, officials discovered that two of the men hanged were not on Lincoln's list, but nothing was said of this publicly until nine years afterward. "It was a matter of regret that any mistakes were made," declared one of those responsible. "I feel sure they were not made intentionally." One of the innocent men hanged had saved a white woman's life during the raiding.[24]

Several others who were executed that day maintained their innocence until the end. One of them was Rda-in-yan-ka, who had tried to stop the war from starting, but later joined with Little Crow. When Little Crow and his followers left for Dakota, Wabasha had persuaded Rda-in-yan-ka not to go.

Shortly before his execution, Rda-in-yan-ka dictated a farewell letter to his chief:

> Wabasha—You have deceived me. You told me that if we followed the advice of General Sibley, and gave ourselves up to the whites, all would be well; no innocent man would be injured. I have not killed, wounded, or injured a white man, or any white persons. I have not participated in the plunder of their property; and yet today I am set apart for execution, and must die in a few days, while men who are guilty will remain in prison. My wife is your daughter, my children are your grandchildren. I leave them all in your care and under your protection. Do not let them suffer; and when my children are grown up, let them know that their father died because he followed the advice of his chief, and without having the blood of a white man to answer for to the Great Spirit.
>
> My wife and children are dear to me. Let them not grieve for me. Let them remember that the brave should be prepared to meet death; and I will do as becomes a Dakota.
>
> Your son-in-law,
Rda-in-yan-ka [25]

Those who escaped execution were sentenced to prison. One of them was Big Eagle, who readily admitted participating in the battles. "If I had known that I would be sent to the penitentiary," he said, "I would not have surrendered, but when I had been in the penitentiary three years and they were about to turn me out, I told them they might keep me another year if they wished, and I meant what I said. I did not like the way I had been treated. I surrendered in good faith, knowing that many of the whites were acquainted with me and that I had not been a murderer, or present when a murder had been committed, and if I had killed or wounded a man it had been in fair open fight." [26] Many of the others regretted that they had not fled from Minnesota with the warriors.

By the time of the executions, Little Crow and his followers were camped on Devil's Lake, a wintering place for several Sioux tribes. During the winter he tried to unite the chiefs in a military alliance, warning them that unless they were prepared to fight they would all go down before the invading whites. He won their sympathy, but few of the Plains Indians believed they were in any danger. If the white men moved into the Dakota country, the Indians would simply move farther west. The land was big enough for everybody.

In the spring Little Crow, Shakopee, and Medicine Bottle took their bands north into Canada. At Fort Garry (Winnipeg) Little Crow attempted to persuade the British authorities to aid the Santees. For his first meeting with them he dressed in his best clothing—a black coat with a velvet collar, a blue cloth breech-clout, and deerskin leggings. He reminded the British that his grandfather had been their ally in previous wars with the Americans, and that in the War of 1812 the Santees had captured a cannon from the Americans and presented it to the British. On that occasion, Little Crow said, the British had promised the Santees that if they were ever in trouble and wanted help, the British would bring the cannon back to them with men to work it. The Santees were now in trouble and wanted the cannon brought back.

An issue of foodstuffs, however, was all that Little Crow could obtain from the British Canadians. They had no cannon to give the Santees, not even ammunition for the weapons they had.

In the Strawberry Moon, June, 1863, Little Crow decided what he must do. If he and his family were forced to become Plains Indians, they must have horses. The white men who had driven him from his land had horses; he would take their horses in exchange for the land. He decided to return to Minnesota with a small party to capture horses.

His sixteen-year-old son, Wowinapa, later told about it: "Father said he could not fight the white men, but would go below and steal horses from them and give them to his children, so that they could be comfortable, and then he would go away off.

"Father also told me that he was getting old, and wanted me to go with him to carry his bundles. He left his wives and other children behind. There were sixteen men and one squaw in the party that went below with us. We had no horses, but walked all the way down to the settlements." [27]

In the Moon of the Red Blooming Lilies they reached the Big Woods, which only a few years before had been Santee country but now was filling up with farms and settlements. On the afternoon of July 3, Little Crow and Wowinapa left their hidden camping place and went to pick raspberries near the settlement of Hutchinson. About sundown they were sighted by two settlers returning home from a deer hunt. As the state of Minnesota had recently begun paying twenty-five-dollars bounty for Sioux scalps, the settlers immediately opened fire.

Little Crow was hit in the side, just above the hip. "His gun and mine were lying on the ground," Wowinapa said. "He took up my gun and fired it first, and then fired his own gun. The ball struck the stock of his gun, and then hit him in the side, near the shoulder. This was the shot that killed him. He told me that he was killed and asked me for water, which I gave him. He died immediately after. When I heard the first shot fired, I lay down, and the men did not see me before father was killed."

Wowinapa hurriedly dressed his dead father in new moccasins for the journey to the Land of Ghosts. He covered the body with a coat and fled to the camp. After warning the other members of the party to scatter, he started back to Devil's Lake. "I traveled only at night, and as I had no ammunition to kill anything to eat, I had not strength enough to travel fast." In an abandoned village near Big Stone Lake he found a single cartridge and managed to shoot a wolf. "I ate some of it, which gave me strength to travel, and I went on up the lake until the day I was captured." [28]

Wowinapa was captured by some of Long Trader Sibley's soldiers who had marched into the Dakota country that summer to kill Sioux. The soldiers returned the sixteen-year-old boy to Minnesota, where he was given a military trial and sentenced to be hanged. He learned then that his father's scalp and skull had been preserved and placed on exhibition in St. Paul. The state of Minnesota presented the settlers who had killed Little Crow with the regular scalp bounty and a bonus of five hundred dollars.

When Wowinapa's trial record was sent to Washington, military authorities disapproved of the proceedings and commuted the boy's sentence to imprisonment. (Some years later, after his release from prison, Wowinapa changed his name to Thomas Wakeman, became a church deacon, and founded the first Young Men's Christian Association among the Sioux.)

Meanwhile Shakopee and Medicine Bottle remained in Canada, believing themselves beyond reach of the vengeful Minnesotans. In December, 1863, however, one of the Long Trader's little chiefs, Major Edwin Hatch, marched a battalion of Minnesota cavalry to Pembina, just below the Canadian frontier.

From there Hatch sent a lieutenant across the line to Fort Garry to meet secretly with an American citizen, John McKenzie. With the aid of McKenzie and two Canadians, the lieutenant arranged the capture of Shakopee and Medicine Bottle. During a friendly meeting with the two Santee war chiefs, the conspirators gave them wine mixed with laudanum, chloroformed them while they slept, bound their hands and feet, and strapped them to a dog sled. In complete disregard of international law, the lieutenant hauled his captives across the border and delivered them to Major Hatch at Pembina. A few months later Sibley staged another spectacular trial, and Shakopee and Medicine Bottle were sentenced to be hanged. Of the verdict the St. Paul *Pioneer* commented: "We do not believe that serious injustice will be done by the executions tomorrow, but it would have been more creditable if some tangible evidence of their guilt had been obtained . . . no white man, tried before a jury of his peers, would be executed upon the testimony thus produced." After the hangings, the Minnesota legislature gratefully appropriated a thousand dollars as payment to John McKenzie for his services in Canada.[29]

The day of the Santee Sioux in Minnesota now came to an end. Although most of the war chiefs and warriors were dead, in prison, or far beyond the borders of the state, the uprising had given the white citizens an opportunity to seize the Santees' remaining lands without even a pretense of payment. Previous treaties were abrogated, and the surviving Indians were informed that they would be removed to a reservation in Dakota Territory. Even those leaders who had collaborated with the white men had to go. "Exterminate or banish," was the cry of the land-hungry settlers. The first shipment of 770 Santees left St. Paul by steamboat on May 4, 1863. White Minnesotans lined the river landing to see them off with shouts of derision and showers of hurled stones.

Crow Creek on the Missouri River was the site chosen for the Santee reservation. The soil was barren, rainfall scanty, wild game scarce, and the alkaline water unfit for drinking. Soon the surrounding hills were covered with graves; of the 1,300 Santees brought there in 1863, less than a thousand survived their first winter.

Among the visitors to Crow Creek that year was a young Teton Sioux. He looked with pity upon his Santee cousins and listened to their stories of the Americans who had taken their land and driven them away. Truly, he thought, that nation of white men is like a spring freshet that overruns its banks and destroys all who are in its path. Soon they would take the buffalo country unless the hearts of the Indians were strong enough to hold it. He resolved that he would fight to hold it. His name was Tatanka Yotanka, the Sitting Bull.

FOUR

War Comes to the Cheyennes

1864—January 13, Stephen Foster, composer of songs and ballads, dies at age 38. April 10, Archduke Maximilian, supported by a French army, becomes Emperor of Mexico. April 17, bread riot in Savannah, Georgia. May 19, Nathaniel Hawthorne dies at age 60. June 30, Secretary of the Treasury Chase resigns; charges speculators are plotting to prolong war for monetary gain. Legislator and historian Robert C. Winthrop says: "Professed patriotism may be made the cover for a multitude of sins." September 2, Atlanta, Georgia, taken by Union Army. November 8, Lincoln reelected President. December 8, in Rome, Pius IX issues *Syllabus Errorum*, condemning Liberalism, Socialism, and Rationalism. December 21, Savannah falls to Sherman's army. December, Edwin Booth playing in *Hamlet* at New York's Winter Garden Theater.

Although wrongs have been done me I live in hopes. I have not got two hearts. . . . Now we are together again to make peace. My shame is as big as the earth, although I will do what my friends advise me to do. I once thought that I was the only man that persevered to be the friend of the white man, but since they have come and cleaned out our lodges, horses, and everything else, it is hard for me to believe white men any more.

— MOTAVATO (BLACK KETTLE) OF THE SOUTHERN CHEYENNES

In 1851 the Cheyennes, Arapahos, Sioux, Crows, and other tribes met at Fort Laramie with representatives of the United States and agreed to permit the Americans to establish roads and military posts across their territory. Both parties to the treaty swore "to maintain good faith and friendship in all their mutual intercourse, and to make an effective and lasting peace." By the end of the first decade following the treaty signing, the white men had driven a hole through the Indian country along the valley of the Platte River. First came the wagon trains and then a chain of forts; then the stagecoaches and a closer-knit chain of forts; then the pony-express riders, followed by the talking wires of the telegraph.

In that treaty of 1851 the Plains Indians did not relinquish any rights or claims to their lands, nor did they "surrender the privilege of hunting, fishing or passing over any of the tracts of country heretofore described." The Pike's Peak gold rush of 1858 brought white miners by the thousands to dig yellow metal out of the Indians' earth. The miners built little wooden villages everywhere, and in 1859 they built a big village which they called Denver City. Little Raven, an Arapaho chief who was amused by the activities of white men, paid a visit to Denver; he learned to smoke cigars and to eat meat with a knife and fork. He also told the miners he was glad to see them getting gold, but reminded them that the land belonged to the Indians, and expressed the hope they would not stay around after they found all the yellow metal they needed.

The miners not only stayed, but thousands more of them came. The Platte Valley, which had once teemed with buffalo, began to fill with settlers staking out ranches and land claims on territory assigned by the Laramie treaty to Southern Cheyennes and Arapahos. Only ten years after the treaty signing, the Great Council in Washington created the Territory of Colorado; the Great Father sent out a governor; and politicians began maneuvering for a land cession from the Indians.

Through all of this the Cheyennes and Arapahos kept the peace, and when United States officials invited their leaders to gather at Fort Wise on the Arkansas River to discuss a new treaty, several chiefs responded. According to later statements of chiefs of both tribes, what they were told would be in the treaty and what was actually written into it were quite different. It was the understanding of the chiefs that the Cheyennes and Arapahos would retain their land rights and freedom of movement to hunt buffalo, but that they would agree to live within a triangular section of territory bounded by Sand Creek and the Arkansas River. Freedom of movement was an especially vital matter because the reservation assigned the two tribes had almost no wild game upon it and was unsuited to agriculture unless irrigated.

The treaty making at Fort Wise was a gala affair. Because of its importance, Colonel A. B. Greenwood, Commissioner of Indian Affairs, put in an appearance to pass out medals, blankets, sugar, and tobacco. The Little White Man (William Bent), who had married into the Cheyenne tribe, was there to look after the Indians' interests. When the Cheyennes pointed out that only six of their forty-four chiefs were present, the United States officials replied that the others could sign later. None of the others ever did, and for that reason the legality of the treaty was to remain in doubt. Black Kettle, White Antelope, and Lean Bear were among the signers for the Cheyennes. Little Raven, Storm, and Big Mouth signed for the Arapahos. Witnesses to the signatures were two officers of the United States Cavalry, John Sedgwick and J. E. B. Stuart. (A few months later Sedgwick and Stuart, who urged the Indians to peaceful pursuits, were fighting on opposite sides in the Civil War, and by one of the ironies of history they died within a few hours of each other in the battles of the Wilderness.)

During the first years of the white man's Civil War, Cheyenne and Arapaho hunting parties found it increasingly difficult to stay clear of Bluecoat soldiers who were scouting southward in search of Graycoats. They heard about the troubles of the Navahos, and from friends among the Sioux they learned of the awful fate of the Santees who dared challenge the power of the soldiers in Minnesota. Cheyenne and Arapaho chiefs tried to keep their young men busy hunting buffalo away from the white men's

routes of travel. Each summer, however, the numbers and arrogance of the Bluecoats increased. By the spring of 1864, soldiers
were prowling into remote hunting grounds between the Smoky
Hill and Republican rivers.

When the grass was well up that year, Roman Nose and quite
a number of the Dog Soldier Cheyennes went north for better
hunting in the Powder River country with their Northern
Cheyenne cousins. Black Kettle, White Antelope, and Lean Bear
kept their bands below the Platte, however, and so did Little
Raven of the Arapahos. They were careful to avoid soldiers and
white buffalo hunters by staying away from forts and trails and
settlements.

Black Kettle and Lean Bear did go down to Fort Larned (Kansas) that spring to trade. Only the year before the two chiefs had
been invited on a visit to see the Great Father, Abraham Lincoln,
in Washington, and they were sure the Great Father's soldiers at
Fort Larned would treat them well. President Lincoln gave them
medals to wear on their breasts, and Colonel Greenwood presented Black Kettle with a United States flag, a huge garrison
flag with white stars for the thirty-four states bigger than glittering stars in the sky on a clear night. Colonel Greenwood had told
him that as long as that flag flew above him no soldiers would
ever fire upon him. Black Kettle was very proud of his flag and
when in permanent camp always mounted it on a pole above his
tepee.

In the middle of May, Black Kettle and Lean Bear heard that
soldiers had attacked some Cheyennes on the South Platte River.
They decided to break camp and move northward to join the rest
of the tribe for strength and protection. After one day's march
they went into camp near Ash Creek. Next morning, as was the
custom, the hunters went out early for game, but they soon came
hurrying back. They had seen soldiers with cannons approaching
the camp.

Lean Bear liked excitement, and he told Black Kettle he would
go out and meet the soldiers and find out what they wanted. He
hung the medal from the Great Father Lincoln outside his coat
and took some papers that had been given him in Washington
certifying that he was a good friend of the United States, and

then rode out with an escort of warriors. Lean Bear rode up on a hill near camp and saw the soldiers approaching in four bunches of cavalry. They had two cannons in the center and several wagons strung out in the rear.

Wolf Chief, one of the young warriors escorting Lean Bear, said afterward that as soon as the Cheyennes were seen by the soldiers, the latter formed a line front. "Lean Bear told us warriors to stay where we were," Wolf Chief said, "so as not to frighten the soldiers, while he rode forward to shake hands with the officer and show his papers. . . . When the chief was within only twenty or thirty yards of the line, the officer called out in a very loud voice and the soldiers all opened fire on Lean Bear and the rest of us. Lean Bear fell off his horse right in front of the troops, and Star, another Cheyenne, also fell off his horse. The soldiers then rode forward and shot Lean Bear and Star again as they lay helpless on the ground. I was off with a party of young men to one side. There was a company of soldiers in front of us, but they were all shooting at Lean Bear and the other Cheyennes who were near to him. They paid no attention to us until we began firing on them with bows and guns. They were so close that we shot several of them with arrows. Two of them fell backward off their horses. By this time there was a great deal of confusion. More Cheyennes kept coming up in small parties, and the soldiers were bunching up and seemed badly frightened. They were shooting at us with the cannon. The grapeshot struck the ground around us, but the aim was bad." [1]

In the midst of the fighting, Black Kettle appeared on his horse and began riding up and down among the warriors. "Stop the fighting!" he shouted. "Do not make war!" It was a long time before the Cheyennes would listen to him. "We were very mad," Wolf Chief said, "but at last he stopped the fight. The soldiers ran off. We captured fifteen cavalry horses, with saddles, bridles, and saddle bags on them. Several soldiers were killed; Lean Bear, Star, and one more Cheyenne were killed, and many were wounded."

The Cheyennes were sure that they could have killed all the soldiers and captured their mountain howitzers, because five hundred Cheyenne warriors were in the camp against a hundred soldiers. As it was, many of the young men, infuriated by the cold-blooded killing of Lean Bear, chased the retreating soldiers in a running fight all the way to Fort Larned.

Black Kettle was bewildered by this sudden attack. He grieved for Lean Bear; they had been friends for almost half a century. He remembered how Lean Bear's curiosity was always getting him into trouble. Sometime before, when the Cheyennes paid a friendly visit to Fort Atkinson on the Arkansas River, Lean Bear noticed a bright shiny ring worn by an officer's wife. Impulsively he took hold of the woman's hand to look at her ring. The woman's husband rushed up and slashed Lean Bear with a big whip. Lean Bear turned and jumped on his horse and rode back to the Cheyenne camp. He painted his face and rode through the camp, urging the warriors to join him in attacking the fort. A Cheyenne chief had been insulted, he cried. Black Kettle and the other chiefs had a hard time calming him down that day. Now Lean Bear was dead, and his death had stirred the warriors to a far deeper anger than the insult at Fort Atkinson.

Black Kettle could not understand why the soldiers had attacked a peaceful Cheyenne camp without warning. He supposed that if anyone would know, it would be his old friend the Little White Man, William Bent. More than thirty years had passed since the Little White Man and his brothers had come to the Arkansas River and built Bent's Fort. William had married Owl Woman, and after she died he married her sister, Yellow Woman. In all those years the Bents and the Cheyennes had lived in close friendship. The Little White Man had three sons and two daughters, and they lived much of the time with their mother's people. That summer two of the half-breed sons, George and Charlie, were hunting buffalo with the Cheyennes on Smoky Hill River.

After some thought about the matter, Black Kettle sent a messenger on a fast pony to find the Little White Man. "Tell him we have had a fight with the soldiers and killed several of them," Black Kettle said. "Tell him we do not know what the fight was about or for, and that we would like to see him and talk with him about it." [2]

By chance Black Kettle's messenger found William Bent on the road between Fort Larned and Fort Lyon. Bent sent the mes-

senger back with instructions for Black Kettle to meet him on
Coon Creek. A week later the old friends met, both concerned
over the future of the Cheyennes, Bent especially worried about
his sons. He was relieved to learn that they were hunting on
the Smoky Hill. No trouble had been reported from there, but
he knew of two fights that had occurred elsewhere. At Fremont's
Orchard north of Denver, a band of Dog Soldiers was attacked
by a patrol of Colonel John M. Chivington's Colorado Volunteers who were out looking for stolen horses. The Dog Soldiers
were herding a horse and a mule picked up as strays, but Chivington's soldiers opened fire before giving the Cheyennes an opportunity to explain where they had obtained the animals. After
this engagement Chivington sent out a larger force, which attacked a Cheyenne camp near Cedar Bluffs, killing two women
and two children. The artillery soldiers who had attacked Black
Kettle's camp on May 16 were also Chivington's men, sent out
from Denver with no authority to operate in Kansas. The officer
in command, Lieutenant George S. Eayre, was under orders from
Colonel Chivington to "kill Cheyennes whenever and wherever
found." [3]

If such incidents continued, William Bent and Black Kettle
agreed, a general war was bound to break out all over the plains.
"It is not my intention or wish to fight the whites," Black Kettle
said. "I want to be friendly and peaceable and keep my tribe so.
I am not able to fight the whites. I want to live in peace."

Bent told Black Kettle to keep his young men from making
revenge raids, and promised he would return to Colorado and
try to persuade the military authorities not to continue on the
dangerous road they were taking. He then set out for Fort Lyon.

"On my arrival there," he later testified under oath, "I met
Colonel Chivington, related to him the conversation that had
taken place between me and the Indians, and that the chiefs
desired to be friendly. In reply he said he was not authorized to
make peace, and that he was then on the warpath—I think
were the words he used. I then stated to him that there was
great risk to run in keeping up the war; that there were a great
many government trains traveling to New Mexico and other
points; also a great many citizens, and that I did not think there

was sufficient force to protect the travel, and that the citizens and settlers of the country would have to suffer. He said the citizens would have to protect themselves. I then said no more to him." [4]

Late in June the governor of Colorado Territory, John Evans, issued a circular addressed to the "friendly Indians of the plains," informing them that some members of their tribes had gone to war with the white people. Governor Evans declared that "in some instances they have attacked and killed soldiers." He made no mention of soldiers attacking Indians, although this was the way all three fights with the Cheyennes had begun. "For this the Great Father is angry," he went on, "and will certainly hunt them out and punish them, but he does not want to injure those who remain friendly to the whites; he desires to protect and take care of them. For this purpose I direct that all friendly Indians keep away from those who are at war, and go to places of safety." Evans ordered friendly Cheyennes and Arapahos to report to Fort Lyon on their reservation, where their agent, Samuel G. Colley, would furnish them with provisions and show them a place of safety. "The object of this is to prevent friendly Indians from being killed through mistake. . . . The war on hostile Indians will be continued until they are all effectually subdued." [5]

As soon as William Bent learned of Governor Evans' decree he started immediately to warn the Cheyennes and Arapahos to come in to Fort Lyon. Because the various bands were scattered across western Kansas for their summer hunts, several weeks passed before runners could reach all of them. During this period clashes between soldiers and Indians steadily increased. Sioux warriors, aroused by General Alfred Sully's punitive expeditions of 1863 and 1864 into Dakota, swarmed down from the north to raid wagon trains, stagecoach stations, and settlers along the Platte route. For these actions the Southern Cheyennes and Arapahos received much of the blame, and most of the attention of the Colorado soldiers. William Bent's half-breed son George, who was with a large band of Cheyennes on the Solomon River in July, said they were attacked again and again by the troops without any cause, until they began retaliating in the only way they knew how—burning the stage stations, chasing the coaches, running off stock, and forcing the freighters to corral their trains and fight.

Black Kettle and the older chiefs tried to stop these raids, but their influence was weakened by the appeal of younger leaders such as Roman Nose and by the members of the *Hotamitanio,* or Dog Soldier Society. When Black Kettle discovered that seven white captives—two women and five children—had been brought into the Smoky Hill camps by the raiders, he ransomed four of them from the captors with his own ponies so that he could return them to their relatives. About this time, he finally received a message from William Bent informing him of Governor Evans' order to report to Fort Lyon.

It was now late August, and Evans had issued a second proclamation "authorizing all citizens of Colorado, either individually or in such parties as they may organize, to go in pursuit of all hostile Indians on the plains, scrupulously avoiding those who have responded to my call to rendezvous at the points indicated; also to kill and destroy as enemies of the country wherever they may be found, all such hostile Indians." [6] The hunt was already on for all Indians not confined to one of the assigned reservations.

Black Kettle immediately held a council, and all the chiefs in camp agreed to comply with the governor's requirements for peace. George Bent, who had been educated at Webster College in St. Louis, was asked to write a letter to agent Samuel Colley at Fort Lyon, informing him that they wanted peace. "We heard that you have some prisoners in Denver. We have seven prisoners of yours which we are willing to give up, providing you give up yours. . . . We want true news from you in return." Black Kettle hoped that Colley would give him instructions as to how to bring his Cheyennes across Colorado without being attacked by soldiers or roving bands of Governor Evans' armed citizens. He did not entirely trust Colley; he suspected the agent of selling part of the Indians' allotment of goods for his own profit. (Black Kettle did not yet know how deeply involved Colley was with Governor Evans and Colonel Chivington in their scheme to drive the Plains Indians from Colorado.) On July 26, the agent had

written Evans that they could not depend on any of the Indians
to keep the peace. "I now think a little powder and lead is the
best food for them," he concluded.[7]

Because of his distrust of Colley, Black Kettle had a second
copy of the letter written out and addressed to William Bent.
He gave the separate copies to Ochinee (One-Eye) and Eagle
Head, and ordered them to ride for Fort Lyon. Six days later,
as One-Eye and Eagle Head were approaching the fort, they
were suddenly confronted by three soldiers. The soldiers took
firing positions, but One-Eye quickly made signs for peace and
held up Black Kettle's letter. In a few moments the Indians were
being escorted into Fort Lyon as prisoners and handed over to
the commanding officer, Major Edward W. Wynkoop.

Tall Chief Wynkoop was suspicious of the Indians' motives.
When he learned from One-Eye that Black Kettle wanted him
to come out to the Smoky Hill camp and guide the Indians back
to the reservation, he asked how many Indians were there. Two
thousand Cheyennes and Arapahos, One-Eye replied, and perhaps two hundred of their Sioux friends from the north who
were tired of being chased by soldiers. Wynkoop made no reply
to this. He had scarcely more than a hundred mounted soldiers,
and he knew the Indians knew the size of his force. Suspecting
a trap, he ordered the Cheyenne messengers imprisoned in the
guardhouse and called his officers together for a council. The
Tall Chief was young, in his mid-twenties, and his only military
experience was one battle against Texas Confederates in New
Mexico. For the first time in his career he was faced with a decision that could mean disaster for his entire command.

After a day's delay, Wynkoop finally decided that he would
have to go to the Smoky Hill—not for the sake of the Indians,
but to rescue the white prisoners. No doubt it was for this reason that Black Kettle had mentioned the prisoners in his letter;
he knew that white men could not abide the thought of white
women and children living with Indians.

On September 6 Wynkoop was ready to march with 127
mounted troops. Releasing One-Eye and Eagle Head from the
guardhouse, he told them that they would be serving as both
guides and hostages for the expedition. "At the first sign of

treachery from your people," Wynkoop warned them, "I will kill you."

"The Cheyennes do not break their word," One-Eye replied. "If they should do so, I would not care to live longer."

(Wynkoop said afterward that his conversations with the two Cheyennes on this march caused him to change his long-held opinions of Indians. "I felt myself in the presence of superior beings; and these were the representatives of a race that I heretofore looked upon without exception as being cruel, treacherous, and bloodthirsty without feeling or affection for friend or kindred.") [8]

Five days later, along the headwaters of the Smoky Hill, Wynkoop's advance scouts sighted a force of several hundred warriors drawn up as though for battle.

George Bent, who was still with Black Kettle, said that when Wynkoop's soldiers appeared the Dog Soldiers "got ready for a fight and rode out to meet the troops with bows strung and arrows in their hands, but Black Kettle and some of the chiefs interfered, and requesting Major Wynkoop to move his troops off to a little distance, they prevented a fight." [9]

Next morning Black Kettle and the other chiefs met Wynkoop and his officers for a council. Black Kettle let the others speak first. Bull Bear, a leader of the Dog Soldiers, said that he and his brother Lean Bear had tried to live in peace with white men, but that soldiers had come without cause or reason and killed Lean Bear. "The Indians are not to blame for the fighting," he added. "The white men are foxes and peace cannot be brought about with them; the only thing the Indians can do is fight."

Little Raven of the Arapahos agreed with Bull Bear. "I would like to shake hands with the white men," he said, "but I am afraid they do not want peace with us." One-Eye asked to speak then, and said he was ashamed to hear such talk. He had risked his life to go to Fort Lyon, he said, and pledged his word to Tall Chief Wynkoop that the Cheyennes and Arapahos would come in peacefully to their reservation. "I pledged the Tall Chief my word and my life," One-Eye declared. "If my people do not act in good faith I will go with the whites and fight for them, and I have a great many friends who will follow me."

Wynkoop promised that he would do everything that he could to stop the soldiers from fighting the Indians. He said he was not a big chief and could not speak for all the soldiers, but that if the Indians would deliver the white captives to him, he would go with the Indian leaders to Denver and help them make peace with the bigger chiefs.

Black Kettle, who had been listening silently through the proceedings ("immovable with a slight smile upon his face," according to Wynkoop), arose and said he was glad to hear Tall Chief Wynkoop speak. "There are bad white men and bad Indians," he said. "The bad men on both sides brought about this trouble. Some of my young men joined in with them. I am opposed to fighting and have done everything in my power to prevent it. I believe the blame rests with the whites. They commenced the war and forced the Indians to fight." He promised then to deliver the four white prisoners he had purchased; the remaining three were in a camp farther north, and some time would be required to negotiate for them.

The four captives, all children, appeared to be unharmed; in fact, when a soldier asked eight-year-old Ambrose Archer how the Indians had treated him, the boy replied that he "would just as lief stay with the Indians as not." [10]

After more parleying it was finally agreed that the Indians would remain camped on the Smoky Hill while seven chiefs went to Denver with Wynkoop to make peace with Governor Evans and Colonel Chivington. Black Kettle, White Antelope, Bull Bear, and One-Eye represented the Cheyennes; Neva, Bosse, Heaps-of-Buffalo, and Notanee the Arapahos. Little Raven and Left Hand, who were skeptical of any promises from Evans and Chivington, remained behind to keep their young Arapahos out of trouble. War Bonnet would look after the Cheyennes in camp.

Tall Chief Wynkoop's caravan of mounted soldiers, the four white children, and the seven Indian leaders reached Denver on September 28. The Indians rode in a mule-drawn flatbed wagon fitted with board seats. For the journey, Black Kettle mounted his big garrison flag above the wagon, and when they entered the dusty streets of Denver the Stars and Stripes fluttered protectively over the heads of the chiefs. All of Denver turned out for the procession.

Before the council began, Wynkoop visited Governor Evans for an interview. The governor was reluctant to have anything to do with the Indians. He said that the Cheyennes and Arapahos should be punished before giving them any peace. This was also the opinion of the department commander, General Samuel R. Curtis, who telegraphed Colonel Chivington from Fort Leavenworth that very day: "I want no peace till the Indians suffer more." [11]

Finally Wynkoop had to beg the governor to meet with the Indians. "But what shall I do with the Third Colorado Regiment if I make peace?" Evans asked. "They have been raised to kill Indians, and they must kill Indians." He explained to Wynkoop that Washington officials had given him permission to raise the new regiment because he had sworn it was necessary for protection against hostile Indians, and if he now made peace the Washington politicians would accuse him of misrepresentation. There was political pressure on Evans from Coloradans who wanted to avoid the military draft of 1864 by serving in uniform against a few poorly armed Indians rather than against the Confederates farther east. Eventually Evans gave in to Major Wynkoop's pleadings; after all, the Indians had come four hundred miles to see him in response to his proclamation.[12]

The council was held at Camp Weld near Denver, and consisted of the chiefs, Evans, Chivington, Wynkoop, several other Army officers, and Simeon Whitely, who was there by the governor's order to record every word said by the participants. Governor Evans opened the proceedings brusquely, asking the chiefs what they had to say. Black Kettle replied in Cheyenne, with the tribe's old trader friend, John S. Smith, translating:

"On sight of your circular of June 27, 1864, I took hold of the matter, and have now come to talk to you about it. . . . Major Wynkoop proposed that we come to see you. We have come with our eyes shut, following his handful of men, like coming through the fire. All we ask is that we may have peace with the whites. We want to hold you by the hand. You are our father. We have been traveling through a cloud. The sky has been dark ever since the war began. These braves who are with me are willing to do what I say. We want to take good tidings home to our people, that they may sleep in peace. I want you to give all these chiefs of the soldiers here to understand that we are for peace, and that we have made peace, that we may not be mistaken by them for enemies. I have not come here with a little wolf bark, but have come to talk plain with you. We must live near the buffalo or starve. When we came here we came free, without any apprehension, to see you, and when I go home and tell my people that I have taken your hand, and the hands of all the chiefs here in Denver, they will feel well, and so will all the different tribes of Indians on the plains, after we have eaten and drunk with them."

Evans replied: "I am sorry you did not respond to my appeal at once. You have gone into an alliance with the Sioux, who are at war with us."

Black Kettle was surprised. "I don't know who could have told you this," he said.

"No matter who said this," Evans countered, "but your conduct has proved to my satisfaction that was the case."

Several of the chiefs spoke at once then: "This is a mistake; we have made no alliance with the Sioux or anyone else."

Evans changed the subject, stating that he was in no mood to make a treaty of peace. "I have learned that you understand that as the whites are at war among themselves," he went on, "you think you can now drive the whites from this country, but this reliance is false. The Great Father at Washington has men enough to drive all the Indians off the plains, and whip the Rebels at the same time. . . . My advice to you is to turn on the side of the government, and show by your acts that friendly disposition you profess to me. It is utterly out of the question for you to be at peace with us while living with our enemies, and being on friendly terms with them."

White Antelope, the oldest of the chiefs, now spoke: "I understand every word you have said, and will hold on to it. . . . The Cheyennes, all of them, have their eyes open this way, and they will hear what you say. White Antelope is proud to have seen the chief of all the whites in this country. He will tell his people. Ever since I went to Washington and received this medal, I

6. *Cheyenne and Arapaho chiefs meeting at the Camp Weld Council on September 28, 1864. Standing, third from left: John Smith, interpreter; to his left, White Wing and Bosse. Seated left to right: Neva, Bull Bear, Black Kettle, One-Eye, and an unidentified Indian. Kneeling left to right: Major Edward Wynkoop, Captain Silas Soule.*

have called all white men as my brothers. But other Indians have been to Washington and got medals, and now the soldiers do not shake hands, but seek to kill me. . . . I fear that these new soldiers who have gone out may kill some of my people while I am here."

Evans told him flatly: "There is great danger of it."

"When we sent our letter to Major Wynkoop," White Antelope continued, "it was like going through a strong fire or blast for Major Wynkoop's men to come to our camp; it was the same for us to come to see you."

Governor Evans now began to question the chiefs about specific incidents along the Platte, trying to trap some of them into admitting participation in raids. "Who took the stock from Fremont's Orchard," he asked, "and had the first fight with the soldiers this spring north of there?"

"Before answering that question," White Antelope replied boldly, "I would like for you to know that this was the beginning of the war, and I should like to know what it was for. A soldier fired first."

"The Indians had stolen about forty horses," Evans charged. "The soldiers went to recover them, and the Indians fired a volley into their ranks."

White Antelope denied this. "They were coming down the Bijou," he said, "and found one horse and one mule. They returned one horse before they got to Gerry's to a man, then went to Gerry's expecting to turn the other one over to someone. They then heard that the soldiers and Indians were fighting down the Platte; then they took fright and all fled."

"Who committed depredations at Cottonwood?" Evans demanded.

"The Sioux; what band, we do not know."

"What are the Sioux going to do next?"

Bull Bear answered the question: "Their plan is to clean out all this country," he declared. "They are angry, and will do all the damage to the whites they can. I am with you and the troops, to fight all those who have no ears to listen to what you say. . . . I have never hurt a white man. I am pushing for something good. I am always going to be friends with whites; they can do me good. . . . My brother Lean Bear died in trying to keep peace with the whites. I am willing to die the same way, and expect to do so."

As there seemed little more to discuss, the governor asked Colonel Chivington if he had anything to say to the chiefs. Chivington arose. He was a towering man with a barrel chest and a thick neck, a former Methodist preacher who had devoted much of his time to organizing Sunday schools in the mining camps. To the Indians he appeared like a great bearded bull buffalo with a glint of furious madness in his eyes. "I am not a big war chief," Chivington said, "but all the soldiers in this country are at my command. My rule of fighting white men or Indians is to fight them until they lay down their arms and submit to military authority. They [the Indians] are nearer to Major Wynkoop than anyone else, and they can go to him when they are ready to do that."[13]

And so the council ended, leaving the chiefs confused as to whether they had made peace or not. They were sure of one thing—the only real friend they could count on among the soldiers was Tall Chief Wynkoop. The shiny-eyed Eagle Chief, Chivington, had said they should go to Wynkoop at Fort Lyon, and that is what they decided to do.

"So now we broke up our camp on the Smoky Hill and moved down to Sand Creek, about forty miles northeast of Fort Lyon," George Bent said. "From this new camp the Indians went in and visited Major Wynkoop, and the people at the fort seemed so friendly that after a short time the Arapahos left us and moved right down to the fort, where they went into camp and received regular rations." [14]

Wynkoop issued the rations after Little Raven and Left Hand told him the Arapahos could find no buffalo or other wild game on the reservation, and they were fearful of sending hunting parties back to the Kansas herds. They may have heard about Chivington's recent order to his soldiers: "Kill all the Indians you come across." [15]

Wynkoop's friendly dealings with the Indians soon brought him into disfavor with military officials in Colorado and Kansas. He was reprimanded for taking the chiefs to Denver without authorization, and was accused of "letting the Indians run things at Fort Lyon." On November 5, Major Scott J. Anthony, an officer of Chivington's Colorado Volunteers, arrived at Fort Lyon with orders to relieve Wynkoop as commander of the post.

One of Anthony's first orders was to cut the Arapahos' rations and to demand the surrender of their weapons. They gave him three rifles, one pistol, and sixty bows with arrows. A few days later when a group of unarmed Arapahos approached the fort to trade buffalo hides for rations, Anthony ordered his guards to fire on them. Anthony laughed when the Indians turned and ran. He remarked to one of the soldiers "that they had annoyed him enough, and that was the only way to get rid of them." [16]

The Cheyennes who were camped on Sand Creek heard from the Arapahos that an unfriendly little red-eyed soldier chief had taken the place of their friend Wynkoop. In the Deer Rutting Moon of mid-November, Black Kettle and a party of Cheyennes journeyed to the fort to see this new soldier chief. His eyes were indeed red (the result of scurvy), but he pretended to be friendly. Several officers who were present at the meeting between Black Kettle and Anthony testified afterward that Anthony assured the Cheyennes that if they returned to their camp at Sand Creek they would be under the protection of Fort Lyon. He also told them that their young men could go east toward the Smoky Hill to hunt buffalo until he secured permission from the Army to issue them winter rations.

Pleased with Anthony's remarks, Black Kettle said that he and the other Cheyenne leaders had been thinking of moving far south of the Arkansas so that they would feel safe from the soldiers, but that the words of Major Anthony made them feel safe at Sand Creek. They would stay there for the winter.

After the Cheyenne delegation departed, Anthony ordered Left Hand and Little Raven to disband the Arapaho camp near Fort Lyon. "Go and hunt buffalo to feed yourselves," he told them. Alarmed by Anthony's brusqueness, the Arapahos packed up and began moving away. When they were well out of view of the fort, the two bands of Arapahos separated. Left Hand went with his people to Sand Creek to join the Cheyennes. Little Raven led his band across the Arkansas River and headed south; he did not trust the Red-Eyed Soldier Chief.

Anthony now informed his superiors that "there is a band of Indians within forty miles of the post. . . . I shall try to keep

7. *Little Raven, chief of the Arapahos. Photographer not recorded, but taken prior to 1877. Courtesy of the Smithsonian Institution.*

the Indians quiet until such time as I receive reinforcements." [17]

On November 26, when the post trader, Gray Blanket John Smith, requested permission to go out to Sand Creek to trade for hides, Major Anthony was unusually cooperative. He provided Smith with an Army ambulance to haul his goods, and also a driver, Private David Louderback of the Colorado Cavalry. If nothing else would lull the Indians into a sense of security and keep them camped where they were, the presence of a post trader and a peaceful representative of the Army should do so.

Twenty-four hours later the reinforcements which Anthony said he needed to attack the Indians were approaching Fort Lyon. They were six hundred men of Colonel Chivington's Colorado regiments, including most of the Third, which had been formed by Governor John Evans for the sole purpose of fighting Indians. When the vanguard reached the fort, they surrounded it and forbade anyone to leave under penalty of death. About the same time a detachment of twenty cavalrymen reached William Bent's ranch a few miles to the east, surrounded Bent's house, and forbade anyone to enter or leave. Bent's two half-breed sons, George and Charlie, and his half-breed son-in-law Edmond Guerrier were camped with the Cheyennes on Sand Creek.

When Chivington rode up to the officers' quarters at Fort Lyon, Major Anthony greeted him warmly. Chivington began talking of "collecting scalps" and "wading in gore." Anthony responded by saying that he had been "waiting for a good chance to pitch into them," and that every man at Fort Lyon was eager to join Chivington's expedition against the Indians.[18]

Not all of Anthony's officers, however, were eager or even willing to join Chivington's well-planned massacre. Captain Silas Soule, Lieutenant Joseph Cramer, and Lieutenant James Connor protested that an attack on Black Kettle's peaceful camp would violate the pledge of safety given the Indians by both Wynkoop and Anthony, "that it would be murder in every sense of the word," and any officer participating would dishonor the uniform of the Army.

Chivington became violently angry at them and brought his fist down close to Lieutenant Cramer's face. "Damn any man who sympathizes with Indians!" he cried. "I have come to kill

Indians, and believe it is right and honorable to use any means under God's heaven to kill Indians." [19]

Soule, Cramer, and Connor had to join the expedition or face a court-martial, but they quietly resolved not to order their men to fire on the Indians except in self-defense.

At eight o'clock on the evening of November 28, Chivington's column, now consisting of more than seven hundred men by the addition of Anthony's troops, moved out in column of fours. Four twelve-pounder mountain howitzers accompanied the cavalry. Stars glittered in a clear sky; the night air carried a sharp bite of frost.

For a guide Chivington conscripted sixty-nine-year-old James Beckwourth, a mulatto who had lived with the Indians for half a century. Medicine Calf Beckwourth tried to beg off, but Chivington threatened to hang the old man if he refused to guide the soldiers to the Cheyenne-Arapaho encampment.

As the column moved on, it became evident that Beckwourth's dimming eyes and rheumatic bones handicapped his usefulness as a guide. At a ranch house near Spring Bottom, Chivington stopped and ordered the rancher hauled out of his bed to take Beckwourth's place as guide. The rancher was Robert Bent, eldest son of William Bent; all three of Bent's half-Cheyenne sons would soon be together at Sand Creek.

The Cheyenne camp lay in a horseshoe bend of Sand Creek north of an almost dry stream bed. Black Kettle's tepee was near the center of the village, with White Antelope's and War Bonnet's people to the west. On the east side and slightly separated from the Cheyennes was Left Hand's Arapaho camp. Altogether there were about six hundred Indians in the creek bend, two-thirds of them being women and children. Most of the warriors were several miles to the east hunting buffalo for the camp, as they had been told to do by Major Anthony.

So confident were the Indians of absolute safety, they kept no night watch except of the pony herd which was corralled below the creek. The first warning they had of an attack was about sunrise—the drumming of hooves on the sand flats. "I was sleeping in a lodge," Edmond Guerrier said. "I heard, at

first, some of the squaws outside say there were a lot of buffalo
coming into camp; others said they were a lot of soldiers."
Guerrier immediately went outside and started toward Gray
Blanket Smith's tent.[20]

George Bent, who was sleeping in the same area, said that he
was still in his blankets when he heard shouts and the noise of
people running about the camp. "From down the creek a large
body of troops was advancing at a rapid trot . . . more soldiers
could be seen making for the Indian pony herds to the south of
the camps; in the camps themselves all was confusion and noise
—men, women, and children rushing out of the lodges partly
dressed; women and children screaming at sight of the troops;
men running back into the lodges for their arms. . . . I looked
toward the chief's lodge and saw that Black Kettle had a large
American flag tied to the end of a long lodgepole and was standing in front of his lodge, holding the pole, with the flag fluttering
in the gray light of the winter dawn. I heard him call to the
people not to be afraid, that the soldiers would not hurt them;
then the troops opened fire from two sides of the camp." [21]

Meanwhile young Guerrier had joined Gray Blanket Smith
and Private Louderback at the trader's tent. "Louderback proposed we should go out and meet the troops. We started. Before
we got outside the edge of the tent I could see soldiers begin
to dismount. I thought they were artillerymen and were about
to shell the camp. I had hardly spoken when they began firing
with their rifles and pistols. When I saw I could not get to them,
I struck out; I left the soldier and Smith."

Louderback halted momentarily, but Smith kept moving
ahead toward the cavalrymen. "Shoot the damned old son of a
bitch!" a soldier shouted from the ranks. "He's no better than
an Indian." At the first scattered shots, Smith and Louderback
turned and ran for their tent. Smith's half-breed son, Jack, and
Charlie Bent had already taken cover there.[22]

By this time hundreds of Cheyenne women and children were
gathering around Black Kettle's flag. Up the dry creek bed, more
were coming from White Antelope's camp. After all, had not
Colonel Greenwood told Black Kettle that as long as the United
States flag flew above him no soldier would fire upon him? White
Antelope, an old man of seventy-five, unarmed, his dark face

seamed from sun and weather, strode toward the soldiers. He was still confident that the soldiers would stop firing as soon as they saw the American flag and the white surrender flag which Black Kettle had now run up.

Medicine Calf Beckwourth, riding beside Colonel Chivington, saw White Antelope approaching. "He came running out to meet the command," Beckwourth later testified, "holding up his hands and saying 'Stop! stop!' He spoke it in as plain English as I can. He stopped and folded his arms until shot down." [23] Survivors among the Cheyennes said that White Antelope sang the death song before he died:

> Nothing lives long
> Only the earth and the mountains.

From the direction of the Arapaho camp, Left Hand and his people also tried to reach Black Kettle's flag. When Left Hand saw the troops, he stood with his arms folded, saying he would not fight the white men because they were his friends. He was shot down.

Robert Bent, who was riding unwillingly with Colonel Chivington, said that when they came in sight of the camp "I saw the American flag waving and heard Black Kettle tell the Indians to stand around the flag, and there they were huddled—men, women, and children. This was when we were within fifty yards of the Indians. I also saw a white flag raised. These flags were in so conspicuous a position that they must have been seen. When the troops fired, the Indians ran, some of the men into their lodges, probably to get their arms. . . . I think there were six hundred Indians in all. I think there were thirty-five braves and some old men, about sixty in all . . . the rest of the men were away from camp, hunting. . . . After the firing the warriors put the squaws and children together, and surrounded them to protect them. I saw five squaws under a bank for shelter. When the troops came up to them they ran out and showed their persons to let the soldiers know they were squaws and begged for mercy, but the soldiers shot them all. I saw one squaw lying on the bank whose leg had been broken by a shell; a soldier came up to her with a drawn saber; she raised her arm to protect herself, when he struck, breaking her arm; she rolled over and raised her other arm, when he struck, breaking it, and then left her without killing her. There seemed to be indiscriminate slaughter of men, women, and children. There were some thirty or forty squaws collected in a hole for protection; they sent out a little girl about six years old with a white flag on a stick; she had not proceeded but a few steps when she was shot and killed. All the squaws in that hole were afterwards killed, and four or five bucks outside. The squaws offered no resistance. Every one I saw dead was scalped. I saw one squaw cut open with an unborn child, as I thought, lying by her side. Captain Soule afterwards told me that such was the fact. I saw the body of White Antelope with the privates cut off, and I heard a soldier say he was going to make a tobacco pouch out of them. I saw one squaw whose privates had been cut out. . . . I saw a little girl about five years of age who had been hid in the sand; two soldiers discovered her, drew their pistols and shot her, and then pulled her out of the sand by the arm. I saw quite a number of infants in arms killed with their mothers." [24]

(In a public speech made in Denver not long before this massacre, Colonel Chivington advocated the killing and scalping of all Indians, even infants. "Nits make lice!" he declared.)

Robert Bent's description of the soldiers' atrocities was corroborated by Lieutenant James Connor: "In going over the battleground the next day I did not see a body of man, woman, or child but was scalped, and in many instances their bodies were mutilated in the most horrible manner—men, women, and children's privates cut out, &c; I heard one man say that he had cut out a woman's private parts and had them for exhibition on a stick; I heard another man say that he had cut the fingers off an Indian to get the rings on the hand; according to the best of my knowledge and belief these atrocities that were committed were with the knowledge of J. M. Chivington, and I do not know of his taking any measures to prevent them; I heard of one instance of a child a few months old being thrown in the feed-box of a wagon, and after being carried some distance left on the ground to perish; I also heard of numerous instances in which men had cut out the private parts of females and stretched them over the saddle-bows and wore them over their hats while riding in the ranks." [25]

A trained and well-disciplined regiment of soldiers undoubtedly could have destroyed almost all of the defenseless Indians at Sand Creek. Lack of discipline, combined with heavy drinking of whiskey during the night ride, cowardice, and poor marksmanship among the Colorado troops made it possible for many Indians to escape. A number of Cheyennes dug rifle pits below high banks of the dry creek, and held out until nightfall. Others fled singly or in small groups across the plain. When the shooting ended, 105 Indian women and children and 28 men were dead. In his official report Chivington claimed between four and five hundred dead warriors. He had lost nine killed, 38 wounded, many of the casualties resulting from careless firing by the soldiers upon each other. Among the dead chiefs were White Antelope, One-Eye, and War Bonnet. Black Kettle miraculously escaped by running up a ravine, but his wife was badly wounded. Left Hand, although shot down, also managed to survive.

Captives at the end of the fighting totaled seven—John Smith's Cheyenne wife, the wife of another white civilian at Fort Lyon and her three children, and the two half-breed boys, Jack Smith and Charlie Bent. The soldiers wanted to kill the half-breed boys because they were wearing Indian dress. Old Medicine Calf Beckwourth rescued Charlie Bent by concealing him in a wagon with a wounded officer, later turning him over to his brother Robert. But Beckwourth could not save Jack Smith's life; a soldier shot the trader's son by firing at him through a hole in the tent where the boy was being held prisoner.

The third Bent son, George, became separated from Charlie early in the fighting. He joined the Cheyennes who dug rifle pits under the high banks of the creek. "Just as our party reached this point," he said, "I was struck in the hip by a bullet and knocked down; but I managed to tumble into one of the holes and lay there among the warriors, women, and children." After nightfall the survivors crawled out of the holes. It was bitter cold, and blood had frozen over their wounds, but they dared not make fires. The only thought in their minds was to flee eastward toward the Smoky Hill and try to join their warriors. "It was a terrible march," George Bent remembered, "most of us being on foot, without food, ill-clad, and encumbered with the women and children." For fifty miles they endured icy winds, hunger, and pain of wounds, but at last they reached the hunting camp. "As we rode into that camp there was a terrible scene. Everyone was crying, even the warriors, and the women and children screaming and wailing. Nearly everyone present had lost some relatives or friends, and many of them in their grief were gashing themselves with their knives until the blood flowed in streams." [26]

As soon as his wound healed, George made his way back to his father's ranch. There from his brother Charlie he heard more details of the soldiers' atrocities at Sand Creek—the horrible scalpings and mutilations, the butchery of children and infants. After a few days the brothers agreed that as half-breeds they wanted no part of the white man's civilization. They renounced the blood of their father, and quietly left his ranch. With them went Charlie's mother, Yellow Woman, who swore that she would never again live with a white man. They started north to join the Cheyennes.

It was now January, the Moon of Strong Cold, when Plains Indians traditionally kept fires blazing in their lodges, told stories through the long evenings, and slept late in the mornings. But this was a bad time, and as news of the Sand Creek massacre spread across the plains, the Cheyennes, Arapahos, and Sioux sent runners back and forth with messages calling for a war of revenge against the murdering white men.

By the time Yellow Woman and the young Bent brothers reached their relatives on the Republican River, the Cheyennes were supported by thousands of sympathetic allies—Spotted Tail's Brulé Sioux, Pawnee Killer's Oglala Sioux, and large bands of Nothern Arapahos. Cheyenne Dog Soldiers (now led by Tall Bull) who had refused to go to Sand Creek were there, and also Roman Nose and his following of young warriors. While the Cheyennes mourned their dead, the leaders of the tribes smoked war pipes and planned their strategy.

In a few hours of madness at Sand Creek, Chivington and his soldiers destroyed the lives or the power of every Cheyenne and Arapaho chief who had held out for peace with the white men. After the flight of the survivors, the Indians rejected Black Ket-

8. *George Bent and his wife, Magpie. Photographed in 1867. Courtesy of State Historical Society of Colorado.*

tle and Left Hand, and turned to their war leaders to save them from extermination.

At the same time, United States officials were calling for an investigation of Governor Evans and Colonel Chivington, and although they must have known it was too late to avoid a general Indian war, they sent Medicine Calf Beckwourth as an emissary to Black Kettle to see if there was any possibility of peace.

Beckwourth found the Cheyennes but soon learned that Black Kettle had drifted off somewhere with a handful of relatives and old men. The leading chief was now Leg-in-the-Water.

"I went into the lodge of Leg-in-the-Water," Beckwourth said. "When I went in he raised up and he said, 'Medicine Calf, what have you come here for; have you fetched the white man to finish killing our families again?' I told him I had come to talk to him; call in your council. They came in a short time afterwards, and wanted to know what I had come for. I told them I had come to persuade them to make peace with the whites, as there was not enough of them to fight the whites, as they were as numerous as the leaves of the trees. 'We know it,' was the general response of the council. 'But what do we want to live for? The white man has taken our country, killed all of our game; was not satisfied with that, but killed our wives and children. Now no peace. We want to go and meet our families in the spirit land. We loved the whites until we found out they lied to us, and robbed us of what we had. We have raised the battle ax until death.'

"They asked me then why I had come to Sand Creek with the soldiers to show them the country. I told them if I had not come the white chief would have hung me. 'Go and stay with your white brothers, but we are going to fight till death.' I obeyed orders and came back, willing to play quits." [27]

In January, 1865, the alliance of Cheyenne, Arapaho, and Sioux launched a series of raids along the South Platte. They attacked wagon trains, stage stations, and small military outposts. They burned the town of Julesburg, scalping the white defenders in revenge for the scalping of Indians at Sand Creek. They ripped out miles of telegraph wire. They raided and plundered up and down the Platte route, halting all communications

9. *Edmond Guerrier, interpreter. Photographer not recorded, but taken prior to 1877. Courtesy of the Smithsonian Institution.*

and supplies. In Denver there was panic as food shortages began to grow.

When the warriors returned to their winter camp in the Big Timbers on the Republican, they had a big dance to celebrate their first blows for revenge. Snow blanketed the Plains, but the chiefs knew that soldiers would soon come marching from all directions with their big-talking guns. While the dances were still going on, the chiefs held a council to decide where they should go to escape the pursuing soldiers. Black Kettle was there, and he spoke for going south, below the Arkansas, where summers were long and buffalo were plentiful. Most of the other chiefs spoke for going north across the Platte to join their relatives in the Powder River country. No soldiers would dare march into that great stronghold of the Teton Sioux and Northern Cheyennes. Before the council ended, the alliance agreed to send runners to the Powder River country to tell the tribes there that they were coming.

Black Kettle, however, would not go, and some four hundred Cheyennes—mostly old men, women, and a few badly wounded warriors—agreed to follow him southward. On the last day before the camp moved out, George Bent said farewell to this last remnant of his mother's people, the Southern Cheyennes. "I went around among the lodges and shook hands with Black Kettle and all my friends. These lodges under Black Kettle moved south of the Arkansas and joined the Southern Arapahos, Kiowas, and Comanches." [28]

With about three thousand Sioux and Arapahos, the Cheyennes (including Yellow Woman and the Bent brothers) moved northward, exiled into a land that few of them had seen before. Along the way they had fights with soldiers who marched out from Fort Laramie, but the alliance was too strong for the soldiers, and the Indians brushed them off as though they were coyotes snapping at a mighty buffalo herd.

When they reached the Powder River country, the Southern Cheyennes were welcomed by their kinsmen, the Northern Cheyennes. The Southerners, who wore cloth blankets and leggings, traded from white men, thought the Northerners looked very wild in their buffalo robes and buckskin leggings. The Northern Cheyennes wrapped their braided hair with strips of red-painted buckskin, wore crow feathers on their heads, and used so many Sioux words that the Southern Cheyennes had difficulty understanding them. Morning Star, a leading chief of the Northern Cheyennes, had lived and hunted so long with the Sioux that almost everyone called him by his Sioux name, Dull Knife.

At first the Southerners camped on the Powder about half a mile apart from the Northerners, but there was so much visiting back and forth that they soon decided to camp together, pitching their tepees in an old-time tribal circle with clans grouped together. From that time on, there was little talk of Southerners and Northerners among these Cheyennes.

In the spring of 1865, when they moved their ponies over to Tongue River for better grazing, they camped near Red Cloud's Oglala Sioux. The Cheyennes from the south had never seen so many Indians camped all together, more than eight thousand, and the days and nights were filled with hunts and ceremonies and feasts and dances. George Bent later told of inducting Young-Man-Afraid-of-His-Horses, a Sioux, into his Cheyenne clan, the Crooked Lances. This indicated how close the Sioux and Cheyennes were in that time.

Although each tribe kept its own laws and customs, these Indians had come to think of themselves as the People, confident of their power and sure of their right to live as they pleased. White invaders were challenging them on the east in Dakota and on the south along the Platte, but they were ready to meet all challenges. "The Great Spirit raised both the white man and the Indian," Red Cloud said. "I think he raised the Indian first. He raised me in this land and it belongs to me. The white man was raised over the great waters, and his land is over there. Since they crossed the sea, I have given them room. There are now white people all about me. I have but a small spot of land left. The Great Spirit told me to keep it." [29]

Through the springtime the Indians sent scouting parties down to watch the soldiers who were guarding the roads and telegraph lines along the Platte. The scouts reported many more soldiers than usual, some of them prowling northward along Bozeman's Trail through the Powder River country. Red Cloud and the other chiefs decided it was time to teach the soldiers a lesson; they would strike them at the point where they were farthest north, a place the white men called Platte Bridge Station.

Because the Cheyenne warriors from the south wanted revenge for the relatives massacred at Sand Creek, most of them were invited to go along on the expedition. Roman Nose of the Crooked Lances was their leader, and he rode with Red Cloud, Dull Knife, and Old-Man-Afraid-of-His-Horses. Almost three thousand warriors formed the war party. Among them were the Bent brothers, painted and dressed for battle.

On July 24 they reached the hills overlooking the bridge across the North Platte. At the opposite end of the bridge was the military post—a stockade, stage station, and telegraph office. About a hundred soldiers were inside the stockade. After looking at the place through their field glasses, the chiefs decided they would burn the bridge, cross the river at a shallow ford below, and then lay siege to the stockade. But first they would try to draw the soldiers outside with decoys and kill as many as possible.

Ten warriors went down in the afternoon, but the soldiers would not come out of their stockade. Next morning another set of decoys lured the soldiers out on the bridge, but they would come no farther. On the third morning, to the Indians' surprise, a platoon of cavalrymen marched out of the fort, crossed the bridge, and turned westward at a trot. In a matter of seconds, several hundred Cheyennes and Sioux were mounted on their ponies and swarming down the hills toward the Bluecoats. "As we went into the troops," George Bent said, "I saw an officer on a bay horse rush past me through the dense clouds of dust and smoke. His horse was running away from him . . . the lieutenant had an arrow sticking in his forehead and his face was streaming with blood." (The fatally wounded officer was Lieutenant Caspar Collins.) A few of the cavalrymen escaped and reached a rescue platoon of infantrymen on the bridge. Cannon from the fort broke off further pursuit by the Indians.

While the fighting was going on, some of the Indians still on the hills discovered why the cavalrymen had marched out of the fort. They had been riding to meet a wagon train approaching from the west. In a few minutes, the Indians had the wagon train surrounded, but the soldiers dug in under the wagons and put up a stubborn fight. During the first minutes of the fighting, Roman Nose's brother was killed. When Roman Nose heard of this, he was angry for revenge. He called out for all the Cheyennes to prepare for a charge. "We are going to empty the soldiers' guns!" he shouted. Roman Nose was wearing his medicine bonnet and shield, and he knew that no bullets could strike him. He led the Cheyennes into a circle around the wagons, and they lashed their ponies so that they ran very fast. As the circle tightened closer to the wagons, the soldiers emptied all their guns at once, and then the Cheyennes charged straight for the wagons and killed all the soldiers. They were disappointed by what they found in the wagons; nothing was there but soldiers' bedding and mess chests.

That night in camp Red Cloud and the other chiefs decided they had taught the soldiers to fear the power of the Indians. And so they returned to the Powder River country, hopeful that the white men would now obey the Laramie treaty and quit prowling without permission into the Indians' country north of the Platte.

Meanwhile, Black Kettle and the last remnants of the Southern Cheyennes had moved south of the Arkansas River. They joined Little Raven's Arapahos, who by this time had heard of the Sand Creek massacre and were mourning friends and relatives lost there. During the summer (1865) their hunters found only a few buffalo below the Arkansas, but they were afraid to go back north where the big herds grazed between the Smoky Hill and Republican rivers.

Late in the summer, runners and messengers began coming from all directions looking for Black Kettle and Little Raven. Suddenly they had become very important. Some white officials had journeyed from Washington to find the Cheyennes and Arapahos and tell them the Great Father and his Council were filled with pity for them. The government officials wanted to make a new treaty.

Although the Cheyennes and Arapahos had been driven from Colorado, and settlers were claiming their lands, it seemed that the titles to the lands were not clear. By the law of the old treaties it could be proven that Denver City itself stood upon Cheyenne and Arapaho land. The government wanted all Indian land claims in Colorado extinguished so that white settlers would be certain they owned the land once they had claimed it.

Black Kettle and Little Raven would not agree to meet with the officials until they heard from the Little White Man, William Bent. He told them that he had tried to persuade the United States to give the Indians permanent rights to the buffalo country between the Smoky Hill and Republican, but the government refused to do this because a stage line and later a railroad would pass through that country, bringing more white settlers. The Cheyennes and Arapahos would have to live south of the Arkansas River.

In the Drying Grass Moon, Black Kettle and Little Raven met the commissioners at the mouth of the Little Arkansas. The Indians had seen two of these treaty makers before—Black Whiskers Sanborn and White Whiskers Harney. They believed Sanborn to be a friend, but they remembered Harney had massacred the Brulé Sioux at the Blue Water in Nebraska in 1855. Agents Murphy and Leavenworth were there, and a straight-talking man, James Steele. Rope Thrower Carson, who had separated the Navahos from their tribal lands, was also there. Gray Blanket Smith, who had endured the ordeal of Sand Creek with them, came to translate, and the Little White Man was there to do the best he could for them.

"Here we are, all together, Arapahos and Cheyennes," Black Kettle said, "but few of us, we are one people. . . . All my friends, the Indians that are holding back—they are afraid to come in; are afraid they will be betrayed as I have been."

"It will be a very hard thing to leave the country that God gave us," Little Raven said. "Our friends are buried there, and we hate to leave these grounds. . . . There is something strong for us—that fool band of soldiers that cleared out our lodges and killed our women and children. This is hard on us. There at Sand Creek—White Antelope and many other chiefs lie there; our women and children lie there. Our lodges were destroyed there, and our horses were taken from us there, and I do not feel disposed to go right off to a new country and leave them."

James Steele answered: "We all fully realize that it is hard for any people to leave their homes and graves of their ancestors, but, unfortunately for you, gold has been discovered in your country, and a crowd of white people have gone there to live, and a great many of these people are the worst enemies of the Indians—men who do not care for their interests, and who would not stop at any crime to enrich themselves. These men are now in your country—in all parts of it—and there is no portion where you can live and maintain yourselves but what you will come in contact with them. The consequences of this state of things are that you are in constant danger of being imposed upon, and you have to resort to arms in self-defense. Under the circumstances, there is, in the opinion of the commission, no part of the former country large enough where you can live in peace."

Black Kettle said: "Our forefathers, when alive, lived all over this country; they did not know about doing wrong; since then they have died, and gone I don't know where. We have all lost our way. . . . Our Great Father sent you here with his words to us, and we take hold of them. Although the troops have struck us, we throw it all behind and are glad to meet you in peace and friendship. What you have come here for, and what the President has sent you for, I don't object to, but say yes to it. . . . The white people can go wherever they please and they will not be disturbed by us, and I want you to let them know. . . . We are different nations, but it seems as if we were but one people, whites and all. . . . Again I take you by the hand, and I feel happy. These people that are with us are glad to think that we have peace once more, and can sleep soundly, and that we can live." [30]

And so they agreed to live south of the Arkansas, sharing land that belonged to the Kiowas. On October 14, 1865, the chiefs and head men of what remained of the Southern Cheyennes and Arapahos signed the new treaty agreeing to "perpetual peace." Article 2 of the treaty read: "It is *further agreed* by the Indian parties hereto . . . that henceforth they will, and do hereby, relinquish all claims or rights . . . in and to the country bounded as follows, viz: beginning at the junction of the north and south forks of the Platte River; thence up the north fork to the top of the principal range of the Rocky Mountains, or to the Red Buttes; thence southwardly along the summit of the Rocky Mountains to the headwaters of the Arkansas River; thence down the Arkansas River to the Cimarone crossing of the same; thence to the place of beginning; which country they claim to have originally owned, and never to have relinquished the title thereto." [31]

Thus did the Cheyennes and Arapahos abandon all claims to the Territory of Colorado. And that of course was the real meaning of the massacre at Sand Creek.

PRANCING THEY COME

He - na wa - ći   a - u we   he - na wa - ći   a - u we
he - na wa - ći   a - u we   ho - toŋ a - u   we - lo *he*   o
śuŋ - ka - wa - kaŋ   o - ya - te waŋ   he - na   wa - ći   a - u we
he - na   wa - ći   a - u we   ho - toŋ a - u   we - lo *he*   o

Courtesy of the Bureau of American Ethnology Collection

See them
prancing.
They come
neighing,
they come
a Horse Nation.
See them
prancing.
They come
neighing,
they come.

FIVE

Powder River Invasion

1865—April 2, Confederates abandon Richmond. April **9,** Lee
surrenders to Grant at Appomattox; Civil War ends. April **14,**
John Wilkes Booth assassinates President Lincoln; Andrew
Johnson becomes President. June 13, President Johnson issues
proclamation for reconstruction of former Confederate States.
October, U.S. asks France to recall troops from Mexico.
December 18, Thirteenth Amendment to U.S. Constitution
abolishes slavery. Lewis. Carroll's *Alice in Wonderland* and
Tolstoy's *War and Peace* published.

*Whose voice was first sounded on this land? The voice of the red
people who had but bows and arrows. . . . What has been done in
my country I did not want, did not ask for it; white people going
through my country. . . . When the white man comes in my country
he leaves a trail of blood behind him. . . . I have two mountains in
that country—the Black Hills and the Big Horn Mountain. I want
the Great Father to make no roads through them. I have told these
things three times; now I have come here to tell them the fourth time.*

—Mahpiua Luta (Red Cloud) of the Oglala Sioux

After returning to the Powder River country following the Platte Bridge fight, the Plains Indians began preparing for their usual summer medicine ceremonies. The tribes camped near each other at the mouth of Crazy Woman's Fork of the Powder. Farther north along that river and the Little Missouri were some Teton Sioux who had moved west that year to get away from General Sully's soldiers in Dakota. Sitting Bull and his Hunkpapa people were there, and these cousins of the Oglalas sent emissaries down for a big sun dance, the annual religious renewal of the Tetons. While the sun dance was in progress, the Cheyennes held their medicine-arrows ceremony, which lasted four days. The Arrow Keeper unwrapped the four secret arrows from their coyote fur bag, and all the males in the tribe passed by to make an offering and pray to the arrows.

Black Bear, one of the leading chiefs of the Northern Arapahos, decided to take his people west to Tongue River; he invited some of the Southern Arapahos who had come north after Sand Creek to go with them. They would set up a village on the Tongue, he said, and have many hunts and dances before the coming of the cold moons.

And so by late August, 1865, the tribes in the Powder River country were scattered from the Bighorns on the west to the Black Hills on the east. They were so sure of the country's impregnability that most of them were skeptical when they first began hearing rumors of soldiers coming at them from four directions.

Three of the soldier columns were under command of General Patrick E. Connor, who had transferred from Utah in May to fight Indians along the Platte route. In 1863 Star Chief Connor had surrounded a camp of Paiutes on Bear River and butchered 278 of them. For this he was hailed by the white men as a brave defender of the frontier from the "red foe."

In July, 1865, Connor announced that the Indians north of the Platte "must be hunted like wolves," and he began organizing three columns of soldiers for an invasion of the Powder River country. One column under Colonel Nelson Cole would march from Nebraska to the Black Hills of Dakota. A second column under Colonel Samuel Walker would move straight north from Fort Laramie to link up with Cole in the Black Hills. The third column, with Connor himself in command, would head in a northwesterly direction along the Bozeman Road toward Montana. General Connor thus hoped to trap the Indians between his column and the combined forces of Cole and Walker. He warned his officers to accept no overtures of peace from the Indians, and ordered bluntly: "Attack and kill every male Indian over twelve years of age." [1]

Early in August the three columns were set in motion. If everything went according to plan, they would rendezvous about September 1 on Rosebud River in the heart of hostile Indian country.

A fourth column, which had no connection with Connor's expeditions, was also approaching the Powder River country from the east. Organized by a civilian, James A. Sawyers, to open a new overland route, this column had no objective other than to reach the Montana gold fields. Because Sawyers knew that he would be trespassing on Indian treaty lands, he expected resistance and therefore had obtained two companies of infantrymen to escort his group of seventy-three goldseekers and eighty wagons of supplies.

It was about August 14 or 15 when the Sioux and Cheyennes who were camped along the Powder first learned of Sawyers' approaching train. "Our hunters rode into camp much excited," George Bent recalled afterward, "and said soldiers were up the river. Our village crier, a man named Bull Bear, mounted and rode about our camp, crying that soldiers were coming. Red Cloud got in his herd and mounted and rode through the Sioux camp, crying the same thing for the Sioux. Everybody ran for ponies. At such times a man always took any pony he wanted; if the pony was killed in the fight the rider did not have to pay its owner for it, but everything the rider captured in battle belonged to the owner of the pony he rode. When all were mounted we rode up the Powder about fifteen miles, where we came upon the

Sawyers 'road-building party,' a big train of emigrants moving
along with soldiers marching on each side of it." [2]

As part of their booty taken during the Platte Bridge fight the
Indians had brought back some Army uniforms and bugles. On
leaving camp, George Bent hastily donned an officer's blouse, and
his brother Charlie carried along a bugle. They thought these
things might mystify the soldiers and make them jumpy. About
five hundred Sioux and Cheyennes were in the war party, and
both Red Cloud and Dull Knife went along. The chiefs were
very angry that soldiers had come into their country without
asking permission.

When they first sighted the wagon train, it was moving along
between two hills with a herd of about three hundred cattle in
the rear. The Indians divided and spread out along opposite
ridges, and at a signal began firing upon the soldier escorts. In a
few minutes the train formed in a circular corral with the cattle
herded inside and the wagon wheels interlocked.

For two or three hours the warriors amused themselves by
creeping down gullies and suddenly opening fire at close range.
A few of the more daring riders galloped in close, circled the
wagons, and then swept out of range. After the soldiers started
firing their two howitzers, the warriors kept behind little hil-
locks, uttering war cries and insulting the soldiers. Charlie Bent
blew his bugle several times and shouted all the Anglo-Saxon
profanity he could remember hearing around his father's trading
post. ("They taunted us in a most aggravating manner," one of
the besieged goldseekers said afterward. "Some few of them
could speak enough English to call us all the vile names imagi-
nable." [3])

The wagon train could not move, but neither could the Indians get at it. About midday, to end the stalemate, the chiefs
ordered a white flag hoisted. A few minutes later a man in buckskins came riding out of the wagon corral. Because the Bent
brothers could speak English, they were sent down to meet the
emissary. The man was a good-humored Mexican, Juan Suse,
and he was as much surprised by the Bents' English as he was by
George's blue uniform blouse. Suse, who knew little English, had
to use sign language, but he managed to make them understand

that the commander of the wagon train was willing to parley
with the Indian chiefs.

A meeting was quickly arranged, the Bents becoming interpreters now for Red Cloud and Dull Knife. Colonel Sawyers and
Captain George Williford came out from the corral with a small
escort. Colonel Sawyers' title was honorary, but he considered
himself in command of the wagon train. Captain Williford's
title was genuine; his two companies of soldiers were Galvanized
Yankees, former Confederate prisoners of war. Williford's nerves
were on edge. He was unsure of his men, unsure of his authority
on the expedition. He glared at the blue uniform coat worn by
the half-breed Cheyenne interpreter, George Bent.

When Red Cloud demanded an explanation for the presence
of soldiers in the Indians' country, Captain Williford replied by
asking why the Indians had attacked peaceful white men.
Charlie Bent, still embittered by memories of Sand Creek, told
Williford that the Cheyennes would fight all white men until
the government hanged Colonel Chivington. Sawyers protested
that he had not come to fight Indians; he was seeking a short
route to the Montana gold fields, and only wanted to pass
through the country.

"I interpreted to the chiefs," George Bent said afterward,
"and Red Cloud replied if the whites would go clear out of his
country and make no roads it was all right. Dull Knife said the
same for the Cheyennes; then both chiefs said for the officer
[Williford] to take the train due west from this place, then turn
north and when he had passed the Bighorn Mountains he would
be out of their country." [4]

Sawyers again protested. To follow such a route would take
him too far out of his way; he said he wanted to move north
along the Powder River valley to find a fort that General Connor
was building there.

This was the first news that Red Cloud and Dull Knife had
heard of General Connor and his invasion. They expressed surprise and anger that soldiers would dare build a fort in the heart
of their hunting grounds. Seeing that the chiefs were growing
hostile, Sawyers quickly offered them a wagonload of goods—
flour, sugar, coffee, and tobacco. Red Cloud suggested that gun-

powder, shot, and caps be added to the list, but Captain Williford objected strongly; in fact, the military officer was opposed to giving the Indians anything.

Finally the chiefs agreed to accept a full wagonload of flour, sugar, coffee, and tobacco in exchange for granting permission for the train to move to Powder River. "The officer told me," George Bent later said, "to hold the Indians back away from the train and he would unload the goods on the ground. He wanted to go on to the river and camp. This was at noon. After he reached the river and corralled his train there, another lot of Sioux came up from the village. The wagonload of goods had already been divided by the first party of Indians, so these newcomers demanded more goods, and when the officer refused they began firing on the corral." [5]

This second band of Sioux harassed Sawyers and Williford for several days, but Red Cloud and Dull Knife and their warriors took no part in it. They moved on up the valley to see if there was anything to the rumors of soldiers building a fort on the Powder.

In the meantime, Star Chief Connor had started construction of a stockade about sixty miles south of the Crazy Woman Fork of the Powder and named it in honor of himself, Fort Connor. With Connor's column was a company of Pawnee scouts under command of Captain Frank North. The Pawnees were old tribal enemies of the Sioux, Cheyennes, and Arapahos, and they had been enlisted for the campaign at regular cavalrymen's pay. While the soldiers cut logs for Connor's stockade, the Pawnees scouted the area in search of their enemies. On August 16 they sighted a small party of Cheyennes approaching from the south. With them was Charlie Bent's mother, Yellow Woman.

She was riding with four men slightly in advance of the main party, and when she first saw the Pawnees on a low hill she thought they were Cheyennes or Sioux. The Pawnees signaled with their blankets that they were friends, and the Cheyennes moved on toward them, suspecting no danger. When the Cheyennes came close to the hill, the Pawnees suddenly attacked them. And so Yellow Woman, who had left William Bent because he was a member of the white race, died at the hands of a mercenary of her own race. On that day her son Charlie was

10. *Red Cloud, or Mahpiua-luta, of the Oglala Dakotas. Photographed by Charles M. Bell in Washington, D.C., in 1880. Courtesy of the Smithsonian Institution.*

only a few miles to the east with Dull Knife's warriors, returning from the siege of Sawyers' wagon train.

On August 22 General Connor decided that the stockade on the Powder was strong enough to be held by one cavalry company. Leaving most of his supplies there, he started with the remainder of his column on a forced march toward the Tongue River valley in search of any large concentrations of Indian lodges that his scouts might find. Had he moved north along the Powder he would have found thousands of Indians eager for a fight—Red Cloud's and Dull Knife's warriors who were out searching for Connor's soldiers.

About a week after Connor's column left the Powder, a Cheyenne warrior named Little Horse was traveling across this same country with his wife and young son. Little Horse's wife was an Arapaho woman, and they were making a summer visit to see her relatives at Black Bear's Arapaho camp on Tongue River. Along the way one day, a pack on his wife's horse got loose. When she dismounted to tighten it, she happened to glance back across a ridge. A file of mounted men was coming along the trail far behind them.

"Look over there," she called to Little Horse.

"They're soldiers!" Little Horse cried. "Hurry!"

As soon as they were over the next hill, and out of view of the soldiers, they turned off the trail. Little Horse cut loose the travois on which his young son was riding, took the boy on behind him, and they rode fast—straight across country for Black Bear's camp. They came galloping in, disturbing the peaceful village of 250 lodges pitched on a mesa above the river. The Arapahos were rich in ponies that year; three thousand were corralled along the stream.

None of the Arapahos believed that soldiers could be within hundreds of miles, and when Little Horse's wife tried to get the crier to warn the people, he said: "Little Horse has made a mistake; he just saw some Indians coming over the trail, and nothing more." Certain that the horsemen they had seen were soldiers, Little Horse and his wife hurried on to find her relatives. Her brother, Panther, was resting in front of his tepee, and they told him that soldiers were coming and that he had better move out in a hurry. "Pack up whatever you wish to take along," Little Horse said. "We must go tonight."

Panther laughed at his Cheyenne brother-in-law. "You're always getting frightened and making mistakes about things," he said. "You saw nothing but some buffalo."

"Very well," Little Horse replied, "you need not go unless you want to, but we shall go tonight." His wife managed to persuade some of her other relatives to pack up, and before nightfall they left the village and moved several miles down the Tongue.[6]

Early the next morning, Star Chief Connor's soldiers attacked the Arapaho camp. By chance, a warrior who had taken one of his race horses out for a run happened to see the troops assembling behind a ridge. He galloped back to camp as fast as he could, giving some of the Arapahos a chance to flee down the river.

A few moments later, at the sound of a bugle and the blast of a howitzer, eighty Pawnee scouts and 250 of Connor's cavalrymen charged the village from two sides. The Pawnees swerved toward the three thousand ponies which the Arapaho herders were desperately trying to scatter along the river valley. The village, which had been peaceful and quiet a few minutes before, suddenly became a scene of fearful tumult—horses rearing and whinnying, dogs barking, women screaming, children crying, warriors and soldiers yelling and cursing.

The Arapahos tried to form a line of defense to screen the flight of their noncombatants, but in the first rattle of rifle fire some women and children were caught between the warriors and the cavalrymen. "The troops," said one of Connor's officers, "killed a warrior, who, falling from his horse, dropped two Indian children he had been carrying. In retreating, the Indians left the children about halfway between the two lines, where they could not be reached by either party." The children were shot down.[7]

"I was in the village in the midst of a hand-to-hand fight with warriors and their squaws," another officer said, "for many of the female portion of this band did as brave fighting as their savage lords. Unfortunately for the women and children, our

men had no time to direct their aim . . . squaws and children,
as well as warriors, fell among the dead and wounded." [8]

As quickly as they could catch ponies, the Arapahos mounted
and began retreating up Wolf Creek, the soldiers pressing after
them. With the soldiers was a scout in buckskins, and some of
the older Arapahos recognized him as an old acquaintance who
had trapped along the Tongue and Powder years before and had
married one of their women. They had considered him a friend.
Blanket, they called him, Blanket Jim Bridger. Now he was a
mercenary like the Pawnees.

For ten miles the Arapahos retreated that day, and when the
soldiers' horses grew tired, the warriors turned on them, using
their old trade guns upon the Bluecoats and stinging them with
arrows. By early afternoon Black Bear and his warriors pushed
Connor's cavalrymen back to the village, but artillerymen had
mounted two howitzers there, and the big-talking guns filled
the air with whistling pieces of metal. The Arapahos could go
no farther.

While the Arapahos watched from the hills, the soldiers tore
down all the lodges in the village and heaped poles, tepee covers,
buffalo robes, blankets, furs, and thirty tons of pemmican into
great mounds and set fire to them. Everything the Arapahos
owned—shelter, clothing, and their winter supply of food—went
up in smoke. And then the soldiers and the Pawnees mounted
up and went away with the ponies they had captured, a thousand
animals, one-third of the tribe's pony herd.

During the afternoon Little Horse, the Cheyenne who had
tried to warn the Arapahos that soldiers were coming, heard the
sound of the big guns. As soon as the soldiers left, he and his
wife and those of her relatives who had heeded their warning
came back into the burned village. They found more than fifty
dead Indians. Panther, Little Horse's brother-in-law, was lying
beside a circle of yellowed grass where his lodge had stood that
morning. Many others, including Black Bear's son, were badly
wounded and soon would die. The Arapahos had nothing left
except the ponies they had saved from capture, a few old guns,
their bows and arrows, and the clothing they were wearing when
the soldiers charged into the village. This was the Battle of

Tongue River that happened in the Moon When the Geese Shed Their Feathers.

Next morning some of the warriors followed after Connor's cavalrymen, who were heading north toward the Rosebud. On that same day the Sawyers wagon train, which the Sioux and Cheyennes had besieged two weeks earlier, came rolling through the Arapaho country. Infuriated by the presence of so many intruders, the Indians ambushed soldiers scouting ahead of the train, stampeded cattle in the rear, and picked off an occasional wagon driver. Because they had expended most of their ammunition fighting Connor's cavalrymen, the Arapahos were not strong enough to surround and attack Sawyers' wagons. They constantly harassed the goldseekers, however, until they passed out of the Bighorn country into Montana.

Star Chief Connor meanwhile marched on toward the Rosebud, searching hungrily for more Indian villages to destroy. As he neared the rendezvous point on the Rosebud, he sent scouts out in all directions to look for the other two columns of his expedition, the ones led by the Eagle Chiefs, Cole and Walker. No trace could be found of either column, and they were a week overdue. On September 9 Connor ordered Captain North to lead his Pawnees in a forced march to Powder River in hopes of intercepting the columns. On the second day the Pawnee mercenaries ran into a blinding sleet storm, and then two days later they found where Cole and Walker had camped not long before. The ground was covered with dead horses, nine hundred of them. The Pawnees "were overcome with astonishment and wonder at the sight, for they did not know how the animals had come to their deaths. Many of the horses had been shot through the head." [9] Nearby were charred remains in which they found pieces of metal buckles, stirrups, and rings—the remains of burned saddles and harnesses. Captain North was uncertain what to make of this evidence of a disaster; he immediately turned back toward the Rosebud to report to General Connor.

On August 18 the two columns under Cole and Walker had joined along the Belle Fourche River in the Black Hills. Morale of the two thousand troops was low; they were Civil War volunteers who felt they should have been discharged when the war ended in April. Before leaving Fort Laramie, soldiers of one of Walker's Kansas regiments mutinied and would not march out until artillery was trained upon them. By late August rations for the combined columns were so short that they began slaughtering mules for meat. Scurvy broke out among the men. Because of a shortage of grass and water, their mounts grew weaker and weaker. With men and horses in such condition, neither Cole nor Walker had any desire to press a fight with Indians. Their only objective was to reach the Rosebud for the rendezvous with General Connor.

As for the Indians, there were thousands of them in the sacred places of Paha-Sapa, the Black Hills. It was summer, the time for communing with the Great Spirit, for beseeching his pity and seeking visions. Members of all the tribes were there at the center of the world, singly or in small bands, engaged in these religious ceremonies. They watched the dust streamers of two thousand soldiers and their horses and wagons, and hated them for their desecration of Paha-Sapa, from where the hoop of the world bent to the four directions. But no war parties were formed, and the Indians kept away from the noisy, dusty column.

On August 28, when Cole and Walker reached the Powder, they sent scouts to the Tongue and Rosebud to find General Connor, but he was still far to the south that day preparing to destroy Black Bear's Arapaho village. After their scouts returned to camp without finding any trace of Connor, the two commanders put their men on half-rations and decided to start moving south before starvation brought disaster.

During the few days that the soldiers were camped there on the Powder where it curved north toward the Yellowstone, bands of Hunkpapa and Minneconjou Sioux were following their trail out of the Black Hills. By September 1 the trackers numbered nearly four hundred warriors. With them was the Hunkpapa leader, Sitting Bull, who two years before at the Crow Creek camp of the exiled Santees from Minnesota had sworn that he would fight if necessary to save the buffalo country from land-hungry white men.

When the Sioux war party discovered the soldiers camped in timber along the Powder, several of the young men wanted to

ride in under a truce flag and see if they could persuade the
Bluecoats to give them tobacco and sugar as peace offerings.
Sitting Bull did not trust white men and was opposed to such
begging, but he held back and let the others send a truce party
down toward the camp.

The soldiers waited until the Sioux truce party came within
easy rifle range and then fired on them, killing and wounding
several of them before they could escape. On their way back to
the main body of warriors, the survivors of the truce party made
off with several horses from the soldiers' herd.

Sitting Bull was not surprised at the way the soldiers had
treated their peaceful Indian visitors. After looking at the gaunt
horses taken from the soldiers' herd, he decided that four hundred Sioux on fleet-footed mustangs should be an equal match
for two thousand soldiers on such half-starved Army mounts.
Black Moon, Swift Bear, Red Leaf, Stands-Looking-Back, and
most of the other warriors agreed with him. Stands-Looking-
Back had a saber that he had captured from one of General
Sully's men in Dakota, and he wanted to try it against the
soldiers.

In pictographs that Sitting Bull drew later for his autobiography, he showed himself on that day wearing beaded leggings
and a fur cap with earflaps. He was armed with a single-shot
muzzle-loader, a bow and quiver, and carried his thunderbird
shield.

Riding down to the camp single file, the Sioux encircled the
soldiers guarding the horse herd, and began picking them off
one by one until a company of cavalrymen came charging up
the bank of the Powder. The Sioux quickly withdrew on their
fast ponies, keeping out of range until the Bluecoats' bony
mounts began to falter. Then they turned on their pursuers,
Stands-Looking-Back in the lead, brandishing his saber and
riding right in until he knocked a soldier off his horse. Stands-
Looking-Back then wheeled his pony and dashed safely away,
yelling with glee over his exploit.

After a few minutes the soldiers re-formed, and at the sound of
a bugle came charging after the Sioux again. Once more the
swift mustangs of the Sioux took them out of range, the Indians scattering until the frustrated soldiers came to a halt.

This time the Sioux struck from all sides, racing in among the soldiers and knocking them off their horses. Sitting Bull captured a black stallion, afterward making a pictograph of the event for his autobiography.

Alarmed by the Indian attack, the Eagle Chiefs, Cole and Walker, formed their columns for a forced march southward along the Powder. For a few days the Sioux followed the soldiers, scaring them by appearing suddenly on ridgetops or making little forays against the rear guard. Sitting Bull and the other leaders laughed at how frightened the Bluecoats became, bunching up all the time and looking over their shoulders, and always hurrying, hurrying, trying to get away from them.

When the big sleet storm came, the Indians took shelter for two days, and then one morning they heard scattered firing from the direction the soldiers had gone. The next day they found the abandoned camp with dead horses everywhere. They could see that the horses had been covered with sheets of freezing rain, and the soldiers had shot them because they could not make them go any farther.

Since many of the frightened Bluecoats were now on foot, the Sioux decided to keep following them and drive them so crazy with fear they would never return to the Black Hills again. Along the way these Hunkpapas and Minneconjous began meeting small scouting parties of Oglala Sioux and Cheyennes who were still out looking for Star Chief Connor's column. There was great excitement in these meetings. Only a few miles south was a big Cheyenne village, and as runners brought the leaders of the bands together, they began planning a big ambush for the soldiers.

During that summer Roman Nose had made many medicine fasts to obtain special protection against enemies. Like Red Cloud and Sitting Bull, he was determined to fight for his country, and he was also determined to win. White Bull, an old Cheyenne medicine man, advised him to go alone to a medicine lake nearby and live with the water spirits. For four days Roman Nose lay on a raft in the lake without food or water, enduring the hot sun by day and thunderstorms at night. He prayed to the Great Medicine Man and to the water spirits. After Roman Nose

returned to camp, White Bull made him a protective war bonnet filled with so many eagle feathers that when he was
mounted, the war bonnet trailed almost to the ground.

In September, when the Cheyenne camp first heard about the
soldiers fleeing south up the Powder, Roman Nose asked for
the privilege of leading a charge against the Bluecoats. A day
or two later the soldiers were camped in a bend of the river, with
high bluffs and thick timber on both sides. Deciding that this
was an excellent place for an attack, the chiefs brought several
hundred warriors into position all around the camp and began
the fight by sending small decoy parties in to draw the soldiers
out of their wagon corral. But the soldiers would not come out.

Now Roman Nose rode up on his white pony, his war bonnet
trailing behind him, his face painted for battle. He called to the
warriors not to fight singly as they had always done but to fight
together as the soldiers did. He told them to form a line on the
open ground between the river and the bluffs. The warriors
maneuvered their ponies into a line front facing the soldiers,
who were formed on foot before their wagons. Roman Nose now
danced his white pony along in front of the warriors, telling
them to stand fast until he had emptied the soldiers' guns.
Then he slapped the pony into a run and rode straight as an
arrow toward one end of the line of soldiers. When he was close
enough to see their faces clearly, he turned and rode fast along
the length of the soldiers' line, and they emptied their guns at
him all along the way. At the end of the line, he wheeled the
white pony and rode back along the soldiers' front again.

"He made three, or perhaps four, rushes from one end of the
line to the other," said George Bent. "And then his pony was
shot and fell under him. On seeing this, the warriors set up a
yell and charged. They attacked the troops all along the line,
but could not break through anywhere." [10]

Roman Nose had lost his horse, but his protective medicine
saved his life. He also learned some things that day about fighting Bluecoats—and so did Red Cloud, Sitting Bull, Dull Knife,
and the other leaders. Bravery, numbers, massive charges—they
all meant nothing if the warriors were armed only with bows,
lances, clubs, and old trade guns of the fur-trapper days. ("We
were now attacked from all sides, front, rear, and flanks," Colo-

nel Walker reported, "but the Indians seemed to have but few
fire arms." [11]) The soldiers were armed with modern Civil War
rifles, and had the support of howitzers.

For several days after the fight—which would be remembered
by the Indians as Roman Nose's fight—the Cheyennes and
Sioux continued to harass and punish the soldiers. The Bluecoats were now barefoot and in rags, and had nothing left to
eat but their bony horses, which they devoured raw because
they were too pressed to build fires. At last in the Drying Grass
Moon toward the end of September, Star Chief Connor's returning column arrived to rescue Cole and Walker's beaten soldiers. The soldiers all camped together around the stockade at
Fort Connor on the Powder until messengers from Fort Laramie
arrived with orders recalling the troops (except for two companies, which were to remain at Fort Connor).

The two companies which were ordered to stay through the
winter at Fort Connor (soon to be renamed Fort Reno) were
the Galvanized Yankees who had escorted Sawyers' wagon
trains west to the gold fields. General Connor left these former
Confederate soldiers six howitzers to defend their stockade. Red
Cloud and the other leaders studied the fort from a distance.
They knew they had enough warriors to storm the stockade,
but too many would die under the showers of shot hurled by
the big guns. They finally agreed upon a crude strategy of keeping a constant watch on the fort and its supply trail from Fort
Laramie. They would hold the soldiers prisoners in their fort
all winter and cut off their supplies from Fort Laramie.

Before that winter ended, half the luckless Galvanized Yankees were dead or dying of scurvy, malnutrition, and pneumonia.
From the boredom of confinement, many slipped away and deserted, taking their chances with the Indians outside.

As for the Indians, all except the small bands of warriors
needed to watch the fort moved over to the Black Hills, where
plentiful herds of antelope and buffalo kept them fat in their
warm lodges. Through the long winter evenings the chiefs re-
counted the events of Star Chief Connor's invasion. Because
the Arapahos had been overconfident and careless, they had
lost a village, several lives, and part of their rich pony herd.
The other tribes had lost a few lives but no horses or lodges.

They had captured many horses and mules carrying U.S. brands. They had taken many carbines, saddles, and other equipment from the soldiers. Above all, they had gained a new confidence in their ability to drive the Bluecoat soldiers from their country.

"If white men come into my country again, I will punish them again," Red Cloud said, but he knew that unless he could somehow obtain many new guns like the ones they had captured from the soldiers, and plenty of ammunition for the guns, the Indians could not go on punishing the soldiers forever.

SIX

Red Cloud's War

1866—March 27, President Johnson vetoes Civil Rights Bill. April 1, Congress overrides the President's veto of Civil Rights Bill and gives equal rights to all persons born in United States (except Indians); President empowered to use Army to enforce the law. June 13, Fourteenth Amendment to the U.S. Constitution, giving Negroes rights of citizenship, is forwarded to states for ratification. July 21, several hundred die in London cholera epidemic. July 30, race riot in New Orleans. Werner von Siemens invents the dynamo. Dostoyevsky's *Crime and Punishment* and Whittier's *Snowbound* are published.

1867—February 9, Nebraska admitted to Union as thirty-seventh state. February 17, first ship passes through Suez Canal. March 12, last French troops leave Mexico. March 30, U.S. purchases Alaska from Russia for $7,200,000. May 20, in London, John Stuart Mill's bill to permit women to vote is rejected by Parliament. June 19, Mexicans execute Emperor Maximilian. July 1, Dominion of Canada established. October 27, Garibaldi marches on Rome. November 25, congressional committee resolves that President Johnson "be impeached for high crimes and misdemeanors." Alfred Nobel invents dynamite. Christopher L. Sholes constructs the first practical typewriter. Johann Strauss composes "The Blue Danube." Karl Marx publishes first part of *Das Kapital*.

This war did not spring up here in our land; this war was brought upon us by the children of the Great Father who came to take our land from us without price, and who, in our land, do a great many evil things. The Great Father and his children are to blame for this trouble. . . . It has been our wish to live here in our country peaceably, and do such things as may be for the welfare and good of our people, but the Great Father has filled it with soldiers who think only of our death. Some of our people who have gone from here in order that they may have a change, and others who have gone north to hunt, have been attacked by the soldiers from this direction, and when they have got north have been attacked by soldiers from the other side, and now when they are willing to come back the soldiers stand between them to keep them from coming home. It seems to me there is a better way than this. When people come to trouble, it is better for both parties to come together without arms and talk it over and find some peaceful way to settle it.

—Sinte-Galeshka (Spotted Tail) of the Brulé Sioux

In late summer and autumn of 1865, while the Indians in the Powder River country were demonstrating their military power, a United States treaty commission was traveling along the upper Missouri River. At every Sioux village near the river, the commissioners stopped to parley with whatever leaders they could find. Newton Edmunds, recently appointed governor of the Territory of Dakota, was the prime mover on this commission. Another member was the Long Trader, Henry Sibley, who three years earlier had driven the Santee Sioux from the state of Minnesota. Edmunds and Sibley handed out blankets, molasses, crackers, and other presents to the Indians they visited, and had no difficulty in persuading their hosts to sign new treaties. They also sent runners into the Black Hills and Powder River country inviting the warrior chiefs to come in and sign, but the chiefs were too busy fighting General Connor's invaders, and none responded.

In the spring of that year the white man's Civil War had been brought to an end, and the trickle of white emigration to the West was showing signs of increasing to a flood. What the treaty commissioners wanted was right of passageway for trails, roads, and eventually railroads across the Indian country.

Before autumn ended the commissioners completed nine treaties with the Sioux—including the Brulés, Hunkpapas, Oglalas, and Minneconjous, most of whose warrior chiefs were nowhere near the villages on the Missouri. Government authorities in Washington hailed the treaties as the end of Indian hostilities. At last the Plains Indians were pacified, they said; never again would there be a need for expensive campaigns such as Connor's Powder River expedition, which had been organized to kill Indians "at an expense of more than a million dollars apiece, while hundreds of our soldiers had lost their lives, many of our border settlers been butchered, and much property destroyed." [1]

Governor Edmunds and the other commission members knew very well that the treaties were meaningless because not one warrior chief had signed them. Although the commissioners forwarded copies to Washington to be ratified by Congress, they continued their efforts to persuade Red Cloud and the other Powder River chiefs to meet with them at any convenient location for further treaty signings. As the Bozeman Trail was the most important route out of Fort Laramie to Montana, military officials at the fort were under heavy pressure to coax Red Cloud and other war leaders to cease their blockade of the road and come to Laramie at the earliest possible date.

Colonel Henry Maynadier, who had been assigned to Fort Laramie as commander of one of the Galvanized Yankee regiments, attempted to employ a trustworthy frontiersman such as Blanket Jim Bridger or Medicine Calf Beckwourth to act as an intermediary with Red Cloud, but none was willing to go into the Powder River country so soon after Connor had aroused the tribes to anger with his invasion. At last Maynadier decided to employ as messengers five Sioux who spent much of their time around the fort—Big Mouth, Big Ribs, Eagle Foot, Whirlwind, and Little Crow. Referred to contemptuously as "Laramie Loafers," these trader Indians were actually shrewd entrepreneurs. If a white man wanted a first-rate buffalo robe at a bargain, or if an Indian up on Tongue River wanted supplies from the fort commissary, the Laramie Loafers arranged exchanges. They would play an important role as munitions suppliers to the Indians during Red Cloud's war.

Big Mouth and his party were out for two months, spreading the news that fine presents awaited all warrior chiefs if they would come in to Fort Laramie and sign new treaties. On January 16, 1866, the messengers returned in company with two destitute bands of Brulés led by Standing Elk and Swift Bear. Standing Elk said that his people had lost many ponies in a blizzard and that game was scarce over on the Republican. Spotted Tail, the head man of the Brulés, would come in as soon as his daughter was able to travel. She was ill of the coughing sickness. Standing Elk and Swift Bear were eager to sign the treaty and receive clothing and provisions for their people.

"But what about Red Cloud?" Colonel Maynadier wanted to know. "Where was Red Cloud, Man-Afraid-of-His-Horses, Dull Knife—the leaders who had fought Connor's soldiers?" Big Mouth and the other Laramie Loafers assured him that the warrior chiefs would be there in a short time. They could not be hurried, especially in the Moon of Strong Cold.

Weeks passed, and then early in March a messenger arrived from Spotted Tail informing Colonel Maynadier that the Brulé chief was coming in to discuss the treaty. Spotted Tail's daughter Fleet Foot was very ill, and he hoped the soldiers' doctor would make her well again. A few days later, when Maynadier heard that Fleet Foot had died en route, he rode out with a company of soldiers and an ambulance to meet the mourning procession of Brulés. It was a cold sleety day, the Wyoming landscape bleak, streams locked in ice, brown hills patched with snow. The dead girl had been wrapped in a deerskin, tightly thonged and creosoted with smoke; this crude pall was suspended between her favorite ponies, a pair of white mustangs.

Fleet Foot's body was transferred to the ambulance, her white ponies fastened behind, and the procession continued toward Fort Laramie. When Spotted Tail's party reached the fort, Colonel Maynadier turned the entire garrison out to honor the grieving Indians.

The colonel invited Spotted Tail into his headquarters and

offered sympathy for the loss of his daughter. The chief said that in the days when the white men and the Indians were at peace, he had brought his daughter to Fort Laramie many times, that she loved the fort, and he would like to have her burial scaffold mounted in the post cemetery. Colonel Maynadier immediately granted permission. He was surprised to see tears well up in Spotted Tail's eyes; he did not know that an Indian could weep. Somewhat awkwardly the colonel changed the subject. The Great Father in Washington was sending out a new peace commission in the spring; he hoped that Spotted Tail could stay near the fort until the commissioners arrived; there was a great urgency to make the Bozeman Road safe for travel. "I am informed that the travel next spring will be very great," the colonel said, "to the mines of Idaho and Montana."

"We think we have been much wronged," Spotted Tail replied, "and are entitled to compensation for the damage and distress caused by making so many roads through our country, and driving off and destroying the buffalo and game. My heart is very sad, and I cannot talk on business; I will wait and see the counselors the Great Father will send." [2]

Next day Maynadier arranged a military funeral for Fleet Foot, and just before sunset a procession marched to the post cemetery behind the red-blanketed coffin, which was mounted on an artillery caisson. After the custom of the Brulés, the women lifted the coffin to the scaffold, laid a fresh buffalo skin over it, and bound it down with thongs. The sky was leaden and stormy, and sleet began falling with the dusk. At a word of command the soldiers faced outward and discharged three volleys in succession. They and the Indians then marched back to the post. A squad of artillerymen remained beside the scaffold all night; they built a large fire of pine wood and fired their howitzer every half-hour until daybreak.

Four days later Red Cloud and a large party of Oglalas appeared suddenly outside the fort. They stopped first at Spotted Tail's camp, and the two Teton leaders were enjoying a reunion when Maynadier came out with a soldier escort to conduct both of them to his headquarters with the pomp and ceremony of drums and bugles.

When Maynadier told Red Cloud that the new peace commissioners would not arrive at Fort Laramie for some weeks, the Oglala chief became angry. Big Mouth and the other messengers had told him that if he came in and signed a treaty he would receive presents. He needed guns and powder and provisions. Maynadier replied that he could issue the visiting Oglalas provisions from the Army stores, but he had no authority to distribute guns and powder. Red Cloud then wanted to know what the treaty would give his people; they had signed treaties before, and it always seemed that the Indians gave to the white men. This time the white men must give something to the Indians.

Remembering that the president of the new commission, E. B. Taylor, was in Omaha, Maynadier suggested that Red Cloud send a message to Taylor over the telegraph wires. Red Cloud was suspicious; he did not entirely trust in the magic of the talking wires. After some delay he agreed to go with the colonel to the fort's telegraph office, and through an interpreter dictated a message of peace and friendship to the Great Father's counselor in Omaha.

Commissioner Taylor's reply came clicking back: "The Great Father at Washington . . . wants you all to be his friends and the friends of the white man. If you conclude a treaty of peace, he wishes to make presents to you and your people as a token of his friendship. A train loaded with supplies and presents cannot reach Fort Laramie from the Missouri River before the first of June and he desires that about that time be agreed upon as the day when his commissioners shall meet you to make a treaty." [3]

Red Cloud was impressed. He also liked Colonel Maynadier's straightforward manner. He could wait until the Moon When the Green Grass Is Up for the treaty signing. This would give him time to go back to the Powder and send out runners to all the scattered bands of Sioux, Cheyennes, and Arapahos. It would give the Indians time to gather more buffalo hides and beaver skins for trading when they came down to Fort Laramie.

As a goodwill gesture, Maynadier issued small amounts of powder and lead to the departing Oglalas, and they rode away in fine good humor. Nothing had been said by Maynadier about opening the Bozeman Road; nothing had been said by Red

11. *Spotted Tail, or Sinte-Galeshka, of the Brulé Sioux. From a painting by Henry Ulke made in 1877, now in the National Portrait Gallery of the Smithsonian Institution.*

Cloud about Fort Reno, which was still under siege on the
Powder. These subjects could be postponed until the treaty
council.

Red Cloud did not wait for the green grass to come up. He
returned to Fort Laramie in May, the Moon When the Ponies
Shed, and he brought with him his chief lieutenant, Man-Afraid-
of-His-Horses, and more than a thousand Oglalas. Dull Knife
brought in several lodges of Cheyennes, and Red Leaf arrived
with his band of Brulés. Together with Spotted Tail's people
and the other Brulés, they formed a great camp along the Platte
River. The trading posts and sutlers' stores became a swirl of
activity. Never had Big Mouth and the Laramie Loafers been
so busy arranging trades.

A few days later the peace commissioners arrived, and on
June 5 the formal proceedings began, with the usual long ora-
tions by commission members and the various Indian leaders.
Then Red Cloud unexpectedly asked for a few days' delay while
they awaited the arrival of other Tetons who wanted to participate in the discussions. Commissioner Taylor agreed to ad-
journ the council until June 13.

By a trick of fate, June 13 was the day that Colonel Henry
B. Carrington and seven hundred officers and men of the 18th
Infantry Regiment reached the vicinity of Fort Laramie. The
regiment had marched from Fort Kearney, Nebraska, and was
under orders to establish a chain of forts along the Bozeman
Road in preparation for the expected heavy travel to Montana
during the summer. Although plans for the expedition had been
under way for weeks, none of the Indians invited to attend the
treaty signing had been told anything about this military occu-
pation of the Powder River country.

To avoid friction with the two thousand Indians camped
around Fort Laramie, Carrington halted his regiment four miles
east of the post. Standing Elk, one of the Brulé chiefs who had
come in during the winter, watched from his distant tepee while
the soldiers formed their wagon train into a hollow square. He
then mounted his pony and rode over to the camp, and the soldier guards took him in to see Colonel Carrington. Carrington
summoned one of his guides to interpret, and after they had

gone through the formalities of pipe smoking, Standing Elk asked bluntly: "Where are you going?"

Carrington replied frankly that he was taking his troops to the Powder River country to guard the road to Montana.

"There is a treaty being made in Laramie with the Sioux that are in the country where you are going," Standing Elk told him. "You will have to fight the Sioux warriors if you go there."

Carrington said he was not going to make war on the Sioux, but only to guard the road.

"They will not sell their hunting grounds to the white men for a road," Standing Elk insisted. "They will not give you the road unless you whip them." He added quickly that he was a Brulé, that he and Spotted Tail were friends of the white men, but that Red Cloud's Oglalas and the Minneconjous would fight any white men who came north of the Platte.[4]

Before the next day's treaty proceedings, the presence and purpose of the regiment of Bluecoats were known to every Indian at Fort Laramie. When Carrington rode into the fort next morning, Commissioner Taylor decided to introduce him to the chiefs and quietly inform them of what they already knew— that the United States government intended to open a road through the Powder River country regardless of the treaty.

Carrington's first remarks were drowned out by a chorus of disapproving Indian voices. When he resumed speaking, the Indians continued muttering among themselves and began moving restlessly on the pine-board benches where they were assembled on the fort parade ground. Carrington's interpreter suggested in a whisper that perhaps he should allow the chiefs to speak first.

Man-Afraid-of-His-Horses took the platform. In a torrent of words he made it clear that if the soldiers marched into Sioux country, his people would fight them. "In two moons the command will not have a hoof left," he declared.[5]

Now it was Red Cloud's turn. His lithe figure, clad in a light blanket and moccasins, moved to the center of the platform. His straight black hair, parted in the middle, was draped over his shoulders to his waist. His wide mouth was fixed in a determined slit beneath his hawk nose. His eyes flashed as he began

scolding the peace commissioners for treating the Indians like
children. He accused them of pretending to negotiate for a
country while they prepared to take it by conquest. "The white
men have crowded the Indians back year by year," he said,
"until we are forced to live in a small country north of the Platte,
and now our last hunting ground, the home of the People, is
to be taken from us. Our women and children will starve, but
for my part I prefer to die fighting rather than by starvation.
. . . Great Father sends us presents and wants new road. But
White Chief goes with soldiers to steal road before Indian says
yes or no!" While the interpreter was still trying to translate
the Sioux words into English, the listening Indians became so
disorderly that Commissioner Taylor abruptly ended the day's
session. Red Cloud strode past Carrington as if he were not
there, and continued on across the parade ground toward the
Oglala camp. Before the next dawn, the Oglalas were gone from
Fort Laramie.[6]

During the next few weeks, as Carrington's wagon train moved
north along the Bozeman Road, the Indians had an opportunity
to appraise its size and strength. The two hundred wagons were
loaded to the bows with mowing machines, shingle and brick
machines, wooden doors, window sashes, locks, nails, musical
instruments for a twenty-five-piece band, rocking chairs, churns,
canned goods and vegetable seeds, as well as the usual ammunition, gunpowder, and other military supplies. The Bluecoats
evidently expected to stay in the Powder River country; a number of them had brought their wives and children along, with
an assortment of pets and servants. They were armed with obsolete muzzle-loaders and a few breech-loading Spencer carbines,
and were supported by four pieces of artillery. For guides they
had secured the services of Blanket Jim Bridger and Medicine
Calf Beckwourth, who knew that Indians were watching the
daily progress of the train along the Powder River road.

By June 28 the regiment reached Fort Reno, relieving the
two companies of Galvanized Yankees who during the winter
and spring had been kept virtual prisoners within their own
stockade. To garrison Fort Reno, Carrington left about one-
fourth of his regiment, and then moved on north, searching for
a site for his headquarters post. From Indian camps along the

Powder and Tongue, hundreds of warriors now began gathering along the flanks of the military train.

On July 13 the column halted between the forks of the Little Piney and Big Piney creeks. There in the heart of a luxuriant grassland near the pine-clad slopes of the Bighorns, on the best hunting grounds of the Plains Indians, the Bluecoats pitched their Army tents and began building Fort Phil Kearny.

Three days later a large party of Cheyennes approached the encampment. Two Moon, Black Horse, and Dull Knife were among the leaders, but Dull Knife kept in the background because the other chiefs had been chiding him severely for remaining at Fort Laramie and signing the paper which gave the soldiers permission to build forts and open the Powder River road. Dull Knife insisted that he had touched the pen at Laramie in order to obtain presents of blankets and ammunition, and he did not know what was written on the paper. Yet the others rebuked him for doing this after Red Cloud had turned his back on the white men, disdaining their presents and gathering his warriors to defy them.

Under truce flags the Cheyennes arranged a parley with the Little White Chief Carrington. Forty chiefs and warriors were given permission to visit the soldier camp. Carrington met them with the military band he had brought all the way from Fort Kearney, Nebraska, entertaining the Indians with spirited martial music. Blanket Jim Bridger was there, and they knew they could not fool the Blanket, but they did fool the Little White Chief into believing they had come to talk of peace. While the pipe smoking and preliminary speeches were going on, the chiefs studied the power of the soldiers.

Before they were ready to depart, the Little White Chief sighted one of his howitzers at a hill and exploded a spherical case shot upon it. "It shoots twice," Black Horse said with forced solemnity. "White Chief shoot once. Then White Chief's Great Spirit fires it once more for his white children." [7]

The power of the big gun impressed the Indians, as Carrington had hoped it would, but he did not suspect that Black Horse was deriding him with that bland remark about the Great Spirit firing it "once more for his white children." When the Cheyennes prepared to leave, the Little White Chief gave them pieces of paper saying that they had agreed to a "lasting peace with the whites and all travelers on the road," and they departed. Within a few hours, villages along the Tongue and Powder heard from the Cheyennes that the new fort was too strong to be captured without great loss. They would have to lure the soldiers out into the open, where they could be more easily attacked.

Next morning at dawn, a band of Red Cloud's Oglalas stampeded 175 horses and mules from Carrington's herd. When the soldiers came riding in pursuit, the Indians strung them out in a fifteen-mile chase and inflicted the first casualties upon the Bluecoat invaders of the Powder River country.

From that day all through the summer of 1866, the Little White Chief was engaged in a relentless guerrilla war. None of the numerous wagon trains, civilian or military, that moved along the Bozeman Road was safe from surprise attacks. Mounted escorts were spread thin, and the soldiers soon learned to expect deadly ambushes. Soldiers assigned to cut logs a few miles from Fort Phil Kearny were under constant and deadly harassment.

As the summer wore on, the Indians developed a supply base on the upper Powder, and their grand strategy soon became apparent—make travel on the road difficult and dangerous, cut off supplies for Carrington's troops, isolate them, and attack.

Red Cloud was everywhere, and his allies increased daily. Black Bear, the Arapaho chief whose village had been destroyed by General Connor the previous summer, notified Red Cloud that his warriors were eager to join the fighting. Sorrel Horse, another Arapaho, also brought his warriors into the alliance. Spotted Tail, still believing in peace, had gone to hunt buffalo along the Republican, but many of his Brulé warriors came north to join Red Cloud. Sitting Bull was there during the summer; he later drew a pictograph of his capture of a split-eared horse from white travelers on the Powder River road. Gall, a younger Hunkpapa, was also there. With a Minneconjou named Hump and a young Oglala named Crazy Horse, he invented decoy tricks to taunt, infuriate, and then lure soldiers or emigrants into well-laid traps.

Early in August Carrington decided that Fort Phil Kearny was strong enough to risk dividing his force again. Therefore, in accordance with his instructions from the War Department, he detached 150 men and sent them north ninety miles to build a third fort on the Bozeman Road—Fort C. F. Smith. At the same time, he sent scouts Bridger and Beckwourth out to communicate with Red Cloud. This was a difficult assignment, but the two aging frontiersmen went in search of friendly go-betweens.

In a Crow village north of the Bighorns, Bridger obtained some surprising information. Although the Sioux were hereditary enemies of the Crows and had driven them from their rich hunting grounds, Red Cloud himself had recently made a conciliatory visit in hopes of persuading them to join his Indian alliance. "We want you to aid us in destroying the whites," Red Cloud was reported to have said. The Sioux leader then boasted that he would cut off the soldiers' supplies when the snows came and would starve them out of the forts and kill them all.[8] Bridger heard rumors that a few Crows had agreed to join Red Cloud's warriors, but when he rejoined Beckwourth in another Crow village, Beckwourth claimed that he was enlisting Crows who were willing to join Carrington's soldiers in fighting the Sioux. (Medicine Calf Beckwourth never returned to Fort Phil Kearny. He died suddenly in the Crow village, possibly from poison administered by a jealous husband, more likely from natural causes.)

By late summer Red Cloud had a force of three thousand warriors. Through their friends the Laramie Loafers, they managed to assemble a small arsenal of rifles and ammunition, but the majority of warriors still had only bows and arrows. During the early autumn Red Cloud and the other chiefs agreed that they must concentrate their power against the Little White Chief and the hated fort on the Pineys. And so before the coming of the Cold Moons they moved toward the Bighorns and made their camps along the headwaters of the Tongue. From there they were in easy striking distance of Fort Phil Kearny.

During the summer raiding, two Oglalas, High Back Bone and Yellow Eagle, had made names for themselves with their carefully planned stratagems for tricking the soldiers, as well as for reckless horsemanship and daring hand-to-hand attacks after the soldiers fell into their traps. High Back Bone and Yellow Eagle sometimes worked with young Crazy Horse in planning their elaborate decoys. Early in the Moon of Popping Trees they began tantalizing the woodcutters in the pinery and the soldiers guarding the wagons which brought wood to Fort Phil Kearny.

On December 6, a day with a cold wash of air flowing down the slopes of the Bighorns, High Back Bone and Yellow Eagle took about a hundred warriors and dispersed them at various points along the pinery road. Red Cloud was with another group of warriors who took positions along the ridgetops. They flashed mirrors and waved flags to signal the movements of the troops to High Back Bone and his decoys. Before the day was over, the Indians had the Bluecoats dashing about in all directions. At one time the Little White Chief Carrington came out and gave chase. Choosing just the right moment, Crazy Horse dismounted and showed himself on the trail in front of one of Carrington's hot-blooded young cavalry officers, who immediately led a file of soldiers galloping in pursuit. As soon as the soldiers were strung out along the narrow trail, Yellow Eagle and his warriors sprang from concealment in their rear. In a matter of seconds the Indians swarmed over the soldiers. (This was the fight in which Lieutenant Horatio Bingham and Sergeant G. R. Bowers were killed and several soldiers severely wounded.)

In their camps that night and for several days following, the chiefs and warriors talked of how foolishly the Bluecoats had acted. Red Cloud was sure that if they could entice a large number of troops out of the fort, a thousand Indians armed with only bows and arrows could kill them all. Sometime during the week, the chiefs agreed that after the coming of the next full moon they would prepare a great trap for the Little White Chief and his soldiers.

By the third week of December everything was in readiness, and about two thousand warriors began moving south out of the lodges along the Tongue. The weather was very cold, and they wore buffalo robes with the hair turned in, leggings of dark woolen cloth, high-topped buffalo-fur moccasins, and carried red Hudson's Bay blankets strapped to their saddles. Most of them rode pack horses, leading their fast-footed war ponies by lariats. Some had rifles, but most were armed with bows and arrows, knives, and lances. They carried enough pemmican to last several days, and when an opportunity offered, small groups would turn off the trail, kill a deer, and take as much meat as could be carried on their saddles.

About ten miles north of Fort Phil Kearny, they made a temporary camp in three circles of Sioux, Cheyennes, and Arapahos. Between the camp and the fort was the place selected for the ambush—the little valley of Peno Creek.

On the morning of December 21 the chiefs and medicine men decided the day was favorable for a victory. In the first gray light of dawn, a party of warriors started off in a wide circuit toward the wood-train road, where they were to make a feint against the wagons. Ten young men had already been chosen for the dangerous duty of decoying the soldiers—two Cheyennes, two Arapahos, and two from each of the three Sioux divisions, Oglalas, Minneconjous, and Brulés. Crazy Horse, Hump, and Little Wolf were the leaders. While the decoys mounted and started off toward Lodge Trail Ridge, the main body of warriors moved down the Bozeman Road. Patches of snow and ice lay along the shady sides of the ridges, but the day was bright, the air cold and dry. About three miles from the fort, where the road ran along a narrow ridge and descended to Peno Creek, they began laying a great ambush. The Cheyennes and Arapahos took the west side. Some of the Sioux hid in a grassy flat on the opposite side; others remained mounted and concealed themselves behind two rocky ridges. By midmorning almost two thousand warriors were waiting there for the decoys to bring the Bluecoats into the trap.

While the war party was making its feint against the wood train, Crazy Horse and the decoys dismounted and waited in concealment on a slope facing the fort. At the first sound of gunfire, a company of soldiers dashed out of the fort and galloped off to rescue the woodcutters. As soon as the Bluecoats were out of sight, the decoys showed themselves on the slope and moved down closer to the fort. Crazy Horse waved his red blanket and darted in and out of the brush that fringed the frozen Piney. After a few minutes of this, the Little Soldier Chief in the fort fired off his big twice-shooting gun. The de-

coys scattered along the slope, jumping, zigzagging, and yelling
to make the soldiers believe they were frightened. By this time
the war party had withdrawn from the wood train and doubled
back toward Lodge Trail Ridge. In a few minutes the soldiers
came in pursuit, some mounted, some on foot. (They were commanded by Captain William J. Fetterman, who had explicit
orders not to pursue beyond Lodge Trail Ridge.)

Crazy Horse and the other decoys now jumped on their ponies
and began riding back and forth along the slope of Lodge Trail
Ridge, taunting the soldiers and angering them so that they fired
recklessly. Bullets ricocheted off the rocks, and the decoys moved
back slowly. When the soldiers slowed their advance or halted,
Crazy Horse would dismount and pretend to adjust his bridle
or examine his pony's hooves. Bullets whined all around him,
and then the soldiers finally moved up on the ridgetop to chase the
decoys down toward Peno Creek. They were the only Indians
in sight, only ten of them, and the soldiers were charging their
horses to catch them.

When the decoys crossed Peno Creek, all eighty-one of the
cavalrymen and infantrymen were within the trap. Now the
decoys divided into two parties and quickly rode across each
other's trail. This was the signal for attack.

Little Horse, the Cheyenne who a year earlier gave warning
to the Arapahos of General Connor's approach, had the honor
of signaling his people, who were concealed in gullies on the
west side. He raised his lance, and all the mounted Cheyennes
and Arapahos charged with a sudden thunder of hooves.

From the opposite side came the Sioux, and for a few minutes
the Indians and the walking soldiers were mixed in confused
hand-to-hand fighting. The infantrymen were soon all killed,
but the cavalrymen retreated to a rocky height near the end of
the ridge. They turned their horses loose and tried to take cover
among the ice-crusted boulders.

Little Horse made a name for himself that day, leaping over
rocks and in and out of gullies until he was within forty feet of
the besieged cavalrymen. White Bull of the Minneconjous also
distinguished himself in the bloody fighting on the hillside.
Armed only with a bow and a lance, he charged a dismounted
cavalryman who was firing at him with a carbine. In a picto-

graph that White Bull later drew of the event, he showed himself clad in a red war cape, firing an arrow into the soldier's heart and cracking him over the head with his lance to count first coup.

Toward the end of the fighting the Cheyennes and Arapahos on one side and the Sioux on the other were so close together that they began hitting each other with their showers of arrows. Then it was all over. Not a soldier was left alive. A dog came out from among the dead, and a Sioux started to catch it to take home with him, but Big Rascal, a Cheyenne, said, "Don't let the dog go," and somebody shot it with an arrow. This was the fight the white men called the Fetterman Massacre; the Indians called it the Battle of the Hundred Slain.[9]

Casualties were heavy among the Indians, almost two hundred dead and wounded. Because of the intense cold, they decided to take the wounded back to the temporary camp, where they could be kept from freezing. Next day a roaring blizzard trapped the warriors there in improvised shelters, and when the storm abated they went back to their villages on the Tongue.

Now it was the Moon of Strong Cold, and there would be no more fighting for a while. The soldiers who were left alive in the fort would have a bitter taste of defeat in their mouths. If they had not learned their lesson and were still there when the grass greened in the spring, the war would continue.

The Fetterman Massacre made a profound impression upon Colonel Carrington. He was appalled by the mutilations—the disembowelings, the hacked limbs, the "private parts severed and indecently placed on the person." He brooded upon the reasons for such savagery, and eventually wrote an essay on the subject, philosophizing that the Indians were compelled by some paganistic belief to commit the terrible deeds that remained forever in his mind. Had Colonel Carrington visited the scene of the Sand Creek Massacre, which occurred only two years before the Fetterman Massacre, he would have seen the same mutilations—committed upon Indians by Colonel Chivington's soldiers. The Indians who ambushed Fetterman were only imitating their enemies, a practice which in warfare, as in civilian life, is said to be the sincerest form of flattery.

The Fetterman Massacre also made a profound impression upon the United States government. It was the worst defeat the Army had yet suffered in Indian warfare, and the second in American history from which came no survivors. Carrington was recalled from command, reinforcements were sent to the forts in the Powder River country, and a new peace commission was dispatched from Washington to Fort Laramie.

The new commission was headed by Black Whiskers John Sanborn, who in 1865 had persuaded Black Kettle's Southern Cheyennes to give up their hunting grounds in Kansas and live below the Arkansas River. Sanborn and General Alfred Sully arrived at Fort Laramie in April, 1867, and their mission at this time was to persuade Red Cloud and the Sioux to give up their hunting grounds in the Powder River country and live on a reservation. As in the previous year, the Brulés were the first to come in—Spotted Tail, Swift Bear, Standing Elk, and Iron Shell.

Little Wound and Pawnee Killer, who had brought their Oglala bands down to the Platte in hopes of finding buffalo, came in to see what kind of presents the commissioners might be handing out. Man-Afraid-of-His-Horses arrived as a representative for Red Cloud. When the commissioners asked him if Red Cloud was coming in to talk peace, Man-Afraid replied that the Oglala leader would not talk about peace until all soldiers were removed from the Powder River country.

During these parleys, Sanborn asked Spotted Tail to address the assembled Indians. Spotted Tail advised his listeners to abandon warfare with the white men and live in peace and happiness. For this, he and the Brulés received enough powder and lead to go off on a buffalo hunt to the Republican River. The hostile Oglalas received nothing. Man-Afraid returned to join Red Cloud, who had already resumed raiding along the Bozeman Road. Little Wound and Pawnee Killer followed the Brulés to the buffalo ranges, joining their old Cheyenne friend Turkey Leg. Black Whiskers Sanborn's peace commission had accomplished nothing.

Before the summer was done, Pawnee Killer and Turkey Leg became involved with a soldier chief whom they named Hard Backsides because he chased them over long distances for many hours without leaving his saddle. Later on they would call him Long Hair Custer. When General Custer invited them to come to Fort McPherson for a parley, they approached the fort and accepted sugar and coffee. They told Hard Backsides they were friends of the white men but did not like the Iron Horse that ran on the iron tracks, whistling and snorting smoke and frightening all the game out of the Platte Valley. (The Union Pacific Railroad tracks were being laid across western Nebraska in 1867.)

In their search for buffalo and antelope, the Oglalas and Cheyennes crossed the railroad tracks several times that summer. Sometimes they saw Iron Horses dragging wooden houses on wheels at great speed along the tracks. They puzzled over what could be inside the houses, and one day a Cheyenne decided to rope one of the Iron Horses and pull it from the tracks. Instead, the Iron Horse jerked him off his pony and dragged him unmercifully before he could get loose from his lariat.

It was Sleeping Rabbit who suggested they try another way to catch one of the Iron Horses. "If we could bend the track up and spread it out, the Iron Horse might fall off," he said. "Then we could see what is in the wooden houses on wheels." They did this, and waited for the train. Sure enough, the Iron Horse fell over on its side, and much smoke came out of it. Men came running from the train, and the Indians killed all but two, who escaped and ran away. Then the Indians broke open the houses on wheels and found sacks of flour, sugar, and coffee; boxes of shoes; and barrels of whiskey. They drank some of the whiskey and began tying the ends of bolts of cloth to their ponies' tails. The ponies went dashing off across the prairie with long streamers of cloth unrolling and flying out behind them. After a while the Indians took hot coals from the wrecked engine and set the boxcars on fire. Then they rode away before soldiers could come to punish them.[10]

Incidents such as this, combined with Red Cloud's continuing war, which had brought civilian travel to an end through the Powder River country, had a strong effect upon the United States government and its high military command. The government was determined to protect the route of the Union Pacific Railroad, but even old war dogs such as General Sherman were

beginning to wonder if it might not be advisable to leave the
Powder River country to the Indians in exchange for peace
along the Platte Valley.

Late in July, after holding their sun-dance and medicine-arrow
ceremonies, the Sioux and Cheyennes decided to wipe out one
of the forts on the Bozeman Road. Red Cloud wanted to attack
Fort Phil Kearny, but Dull Knife and Two Moon thought it
would be easier to take Fort C. F. Smith, because Cheyenne
warriors had already killed or captured nearly all the soldiers'
horses there. Finally, after the chiefs could reach no agreement,
the Sioux said they would attack Fort Phil Kearny, and the
Cheyennes went north to Fort C. F. Smith.

On August 1 five or six hundred Cheyenne warriors caught
thirty soldiers and civilians in a hayfield about two miles from
Fort C. F. Smith. Unknown to the Cheyennes, the defenders
were armed with new repeating rifles, and when they charged
the soldiers' log corral they met such a withering fire that only
one warrior was able to penetrate the fortifications, and he was
killed. The Cheyennes then set fire to the high dry grass around
the corral. ("The fire came on in rolling billows, like the waves
of the ocean," one of the soldiers said afterward. "When it arrived within twenty feet of the barricade it stopped, as though
arrested by supernatural power. The flames arose to a perpendic-
ular height of at least forty feet, made one or two undulating
movements, and were extinguished with a spanking slap, like the
flapping sound of a heavy canvas in a hard gale; the wind, the
succeeding instant, carried the smoke . . . into the faces of the
attacking Indians, who improved the opportunity, under cover
of it, to carry away their dead and wounded." [11])

This was enough for the Cheyennes that day. Many warriors
suffered bad wounds from the fast-firing guns, and about twenty
were dead. They started back south to see if the Sioux had found
any better luck at Fort Phil Kearny.

. The Sioux had not. After making several feints around the
fort, Red Cloud decided to use the decoy trick which had worked
so well with Captain Fetterman. Crazy Horse would attack the
woodcutters' camp, and when the soldiers came out of the fort,
High Back Bone would swarm down on them with eight hundred warriors. Crazy Horse and his decoys carried out their

assignment perfectly, but for some reason several hundred warriors prematurely rushed out of concealment to stampede the horse herd near the fort, giving the soldiers warning of their presence.

To salvage something from the fight, Red Cloud turned the attack against the woodcutters, who had taken cover behind a corral of fourteen wagon beds reinforced with logs. Several hundred mounted warriors made a circling approach, but as at Fort C. F. Smith, the defenders were armed with breech-loading Springfields. Faced with rapid and continuous fire from the new weapons, the Sioux quickly pulled their ponies out of range. "Then we left our horses in a gulch and charged on foot," a warrior named Fire Thunder said afterward, "but it was like green grass withering in a fire. So we picked up our wounded and went away. I do not know how many of our people were killed, but there were very many. It was bad." [12]

(The two engagements were called the Hayfield and Wagon Box fights by white men, who created a great many legends around them. One imaginative chronicler described the wagon boxes as being ringed by the bodies of dead Indians; another reported Indian casualties at 1,137, although fewer than a thousand were there.)

The Indians considered neither fight a defeat, and although some soldiers may have thought of the Hayfield and Wagon Box fights as victories, the United States government did not. Only a few weeks later, General Sherman himself was traveling westward with a new peace council. This time the military authorities were determined to end Red Cloud's war by any means short of surrender.

In late summer of 1867 Spotted Tail received a message from the new Indian commissioner, Nathaniel Taylor. The Brulés had been roaming peacefully below the Platte, and the commissioner asked Spotted Tail to inform as many Plains chiefs as possible that ammunition would be issued to all friendly Indians sometime during the Drying Grass Moon. The chiefs were to assemble at the end of the Union Pacific Railroad track, which was then in western Nebraska. The Great Warrior Sherman and six new peace commissioners would come there on the Iron

Horse to parley with the chiefs about ending Red Cloud's war.

Spotted Tail sent for Red Cloud, but the Oglala declined again, sending Man-Afraid to represent him. Pawnee Killer and Turkey Leg came in, and so did Big Mouth and the Laramie Loafers. Swift Bear, Standing Elk, and several other Brulé chiefs also responded to the invitation.

On September 19 a shiny railroad car arrived at Platte City station, and the Great Warrior Sherman, Commissioner Taylor, White Whiskers Harney, Black Whiskers Sanborn, John Henderson, Samuel Tappan, and General Alfred Terry alighted. These men were well known to the Indians, excepting the long-legged sad-eyed one who was called General Terry. Some of them would confront One Star Terry's power under quite different circumstance nine years late on the Little Bighorn.

Commissioner Taylor began the proceedings: "We are sent out here to inquire and find out what has been the trouble. We want to hear from your own lips your grievances and complaints. My friends, speak fully, speak freely, and speak the whole truth. . . . War is bad, peace is good. We must choose the good and not the bad. . . . I await what you have to say."

Spotted Tail replied: "The Great Father has made roads stretching east and west. Those roads are the cause of all our troubles. . . . The country where we live is overrun by whites. All our game is gone. This is the cause of great trouble. I have been a friend of the whites, and am now. . . . If you stop your roads we can get our game. That Powder River country belongs to the Sioux. . . . My friends, help us; take pity on us."

All through that first day's meeting, the other chiefs echoed Spotted Tail's words. Although few of these Indians considered the Powder River country as their home (they preferred the plains of Nebraska and Kansas), all supported Red Cloud's determination to keep that last great hunting ground inviolate. "These roads scared all our game away," said one. "I want you to stop the Powder River road." "Let our game alone," said another. "Don't disturb it, and then you will have life." "Who is our Great Father?" Pawnee Killer asked with genuine wonderment. "What is he? Is it true that he sent you here to settle our troubles? The cause of our troubles is the Powder River road. . . . If the Great Father stops the Powder River road, I know that your people can travel on this iron road without being molested."

On the following day the Great Warrior Sherman addressed the chiefs, blandly assuring them that he had thought of their words all night and was ready to give a reply. "The Powder River road was built to furnish our men with provisions," he said. "The Great Father thought that you consented to give permission for that road at Laramie last spring, but it seems that some of the Indians were not there, and have gone to war." Subdued laughter from the chiefs may have surprised Sherman, but he went on, his voice taking a harsher tone: "While the Indians continue to make war upon the road it will not be given up. But if, on examination, at Laramie in November, we find that the road hurts you, we will give it up or pay for it. If you have any claims, present them to us at Laramie."

Sherman launched into a discussion of the Indians' need for land of their own, advised them to give up their dependence upon wild game, and then he dropped a thunderbolt: "We therefore propose to let the whole Sioux nation select their country up the Missouri River, embracing the White Earth and Cheyenne rivers, to have their lands like the white people, forever, and we propose to keep all white men away except such agents and traders as you may choose."

As these words were translated, the Indians expressed surprise, murmuring among themselves. So this was what the new commissioners wanted them to do! Pack up and move far away to the Missouri River? For years the Teton Sioux had been following wild game westward from there; why should they go back to the Missouri to starve? Why could they not live in peace where game could still be found? Had the greedy eyes of the white men already chosen these bountiful lands for their own?

During the remainder of the discussions the Indians were uneasy. Swift Bear and Pawnee Killer made friendly speeches in which they asked for powder and lead, but the meeting ended with an uproar when the Great Warrior Sherman proposed that only the Brulés should receive ammunition. When Commissioner Taylor and White Whiskers Harney pointed out that all the chiefs had been invited to the council with the promise of an issue of hunting ammunition, the Great Warrior withdrew his opposition, and small amounts of powder and lead were given to the Indians.[13]

Man-Afraid wasted no time in returning to Red Cloud's camp on the Powder. If Red Cloud had had any intention of meeting the new peace commissioners at Laramie during the Moon of Falling Leaves, he changed his mind after hearing Man-Afraid's account of the Great Warrior Sherman's high-handed attitude and his remarks about removing the Sioux nation to the Missouri River.

On November 9, when the commissioners arrived at Fort Laramie, they found only a few Crow chiefs waiting to meet with them. The Crows were friendly, but one of them—Bear Tooth—made a surprising speech in which he condemned all white men for their reckless destruction of wildlife and the natural environment: "Fathers, fathers, fathers, hear me well. Call back your young men from the mountains of the bighorn sheep. They have run over our country; they have destroyed the growing wood and the green grass; they have set fire to our lands. Fathers, your young men have devastated the country and killed my animals, the elk, the deer, the antelope, my buffalo. They do not kill them to eat them; they leave them to rot where they fall. *Fathers, if I went into your country to kill your animals, what would you say? Should I not be wrong, and would you not make war on me?*" [14]

A few days after the commissioners' meeting with the Crows, messengers arrived from Red Cloud. He would come to Laramie to talk peace, he informed the commissioners, as soon as the soldiers were withdrawn from the forts on the Powder River road. The war, he repeated, was being fought for one purpose—to save the valley of the Powder, the only hunting ground left his nation, from intrusion by white men. "The Great Father sent his soldiers out here to spill blood. I did not first commence the spilling of blood. . . . If the Great Father kept white men out of my country, peace would last forever, but if they disturb me, there will be no peace. . . . The Great Spirit raised me in this land, and has raised you in another land. What I have said I mean. I mean to keep this land." [15]

For the third time in two years, a peace commission had failed. Before the commissioners returned to Washington, however, they sent Red Cloud a shipment of tobacco with another plea to come to Laramie as soon as the winter snows melted in the spring. Red Cloud politely replied that he had received the tobacco of peace and would smoke it, and that he would come to Laramie as soon as the soldiers left his country.

In the spring of 1868 the Great Warrior Sherman and the same peace commission returned to Fort Laramie. This time they had firm orders from an impatient government to abandon the forts on the Powder River road and obtain a peace treaty with Red Cloud. This time they sent a special agent from the Indian Bureau to personally invite the Oglala leader to a peace signing. Red Cloud told the agent he would need about ten days to consult with his allies, and would probably come to Laramie during May, the Moon When the Ponies Shed.

Only a few days after the agent returned to Laramie, however, a message arrived from Red Cloud: "We are on the mountains looking down on the soldiers and the forts. When we see the soldiers moving away and the forts abandoned, then I will come down and talk." [16]

This was all very humiliating and embarrassing to the Great Warrior Sherman and the commissioners. They managed to obtain the signatures of a few minor chiefs who came in for presents, but as the days passed, the frustrated commissioners quietly departed one by one for the East. By late spring only Black Whiskers Sanborn and White Whiskers Harney were left to negotiate, but Red Cloud and his allies remained on the Powder through the summer, keeping a close watch on the forts and the road to Montana.

At last the reluctant War Department issued orders for abandonment of the Powder River country. On July 29 the troops at Fort C. F. Smith packed their gear and started marching southward. Early the next morning Red Cloud led a band of celebrating warriors into the post, and they set fire to every building. A month later Fort Phil Kearny was abandoned, and the honor of burning was given to the Cheyennes under Little Wolf. A few days after that, the last soldier departed from Fort Reno, and the Powder River road was officially closed.

After two years of resistance, Red Cloud had won his war. For a few more weeks he kept the treaty makers waiting, and then on November 6, surrounded by a coterie of triumphant warriors, he came riding into Fort Laramie. Now a conquering hero, he would sign the treaty: "From this day forward all war between the parties to this agreement shall forever cease. The government of the United States desires peace, and its honor is hereby pledged to keep it. The Indians desire peace, and they now pledge their honor to maintain it."

For the next twenty years, however, the contents of the other sixteen articles of that treaty of 1868 would remain a matter of dispute between the Indians and the government of the United States. What many of the chiefs understood was in the treaty and what was actually written therein after Congress ratified it were like two horses whose colorations did not match.

(Spotted Tail, nine years later: "These promises have not been kept. . . . All the words have proved to be false. . . . There was a treaty made by General Sherman, General Sanborn, and General Harney. At that time the general told us we should have annuities and goods from that treaty for thirty-five years. He said this but yet he didn't tell the truth." [17])

SUN DANCE CHANT

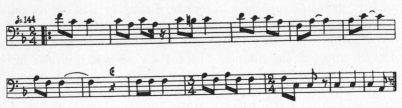

Courtesy of the Bureau of American Ethnology Collection

Look at that young man.
He is feeling good
Because his sweetheart
Is watching him.

SEVEN

"The Only Good Indian
Is a Dead Indian"

1868—February 24, U.S. House of Representatives resolves to impeach President Johnson. March 5, Senate convenes as Court of Impeachment; President Johnson is summoned to appear. May 22, the world's first robbery of a railroad train occurs in Indiana. May 26, Senate fails to convict President Johnson. July 28, Fourteenth Amendment (equal rights to all except Indians) becomes a part of U.S. Constitution. July 25, Congress organizes Wyoming Territory out of parts of Dakota, Utah, and Idaho. October 11, Thomas Edison patents his first invention, an electrical vote recorder. November 3, Ulysses Grant elected President. December 1, John D. Rockefeller begins relentless war on competitors in oil business.

We never did the white man any harm; we don't intend to. . . . We are willing to be friends with the white man. . . . The buffalo are diminishing fast. The antelope, that were plenty a few years ago, they are now thin. When they shall all die we shall be hungry; we shall want something to eat, and we will be compelled to come into the fort. Your young men must not fire at us; whenever they see us they fire, and we fire on them.
  —Tonkahaska (Tall Bull) to General Winfield Scott Hancock

Are not women and children more timid than men? The Cheyenne warriors are not afraid, but have you never heard of Sand Creek? Your soldiers look just like those who butchered the women and children there.
  —Woquini (Roman Nose) to General Winfield Scott Hancock

We were once friends with the whites, but you nudged us out of the way by your intrigues, and now when we are in council you keep nudging each other. Why don't you talk, and go straight, and let all be well?
  —Motavato (Black Kettle) to the Indians at Medicine Creek Lodge

I N the spring of 1866, as Red Cloud was preparing to fight for the Powder River country, a considerable number of homesick Southern Cheyennes who had been with him decided to go south for the summer. They wanted to hunt buffalo again along their beloved Smoky Hill and hoped to see some of their old friends and relatives who had gone with Black Kettle below the Arkansas. Among them were Tall Bull, White Horse, Gray Beard, Bull Bear, and other Dog Soldier chiefs. The great war leader Roman Nose also went along, and so did the two half-breed Bent brothers.

In the valley of the Smoky Hill they found several bands of young Cheyennes and Arapahos who had slipped away from the camps of Black Kettle and Little Raven below the Arkansas. They had come into Kansas to hunt, against the wishes of their chiefs, who by signing the treaty of 1865 had given up tribal rights to their old hunting grounds. Roman Nose and the Dog Soldier chiefs scoffed at the treaty; none of them had signed it, and none accepted it. Fresh from the freedom and independence of the Powder River country, they had no use for chiefs who signed away tribal lands.

Not many of the returned exiles went on south to visit Black Kettle's people. Among the few who did was George Bent. He especially wanted to see Black Kettle's niece, Magpie, and not long after their reunion he made her his wife. On rejoining Black Kettle, Bent discovered that the Southern Cheyennes' old friend, Edward Wynkoop, was now the agent for the tribe. "These were happy days for us," George Bent said afterward. "Black Kettle was a fine man and highly respected by all who knew him." [1]

When agent Wynkoop learned that the Dog Soldiers were hunting again along the Smoky Hill, he went to see the chiefs and tried to persuade them to sign the treaty and join Black Kettle. They refused flatly, saying that they would never leave their country again. Wynkoop warned them that soldiers would probably attack them if they stayed in Kansas, but they replied that they would "live or die there." The only promise they would give the agent was that they would hold their young men in check.

By late summer the Dog Soldiers were hearing rumors of Red Cloud's successes against the soldiers in the Powder River country. If the Sioux and Northern Cheyennes could fight a war to hold their country, then why should not the Southern Cheyennes and Arapahos fight to hold their country between the Smoky Hill and the Republican?

With Roman Nose as a unifying leader, many bands came together, and the chiefs made plans to stop travel along the Smoky Hill road. While the Cheyennes had been up north, a new stagecoach line had been opened right through the heart of their best buffalo range. Chains of stations were springing up all along the Smoky Hill route, and the Indians agreed that these stations must be rubbed out if they hoped to stop the coaches and wagon trains.

It was during this time that George and Charlie Bent came to a parting in their lives. George made up his mind to follow Black Kettle, but Charlie was an ardent disciple of Roman Nose. In October, during a meeting with their white father at Fort Zarah, Charlie flew into a rage and accused his brother and father of betraying the Cheyennes. After threatening to kill both of them, he had to be forcibly disarmed. (Charlie rejoined the Dog Soldiers and led several raids against the stage stations; in 1868 he was wounded, then contracted malaria, and died in one of the Cheyenne camps.)

Late in the autumn of 1866 Roman Nose and a party of warriors visited Fort Wallace and notified the Overland Stage Company's agent that if he did not stop running coaches through their country within fifteen days, the Indians would begin attacking them. A series of early snowstorms, however, halted travel before Roman Nose could begin his attacks; the Dog Soldiers had to content themselves with a few raids against livestock corrals at the stations. Faced with a long winter, the Dog Soldiers decided to make a permanent camp in the Big Timbers on the Republican, and there they awaited the spring of 1867.

To earn some money that winter, George Bent spent several weeks with the Kiowas trading for buffalo robes. When he returned to Black Kettle's village in the spring, he found everyone excited about rumors of a large force of Bluecoats marching westward across the Kansas plains toward Fort Larned. Black Kettle called a council and told his people that soldiers could mean nothing but trouble; then he ordered them to pack up and move south toward the Canadian River. This was why messengers sent out by agent Wynkoop did not find Black Kettle until after the trouble—which the chief so accurately predicted—had already started.

Wynkoop's runners did find most of the Dog Soldier leaders, and fourteen of them agreed to come to Fort Larned and hear what General Winfield Scott Hancock had to say to them. Tall Bull, White Horse, Gray Beard, and Bull Bear brought about five hundred lodges down to Pawnee Creek, made a big camp there about thirty-five miles from Fort Larned, and then after a few days' delay caused by a snowstorm, rode on into the fort.

Several of them wore the big blue Army coats they had captured up north, and they could see that General Hancock did not like this. He was wearing the same kind of coat with shoulder ornaments and shiny medals on it. He received them in a haughty, blustery manner, letting them see the power of his 1,400 soldiers, including the new Seventh Cavalry commanded by Hard Backsides Custer. After General Hancock had his artillerymen fire off some cannons for their benefit, they decided to name him Old Man of the Thunder.

Although their friend Tall Chief Wynkoop was there, they were suspicious from the very beginning of Old Man of the Thunder. Instead of waiting until the next day to talk, he summoned them to a night council. They considered this a bad sign, to hold council at night.

"I don't find many chiefs here," Hancock complained. "What is the reason? I have a great deal to say to the Indians, but I want to talk to them all together. . . . Tomorrow I am going to your camp." The Cheyennes did not like to hear this. Their women and children were back in the camp, many of them survivors of the horrors of Sand Creek three years before. Would Hancock bring his 1,400 soldiers and his thundering guns down upon them again? The chiefs sat in silence, with the light of the campfire playing upon their grave faces, waiting for Hancock to continue. "I have heard that a great many Indians want to fight. Very well, we are here, and are come prepared for war. If you are for peace, you know the conditions. If you are for war, look out for the consequences." He told them then about the railroad. They had heard rumors of it, the iron track coming out past Fort Riley, heading straight for the Smoky Hill country.

"The white man is coming out here so fast that nothing can stop him," Hancock boasted. "Coming from the East, and coming from the West, like a prairie on fire in a high wind. Nothing can stop him. The reason for it is, that the whites are a numerous people, and they are spreading out. They require room and cannot help it. Those on one sea in the West wish to communicate with those living on another sea in the East, and that is the reason they are building these roads, these wagon roads and railroads, and telegraphs. . . . You must not let your young men stop them; you must keep your men off the roads. . . . I have no more to say. I will await the end of your council, to see whether you want war or peace." [2]

Hancock sat down, his face expectant as the interpreter completed his last remark, but the Cheyennes remained silent, staring across the campfire at the general and his officers. At last Tall Bull lighted a pipe, exhaled smoke, and passed it around the circle. He arose, folded his red-and-black blanket to free his right arm, and offered his hand to the Old Man of the Thunder.

"You sent for us," Tall Bull said. "We came here. . . . We never did the white man any harm; we don't intend to. Our agent, Colonel Wynkoop, told us to meet you here. Whenever you want to go to the Smoky Hill you can go; you can go on any road. When we come on the road, your young men must not shoot us. We are willing to be friends with the white man. . . . You say you are going to our village tomorrow. If you go, I shall have no more to say to you there than here. I have said all I want to say." [3]

The Old Man of the Thunder arose and put on his haughty manner again. "Why is Roman Nose not here?" he asked. The chiefs tried to tell him that although Roman Nose was a mighty warrior he was not a chief, and only the chiefs had been invited to council.

"If Roman Nose will not come to me I will go to see him," Hancock declared. "I will march my troops to your village tomorrow."

As soon as the meeting broke up, Tall Bull went to Wynkoop and begged him to stop the Old Man of the Thunder from marching his soldiers to the Cheyenne camp. Tall Bull was afraid that if the Bluecoats came near the camp, there would be trouble between them and the hot-headed young Dog Soldiers.

Wynkoop agreed. "Previous to General Hancock's departure," Wynkoop said afterward, "I expressed to him my fears of the result of his marching his troops immediately on to the Indian village; but, notwithstanding, he persisted in doing so." Hancock's column consisted of cavalry, infantry, and artillery, "and had as formidable an aspect and presented as warlike an appearance as any that ever marched to meet an enemy on a battlefield."

On this march toward the Pawnee Fork, some of the chiefs went ahead to warn the Cheyenne warriors that soldiers were coming. Others rode with Wynkoop, who later said they exhibited in various ways "their fear of the result of the expedition—not fearful of their own lives or liberty . . . but fearful of the panic which they expected to be created among their women and children upon the arrival of the troops." [4]

Meanwhile, the Cheyenne camp had learned that the column of soldiers was coming. Messengers reported that the Old Man of the Thunder was angry because Roman Nose had not come to see him at Fort Larned. Roman Nose was flattered, but neither he nor Pawnee Killer (whose Sioux were camped nearby) had any intention of allowing the Old Man of the Thunder to bring his soldiers near their unprotected villages. Gathering about three hundred warriors, Roman Nose and Pawnee Killer led them out to scout the approaching column. All around their villages they set fire to the prairie grass so the soldiers would not find it easy to camp nearby.

During the day Pawnee Killer went ahead to meet the column and parley with Hancock. He told the general that if the soldiers would not camp too near the villages, he and Roman Nose would meet him in council the next morning. About sundown the soldiers halted to camp; they were still several miles from the lodges on Pawnee Fork. This was on the thirteenth day of April, the Moon of the Red Grass Appearing.

That night Pawnee Killer and several of the Cheyenne chiefs left the soldier camp and went on to their villages to hold council and decide what they should do. There was so much disagreement among the chiefs, however, that nothing was done. Roman Nose wanted to dismantle the tepees and start moving northward, scattering so the soldiers could not catch them, but the chiefs who had seen the power of Hancock's soldiers did not want to provoke them to a merciless pursuit.

Next morning the chiefs tried to persuade Roman Nose to go with them to counsel with Hancock, but the warrior leader suspected a trap. After all, had not the Old Man of the Thunder singled him out, had he not marched an army of soldiers across the plains in search of Roman Nose? As the morning grew late, Bull Bear decided he had better ride to the soldier camp. He

found Hancock in an arrogant mood, demanding to know where
Roman Nose was. Bull Bear tried to be diplomatic; he said
Roman Nose and the other chiefs had been delayed by a buffalo
hunt. This only angered Hancock. He told Bull Bear he was
going to march his troops up to the village and camp there until
he saw Roman Nose. Bull Bear made no reply; he mounted
casually, rode away at a slow pace for a few minutes, and then
galloped back to the village as fast as his horse would run.

The news that the soldiers were coming stirred the Indian
camp into immediate action. "I will ride out alone and kill this
Hancock!" Roman Nose shouted. There was no time to dismantle the lodges or pack anything. They put the women and children on ponies and sent them racing northward. Then all the
warriors armed themselves with bows, lances, guns, knives, and
clubs. The chiefs named Roman Nose their war leader, but they
assigned Bull Bear to ride beside him to make sure that in his
anger he did nothing foolish.

Roman Nose put on his officer's blouse with gold epaulets as
shiny as Hancock's. He thrust a carbine into his dragoon scab-
bard and two pistols into his belt, and because he had little
ammunition he added his bow and quiver. At the last moment he
took along a truce flag. He formed his force of three hundred
fighters into a line front extending a mile across the plain. With
pennanted lances up, bows strung, rifles and pistols at the ready,
he led them out slowly to meet the 1,400 soldiers and their big
thundering guns.

"This officer they call Hancock," Roman Nose said to Bull
Bear, "is spoiling for a fight. I will kill him in front of his own
men and give them something to fight about." [5]

Bull Bear replied cautiously, pointing out that the soldiers
outnumbered them almost five to one; they were armed with
fast-shooting rifles and big guns; the soldiers' ponies were sleek
and fat from grain, while the ponies their women and children
were fleeing on were weak after a winter without grass. If there
was a fight, the soldiers could catch them and kill all of them.

In a few minutes they saw the column coming, and they knew
the soldiers had sighted them, because the troops formed into a
line front. Hard Backsides Custer deployed his cavalry for fighting and they came into line at a gallop with sabers drawn.

12. *Roman Nose, of the Southern Cheyennes. Either photographed or copied by A. Zeno Shindler in Washington, D.C., 1868. Courtesy of the Smithsonian Institution.*

Roman Nose calmly signaled the warriors to halt. He raised his truce flag. At this the soldiers slowed their pace; they moved up to about a hundred and fifty yards of the Indians and also halted. A high wind made the flags and pennants snap along both lines. After a minute or so the Indians saw Tall Chief Wynkoop riding forward alone. "They surrounded my horse," Wynkoop said afterward, "expressing their delight at seeing me there, saying that now they knew everything was all right, and they would not be harmed. . . . I conducted the principal men, and met General Hancock, with his officers and their staffs, nearly midway between the two lines." [6]

Roman Nose drew up near the officers; he sat on his horse facing the Old Man of the Thunder and looked him straight in the eyes.

"Do you want peace or war?" Hancock asked sharply.

"We do not want war," Roman Nose replied. "If we did, we would not come so close to your big guns."

"Why did you not come to the council at Fort Larned?" Hancock continued.

"My horses are poor," Roman Nose answered, "and every man that comes to me tells me a different tale about your intentions."

Tall Bull, Gray Beard, and Bull Bear had gathered close by. They were worried because Roman Nose was acting so calmly. Bull Bear spoke, asking the general not to bring his soldiers any nearer the Indian camp. "We have not been able to hold our women and children," he said. "They are frightened and have run away and they will not come back. They fear the soldiers."

"You must get them back," Hancock ordered harshly, "and I expect you to do so."

When Bull Bear turned away with a gesture of frustration, Roman Nose spoke softly to him, telling him to take the chiefs back to the Indian line. "I'm going to kill Hancock," he said. Bull Bear grabbed the bridle of Roman Nose's horse and led him aside, warning him that this would surely bring death to all the tribe.

The wind had increased, blowing sand and making conversation difficult. After ordering the chiefs to start out immediately to bring back their women and children, Hancock announced that the council was ended.[7]

Although the chiefs and warriors obediently rode away in the direction their women and children had taken, they did not bring them back. Nor did they return. Hancock waited, his anger rising, for a day or two. Then, after ordering Custer to take the cavalry in pursuit of the Indians, he moved the infantry into the abandoned camp. In a methodical manner the lodges and their contents were inventoried, and then everything was burned— 251 tepees, 962 buffalo robes, 436 saddles, hundreds of parfleches, lariats, mats, and articles for cooking, eating, and living. The soldiers destroyed everything these Indians owned except the ponies they were riding and the blankets and clothing on their backs.

The frustrated rage of the Dog Soldiers and their Sioux allies at the burning of their villages exploded across the plains. They raided stage stations, ripped out telegraph lines, attacked railroad workers' camps, and brought travel to a halt along the Smoky Hill road. The Overland Express issued an order to its agents: "If Indians come within shooting distance, shoot them. Show them no mercy for they will show you none. General Hancock will protect you and our property." [8] The war that Hancock had come to prevent, he had now foolishly precipitated. Custer galloped his Seventh Cavalry from fort to fort, but he found no Indians.

"General Hancock's expedition, I regret to say, has resulted in no good, but, on the contrary, has been productive of much evil," wrote Superintendent of Indian Affairs Thomas Murphy to Commissioner Taylor in Washington.

"The operations of General Hancock," Black Whiskers Sanborn informed the Secretary of the Interior, "have been so disastrous to the public interests, and at the same time seem to me to be so inhuman, that I deem it proper to communicate my views to you on the subject. . . . For a mighty nation like us to be carrying on a war with a few straggling nomads, under such circumstances, is a spectacle most humiliating, an injustice unparalleled, a national crime most revolting, that must, sooner or later, bring down upon us or our posterity the judgment of Heaven."

The Great Warrior Sherman took a different view in his report to Secretary of War Stanton: "My opinion is, if fifty Indians are allowed to remain between the Arkansas and the Platte we will have to guard every stage station, every train, and all railroad working parties. In other words, fifty hostile Indians will checkmate three thousand soldiers. Rather get them out as soon as possible, and it makes little difference whether they be coaxed out by Indian commissioners or killed." [9]

Sherman was persuaded by higher government authorities to try coaxing them out with a peace commission, and so in that summer of 1867 he formed the commission of Taylor, Henderson, Tappan, Sanborn, Harney, and Terry—the same group which tried to make peace with Red Cloud at Fort Laramie later in the autumn. (See preceding chapter.) Hancock was recalled from the plains, and his soldiers were scattered among forts along the trails.

The new peace plan for the southern plains included not only the Cheyennes and Arapahos but the Kiowas, Comanches, and Prairie Apaches. All five tribes would be established on one great reservation south of the Arkansas River, and the government would provide them with cattle herds and teach them how to grow crops.

Medicine Lodge Creek, sixty miles south of Fort Larned, was chosen as the site of a peace council, the meetings to be held early in October. To make certain that all important chiefs were there, the Bureau of Indian Affairs stockpiled presents at Fort Larned and sent out a number of carefully chosen messengers. George Bent, who was now employed as an interpreter by Tall Chief Wynkoop, was one of the emissaries. He had no difficulty in persuading Black Kettle to come. Little Raven of the Arapahos and Ten Bears of the Comanches were also willing to travel to Medicine Lodge Creek for a council. But when Bent went to the Dog Soldier camps, he found their leaders reluctant to listen to him. The Old Man of the Thunder had made them wary of meetings with soldier chiefs. Roman Nose said flatly that he would not go to Medicine Lodge Creek if the Great Warrior Sherman was going to be there.

Bent knew and the commissioners knew that Roman Nose was the key to any Cheyenne peace settlement. The warrior leader now commanded the allegiance of several hundred fighting men from all the Cheyenne societies. If Roman Nose did not sign the treaty, it would be meaningless so far as peace in

Kansas was concerned. Probably at Bent's suggestion, Edmond Guerrier was chosen to visit Roman Nose and convince him that he should come to Medicine Lodge Creek for at least a preliminary discussion. Guerrier, who had survived Sand Creek, was married to Bent's sister; Roman Nose was married to Guerrier's cousin. With such family ties, diplomacy was not difficult.

On September 27 Guerrier arrived at Medicine Lodge Creek with Roman Nose and Gray Beard. Roman Nose had insisted that Gray Beard come along as his spokesman; Gray Beard understood a few words of English and could not be so easily deceived by interpreters. Superintendent Thomas Murphy, who was handling arrangements preceding arrival of the commissioners, greeted the Cheyenne leaders warmly, told them the forthcoming council would be most important to them, and promised that the commissioners would guarantee them provisions and take them "by the hand and make a good road for peace."

"A dog will rush to eat provisions," Gray Beard said in reply. "The provisions you bring us make us sick. We can live on buffalo but the main articles that we need we do not see— powder, lead, and caps. When you bring us these we will believe you are sincere."

Murphy replied that the United States gave presents of ammunition only to friendly Indians and wanted to know why some of the Cheyennes were so unfriendly as to continue raiding. "Because Hancock burned our village," Roman Nose and Gray Beard both replied. "We are only revenging that one thing." [10]

Murphy assured them that the Great Father had not authorized the burning of the village; the Great Father had already removed Hancock from the plains for doing this bad thing. As for the Great Warrior Sherman, whose presence Roman Nose objected to, the Great Father had also recalled him to Washington. Roman Nose finally agreed to a compromise. He and his followers would camp sixty miles away on the Cimarron; they would watch the council from that distance, and if it pleased them they would come in and participate.

It was the Moon of the Changing Season, October 16, when

the council began in a beautiful grove of tall trees on Medicine Lodge Creek. The Arapahos, Comanches, Kiowas, and Prairie Apaches camped along the wooded bank beside the council grounds. Black Kettle chose the opposite side of the stream. In case of trouble he would at least have the creek between him and the two hundred cavalrymen who were guarding the commissioners. Roman Nose and the Dog Soldier chiefs kept runners in Black Kettle's camp to inform them of the peace talks. These runners were as watchful of Black Kettle as they were of the commissioners; they did not intend to permit Black Kettle to sign a bad treaty in the name of the Cheyenne people.

Although more than four thousand Indians were gathered at Medicine Lodge, so few Cheyennes were present that it began almost entirely as a Kiowa-Comanche-Arapaho affair. This worried the commissioners, whose main objective was to secure a peace with the hostile Dog Soldiers by convincing them that their best interests lay in the proposed reservation below the Arkansas. Black Kettle, Little Robe, and George Bent won over some of the reluctant chiefs, but others became so hostile they threatened to kill all of Black Kettle's horses unless he withdrew from the council.

On October 21, the Kiowas and Comanches signed the treaty, promising to share in a reservation with the Cheyennes and Arapahos, and among other things to confine their buffalo hunting to ranges below the Arkansas and to withdraw all opposition to construction of the railroad being built along the Smoky Hill route. Black Kettle, however, would not agree to sign until more Cheyenne chiefs came to Medicine Lodge; Little Raven and the Arapahos would not sign until the Cheyennes signed. The frustrated commissioners agreed to wait one more week while Black Kettle and Little Robe went to the Dog Soldier camp to carry on their persuasive diplomacy. Five days passed, but no Cheyennes appeared. Then, late in the afternoon of October 26, Little Robe returned from the Dog Soldier camp.

The Cheyenne chiefs were coming, Little Robe announced, with about five hundred warriors. They would be armed and would probably fire off their guns to express their desire for ammunition needed in the autumn buffalo hunts. They would harm no one, and if they received gifts of ammunition they would sign the treaty.

At noon the next day under a warm autumn sun, the Cheyennes came in at a gallop. As they crested a ridge south of the council grounds they formed four abreast like Hard Backsides' cavalrymen. Several were dressed in captured Army blouses; others wore red blankets. Their lances and silver ornaments glittered in the sunlight. As the column came opposite the council grounds, the warriors wheeled into a platoon front, facing the commissioners across the creek. One of the Cheyennes sounded a bugle call, and the ponies leaped forward in a charge, five hundred voices shouting "Hiya hi-i-i-ya!" They brandished their lances, lifted their strung bows, fired a few rifles and pistols into the air, and plunged into the creek with a spray of water. The front ranks whipped their ponies up the bank to within a few feet of White Whiskers Harney, who stood motionless to receive them. The other commissioners were scurrying for cover. Reining their mounts to quick halts, the chiefs and warriors slid off, surrounded the startled commissioners, and began laughing and shaking hands. They had satisfactorily demonstrated the dash and bravery of the fighting Cheyennes.

After preliminary ceremonies were out of the way, the speeches began. Tall Bull, White Horse, Bull Bear, and Buffalo Chief all spoke. They did not want war, they said, but would accept it if they could not get an honorable peace.

Buffalo Chief made one final plea for use of the hunting grounds along the Smoky Hill. The Cheyennes would leave the railroad alone, he promised, and then added in a voice of reason: "Let us own the country together—the Cheyennes should still hunt there." But the white men of the council did not believe in sharing any of the country north of the Arkansas. Next morning, after coffee was served, the Cheyenne and Arapaho chiefs listened to a reading of the treaty, with George Bent interpreting. At first Bull Bear and White Horse refused to sign, but Bent took them aside and convinced them it was the only way to keep their power and live with the tribe. After the signing, the commissioners issued presents, including ammunition for hunting. The Medicine Lodge council was ended. Now most of the Cheyennes and Arapahos would move south as they had promised. But there were others who would not go. Three or four hundred were already heading north from the Cimarron, their fortunes cast with a warrior who would not surrender. The name of Roman Nose was not signed to the treaty.[11]

During the winter of 1867–68, most of the Cheyennes and Arapahos were camped below the Arkansas near Fort Larned. From their autumn hunts they had enough meat to survive the cold moons, but by springtime the food shortage grew serious. Tall Chief Wynkoop came out from the fort occasionally to distribute what scanty supplies he was able to obtain from the Indian Bureau. He told the chiefs that the Great Council in Washington was still arguing over the treaty and had not provided money to buy food and clothing for them as promised. The chiefs replied that if they had arms and ammunition they could go down on Red River and kill enough buffalo to supply their people. But Wynkoop had no arms or ammunition to give them.

As the warm spring days lengthened, the young men grew increasingly restless, grumbling because there was not enough to eat, cursing the broken promises of the white men at Medicine Lodge. In small bands they began drifting northward toward their old Smoky Hill hunting grounds. Tall Bull, White Horse, and Bull Bear gave in to demands of their proud Dog Soldiers, and also crossed the Arkansas. Along the way, some of the wild young men raided isolated settlements in hopes of finding food and guns.

Agent Wynkoop hastened to Black Kettle's village, begging the chiefs to be patient and keep their young men off the warpath, even though the Great Father had broken faith with them.

"Our white brothers are pulling away from us the hand they gave us at Medicine Lodge," Black Kettle said, "but we will try to hold on to it. We hope the Great Father will take pity on us and let us have the guns and ammunition he promised us so we can go hunt buffalo to keep our families from going hungry." [12]

Wynkoop was hopeful that arms and ammunition could be obtained now that the Great Father had sent out a new Star Chief, General Philip Sheridan, to command the soldiers in the

Kansas forts. The agent arranged for several leaders, including
Black Kettle and Stone Calf, to meet with Sheridan at Fort
Larned.

When the Indians saw Sheridan, with his short legs and thick
neck and long swinging arms, they thought he looked like a
bad-tempered bear. During the council Wynkoop asked the
general if he could issue arms to the Indians. "Yes, give them
arms," Sheridan growled, "and if they go to war my soldiers
will kill them like men."

Stone Calf retorted: "Let your soldiers grow long hair, so that
we can have some honor in killing *them*."

It was not a friendly council, and although Wynkoop was able
to obtain a few obsolete rifles for them, the Cheyennes and
Arapahos who remained to hunt below the Arkansas were very
uneasy. Too many of their young men and most of the Dog Soldier bands were still north of the river, some of them raiding
and killing white men wherever they could find them.

By late August most of the Cheyennes in the north were
gathered along the Arikaree fork of the Republican River. Tall
Bull, White Horse, and Roman Nose were there with about
three hundred warriors and their families. A few Arapahos and
Pawnee Killer's Sioux were camped nearby. From Bull Bear,
who was camped with his band on the Solomon, they heard that
General Sheridan had organized a company of scouts to hunt
down Indian camps, but these Indians were too busy gathering
meat for winter to worry about scouts or soldiers finding them.

And then one day in the Moon When the Deer Paw the Earth,
September 16, a hunting party of Sioux from Pawnee Killer's
camp saw about fifty white men going into camp on the Arikaree,
about twenty miles below the Indian camps. Only three or four
of the white men wore blue uniforms; the others were dressed
in rough frontier clothing. This was the special company organized by Sheridan to search out Indian camps; they were known
as Forsyth's Scouts.

As soon as the Sioux hunters alerted their people, Pawnee
Killer sent runners to the Cheyenne camp to ask them to join
in an attack on the white scouts who had invaded their hunting grounds. Tall Bull and White Horse immediately sent criers
through their camps, urging the warriors to make ready their

war rigs and put on their battle paint. They went to see Roman Nose, who was in his tepee undergoing purification ceremonies. A few days before, when the Cheyennes had gone to feast with the Sioux, one of the Sioux women had used an iron fork to cook fried bread, and Roman Nose did not discover this until after he had eaten the bread. Any metal touching his food was against his medicine; Roman Nose's magic power to escape the white men's bullets was worthless until he had completed the purification ceremonies.

The Cheyenne chiefs accepted this belief as a matter of course, but Tall Bull told Roman Nose to hurry up the ceremonies to restore his medicine. Tall Bull was sure the Cheyennes and Sioux together could destroy fifty white scouts, but there might be companies of Bluecoats nearby, and if so, the Indians would soon need Roman Nose to lead them in the charges. Roman Nose told them to go ahead. When he was ready he would come.

Because of the long distance to the soldier scouts' camp, the chiefs decided to wait until next daylight to attack. Riding their best war ponies and armed with their best lances, bows, and rifles, five or six hundred warriors moved down the Arikaree Valley. The Sioux wore their eagle-feather bonnets; the Cheyennes wore their crow-feather bonnets. Not far from the scouts' camp they halted, the chiefs issuing strict orders that no small parties were to go out alone to attack the enemy. All would attack together, as Roman Nose had taught them; they would ride over the scouts and rub them out.

In spite of the warnings, six Sioux and two Cheyennes—all very young men—slipped out before sunrise and tried to capture the white men's horse herd. They charged in just at dawn, yelling and waving blankets to stampede the stock. A few animals were captured, but the young braves had alerted Forsyth's Scouts to the presence of Indians. Before the main body of Sioux and Cheyennes could charge the exposed camp, the scouts had time to move to a small island in the dry bed of the Arikaree and there take cover among the willow brush and high grass.

Across the misted valley, the Indians charged in a broad front, their ponies' hooves drumming on the earth. When they were close enough to see the scouts hurrying to the brushy island, one of the Cheyenne warriors sounded a blast on a bugle. They

had intended to overrun the camp. Now they had to swerve into
the dry stream bed. A burst of fire from the scouts' Spencer repeating rifles raked the first ranks, and the charging warriors divided, some to the left and some to the right, thus sweeping
around the island.

For most of the morning the Indians circled the island. The
only targets were the scouts' horses standing in the high grass,
and as the warriors shot the animals down, the scouts used them
for breastworks. A few warriors made individual charges upon
the island, dismounting and trying to creep up on the scouts
through the brush. But the quick rifle fire was too strong for
them. A Cheyenne named Wolf Belly made two mounted charges
right through the defense ring of scouts. He was wearing his
magic panther skin, and it gave him such strong medicine that
not a single bullet touched him.

Early in the afternoon Roman Nose arrived on the field and
took a position on high ground overlooking the island. Most
of the warriors stopped fighting and waited to see what Roman
Nose would do. Tall Bull and White Horse went to talk with
him, but did not ask him to lead them in battle. Then an old
man, White Contrary, came by and said: "Here is Roman Nose,
the man we depend upon, sitting behind this hill."

Roman Nose laughed. He had already made up his mind what
he was going to do that day, and he knew he was going to die,
but he laughed at what the old man said.

"All those people fighting out there feel that they belong to
you," White Contrary went on, "and they will do all that you
tell them, and here you are behind this hill." [13]

Roman Nose went off to one side and prepared himself for
battle, painting his forehead yellow, his nose red, his chin black.
Then he put on his single-horned war bonnet with the forty
feathers in its tail. When he was ready, he mounted and rode
down to the dry riverbed, where the warriors were waiting in
formation for him to lead them in a victorious charge.

They started out in a slow trot, increased speed to a gallop,
and then lashed their ponies without mercy so that nothing
could stop them from riding over the island. But once again
the fire power of Forsyth's Scouts cut down the front ranks, re-
ducing the force of the desperate charge. Roman Nose reached

the outer fringes of willows; then crossfire caught him above
the hips, a bullet penetrating his spine. He fell into the brush,
lying there until dusk, when he managed to crawl to the bank.
Some young warriors were there searching for him. They carried him up to the high ground, where Cheyenne and Sioux
women had come to take care of the wounded. During the night
Roman Nose died.

For the young Cheyenne warriors, the death of Roman Nose
was like a great light going out in the sky. He had believed and
made them believe that if they would fight for their country as
Red Cloud was doing, they would someday win.

Neither the Cheyennes nor the Sioux had any taste for more
fighting, but they kept Forsyth's Scouts besieged there in the
brush and sand for eight days. The scouts had to eat their dead
horses and dig in the sand for water. On the eighth day, when
a relief column of soldiers came, the Indians were ready to leave
the stench of the island.

The white men made much of this fight; they called it the
Battle of Beecher's Island, after young Lieutenant Frederick
Beecher, who was killed there. The survivors boasted they had
killed "hundreds of redskins," and although the Indians could
count no more than thirty, the loss of Roman Nose was incal-
culable. They would always remember it as the Fight When
Roman Nose Was Killed.

After they had rested from the siege, a considerable number
of Cheyennes started moving south. With soldiers hunting everywhere for them now, their only hope of survival lay with their
relatives below the Arkansas. They looked upon Black Kettle
as a beaten old man, but he was still alive, and he was chief
of the Southern Cheyennes.

They had no way of knowing, of course, that the soldier chief
who looked like an angry bear, Sheridan, was planning a winter
campaign below the Arkansas. When the snows of the cold
moons came, he would send Custer and his pony soldiers to
destroy the villages of the "savage" Indians, most of whom had
kept their treaty obligations. To Sheridan, any Indian who resisted when fired upon was a "savage."

During that autumn Black Kettle established a village on the

Washita River forty miles east of the Antelope Hills, and as the young men drifted back from Kansas he scolded them for their errant ways, but like a forgiving father accepted them back into his band. In November, when he heard rumors of soldiers coming, he and Little Robe and two Arapaho leaders made a journey of almost a hundred miles down the valley of the Washita to Fort Cobb, headquarters for their new agency south of the Arkansas. General William B. Hazen was commander of the fort, and on their summer visits the Cheyennes and Arapahos had found him to be friendly and sympathetic.

On this urgent occasion, however, Hazen was not cordial. When Black Kettle asked for permission to move his 180 lodges near Fort Cobb for protection, Hazen refused to grant it. He also refused permission for the Cheyennes and Arapahos to join the Kiowa and Comanche villages. He assured Black Kettle that if his delegation would return to their villages and keep their young men there, they would not be attacked. After issuing his visitors some sugar, coffee, and tobacco, Hazen sent them away, knowing that he would probably never see any of them again. He was fully aware of Sheridan's war plans.

Facing into a raw north wind that turned into a snowstorm, the disappointed chiefs made their way back to their villages, arriving on the night of November 26. Weary as he was from the long journey, Black Kettle immediately called a council of the tribe's leaders. (George Bent was not present; he had taken his wife, Black Kettle's niece, on a visit to William Bent's ranch in Colorado.)

This time, Black Kettle told his people, they must not be caught by surprise as they had at Sand Creek. Instead of waiting for the soldiers to come to them, he would take a delegation to meet the soldiers and convince them that the Cheyenne village was peaceful. Snow was deep and still falling, but as soon as the clouds left the sky they would start to meet the soldiers.

Although Black Kettle went to bed late that night, he awoke just before dawn as he always did. He stepped outside his lodge, and was glad to see that the skies were clearing. A heavy fog blanketed the valley of the Washita, but he could see deep snow on the ridges across the river.

Suddenly he heard a woman crying, her voice becoming clearer as she came closer. "Soldiers! soldiers!" she was shouting. Reacting automatically, Black Kettle rushed inside his lodge for his rifle. In the few seconds that passed before he was outside again he had made up his mind what he must do—arouse the camp and put everyone to flight. There must not be another Sand Creek. He would meet the soldiers alone at the Washita ford and parley with them. Pointing his rifle skyward, he pulled the trigger. The report brought the village wide awake. As he shouted commands to everyone to mount and ride away, his wife untied his pony and brought it to him.

He was preparing to hurry toward the ford when a bugle blared out of the fog, followed by shouted commands and wild yells of charging soldiers. Because of the snow there was no thunder of hoofbeats, but only a rattle of packs and a jingle of harness metal, a hoarse yelling, and bugles blowing everywhere. (Custer had brought his military band through the snow and had ordered them to play "Garry Owen" for the charge.)

Black Kettle expected the soldiers to come riding across the Washita ford, but instead they were dashing out of the fog from four directions. How could he meet four charging columns and talk to them of peace? It was Sand Creek all over again. He reached for his wife's hand, lifted her up behind him, and lashed the pony into quick motion. She had survived Sand Creek with him; now, like tortured dreamers dreaming the same nightmare over again, they were fleeing again from screaming bullets.

They were almost to the ford when he saw the charging cavalrymen in their heavy blue coats and fur caps. Black Kettle slowed his pony and lifted his hand in the sign gesture of peace. A bullet burned into his stomach, and his pony swerved. Another bullet caught him in the back, and he slid into the snow at the river's edge. Several bullets knocked his wife off beside him, and the pony ran way. The cavalrymen splashed on across the ford, riding right over Black Kettle and his wife, splattering mud upon their dead bodies.

Custer's orders from Sheridan were explicit: "to proceed south in the direction of the Antelope Hills, thence toward the Washita River, the supposed winter seat of the hostile tribes; to destroy their villages and ponies, to kill or hang all warriors, and bring back all women and children." [14]

In a matter of minutes Custer's troopers destroyed Black Kettle's village; in another few minutes of gory slaughter they destroyed by gunfire several hundred corralled ponies. To kill or hang all the warriors meant separating them from the old men, women, and children. This work was too slow and dangerous for the cavalrymen; they found it much more efficient and safe to kill indiscriminately. They killed 103 Cheyennes, but only eleven of them were warriors. They captured 53 women and children.

By this time, gunfire echoing down the valley brought a swarm of Arapahos from their nearby village, and they joined the Cheyennes in a rearguard action. A party of Arapahos surrounded a pursuit platoon of nineteen soldiers under Major Joel Elliott and killed every man. About noontime, Kiowas and Comanches were arriving from farther downriver. When Custer saw the increasing number of warriors on the nearby hills, he rounded up his captives and without searching for the missing Major Elliott started back north in a forced march toward his temporary base at Camp Supply on the Canadian River.

At Camp Supply, General Sheridan was eagerly awaiting news of a Custer victory. When he was informed that the cavalry regiment was returning, he ordered the entire post out for a formal review. With the band blaring triumphantly, the victors marched in, waving the scalps of Black Kettle and the other dead "savages," and Sheridan publicly congratulated Custer for "efficient and gallant services rendered."

In his official report of victory over the "savage butchers" and "savage bands of cruel marauders," General Sheridan rejoiced that he had "wiped out old Black Kettle . . . a worn-out and worthless old cypher." He then stated that he had promised Black Kettle sanctuary if he would come into a fort before military operations began. "He refused," Sheridan lied, "and was killed in the fight." [15]

Tall Chief Wynkoop, who had already resigned in a gesture of protest against Sheridan's policies, was far away in Philadelphia when he heard the news of Black Kettle's death. Wynkoop charged that his old friend had been betrayed, and "met his death at the hands of white men in whom he had too often fatally trusted and who triumphantly report the fact of his scalp in their possession." Other white men who had known and liked

Black Kettle also attacked Sheridan's war policy, but Sheridan brushed them aside as "good and pious ecclesiastics . . . aiders and abettors of savages who murdered, without mercy, men, women, and children." [16]

The Great Warrior Sherman gave Sheridan his support, however, and ordered him to continue killing hostile Indians and their ponies, but at the same time advised that he establish the friendly Indians in camps where they could be fed and exposed to the white man's civilized culture.

In response to this, Sheridan and Custer moved on to Fort Cobb, and from there sent out runners to the four tribes in the area, warning them to come in and make peace or else they would be hunted down and killed. Custer himself went out in search of friendly Indians. For this field operation he requisitioned one of the more attractive young women from his Cheyenne prisoners to go with him. She was listed as an interpreter, although she knew no English.

Late in December the survivors of Black Kettle's band began arriving at Fort Cobb. They had to come on foot, because Custer had killed all of their ponies. Little Robe was now the nominal leader of the tribe, and when he was taken to see Sheridan he told the bearlike soldier chief that his people were starving. Custer had burned their winter meat supply; they could find no buffalo along the Washita; they had eaten all their dogs.

Sheridan replied that the Cheyennes would be fed if they all came into Fort Cobb and surrendered unconditionally. "You cannot make peace now and commence killing whites again in the spring," Sheridan added. "If you are not willing to make a complete peace, you can go back and we will fight this thing out."

Little Robe knew there was but one answer he could give. "It is for you to say what we have to do," he said.[17]

Yellow Bear of the Arapahos also agreed to bring his people to Fort Cobb. A few days later, Tosawi brought in the first band of Comanches to surrender. When he was presented to Sheridan, Tosawi's eyes brightened. He spoke his own name and added two words of broken English. "Tosawi, good Indian," he said.

It was then that General Sheridan uttered the immortal words: "The only good Indians I ever saw were dead." [18] Lieutenant Charles Nordstrom, who was present, remembered the

13. *Tosawi, or Silver Knife, chief of the Comanches. Photographed by Alexander Gardner in Washington, D.C., 1872. Courtesy of the Smithsonian Institution.*

words and passed them on, until in time they were honed into
an American aphorism: *The only good Indian is a dead Indian.*

During that winter the Cheyennes and Arapahos and some
of the Comanches and Kiowas lived off the white man's handouts at Fort Cobb. In the spring of 1869 the United States
government decided to concentrate the Comanches and Kiowas
around Fort Sill, while the Cheyennes and Arapahos were assigned a reservation around Camp Supply. Some of the Dog
Soldier bands had remained far north in their camps on the
Republican; others under Tall Bull had come south for rations
and protection.

While the Cheyennes were moving up the Washita from Fort
Cobb to Camp Supply, Little Robe quarreled with Tall Bull,
accusing him and his young men of causing much of the trouble
with the soldiers. The Dog Soldier chief in turn accused Little
Robe of being weak like Black Kettle, of bowing before the white
men. Tall Bull declared that he would not settle down within the
confines of the poor reservation chosen for the Cheyennes below
the Arkansas. The Cheyennes had always been a free people, he
said. What right had the white men to tell them where they
should live? They should remain free or die.

Little Robe angrily ordered Tall Bull and his Dog Soldiers
to leave the Cheyenne reservation forever. If they failed to do
so, he would join with the whites and drive them out. Tall Bull
proudly replied that he would take his people north and join
the Northern Cheyennes, who with Red Cloud's Sioux had
driven the white men from the Powder River country.

And so, as they had done after Sand Creek, the Southern
Cheyennes divided again. Almost two hundred Dog Soldier
warriors and their families started north with Tall Bull. In
May, the Moon When the Ponies Shed, they joined the bands
who had stayed through the winter on the Republican. As they
were preparing for the long and dangerous march to the Powder
River country, Sheridan sent a cavalry force under General Eugene A. Carr to search them out and destroy them. Carr's soldiers found the Dog Soldier camp and attacked it as forcefully
as Custer had struck Black Kettle's village. This time, however,

a band of warriors sacrificed their lives in a delaying action and thus managed to keep their women and children from being captured.

By scattering in small groups, the Indians escaped Carr's pursuit parties. After a few days Tall Bull reassembled the warriors and led them on a revenge raid to the Smoky Hill. They ripped out two miles of track along the hated railroad, and attacked small settlements, killing as mercilessly as the soldiers had killed their people. Remembering that Custer had taken Cheyenne women as prisoners, Tall Bull took two surviving white women from a ranch house. Both were German immigrants (Maria Weichel and Susannah Allerdice), and none of the Cheyennes could understand any words they said. These white women were troublesome, but Tall Bull insisted that they be taken along as prisoners and treated as the Cheyenne women had been treated by the Bluecoats.

To avoid the pony soldiers who were searching everywhere now, Tall Bull and his people had to keep changing camps and moving about. They worked their way gradually westward across Nebraska into Colorado. It was July before Tall Bull could bring his band together at Summit Springs, where he hoped to cross the Platte. Because of high water in the river, they had to make a temporary camp. Tall Bull sent some of the young men to mark a crossing in the stream with sticks. This was in the Moon When the Cherries Are Ripe, and the day was very hot. Most of the Cheyennes were resting in the shade of their lodges.

By chance that day Major Frank North's Pawnee scouts found the trail of the fleeing Cheyennes. (These Pawnees were the same mercenaries who four years before had gone into the Powder River country with General Connor and had been chased out by Red Cloud's warriors.) With scarcely any warning, the Pawnees and General Carr's Bluecoats charged into Tall Bull's camp. They came in from east and west, so the only way of escape for the Cheyennes was to the south. Ponies were running in every direction; the men were trying to catch them, and the women and children were fleeing on foot.

Many could not get away. Tall Bull and about twenty others took cover in a ravine. Among them were his wife and child and the two German women captives. When the Pawnee mercenaries and the soldiers charged into the camp, a dozen warriors died defending the mouth of the ravine.

Tall Bull took his hatchet and cut holes in the side of the ravine so that he could climb up to the top and fire at the attackers. He fired once, then ducked down, and when he rose to fire again, a bullet smashed into his skull.

During the next few minutes the Pawnees and the soldiers overran the ravine. All the Cheyennes except Tall Bull's wife and child were dead. Both of the German women had been shot, but one was still alive. The white men said that Tall Bull had shot the white captives, but the Indians never believed that he would have wasted his bullets in such a foolish way.

Roman Nose was dead; Black Kettle was dead; Tall Bull was dead. Now they were all good Indians. Like the antelope and the buffalo, the ranks of the proud Cheyennes were thinning to extinction.

EIGHT

The Rise and Fall of Donehogawa

1869—March 4, Ulysses Grant inaugurated as President. May 10, Union Pacific and Central Pacific railroads join at Promontory Point, establishing first transcontinental rail line. September 13, Jay Gould and James Fisk attempt to corner gold market. September 24, government dumps gold on market to force down price; "Black Friday" brings financial disaster to small speculators. November 24, American Woman's Suffrage Association organized. December 10, Wyoming enacts law giving women right to vote and hold office. December 30, Knights of Labor organized in Philadelphia. Mark Twain's *Innocents Abroad* is published.

1870—January 10, John D. Rockefeller organizes Standard Oil Company to monopolize the industry. February 15, construction of Northern Pacific Railroad begins in Minnesota. June, population of United States reaches 38,558,371. July 18, in Rome, Vatican Council declares Papal Infallibility a doctrine of the Church. July 19, France declares war on Prussia. September 2, Napoleon III capitulates to Prussia. September 19, Siege of Paris begins. September 20, William M. Tweed, Tammany boss, accused of robbing New York City treasury. November 29, compulsory education introduced in England. Production of paper from pulpwood begins in New England.

Although this country was once wholly inhabited by Indians, the tribes, and many of them once powerful, who occupied the countries now constituting the states east of the Mississippi, have, one by one, been exterminated in their abortive attempts to stem the western march of civilization. . . . If any tribe remonstrated against the violation of their natural and treaty rights, members of the tribe were inhumanly shot down and the whole treated as mere dogs. . . . It is presumed that humanity dictated the original policy of the removal and concentration of the Indians in the West to save them from threatened extinction. But today, by reason of the immense augmentation of the American population, and the extension of their settlements throughout the entire West, covering both slopes of the Rocky Mountains, the Indian races are more seriously threatened with a speedy extermination than ever before in the history of the country.

—DONEHOGAWA (ELY PARKER), THE FIRST
INDIAN COMMISSIONER OF INDIAN AFFAIRS

WHEN the Cheyenne survivors of the Summit Springs fight at last reached the Powder River country, they found that many things had changed during the three winters they were in the south. Red Cloud had won his war, the forts had been abandoned, and no Bluecoats came north of the Platte. But the camps of the Sioux and Northern Cheyennes were filled with rumors that the Great Father in Washington wanted them to move far eastward to the Missouri River, where wild game was very scarce. Some of their white trader friends told them that it was written in the treaty of 1868 that the Teton Sioux agency was to be on the Missouri. Red Cloud scorned such talk. When he went down to Laramie to sign the treaty he had told the Bluecoat officers who witnessed his touching the pen that he wanted Fort Laramie to be the Teton Sioux trading post, or he would not sign. They had agreed to this.

In the spring of 1869 Red Cloud took a thousand Oglalas to Laramie to trade for goods and collect provisions promised in the treaty. The post commander told him the Sioux trading post was at Fort Randall on the Missouri River, and that they should go there to trade and draw supplies. As Fort Randall was three hundred miles away, Red Cloud laughed at the commander and demanded permission to trade at Laramie. With a thousand armed warriors threatening outside the open post, the commander acquiesced, but he advised Red Cloud to move his people closer to Fort Randall before another trading season arrived.

It was soon apparent that the military authorities at Fort Laramie meant what they said. Spotted Tail and his peaceful Brulés were not even permitted to camp near Laramie. When Spotted Tail was told that if he wanted supplies he would have to go to Fort Randall, he led his people across the plains and settled down near that fort. The easy life of the Laramie Loafers also came to an end; they were sent packing to Fort Randall, where in unfamiliar surroundings they had to build up a completely new enterprise.

Red Cloud remained adamant, however. He had won the Powder River country after a hard-fought war. Fort Laramie was the nearest trading post, and he had no intention of moving to the Missouri or traveling there for supplies.

During the autumn of 1869 Indians everywhere on the Plains were at peace, and rumors of great changes came and went through the camps. It was said that a new Great Father had been chosen in Washington, President Grant. It was also said that the new Great Father had chosen an Indian to be the Little Father of the Indians. This was not easy to believe. Always the Commissioner of Indian Affairs had been a white man who could read and write. Had the Great Spirit at last taught a red man to read and write so that he could be the Little Father of the Indians?

In the Moon When the Snow Drifts into the Tepees (January, 1870) an ugly rumor came from the country of the Blackfeet. Somewhere on the Marias River in Montana, soldiers had surrounded a camp of Piegan Blackfeet and slain them like rabbits trapped in a hole. These mountain Indians were old enemies of the Plains tribes, but everything was changing now, and when soldiers killed Indians anywhere it made all the tribes uneasy. The Army tried to keep the massacre secret, announcing only that Major Eugene M. Baker had led a cavalry command out of Fort Ellis, Montana, to punish a band of Blackfeet horse thieves. The Plains Indians knew the true story, however, long before it ever reached the Indian Bureau in Washington.

During the weeks following that rumored massacre, some strange things happened across the upper Plains. In several agencies, Indians demonstrated their anger by holding meetings in which they condemned the Bluecoats and called the Great Father "a fool and dog, without ears or brains." At two agencies, feelings ran so high that buildings were set on fire; agents were held as prisoners for a time, and some white government employees were chased off the reservations.[1]

Because of the secrecy surrounding the January 23 massacre, the Commissioner of Indian Affairs did not learn about it until three months later. A young Army officer, Lieutenant William B. Pease, acting as agent for the Blackfeet, jeopardized his career in submitting the facts to the commissioner. Using the pretext of the theft of a few mules from a wagon freighter, Major Baker had organized his winter expedition and attacked the first camp in his line of march. The camp was undefended, consisting mostly of old men, women, and children, several of whom were ill with smallpox. Of the 219 Piegans in the camp, only 46 escaped to tell the story; 33 men, 90 women, and 50 children were shot to death as they ran from their lodges.

As soon as he received the report, the commissioner demanded an immediate investigation by government authorities.

Although the commissioner's anglicized name was Ely Samuel Parker, his real name was Donehogawa, Keeper of the Western Door of the Long House of the Iroquois. As a youth on the Tonawanda reservation in New York, he was Hasanoanda of the Seneca Iroquois, but he had soon learned that the owner of an Indian name was not taken seriously in the world of white men. Hasanoanda changed his name to Parker because he was ambitious and expected to be taken seriously as a man.

For almost half a century Parker had been battling racial prejudice, sometimes winning, sometimes losing. Before he was ten years old he went to work as a stable boy on an Army post;

his pride was hurt when the officers teased him because of his poor command of the English language. The proud young Seneca immediately arranged to enter a missionary school. He was determined to learn to read and speak and write English so well that no white man would ever laugh at him again. After graduation he decided that he could best help his people by becoming a lawyer. In those days a young man became a lawyer by working in a law office and then taking a state bar examination. Ely Parker worked for three years with a firm in Ellicottville, New York, but when he applied for admission to the bar he was told that only *white* male citizens could be admitted to law practice in New York. No *Indians* need apply. Adoption of an English name had not changed the bronze color of his skin.

Parker refused to quit. After making careful inquiries as to which of the white man's professions or trades an Indian could be admitted to, he entered Rensselaer Polytechnic Institute and mastered all the courses in civil engineering. He soon found employment on the Erie Canal. Before he was thirty years old, the United States government sought him out to supervise construction of levees and buildings. In 1860 his duties took him to Galena, Illinois, and there he met and made friends with a clerk in a harness store. The clerk was a former Army captain named Ulysses S. Grant.

When the Civil War began, Parker returned to New York with plans to raise a regiment of Iroquois Indians to fight for the Union. His request for permission to do so was turned down by the governor, who told him bluntly that he had no place for Indians in the New York Volunteers. Parker shrugged off the rebuff and journeyed to Washington to offer his services as an engineer to the War Department. The Union Army was in acute need of trained engineers, but not *Indian* engineers. "The Civil War is a white man's war," Parker was told. "Go home, cultivate your farm, and we will settle our own troubles without any Indian aid." [2]

Parker returned to the Tonawanda reservation, but he let his friend Ulysses Grant know that he was having difficulty getting into the Union Army. Grant needed engineers, and after battling Army red tape for months, he finally managed to have orders sent to his Indian friend, who joined him at Vicksburg.

They campaigned together from Vicksburg to Richmond. When Lee surrendered at Appomattox, Lieutenant Colonel Ely Parker was there, and because of his excellent penmanship Grant asked him to write out the terms of surrender.

During the four years following the end of the war, Brigadier General Parker served on various missions to settle differences with Indian tribes. In 1867, after the Fort Phil Kearny fight, he journeyed up the Missouri River to investigate the causes of unrest among the northern Plains Indians. He returned to Washington with many ideas for reformation of the nation's Indian policy, but he had to wait a year before he could start putting them into effect. When Grant was elected President he chose Parker to be the new Commissioner of Indian Affairs, believing that he could deal more intelligently with Indians than any white man.

Parker entered upon his new duties with enthusiasm, but found the Indian Office even more corrupt than he had expected. A clean sweep of the long-entrenched bureaucrats appeared necessary, and with Grant's support he established a system of appointing agents recommended by various religious bodies of the nation. Because so many Quakers volunteered to serve as Indian agents, the new plan became known as Grant's "Quaker policy," or "peace policy," for the Indians.

In addition, a Board of Indian Commissioners composed of public-spirited citizens was formed to act as a watchdog over operations of the Bureau of Indian Affairs. Parker recommended that this board be a mixed commission of white men and Indians, but politics interfered. Because no Indians could be found who had political influence, no Indians were appointed.

During the winter of 1869–70, Commissioner Parker (or Donehogawa of the Iroquois, as he thought of himself more and more) was gratified by the peaceful condition of the western frontier. By the spring of 1870, however, he was becoming disturbed over reports of rebellion coming from Indian agencies on the Plains. The first inkling he had of the cause of unrest was Lieutenant Pease's shocking account of the Piegan massacre. Parker knew that unless something was done to reassure the Indians of the government's good intentions, a general war would probably break out during the summer.

14. *Ely Parker, or Donehogawa, Seneca chief, military secretary to U. S. Grant and Commissioner of Indian Affairs. Photographed around 1867. Courtesy of the Smithsonian Institution.*

The commissioner was well aware of Red Cloud's dissatisfaction, of the Sioux leader's determination to keep the country he had won by treaty, and of his desire for a trading post near that country. Although Spotted Tail had gone to Fort Randall on the Missouri River, the Brulés were already among the most rebellious of the reservation Indians. With their enormous followings among the Plains tribes, Red Cloud and Spotted Tail seemed to the commissioner to be the keys to peace. Could an Iroquois chief win the confidence of the Sioux chiefs? Donehogawa was not certain, but he decided to try.

The commissioner sent a polite invitation to Spotted Tail, but he was too shrewd an Indian to use a direct message to solicit a visit from Red Cloud. Such an invitation most likely would have been received by Red Cloud as a summons to be proudly scorned. Through an intermediary, Red Cloud was informed that he would be a welcome visitor to the Great Father's house in Washington if he wanted to come.

The idea of such a journey intrigued Red Cloud; it would give him an opportunity to talk with the Great Father and tell him that the Sioux did not want a reservation on the Missouri. He could also see for himself if the Little Father of the Indians, the commissioner named Parker, was truly an Indian and could write like a white man.

As soon as the commissioner heard that Red Cloud wanted to come to Washington, he sent Colonel John E. Smith out to Fort Laramie to act as escort. Red Cloud selected fifteen Oglalas to accompany him, and on May 26 the party boarded a special coach on the Union Pacific and started the long journey eastward.

It was a great experience, riding on their old enemy the Iron Horse. Omaha (a city named for Indians) was a beehive of white people, and Chicago (another Indian name) was terrifying with its noise and confusion and buildings that seemed to reach to the sky. The white men were as thick and numerous and aimless as grasshoppers, moving always in a hurry but never seeming to get to whatever place it was they were going to.

After five days of clatter and motion, the Iron Horse brought them into Washington. Except for Red Cloud, the members of the delegation were dazed and ill at ease. Commissioner Parker, who truly was an Indian, greeted them warmly: "I am very glad to see you here today. I know that you have come a great distance to see the Great Father, the President of the United States. I am glad that you have had no accident, and that you have arrived here all safe. I want to hear what Red Cloud has to say for himself and his people."

"I have but a few words to say," Red Cloud responded. "When I heard that my Great Father would permit me to come to see him I was glad, and came right off. Telegraph to my people, and say that I am safe. That is all I have to say today." [3]

When Red Cloud and the Oglalas arrived at the Washington House on Pennsylvania Avenue, where a suite had been reserved for them, they were surprised to find Spotted Tail and a delegation of Brulés waiting for them there. Because Spotted Tail had obeyed the government and moved his people to the Missouri River agency, Commissioner Parker feared there would be trouble between the two rival Tetons. They shook hands, however, and as soon as Spotted Tail told Red Cloud that he and his Brulés thoroughly hated the Dakota reservation and wanted to return to their Nebraska hunting grounds east of Fort Laramie, the Oglala accepted the Brulé as a returned ally.

Next day, Donehogawa of the Iroquois took his Sioux guests on a tour of the capital, visiting the Senate in session, the Navy Yard, and the Arsenal. For their journey, the Sioux had been outfitted with white man's clothing, and it was obvious that most of them were ill at ease in their tight-fitting black coats and button shoes. When Donehogawa told them that Mathew Brady had invited them to his studio to have their photographs taken, Red Cloud said it did not suit him to do so. "I am not a white man, but a Sioux," he explained. "I am not dressed for such an occasion." [4]

Donehogawa understood immediately, and let his visitors know that if it so pleased them they could dress in buckskins, blankets, and moccasins for dinner at the White House with President Grant.

At the White House reception the Sioux were more impressed by the hundreds of blazing candles in glittering chandeliers than they were by the Great Father and his cabinet members, the foreign diplomats, and congressmen who had come to stare at these wild men in the midst of Washington. Spotted Tail, who enjoyed good food, especially liked the strawberries and ice cream. "Surely the white men have many more good things to eat than they send to the Indians," he remarked.

During the next few days, Donehogawa set about bargaining with Red Cloud and Spotted Tail. To obtain a permanent peace, he had to know exactly what they wanted so that he could balance this against the pressures of politicians representing white men who wanted the Indians' land. It was not an enviable position for a sympathetic Indian to be in. He arranged a meeting at the Interior Department, inviting representatives from all branches of the government to meet with the Sioux visitors.

Secretary of the Interior Jacob Cox opened the proceedings with the sort of oration these Indians had heard many times before. The government would like to give the Indians arms and ammunition for hunting, Cox said, but could not do this until it was sure all the Indians were at peace. "Keep the peace," he concluded, "and then we will do what is right for you." He said nothing about the Sioux reservation on the Missouri.

Red Cloud responded by shaking hands with Secretary Cox and the other officials. "Look at me," he said. "I was raised on this land where the sun rises—now I come from where the sun sets. Whose voice was first sounded on this land? The voice of the red people who had but bows and arrows. The Great Father says he is good and kind to us. I don't think so. I am good to his white people. From the word sent me I have come all the way to his house. My face is red; yours is white. The Great Spirit has made you to read and write, but not me. I have not learned. I come here to tell my Great Father what I do not like in my country. You are all close to the Great Father, and are a great many chiefs. The men the Great Father sends to us have no sense—no heart.

"I do not want my reservation on the Missouri; this is the fourth time I have said so." He stopped for a moment, and gestured toward Spotted Tail and the Brulé delegation. "Here are some people from there now. Their children are dying off like sheep; the country does not suit them. I was born at the forks of the Platte and I was told that the land belonged to me from north, south, east, and west. . . . When you send goods to me, they are stolen all along the road, so when they reached me they were only a handful. They held a paper for me to sign, and that is all I got for my land. I know the people you send out there are liars. Look at me. I am poor and naked. I do not want war with my government. . . . I want you to tell all this to my Great Father."

Donehogawa of the Iroquois, the commissioner, replied: "We will tell the President what Red Cloud has said today. The President told me he would talk with Red Cloud very soon."

Red Cloud looked at the red man who had learned to read and write and who was now the Little Father of the Indians. "You might grant my people the powder we ask," he said. "We are but a handful, and you are a great and powerful nation. You make all the ammunition; all I ask is enough for my people to kill game. The Great Spirit has made all things that I have in my country wild. I have to hunt them up; it is not like you, who go out and find what you want. I have eyes; I see all you whites, what you are doing, raising stock, and so forth. I know I will have to come to that in a few years myself; it is good. I have no more to say." [5]

The other Indians, Oglalas and Brulés, crowded around the commissioner, all wishing to speak with him, the red man who had become their Little Father.

The meeting with President Grant was on June 9, in the executive office of the White House. Red Cloud repeated much of what he had said at the Interior Department, emphasizing that his people did not want to live on the Missouri River. The treaty of 1868, he added, gave them the right to trade at Fort Laramie and have an agency on the Platte. Grant avoided a direct reply, but he promised to see that justice was done the Sioux. The President knew that the treaty ratified by Congress made no mention of Fort Laramie or the Platte; it specifically stated that the Sioux agency was to be "at some place on the Missouri." Privately he suggested to Secretary Cox and Commissioner Parker that they call the Indians together the next day and explain to them the terms of the treaty.

Donehogawa spent a restless night; he knew the Sioux had been tricked. When the printed treaty was read and explained to them, they would not like what they heard. Next morning at the Interior Department, Secretary Cox went through the treaty point by point, while Red Cloud listened patiently to the slow interpretation of the English words. When it was finished he declared firmly: "This is the first time I have heard of such a treaty. I never heard of it and do not mean to follow it."

Secretary Cox replied that he did not believe any of the peace commissioners at Laramie would have told a lie about the treaty.

"I did not say the commissioners lied," Red Cloud retorted, "but the interpreters were wrong. When the soldiers left the forts, I signed a treaty of peace, but it was not this treaty. We want to straighten things up." He arose and started to leave the room. Cox offered him a copy of the treaty, suggesting that he have his own interpreter explain it to him and then they would discuss it at another meeting. "I will not take the paper with me," Red Cloud replied. "It is all lies."

That night in their hotel the Sioux talked of going home the next day. Some said they were ashamed to go home to tell their people how they had been lied to and cheated into signing the treaty of 1868. It would be better to die there in Washington. Only the intercession of Donehogawa, the Little Father, persuaded them to come back for one more meeting. He promised to help them interpret the treaty in a better way. He had seen President Grant and convinced him that there was a solution to the difficulty.

At the Interior Department next morning Donehogawa greeted the Sioux by saying simply that Secretary Cox would explain the new interpretation of the treaty. Cox spoke briefly. He was sorry that Red Cloud and his people had misunderstood. Although the Powder River country was *outside* the permanent reservation, it was *inside* the part reserved for hunting grounds. If some of the Sioux preferred to live on their hunting grounds instead of inside the reservation, they could do so. Nor would they have to go to the reservation to trade and receive their goods.

And so for the second time in two years, Red Cloud won a victory over the United States government, but this time he had the help of an Iroquois. He acknowledged this by coming forward and shaking the commissioner's hand. "Yesterday, when I saw the treaty and all the false things in it," he said, "I was mad, and I suppose it made you the same. . . . Now I am pleased. . . . We have thirty-two nations and have a council house, just the same as you have. We held a council before we came here, and the demand I have made upon you is from the chiefs I left behind. We are all alike."

The meeting ended in a spirit of friendliness, with Red Cloud asking Donehogawa to tell the Great Father he had no further business with him; he was ready to board the Iron Horse and go home.

Secretary Cox, all smiles now, informed Red Cloud that the government had planned a visit for the Sioux in New York on their way home.

"I do not want to go that way," Red Cloud replied. "I want a straight line. I have seen enough of towns. . . . I have no business in New York. I want to go back the way I came. The whites are the same everywhere. I see them every day." [6]

Later, when he was told that he had been invited to make a speech to the people of New York, Red Cloud changed his mind. He went to New York, and was astonished by the tumultuous ovation the audience gave him at Cooper Institute. For the first time he had an opportunity to talk to people instead of government officials.

"We want to keep peace," he told them. "Will you help us? In 1868 men came out and brought papers. We could not read them, and they did not tell us truly what was in them. We thought the treaty was to remove the forts, and that we should cease from fighting. But they wanted to send us traders on the Missouri. We did not want to go to the Missouri, but wanted traders where we were. When I reached Washington the Great Father explained to me what the treaty was, and showed me that the interpreters had deceived me. All I want is right and just. I have tried to get from the Great Father what is right and just. I have not altogether succeeded." [7]

Red Cloud indeed had not altogether succeeded in getting what he believed was right and just. Although he returned to Fort Laramie with the good feeling that he had many white friends in the East, he found many white enemies waiting for him in the West. Land seekers, ranchers, freighters, settlers, and others were opposed to a Sioux agency anywhere near the rich Platte Valley, and they made their influence felt in Washington.

Through the summer and autumn of 1870, Red Cloud, with his lieutenant, Man-Afraid-of-His-Horses, worked hard for peace. At the request of Donehogawa, the commissioner, they rounded up dozens of powerful chiefs and brought them into

Fort Laramie for a council that was supposed to decide the location of the Sioux agency. They persuaded Dull Knife and Little Wolf of the Northern Cheyennes; Plenty Bear of the Northern Arapahos; Chief Grass of the Blackfoot Sioux; and Big Foot of the Minneconjous, who had always been suspicious of white men, to join them. Sitting Bull of the Hunkpapas would have nothing to do with any kind of treaty or reservation. "The white people have put bad medicine over Red Cloud's eyes," he said, "to make him see everything and anything they please."

Sitting Bull underestimated Red Cloud's shrewd tenacity. When the Oglala leader discovered at the council that government officials wanted to put the Sioux agency forty miles north of the Platte at Raw Hide Buttes, he would have none of it. "When you go back to the Great Father," he told the officials, "tell him Red Cloud is not willing to go to Raw Hides Buttes." [8] Thereupon he went off to the Powder River country for the winter, confident that Donehogawa the Iroquois would set matters right in Washington.

The power of Commissioner Ely Parker was waning, however. In Washington, his white enemies were closing in on him.

Although Red Cloud's stubborn determination secured a temporary agency for the Sioux thirty-two miles east of Fort Laramie on the Platte, they were permitted to use it for less than two years. By that time Donehogawa was gone from Washington. In 1873 the Sioux agency was moved out of the path of the surging flood of white emigration to the headwaters of White River in northwestern Nebraska. Spotted Tail and his Brulés also were permitted to move from Dakota to the same area. Within a year or so, Camp Robinson was established nearby, and the military would dominate the Red Cloud and Spotted Tail agencies through the troublesome years ahead.

A few weeks after Red Cloud's visit to Washington in 1870, Donehogawa's troubles began in earnest. His reforms had created enemies among political bosses (the so-called Indian Ring) who had long been using the Indian Bureau as a lucrative branch of the spoils system. His thwarting of the Big Horn mining expedition, a group of white frontiersmen who wanted to open the Sioux treaty lands, created enemies in the West.

(The Big Horn Association was formed in Cheyenne, and its members believed in Manifest Destiny: "The rich and beautiful valleys of Wyoming are destined for the occupancy and sustenance of the Anglo-Saxon race. The wealth that for untold ages has lain hidden beneath the snow-capped summits of our mountains has been placed there by Providence to reward the brave spirits whose lot it is to compose the advance-guard of civilization. The Indians must stand aside or be overwhelmed by the ever advancing and ever increasing tide of emigration. The destiny of the aborigines is written in characters not to be mistaken. The same inscrutable Arbiter that decreed the downfall of Rome has pronounced the doom of extinction upon the red men of America.") [9]

In the summer of 1870, a small band of Donehogawa's enemies in Congress attempted to embarrass him by delaying appropriations of funds for purchase of supplies for reservation Indians. By midsummer telegrams began arriving daily in his office from agents pleading for foodstuffs so that hungry Indians would not be forced to break away in search of wild game. Some agents predicted violence if food could not be supplied quickly.

The commissioner responded by purchasing supplies on credit without the delay of advertising for bids. Then he arranged for hasty transportation at slightly higher prices than the contract rates. Only in this way could the reservation Indians have received their rations in time to prevent starvation. Donehogawa, however, had broken a few minor regulations, and this gave his enemies the chance they had been waiting for.

Unexpectedly, the first attack came from William Welsh, a merchant and part-time missionary to the Indians. Welsh had been one of the first members of the watchdog Board of Indian Commissioners, but resigned soon after accepting the appointment. His reasons for resignation were made clear in December, 1870, when he wrote a letter for publication in several Washington newspapers. Welsh charged the commissioner with "fraud and improvidence in the conduct of Indian affairs," and blamed President Grant for putting into office a man "who is but a remove from barbarism." It was evident that Welsh believed the Indians went on the warpath because they were not Christians, and therefore his solution to the Indian problem was to convert all of them to Christianity. When he discovered that Ely Parker (Donehogawa) was tolerant of the Indians' primitive religions, he took a violent dislike to the "heathen" commissioner and resigned.

As soon as Welsh's letter appeared in print, Donehogawa's political enemies seized upon it as a perfect opportunity to remove him from office. Within a week the House of Representatives' Committee on Appropriations adopted a resolution to inquire into the charges against the Commissioner of Indian Affairs, and summoned him to a grilling that continued for days. Welsh submitted a list of thirteen charges of misconduct, which Donehogawa had to prove were unfounded. At the end of the inquiry, however, the commissioner was exonerated of all charges and was complimented for convincing the Indian tribes "that the government is in earnest, and that it may be trusted," and thus saving the Treasury millions of dollars by avoiding another war on the Plains.[10]

Only Donehogawa's closest friends knew how agonizing the entire affair had been to him. He considered Welsh's attack a betrayal, especially the implication that as an Indian "but a remove from barbarism" he was not fit to serve as Commissioner of Indian Affairs.

For several months he debated what his next course of action should be. Above all he wanted to help the advancement of his race, but if he remained in office with political enemies constantly sniping at him because he was an Indian himself, he feared that he might do his people more harm than good. He also wondered if his continuance in office might not be a political embarrassment to his old friend President Grant.

Late in the summer of 1871 he turned in his resignation. Privately he told friends he was leaving because he had become "a rock of offense." Publicly he said he wanted to go into business to better provide for his family. As he had foreseen, the press attacked him, intimating that he must have been a member of the "Indian Ring" himself, a Judas to his own people.

Donehogawa shrugged it all off; after half a century he had grown accustomed to the white man's prejudices. He went to New York City, made himself a fortune in that Gilded Age of finance, and lived out his life as Donehogawa, Keeper of the Western Door of the Long House of the Iroquois.

NINE

Cochise and the Apache Guerrillas

1871—January 28, Paris capitulates to German Army. March 18, Communist uprising in Paris. May 10, Franco-German peace treaty signed; France cedes Alsace-Lorraine to Germany. May 28, uprising in Paris is suppressed. October 8, the Great Chicago Fire. October 12, President Grant issues proclamation against Ku Klux Klan. November 10, in Africa, Henry M. Stanley finds Dr. Livingstone. Impressionist painters hold first exhibition in Paris. Darwin's *Descent of Man* is published.

1872—March 1, Yellowstone National Park is reserved for the people of the United States. James Fisk's and Jay Gould's corrupt Erie Ring collapses. June, U.S. Congress abolishes federal income tax. October, leading Republicans accused of receiving stock of Crédit Mobilier in exchange for political influence to benefit Union Pacific Railroad. November 5, in Rochester, N.Y., Susan B. Anthony and other women's-rights advocates arrested for attempting to vote. November 6, President Grant reelected.

When I was young I walked all over this country, east and west, and saw no other people than the Apaches. After many summers I walked again and found another race of people had come to take it. How is it? Why is it that the Apaches wait to die—that they carry their lives on their fingernails? They roam over the hills and plains and want the heavens to fall on them. The Apaches were once a great nation; they are now but few, and because of this they want to die and so carry their lives on their fingernails.

*—*COCHISE OF THE CHIRICAHUA APACHES

I don't want to run over the mountains anymore; I want to make a big treaty. . . . I will keep my word until the stones melt. . . . God made the white man and God made the Apache, and the Apache has just as much right to the country as the white man. I want to make a treaty that will last, so that both can travel over the country and have no trouble.

*—*DELSHAY OF THE TONTO APACHES

If it had not been for the massacre, there would have been a great many more people here now; but after that massacre who could have stood it? When I made peace with Lieutenant Whitman my heart was very big and happy. The people of Tucson and San Xavier must be crazy. They acted as though they had neither heads nor hearts . . . they must have a thirst for our blood. . . . These Tucson people write for the papers and tell their own story. The Apaches have no one to tell their story.

*—*ESKIMINZIN OF THE ARAVAIPA APACHES

--->---◆>◗<◗---◆---

A FTER the visit of Red Cloud in the summer of 1871, Commissioner Ely Parker and other government officials discussed the advisability of inviting the great Apache chief, Cochise, to Washington. Although there had been no military campaigns in the Apache country since the departure of Star Chief Carleton after the Civil War, there were frequent encounters between roving bands of these Indians and the white settlers, miners, and freighters who kept intruding upon their homelands. The government set aside four reservation areas in New Mexico and Arizona for the various bands, but few Apaches would come in to live on any of them. It was Commissioner Parker's hope that Cochise could help bring about a permanent peace in the Apache country, and he asked his bureau's representatives in that area to invite the chief to come to Washington.

Not until the spring of 1871 was any white man able to find Cochise, and when at last communication was established, the chief declined the government's invitation. He said simply that he could not trust either the military or the civilian representatives of the United States.

Cochise was a Chiricahua Apache. He was taller than most of his people, broad-shouldered, deep-chested, his face intelligent, with black eyes, large straight nose, very high forehead, thick black hair. White men who met him said he was gentle in his manners, and very neat and clean in his appearance.

When the Americans first came to Arizona, Cochise had welcomed them. In 1856, during a meeting with Major Enoch Steen of the First U.S. Dragoons, Cochise promised to let Americans cross the Chiricahua country on the southern route to California. He did not object when the Butterfield Overland Mail established a stage station in Apache Pass; in fact, Chiricahuas living nearby cut wood for the station, trading it for supplies.

Then, one day in February, 1861, Cochise received a message from Apache Pass asking him to come in to the station for a conference with a military officer. Expecting that this would be a routine matter, Cochise took along five members of his family —his brother, two nephews, a woman, and a child. The military officer who wanted to see him was Lieutenant George N. Bascom of the Seventh Infantry, and he had been sent with a company of soldiers to recover cattle and a half-breed boy stolen from the ranch of John Ward. Ward had accused Cochise's Chiricahuas of taking the cattle and the boy.

As soon as Cochise and his relatives entered Bascom's tent, twelve soldiers surrounded it, and the lieutenant peremptorily demanded that the Chiricahuas return the cattle and the boy.

Cochise had heard about the captured boy. A band of Coyoteros from the Gila had raided the Ward ranch, he said, and probably were at Black Mountain. Cochise thought he might be able to arrange a ransom. Bascom's reply was an accusation that the Chiricahuas had the boy and the cattle. At first Cochise thought the young officer was joking. Bascom was short-tempered, however, and when Cochise made light of the accusation, the lieutenant ordered the arrest of Cochise and his relatives, declaring that he would hold them as hostages for return of the cattle and the boy.

At the moment the soldiers moved in to make the arrest, Cochise slashed a hole in the tent and fled under a volley of rifle fire. Although wounded, he managed to escape Bascom's pursuit, but his relatives were held as prisoners. To get them free, Cochise and his warriors captured three white men on the Butterfield Trail, and tried to make an exchange with the lieutenant. Bascom refused the exchange unless the stolen cattle and the boy were included.

Infuriated because Bascom would not believe his people innocent, Cochise blocked Apache Pass and besieged the infantry company at the stage station. After giving Bascom one more chance to exchange, Cochise executed his prisoners, mutilating them with lances, a cruel practice the Apaches had learned from the Spaniards. A few days later Lieutenant Bascom retaliated by hanging Cochise's three male relatives.

It was at this point in history that the Chiricahuas transferred their hatred of the Spaniards to the Americans. For a quarter of a century they and other Apaches would fight an intermittent guerrilla campaign that would be more costly in lives and treasure than any of the other Indian wars.

At this time (1861) the great war chief of the Apaches was Mangas Colorado, or Red Sleeves, a seventy-year-old Mimbreño who was even taller than the towering Cochise. He had followers among many of the bands in southeastern Arizona and southwestern New Mexico. Cochise was married to Mangas' daughter, and after the Bascom affair the two men joined forces to drive the Americans from their homeland. They attacked wagon trains, stopped the movement of stagecoaches and mails, and drove several hundred white miners out of their territory from the Chiricahua Mountains to the Mogollons. After the Blue-

15. *Cochise. Reproduced from a painting in the Arizona Historical Society.*

coats and the Graycoats began their Civil War, Mangas and Cochise fought skirmishes with the Graycoats until they withdrew eastward.

And then, in 1862, Star Chief Carleton came marching from California with his thousands of Bluecoats, using the old trail that ran though the heart of Chiricahua country. They came in small companies at first, always halting for water at a spring near the abandoned stage station in Apache Pass. In the Moon of the Horse, July 15, Mangas and Cochise deployed their five hundred warriors along rocky heights overlooking the pass and spring. Three companies of Bluecoat infantry escorted by a troop of pony soldiers and two wheeled vehicles were approaching from the west. When the column of three hundred soldiers was strung out along the pass, the Apaches attacked suddenly with bullets and arrows. After returning fire for a few minutes, the soldiers hurriedly retreated from the pass.

The Apaches did not pursue. They knew the Bluecoats would come back. After re-forming, the infantrymen pushed into the pass again, this time with the two wagons rolling close behind them. The soldiers came within a few hundred yards of the springs, but there was no cover to shield them there, and the Apaches had the water supply ringed in from above. For several minutes the Bluecoats held their position. Then the wagons came rolling up. Suddenly great flashes of fire burst from the wagons. Clouds of black smoke arose, a great thundering echoed among the high rocks, and bits of flying metal screamed through the air. The Apaches had heard the little cannons of the Spaniards, but these big thundering wagon-guns were filled with terror and death. Now the warriors retreated, and the Bluecoats moved up to take possession of the sweet-flowing waters of the springs.

Mangas and Cochise were not yet ready to quit. If they could draw small bands of soldiers away from the wagon-guns, they might still defeat them. Next morning they saw a platoon of pony soldiers riding back toward the west, probably to warn other soldiers coming from that direction. Mangas took fifty mounted warriors and went dashing down to cut them off. In the running fight which followed, Mangas was wounded in the chest, falling unconscious from his horse. Dismayed by the loss of their leader, the warriors broke off the fight and carried Mangas' bleeding body back up to the heights.

Cochise was determined to save Mangas' life. Instead of trusting to the medicine men and their chants and rattles, he placed his father-in-law in a sling, and with an escort of warriors rode steadily southward for a hundred miles into Mexico to the village of Janos. A Mexican surgeon of great reputation lived there, and as he was presented with the helpless body of Mangas Colorado he was given a terse ultimatum: *Make him well. If he dies, this town will die.*

Some months later Mangas was back in his Mimbres Mountains, wearing a broad-brimmed straw hat, a sarape, leather leggings, and Chinese sandals that he had acquired in Mexico. He was thinner and his face more wrinkled than before, but he could still outride and outshoot warriors half a century younger than he. While he was resting in his mountains he heard that Star Chief Carleton had rounded up the Mescaleros and imprisoned them at Bosque Redondo. He learned that the Bluecoats were searching out Apaches everywhere and killing them with their wagon-guns as they had killed sixty-three of his and Cochise's warriors at Apache Pass.

In the Time of the Flying Ants (January, 1863) Mangas was camped on the Mimbres River. For some time he had been thinking of how he might obtain peace for all the Apaches before he died. He remembered the treaty he had signed at Sante Fe in 1852. In that year the Apaches and the people of the United States had agreed to perpetual peace and friendship. For a few years there had been peace and friendship, but now there was hostility and death. He wanted to see his people live in peace again. He knew that even his bravest and most cunning young warriors such as Victorio and Geronimo could not defeat the great power of the United States. Perhaps it was time for another treaty with the Americans and their Bluecoat soldiers, who had become as numerous as the flying ants.

One day a Mexican approached Mangas' camp under a truce flag. He said that some soldiers were nearby and wanted to talk peace. To Mangas their coming seemed providential. He would have preferred counseling with a star chief, but he agreed to go and see the little *capitán*, Edmond Shirland, of the California

Volunteers. The Mimbreños warriors warned him not to go. Did
he not remember what had happened to Cochise when he went
to see the soldiers at Apache Pass? Mangas shrugged off their
fears. After all, he was but an old man. What harm could the
soldiers do to an old man who wanted only to talk peace? The
warriors insisted that a guard accompany him; he chose fifteen
men, and they started up the trail toward the soldier camp.

When they came within sight of the camp, Mangas and his
party waited for the *capitán* to show himself. A miner who spoke
Spanish came out to escort Mangas into the camp, but the
Apache guards would not let their chief go in until Captain
Shirland mounted a truce flag. As soon as the white banner was
raised, Mangas ordered his warriors to turn back; he would go
in alone. He was protected by a truce, and would be perfectly
safe. Mangas rode on toward the soldier camp, but his warriors
had scarcely disappeared from view when a dozen soldiers sprang
from the underbrush behind him, with rifles cocked and ready.
He was a prisoner.

"We hurried Mangas off to our camp at old Fort McLean," said
Daniel Conner, one of the miners who was traveling with the
California Volunteers, "and arrived in time to see General West
come up with his command. The general walked out to where
Mangas was in custody to see him, and looked like a pigmy beside the old chief, who also towered above everybody about him
in stature. He looked careworn and refused to talk and evidently
felt that he had made a great mistake in trusting the paleface
on this occasion." [1]

Two soldiers were assigned to guard Mangas, and as night
came on and the air turned bitter cold, they built a log fire to
keep themselves and their prisoner from freezing. One of the
California Volunteers, Private Clark Stocking, afterward reported hearing General Joseph West's orders to the guards: "I
want him dead or alive tomorrow morning, do you understand,
I want him dead." [2]

Because of the presence of Mangas' Apaches in the area, extra
sentinels were assigned to patrol the camp after darkness fell.
Daniel Conner was pressed into service, and as he was walking
his post just before midnight he noticed that the soldiers guarding Mangas were annoying the old chief so that he kept

drawing his feet up restlessly under his blanket. Curious as to what the soldiers were doing, Conner stood just outside the firelight and watched them. They were heating their bayonets in the fire and touching them to Mangas' feet and legs. After the chief had endured this torture several times, he raised up and "began to expostulate in a vigorous way by telling the sentinels in Spanish that he was no child to be playing with. But his expostulations were cut short, for he had hardly begun his exclamations when both sentinels promptly brought down their minié muskets to bear on him and fired, nearly at the same time, through his body."

When Mangas fell back, the guards emptied their pistols into his body. A soldier took his scalp, another cut off his head and boiled the flesh away so that he could sell the skull to a phrenologist in the East. They dumped the headless body in a ditch. The official military report stated that Mangas was killed while attempting escape.

After that, as Daniel Conner put it, "the Indians went to war in earnest . . . they seemed bent on avenging his death with all their power."[3]

From the Chiricahua country of Arizona to the Mimbres Mountains of New Mexico, Cochise and his three hundred warriors began a campaign to drive out the treacherous white men or sell their lives in the attempt. Victorio assembled another band, including Mescaleros who had escaped from Bosque Redondo, and they raided settlements and trails along the Rio Grande from the Jornado del Muerto to El Paso. For two years these tiny armies of Apaches kept the Southwest in turmoil. Most were armed only with bows and arrows, and their arrows were frail three-foot reeds, tri-feathered, with triangular inch-long quartz heads chipped to fine points. Held to their shafts by jagged notches instead of thongs or wrappings, these missiles had to be handled with great care, but when the heads reached their marks, they imbedded with the tearing force of minié bullets. With what they had, the Apaches fought well, but they were outnumbered a hundred to one, and they could see nothing in the future but death or imprisonment.

After the Civil War's end and General Carleton's departure, the United States government made overtures of peace toward the Apaches. In the Moon of the Big Leaves (April 21, 1865) Victorio and Nana met at Santa Rita with a representative from the United States. "I and my people want peace," Victorio said. "We are tired of war. We are poor and have little for ourselves and our families to eat or wear. We want to make a peace, a lasting peace, one that will keep. . . . I have washed my hands and mouth with cold fresh water, and what I said is true."

"You can trust us," Nana added.

The agent's reply was brief: "I did not come to ask you to make peace, but to tell you that you can have peace by going to the reservation at the Bosque Redondo."

They had heard much, and all of it bad, about Bosque Redondo. "I have no pockets to put what you say in," Nana commented dryly, "but the words have sunk·deep into my heart. They will not be forgotten." [4]

Victorio asked for a two-day delay before starting to the reservation; he wanted to gather up all his people and their horses. He promised to meet the agent again on April 23, at Pinos Altos.

For four days the agent waited at Pinos Altos, but not a single Apache appeared. Rather than go to the hated Bosque, they preferred to face hunger, privation, and death. Some drifted southward into Mexico; others joined Cochise in the Dragoon Mountains. After his experience at Apache Pass and then the murder of Mangas, Cochise had not even responded to the overtures of peace. During the next five years, the warrior Apaches generally stayed clear of American forts and settlements. Whenever a rancher or miner grew careless, however, a band of raiders would swoop down to capture horses or cattle, and thus they carried on their guerrilla war. By 1870 raids were growing more frequent, and because Cochise was the chief best known to white men, he was usually held responsible for hostile actions no matter where they occurred.

This was why in the spring of 1871 the Commissioner of Indian Affairs so eagerly petitioned Cochise to visit Washington. Cochise, however, did not believe that anything had changed; he still could not trust any representative of the United States government. A few weeks later, after what happened to Eskiminzin and the Aravaipas at Camp Grant, Cochise was even more positive that no Apache should ever again put his life in the hands of the treacherous Americans.

Eskiminzin and his little band of 150 followers lived along Aravaipa Creek, from which they took their name. This was north of Cochise's stronghold, between the San Pedro River and the Galiuro Mountains. Eskiminzin was a stocky, slightly bow-legged Apache with a handsome bulldog face. He could be easy-going at times, fierce at others. One day in February, 1871, Eskiminzin walked into Camp Grant, a small post at the confluence of Aravaipa Creek and the San Pedro. He had heard that the *capitan,* Lieutenant Royal E. Whitman, was friendly, and he asked to see him.

Eskiminzin told Whitman that his people no longer had a home and could make none because the Bluecoats were always pursuing them and shooting at them for no reason other than that they were Apaches. He wanted to make peace so they could settle down and plant crops along the Aravaipa.

Whitman asked Eskiminzin why he did not go to the White Mountains where the government had set aside a reservation. "That is not our country," the chief replied. "Neither are they our people. We are at peace with them [the Coyoteros] but never have mixed with them. Our fathers and their fathers before them have lived in these mountains and have raised corn in this valley. We are taught to make mescal,* our principal article of food, and in summer and winter here we have a never-failing supply. At the White Mountains there is none, and without it now we get sick. Some of our people have been for a short time at the White Mountains, but they are not contented, and they all say, 'Let us go to the Aravaipa and make a final peace and never break it.' " [5]

Lieutenant Whitman told Eskiminzin that he had no authority to make peace with his band, but that if they surrendered their firearms he could permit them to stay near the fort as technical prisoners of war until he received instructions from his superior officers. Eskiminzin agreed to this, and the Aravaipas

---

* Eskiminzin was not referring to the alcoholic beverage known by the same name but to roasted leaves of the agave, a sweet and nutritious food that was cooked in earthen pits. The Mescalero Apaches received their name from it.

came in a few at a time to turn in their guns, some even dispos-
ing of their bows and arrows. They established a village a few
miles up the creek, planted corn, and began cooking mescal.
Impressed by their industry, Whitman employed them to cut
hay for the camp's cavalry horses so they could earn money to
buy supplies. Neighboring ranchers also employed some of them
as laborers. The experiment worked so well that by mid-March
more than a hundred other Apaches, including some Pinals, had
joined Eskiminzin's people, and others were coming in almost
daily.

Whitman meanwhile had written an explanation of the situation to his military superiors, requesting instructions, but late
in April his inquiry was returned for resubmission on proper
government forms. Uneasy because he knew that all responsibility for actions of Eskiminzin's Apaches was his, the lieutenant
kept a close watch on their movements.

On April 10 Apaches raided San Xavier, south of Tucson,
stealing cattle and horses. On April 13 four Americans were
killed in a raid near the San Pedro east of Tucson.

Tucson in 1871 was an oasis of three thousand gamblers,
saloon-keepers, traders, freighters, miners, and a few contractors
who had made fortunes during the Civil War and were hopeful
of continuing their profits with an Indian war. This backwash
of citizens had organized a Committee of Public Safety to protect themselves from Apaches, but as none came near the town,
the committee frequently saddled up and rode out in pursuit of
raiders in the outlying communities. After the two April raids,
some members of the committee announced that the raiders had
come from the Aravaipa village near Camp Grant. Although
Camp Grant was fifty-five miles distant, and it was unlikely that
Aravaipas would have traveled that far to raid, the pronouncement was readily accepted by most of the Tucson citizens. In
general they were opposed to agencies where Apaches worked
for a living and were peaceful; such conditions led to reductions
in military forces and a slackening of war prosperity.

During the last weeks of April, a veteran Indian fighter named
William S. Oury began organizing an expedition to attack the
unarmed Aravaipas near Camp Grant. Six Americans and forty-
two Mexicans agreed to participate, but Oury decided this was

16. *Eskiminzin, head chief of the Aravaipa Apaches. Photographed
probably by Charles M. Bell in Washington, D.C., 1876.
Courtesy of the Smithsonian Institution.*

not enough to ensure success. From the Papago Indians, who years before had been subdued by Spanish soldiers and converted to Christianity by Spanish priests, he recruited ninety-two mercenaries. On April 28 this formidable band of 140 well-armed men was ready to ride.

The first warning that Lieutenant Whitman at Camp Grant had of the expedition was a message from the small military garrison at Tucson informing him that a large party had left there on the twenty-eighth with the avowed purpose of killing all the Indians near Camp Grant. Whitman received the dispatch from a mounted messenger at 7:30 A.M. on April 30.

"I immediately sent the two interpreters, mounted, to the Indian camp," Whitman later reported, "with orders to tell the chiefs the exact state of things, and for them to bring their entire party inside the post. . . . My messengers returned in about an hour, with intelligence that they could find no living Indians." [6]

Less than three hours before Whitman received the warning message, the Tucson expedition was deployed along the creek bluffs and the sandy approaches of the Aravaipas' village. The men on the low ground opened fire on the wickiups, and as the Apaches ran into the open, rifle fire from the bluffs cut them down. In half an hour every Apache in the camp had fled, been captured, or was dead. The captives were all children, twenty-seven of them, taken by the Christianized Papagos to be sold into slavery in Mexico.

When Whitman reached the village it was still burning, and the ground was strewn with dead and mutilated women and children. "I found quite a number of women shot while asleep beside their bundles of hay which they had collected to bring in that morning. The wounded who were unable to get away had their brains beaten out with clubs or stones, while some were shot full of arrows after having been mortally wounded by gunshot. The bodies were all stripped."

Surgeon C. B. Briesly, who accompanied Lieutenant Whitman, reported that two of the women "were lying in such a position, and from the appearance of their genital organs and of their wounds, there can be no doubt that they were first ravished and then shot dead. . . . One infant of some ten months was shot twice and one leg hacked nearly off." [7]

Whitman was concerned that the survivors who had fled into the mountains would blame him for failing to protect them. "I thought the act of caring for their dead would be an evidence to them of our sympathy at least, and the conjecture proved correct, for while at the work many of them came to the spot and indulged in their expressions of grief too wild and terrible to be described . . . of the whole number buried [about a hundred] one was an old man and one was a well-grown boy—all the rest women and children." Death from wounds and the discovery of missing bodies eventually brought the total killed to 144. Eskiminzin did not return, and some of the Apaches believed he would go on the warpath in revenge for the massacre.

"My women and children have been killed before my face," one of the men told Whitman, "and I have been unable to defend them. Most Indians in my place would take a knife and cut his throat." But after the lieutenant pledged his word that he would not rest until they had justice, the grieving Aravaipas agreed to help rebuild the village and start life over again.

Whitman's persistent efforts finally brought the Tucson killers to trial. The defense claimed that the citizens of Tucson had followed the trail of murdering Apaches straight to the Aravaipa village. Oscar Hutton, the post guide at Camp Grant, testified for the prosecution: "I give it as my deliberate judgment that no raiding party was ever made up from the Indians at this post." F. L. Austin, the post trader, Miles L. Wood, the beef contractor, and William Kness, who carried the mail between Camp Grant and Tucson, all made similar statements. The trial lasted for five days; the jury deliberated for nineteen minutes; the verdict was for release of the Tucson killers.

As for Lieutenant Whitman, his unpopular defense of Apaches destroyed his military career. He survived three court-martials on ridiculous charges, and after several more years of service without promotion he resigned.

The Camp Grant massacre, however, fixed the attention of Washington upon the Apaches. President Grant described the attack as "purely murder," and ordered the Army and the Indian Bureau to take urgent actions to bring peace to the Southwest.

In June, 1871, General George Crook arrived at Tucson to take command of the Department of Arizona. A few weeks later Vincent Colyer, a special representative of the Indian Bureau, arrived at Camp Grant. Both men were keenly interested in arranging a meeting with the leading Apache chiefs, especially Cochise.

Colyer first met with Eskiminzin in hopes of persuading him to return to his peaceful ways. Eskiminzin came down out of the mountains and said he would be glad to talk peace with Commissioner Colyer. "The commissioner probably thought he would see a great *capitán*," Eskiminzin remarked quietly, "but he only sees a very poor man and not very much of a *capitán*. If the commissioner had seen me about three moons ago he would have seen me a *capitán*. Then I had many people, but many have been massacred. Now I have got few people. Ever since I left this place, I have been nearby. I knew I had friends here but I was afraid to come back. I never had much to say, but this I can say, I like this place. I have said all I ought to say, since I have few people anywhere to speak for. If it had not been for the massacre, there would have been a great many more people here now; but after that massacre who could have stood it? When I made peace with Lieutenant Whitman my heart was very big and happy. The people of Tucson and San Xavier must be crazy. They acted as though they had neither heads nor hearts . . . they must have a thirst for our blood. . . . These Tucson people write for the papers and tell their own story. The Apaches have no one to tell their story."

Colyer promised to tell the Apaches' story to the Great Father and to the white people who had never heard of it.

"I think it must have been God who gave you a good heart to come and see us, or you must have had a good father and mother to make you so kind."

"It was God," Colyer declared.

"It was," Eskiminzin said, but the white men present could not tell in the translation whether he spoke in confirmation or was asking a question.[8]

The next chief on Colyer's agenda was Delshay of the Tonto Apaches. Delshay was a stocky, broad-shouldered man of about thirty-five. He wore a silver ornament in one ear, his facial expression was fierce, and he usually moved at a half-trot as though in a constant hurry. As early as 1868 Delshay had agreed to keep the Tontos at peace and use Camp McDowell on the west bank of the Rio Verde as his agency. Delshay, however, found the Bluecoat soldiers to be exceedingly treacherous. On one occasion an officer had fired buckshot into Delshay's back for no reason the chief could fathom, and he was quite certain that the post surgeon had tried to poison him. After these occurrences, Delshay stayed clear of Camp McDowell.

Commissioner Colyer arrived at Camp McDowell late in September with authority to use soldiers to open communications with Delshay. Although truce flags, smoke signals, and night fires were used extensively by parties of cavalry and infantry, Delshay would not respond until he had thoroughly tested the intentions of the Bluecoats. By the time he agreed to meet with Captain W. N. Netterville in Sunflower Valley (October 31, 1871), Commissioner Colyer had returned to Washington to make his report. A copy of Delshay's remarks was forwarded to Colyer.

"I don't want to run over the mountains anymore," Delshay said. "I want to make a big treaty. . . . I will make a peace that will last; I will keep my word until the stones melt." He did not want to take the Tontos back to Camp McDowell, however. It was not a good place (after all, he had been shot and poisoned there). The Tontos preferred to live in Sunflower Valley near the mountains so they could gather the fruit and get the wild game there. "If the big *capitán* at Camp McDowell does not put a post where I say," he insisted, "I can do nothing more, for God made the white man and God made the Apache, and the Apache has just as much right to the country as the white man. I want to make a treaty that will last, so that both can travel over the country and have no trouble; as soon as the treaty is made I want a piece of paper so that I can travel over the country as a white man. I will put a rock down to show that when it melts the treaty is to be broken. . . . If I make a treaty, I expect the big *capitán* will come and see me whenever I send for him, and I will do the same whenever he sends for me. If a treaty is made and the big *capitán* does not keep his promises with me I will put his word in a hole and cover it up with dirt. I promise that when a treaty is made the white man or soldiers can turn out all their horses and mules without anyone to look after them, and if any are stolen by the Apaches I will cut my throat. I want to make a big treaty, and if the Americans break the treaty I do not want any more trouble; the white man can take one road and I can take the other. . . . Tell the big *capitán* at Camp McDowell that I will go to see him in twelve days." [9]

The closest that Colyer came to Cochise was Cañada Alamosa, an agency which had been established by the Indian Bureau forty-two miles southwest of Fort Craig, New Mexico. There he talked with two members of Cochise's band. They told him that the Chiricahuas had been in Mexico, but the Mexican government was offering three hundred dollars for Apache scalps, and this had brought out scouting parties who attacked them in the mountains of Sonora. They had scattered and were returning to their old Arizona strongholds. Cochise was somewhere in the Dragoon Mountains.

A courier was sent to find Cochise, but when the man crossed into Arizona Territory he unexpectedly met General Crook, who refused to recognize his authority to go to Cochise's camp. Crook ordered the courier to return immediately to New Mexico.

Crook wanted Cochise for himself, and to find him dead or alive he ordered out five companies of cavalry to scour the Chiricahua Mountains. Gray Wolf was the name the Apaches gave General Crook. Cochise eluded the Gray Wolf by crossing into New Mexico. He sent a messenger to the Star Chief at Santa Fe, General Gordon Granger, informing him that he would meet him at Cañada Alamosa to talk peace.

Granger arrived in a six-mule ambulance with a small escort, and Cochise was waiting for him. The preliminaries were brief. Both men were eager to get the matter settled. For Granger it was an opportunity to win fame as the man who took the surrender of the great Cochise. For Cochise it was the end of the road; he was almost sixty years old and was very tired; streaks of silver dominated his shoulder-length hair.

Granger explained that peace was possible only if the Chiricahuas agreed to settle on a reservation. "No Apache would be allowed to leave the reservation without a written pass from the agent," the general said, "and permission would *never* be given to go on any kind of excursion across the line into Old Mexico."

Cochise replied in a quiet voice, seldom gesturing: "The sun has been very hot on my head and made me as in a fire; my blood was on fire, but now I have come into this valley and drunk of these waters and washed myself in them and they have cooled me. Now that I am cool I have come with my hands open to you to live in peace with you. I speak straight and do not wish to deceive or be deceived. I want a good, strong and lasting peace. When God made the world he gave one part to the white man and another to the Apache. Why was it? Why did they come together? Now that I am to speak, the sun, the moon, the earth, the air, the waters, the birds and beasts, even the children unborn shall rejoice at my words. The white people have looked for me long. I am here! What do they want? They have looked for me long; why am I worth so much? If I am worth so much why not mark where I set my foot and look when I spit? The coyotes go about at night to rob and kill; I cannot see them; I am not God. I am no longer chief of all the Apaches. I am no longer rich; I am but a poor man. The world was not always this way. God made us not as you; we were born like the animals, in the dry grass, not on beds like you. This is why we do as the animals, go about at night and rob and steal. If I had such things as you have, I would not do as I do, for then I would not need to do so. There are Indians who go about killing and robbing. I do not command them. If I did, they would not do so. My warriors have been killed in Sonora. I came in here because God told me to do so. He said it was good to be at peace—so I came! I was going around the world with the clouds, and the air, when God spoke to my thoughts and told me to come in here and be at peace with all. He said the world was for us all; how was it?

"When I was young I walked all over this country, east and west, and saw no other people than the Apaches. After many summers I walked again and found another race of people had

come to take it. How is it? Why is it that the Apaches wait
to die—that they carry their lives on their fingernails. They
roam over the hills and plains and want the heavens to fall on
them. The Apaches were once a great nation; they are now but
few, and because of this they want to die and so carry their
lives on their fingernails. Many have been killed in battle. You
must speak straight so that your words may go as sunlight to
our hearts. Tell me, if the Virgin Mary has walked throughout
all the land, why has she never entered the wickiups of the
Apaches? Why have we never seen or heard her?

"I have no father nor mother; I am alone in the world. No
one cares for Cochise; that is why I do not care to live, and
wish the rocks to fall on me and cover me up. If I had a father
and mother like you, I would be with them and they with me.
When I was going around the world, all were asking for Cochise.
Now he is here—you see him and hear him—are you glad? If
so, say so. Speak, Americans and Mexicans, I do not wish to
hide anything from you nor have you hide anything from me;
I will not lie to you; do not lie to me."

When the discussion came around to a location for the Chiricahua reservation, Granger said that the government wanted to
move the agency from Cañada Alamosa to Fort Tularosa in
the Mogollons. (At Cañada Alamosa, three hundred Mexicans
had settled and made land claims.)

"I want to live in these mountains," Cochise protested. "I
do not want to go to Tularosa. That is a long ways off. The flies
on those mountains eat out the eyes of the horses. The bad
spirits live there. I have drunk of these waters and they have
cooled me; I do not want to leave here." [10]

General Granger said that he would do what he could to persuade the government to let the Chiricahuas live in Cañada
Alamosa with its streams of clear cold water. Cochise promised
that he would keep his people there in peace with their Mexican
neighbors, and he kept his promise. A few months later, however, the government ordered the removal of all Apaches from
Cañada Alamosa to Fort Tularosa. As soon as he heard of the
order, Cochise slipped away with his warriors. They divided
into small parties, fleeing once again to their dry and rocky

mountains in southeastern Arizona. This time, Cochise resolved, he would stay there. Let the Gray Wolf, Crook, come after him if he must; Cochise would fight him with rocks if need be, and then if God willed it, the rocks could fall on Cochise and cover him up.

In the Time When the Corn Is Taken In (September, 1872) Cochise began receiving reports from his lookouts that a small party of white men was approaching his stronghold. They were traveling in one of the Army's little wagons that were made for carrying wounded men. The lookouts reported that Taglito, the Red Beard, was with them—Tom Jeffords. Cochise had not seen Taglito for a long time.

Back in the old days after Cochise and Mangas had gone to war with the Bluecoats, Tom Jeffords contracted to carry the mail between Fort Bowie and Tucson. Apache warriors ambushed Jeffords and his riders so often that he almost gave up the contract. And then one day the red-bearded white man came all alone to Cochise's camp. He dismounted, unbuckled his cartridge belt, and handed it and his weapons to one of the Chiricahua women. With no show of fear whatsoever, Taglito walked over to where Cochise was sitting and sat down beside him. After a proper interval of silence, Taglito Jeffords told Cochise he wanted a personal treaty with him so that he could earn his living carrying the mails. Cochise was baffled. He had never known such a white man. There was nothing he could do but honor Taglito's courage by promising to let him ride his mail route unmolested. Jeffords and his riders were never ambushed again, and many times afterward the tall red-bearded man came back to Cochise's camp and they would talk and drink tiswin together.

Cochise knew that if Taglito was with the party coming into the mountains, they were searching for him. He sent his brother Juan to meet the white men, and then waited in concealment with his family until he was certain that everything was all right. Then he rode down with his son Naiche. Dismounting, he embraced Jeffords, who said in English to a white-bearded man in dusty clothing: "This is Cochise." The right sleeve of the bearded man's coat was empty; he looked like an old warrior, and Cochise was not surprised when Taglito called him a general. He was Oliver Otis Howard. "Buenos días, señor," Cochise said, and they shook hands.

One by one Cochise's guard of warriors came in, and they formed a semicircle, sitting on blankets, for a council with the one-armed graybeard.

"Will the general explain the object of his visit?" Cochise asked in Apache. Taglito translated the words.

"The Great Father, President Grant, sent me to make peace between you and the white people," General Howard said.

"Nobody wants peace more than I do," Cochise assured him.

"Then," said Howard, "we can make peace."

Cochise replied that the Chiricahuas had attacked no white men since their flight from Cañada Alamosa. "My horses are poor and few," he added. "I might have brought in more by raiding the Tucson road, but I did not do it."

Howard suggested that the Chiricahuas could live better if they would agree to move to a big reservation on the Rio Grande.

"I have been there," Cochise said, "and I like the country. Rather than not have peace I will go and take such of my people as I can, but that move will break up my tribe. Why not give me Apache Pass? Give me that, and I will protect all the roads. I will see that nobody's property is taken by Indians."

Howard was surprised. "Perhaps we could do that," he said, and then went on to point out the advantages of living on the Rio Grande.

Cochise was no longer interested in the Rio Grande. "Why shut me up on a reservation?" he asked. "We will make peace. We will keep it faithfully. But let us go around free as Americans do. Let us go wherever we please."

Howard tried to explain that the Chiricahua country did not belong to the Indians, that all Americans had an interest in it. "To keep the peace," he said, "we must fix metes and bounds."

Cochise could not understand why boundaries could not be fixed around the Dragoon Mountains as well as on the Rio Grande. "How long, General, will you stay?" he asked. "Will you wait for my *capitánes* to come in and have a talk?"

"I came from Washington to meet your people and make peace," Howard replied, "and will stay as long as necessary."

General Oliver Otis Howard, straitlaced New Englander, graduate of West Point, hero of Gettysburg, loser of an arm in battle at Fair Oaks, Virginia, remained in the Apache camp for eleven days and was completely won over by the courtesy and direct simplicity of Cochise. He was charmed by the Chiricahua women and children.

"I was forced to abandon the Alamosa scheme," he wrote afterward, "and to give them, as Cochise had suggested, a reservation embracing a part of the Chiricahua Mountains and of the valley adjoining on the west, which included the Big Sulphur Spring and Rodgers' ranch." [11]

One more matter had to be settled. By law a white man must be appointed agent for the new reservation. For Cochise this was no problem; there was only one white man that all the Chiricahuas trusted—Taglito, the red-bearded Tom Jeffords. At first Jeffords objected. He had no experience in that line, and besides, the pay was poor. Cochise insisted, until at last Jeffords gave in. After all, he owed the Chiricahuas his life and prosperity.

Less fortunate were Delshay's Tonto Apaches and Eskiminzin's Aravaipas.

After Delshay's offer to the big *capitán* at Camp McDowell to make a treaty if a Tonto agency was established in Sunflower Valley, the chief received no reply. Delshay accepted this as a refusal. "God made the white man and God made the Apache," he had said, "and the Apache has just as much right to the country as the white man." He had made no treaty and received no piece of paper so that he could travel over the country as a white man; therefore he and his warriors traveled over the country as Apaches. The white men did not like this, and late in 1872 the Gray Wolf sent soldiers hunting through the Tonto Basin for Delshay and his warrior band. Not until the Time of the Big Leaves (April, 1873) did the soldiers come in sufficient numbers to entrap Delshay and the Tontos. They were surrounded, with bullets flying among their women and children, and there was nothing to do but raise a white flag.

The black-bearded soldier chief, Major George M. Randall, took the Tontos to Fort Apache on the White Mountain reservation. In those days the Gray Wolf preferred to use his soldier chiefs instead of civilians as reservation agents. They made the Apaches wear metal tags like dogs, and these tags had numbers on them so that it was impossible for anyone to slip away to the Tonto Basin even for a few days. Delshay and the others grew homesick for their timbered, snowy-topped mountains. On the reservation there was never enough of anything—food, or tools to work with—and they did not get along well with the Coyoteros, who looked upon them as intruders on their reservation. But it was lack of freedom to travel over the country that kept the Tontos miserable.

At last, in the Time of Ripeness (July, 1873), Delshay decided he could no longer bear confinement at White Mountain, and one night he led his people in flight. To keep the Bluecoats from hunting them down again he decided to go to the reservation on Rio Verde. A civilian agent was in charge there, and he promised Delshay that the Tontos could live at Rio Verde if they made no trouble for him. If they ran away again, they would be hunted down and killed. And so Delshay and his people went to work building a *rancheria* on the river near Camp Verde.

That summer there was an uprising at San Carlos agency in which a little soldier chief (Lieutenant Jacob Almy) was killed. The Apache leaders fled, some of them toward the Rio Verde, and they camped near Delshay's *rancheria*. When the Gray Wolf heard of this, he accused Delshay of aiding the fugitives, and sent an order to Camp Verde to have the Tonto chief arrested. Forewarned, Delshay decided he would have to flee once again. He did not want to lose what little freedom he had left, to be locked in irons and shut into the sixteen-foot hole that the soldiers had dug out of the canyon side for Indian prisoners. With a few loyal followers he ran away to the Tonto Basin.

He knew that the hunt would soon begin. The Gray Wolf would not rest until he had tracked Delshay down. For months Delshay and his men eluded the hunters. At last General Crook decided that he could not keep troops forever prowling through the Tonto Basin; only another Apache could find Delshay. And so the general announced that he would pay a reward for Delshay's head. In July, 1874, two mercenary Apaches reported separately to Crook's headquarters. Each presented a severed head, identified as Delshay's. "Being satisfied that both parties were earnest in their beliefs," Crook said, "and the bringing in of an extra head was not amiss, I paid both parties." [12] The heads, with those of other slain Apaches, were mounted on the parade grounds at Rio Verde and San Carlos.

Eskiminzin and the Aravaipas also found it difficult to live in peace. After Commissioner Colyer's visit in 1871, Eskiminzin and his people started life anew at Camp Grant. They rebuilt their wickiup village and replanted their grain fields. Just as everything seemed to be going well, however, the government decided to move Camp Grant sixty miles to the southeast. Using this move as an excuse to clear the San Pedro Valley of Indians, the Army transferred the Aravaipas to San Carlos, a new agency on the Gila River.

The move was made in February, 1873, and the Aravaipas were beginning to build a new *ranchería* and to plant new fields at San Carlos when the uprising occurred in which Lieutenant Almy was killed. Neither Eskiminzin nor any of the other Aravaipas had anything to do with the killing, but because Eskiminzin was a chief, the Gray Wolf ordered him arrested and confined as a "military precaution."

He remained a prisoner until the night of January 4, 1874, when he escaped and led his people away from the reservation. For four cold months they roamed the unfamiliar mountains in search of food and shelter. By April most of the Aravaipas were sick and hungry. To keep them from dying, Eskiminzin returned to San Carlos and sought out the agent.

"We have done nothing wrong," he said. "But we are afraid. That is why we ran away. Now we come back. If we stay in the mountains, we will die of hunger and cold-sickness. If American soldiers kill us here, it will be just the same. We will not run away again."

As soon as the agent reported the return of the Aravaipas, an order came from the Army to arrest Eskiminzin and his subchiefs, hobble them with chains so they could not escape, and transport them as prisoners of war to the new site of Camp Grant.

"What have I done?" Eskiminzin asked the soldier chief who came to arrest him.

The soldier chief did not know. The arrest was a "military precaution."

At the new Camp Grant, Eskiminzin and his subchiefs were kept chained together while they made adobe bricks for the new buildings at the post. At night they slept in their chains on the ground, and they ate food discarded by the soldiers.

One day in that summer a young white man came to see Eskiminzin and told him that he was the new agent at San Carlos. He was John Clum. He said the Aravaipas at San Carlos needed their chief to lead them. "Why are you a prisoner?" Clum asked.

"I have done nothing," Eskiminzin replied. "White men tell lies about me, maybe. I always try to do right." [13]

Clum said he would arrange his release if Eskiminzin would promise to help him improve conditions at San Carlos.

Two months later Eskiminzin rejoined his people. Once again the future looked bright, but the Aravaipa chief was wise enough not to hope for too much. Since the coming of the white men, he was never sure of a place where he could spread his blanket; the future for any Apache was very uncertain.

In the spring of 1874 Cochise became very ill from a debilitating disease. Tom Jeffords, the Chiricahua agent, brought the Army surgeon from Fort Bowie to examine his old friend, but the surgeon could not determine the ailment. His prescriptions brought no improvement, and the muscular body of the great Apache leader began wasting away.

During this time the government decided that money could be saved by consolidating the Chiricahua agency with the new Hot Springs agency in New Mexico. When officials came to discuss the matter with Cochise, he told them the transfer was a matter of indifference to him, that he would be dead before he could be moved. His subchiefs and his sons objected strongly, however, declaring that if the agency was moved, they would not go. Not even the United States had enough troops to move

them, they said, because they would rather die in their mountains than live at the Hot Springs.

After the government officials departed, Cochise grew so weak
and was suffering from such intense internal pain that Jeffords
decided to ride to Fort Bowie for the surgeon. As he was preparing to leave, Cochise asked: "Do you think you will see me
alive again?"

Jeffords replied with the frankness of a brother: "No, I do
not think I will."

"I think I will die about ten o'clock tomorrow morning. Do
you think we will see each other again?"

Jeffords was silent for a moment. "I don't know. What do
you think about it?"

"I don't know," Cochise answered. "It is not clear to my mind,
but I think we will, somewhere up there." [14]

Cochise was dead before Jeffords returned from Fort Bowie.
After a few days the agent announced to the Chiricahuas that
he felt it was time for him to leave. They would not hear of it.
Cochise's sons, Taza and Naiche, were especially insistent that
he remain. If Taglito deserted them, they said, the treaty and
promises made between Cochise and the government would be
worthless. Jeffords promised to stay.

By the springtime of 1875 most of the Apache bands were
either confined to reservations or had fled to Mexico. In March
the Army transferred General Crook from Arizona to the Department of the Platte. The Sioux and Cheyennes, who had
endured reservation life longer than the Apaches, were growing
rebellious.

A forced peace lay over the deserts, peaks, and mesas of the
Apache country. Ironically, its continuance depended largely
upon the patient efforts of two white men who had won the
regard of Apaches simply by accepting them as human beings
rather than as bloodthirsty savages. Tom Jeffords the agnostic
and John Clum of the Dutch Reformed Church were optimistic,
but they were wise enough not to expect too much. For any
white man in the Southwest who defended the rights of Apaches,
the future was very uncertain.

TEN

The Ordeal of Captain Jack

1873—January 6, U.S. Congress begins investigation of Crédit
Mobilier scandal. March 3, "Salary Grab" Act raises salaries
of congressmen and government officials retroactively. May 7,
U.S. Marines land in Panama to protect American lives and
property. September 15, last units of German Army leave
France. September 19, failure of Jay Cooke and Company,
banking firm, precipitates financial panic. September 20, New
York Stock Exchange closes for ten days; severe economic
crisis spreads across nation and world. Jules Verne's *Around
the World in Eighty Days* and Mark Twain's *The Gilded Age*
are published.

*I am but one man. I am the voice of my people. Whatever their hearts
are, that I talk. I want no more war. I want to be a man. You deny
me the right of a white man. My skin is red; my heart is a white man's
heart; but I am a Modoc. I am not afraid to die. I will not fall on the
rocks. When I die, my enemies will be under me. Your soldiers began
on me when I was asleep on Lost River. They drove us to these rocks,
like a wounded deer. . . .*
*I have always told the white man heretofore to come and settle in my
country; that it was his country and Captain Jack's country. That
they could come and live there with me and that I was not mad with
them. I have never received anything from anybody, only what I
bought and paid for myself. I have always lived like a white man, and
wanted to live so. I have always tried to live peaceably and never
asked any man for anything. I have always lived on what I could kill
and shoot with my gun, and catch in my trap.*

—KINTPUASH (CAPTAIN JACK) OF THE MODOCS

CALIFORNIA Indians were gentle as the climate in which they lived. The Spaniards gave them names, established missions for them, converted and debauched them. Tribal organizations were undeveloped among the California Indians; each village had its leaders, but there were no great war chiefs among these unwarlike people. After the discovery of gold in 1848, white men from all over the world poured into California by the thousands, taking what they wanted from the submissive Indians, debasing those whom the Spaniards had not already debased, and then systematically exterminating whole populations now long forgotten. No one remembers the Chilulas, Chimarikos, Urebures, Nipewais, Alonas, or a hundred other bands whose bones have been sealed under a million miles of freeways, parking lots, and slabs of tract housing.

One exception to the nonresistant Indians of California were the Modocs, who lived in the harsher climate of Tule Lake along the border of Oregon. Until the 1850's, white men were almost unknown to the Modocs; then settlers began coming in droves, seizing the best lands and expecting the Modocs to submit meekly. When the Modocs showed fight, the white invaders attempted extermination. The Modocs retaliated with ambushes.

During this time a young Modoc named Kintpuash was coming to manhood, and he could not understand why Modocs and white people could not live together without trying to kill each other. The Tule Lake country was limitless as the sky, with enough deer, antelope, ducks, geese, fish, and camas roots for everybody. Kintpuash scolded his father for not making peace with the white men. His father, who was a chief, told Kintpuash that the white men were treacherous and would have to be driven out before there could be peace. Not long afterward the chief was killed in a fight with white settlers, and Kintpuash became chief of the Modocs.

Kintpuash went into the settlements to find white men he

could trust, so that he could make peace with them. At Yreka he met some good men, and soon all the Modocs were coming there to trade. "I have always told white men when they came to my country," Kintpuash said, "that if they wanted a home to live there they could have it; and I never asked them for any pay for living there as my people lived. I liked to have them come there and live. I liked to be with white people." [1] The young chief also liked the clothes they wore, their houses, wagons, and fine livestock.

The white men around Yreka gave these visiting Indians new names, which the Modocs found amusing, and they often used these names among themselves. Kintpuash was Captain Jack. Some of the others were Hooker Jim, Steamboat Frank, Scarfaced Charley, Boston Charley, Curly Headed Doctor, Shacknasty Jim, Schonchin John, and Ellen's Man.

During the time of the white man's Civil War, troubles arose between the Modocs and the settlers. If a Modoc could not find a deer to kill for his family, he would sometimes kill a rancher's cow; or if he needed a horse he would borrow one out of a settler's pasture. The Modocs' white friends excused this as a "tax" the Indians were levying on the settlers for use of their lands, but most settlers did not like this and through their politicians arranged for a treaty to remove the Modocs from the Tule Lake country.

The treaty commissioners promised Captain Jack and the other head men that if they would move north to a reservation in Oregon every family would have its own land, teams of horses, wagons, farming implements, tools, clothing, and food—all provided by the government. Captain Jack wanted to have his land near Tule Lake, but the commissioners would not agree to this. Somewhat reluctantly Jack signed the treaty, and the Modocs went north to the Klamath reservation. From the very beginning there was trouble. The reservation was on territory that had belonged to Klamath Indians, and the Klamaths treated the Modocs as intruders. When the Modocs cut rails to fence their assigned farmlands, the Klamaths would come and steal the rails. Supplies promised by the government never arrived; the reservation agent issued food and clothing to the Klamaths, but there never seemed to be any for the Modocs. (The Great Council in Washington did not vote any money to buy supplies for the Modocs.)

When Captain Jack saw his people growing hungry, he led them off the reservation. They went down into Lost River Valley, where they had once lived, in search of game and fish and camas roots. White ranchers who lived in the valley did not want the Modocs to be there, however, and they complained frequently to government authorities. Captain Jack cautioned his people to stay clear of white men, but it was not easy for three hundred Indians to remain invisible. During the summer of 1872 the Indian Bureau warned Captain Jack to return to the Klamath reservation. Jack replied that his people could not live with the Klamaths. He requested a Modoc reservation somewhere on Lost River, which had always been Modoc country. The Indian Bureau considered the request a reasonable one, but the ranchers opposed granting any part of the rich grazing lands to Indians. In the autumn of 1872 the government ordered the Modocs to move back to the Klamath reservation. Jack refused to go. The Army was assigned the duty of transferring the Modocs by force. On November 28, 1872, in a freezing rain, Major James Jackson and a company of thirty-eight troopers of the First Cavalry marched out of Fort Klamath, bound south for Lost River.

Just before daylight the cavalrymen arrived at the Modoc camp. They dismounted and with carbines at the ready surrounded the lodges. Scarfaced Charley and several other men came outside with their weapons. Major Jackson asked to see the chief, and when Jack appeared the major told him he had orders from the Great Father to take the Modocs back to the Klamath reservation.

"I will go," Captain Jack said. "I will take all my people with me, but I do not place any confidence in anything you white people tell me. You see, you come here to my camp when it is dark. You scare me and all my people when you do that. I won't run from you. Come up to me like men when you want to see or talk with me." [2]

Major Jackson said he was not there to make trouble. Then he ordered Jack to assemble his men in front of the soldiers.

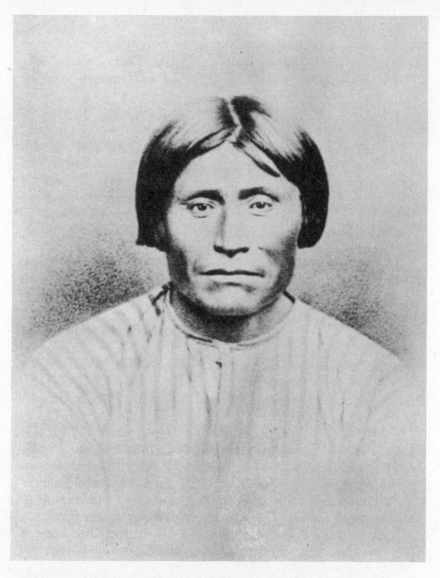

17. *Captain Jack, or Kintpuash, Having the Water Brash. Photographed by L. Heller in 1873. Courtesy of the Smithsonian Institution.*

As soon as this was done, the major pointed to a bunch of sage-brush at the end of the formation. "Lay your gun here," he commanded.

"What for?" Jack asked.

"You are the chief. You lay your gun down, all your men will do the same. You do that, and we'll have no trouble."

Captain Jack hesitated. He knew his men would not want to give up their arms. "I have never fought white people yet," he said, "and I do not want to."

The major insisted that they give up their guns. "I won't let anyone hurt you," he promised.

Captain Jack placed his gun on the sagebrush and signaled the others to do as he had done. They stepped up one by one, stacking their rifles. Scarfaced Charley was the last. He laid his rifle on top of the pile, but kept his pistol strapped around his waist.

The major ordered him to hand over the pistol.

"You got my gun," Scarfaced replied.

The major called to Lieutenant Frazier Boutelle: "Disarm him!"

"Give me that pistol, damn you, quick!" Boutelle ordered as he stepped forward.

Scarfaced Charley laughed. He said he was not a dog to be shouted at.

Boutelle drew his revolver. "You son-of-a-bitch, I'll show you how to talk back to me."

Scarfaced repeated that he was not a dog, adding that he would keep his pistol.[3]

As Boutelle brought his revolver into firing position, Scarfaced quickly drew his pistol from his belt. Both men fired at the same time. The Modoc's bullet tore through the lieutenant's coat sleeve. Scarfaced was not hit. He swung toward the stack of arms, sweeping his rifle from the top, and every Modoc warrior followed his example. The cavalry commander ordered his men to open fire. For a few seconds there was a lively exchange of shots, and then the soldiers retreated, leaving one man dead and seven wounded on the field.

By this time the Modoc women and children were in their log dugouts, paddling southward for Tule Lake. Captain Jack and his warriors followed along the shore, keeping hidden in the thick reeds. They were heading for the Modocs' legendary sanctuary south of the lake—the California Lava Beds.

The Lava Beds was a land of burned-out fires that had turned into rocky fissures, caves, and crevices. Some of the ravines were a hundred feet deep. The cave which Captain Jack chose as his stronghold was a craterlike pit surrounded by a network of natural trenches and lava-rock breastworks. He knew that his handful of warriors could fight off an army if necessary, but he hoped the soldiers would leave them alone now. Surely the white men would not want these useless rocks.

When Major Jackson's soldiers had come to Captain Jack's camp, a small band of Modocs led by Hooker Jim was camped on the opposite side of Lost River. In the early hours of the morning while Captain Jack was fleeing with his people for the Lava Beds, he had heard gunfire from the direction of Hooker Jim's camp. "I ran off and did not want to fight," he said afterward. "They shot some of my women, and they shot my men. I did not stop to inquire anything about it, but left and went away. I had very few people and did not want to fight." [4]

Not for a day or two did he discover what had happened to Hooker Jim's people. Then suddenly Hooker Jim appeared outside Jack's stronghold. With him were Curly Headed Doctor, Boston Charley, and eleven other Modocs. They told Jack that at the time soldiers came to his camp, several settlers had come to their camp and started shooting at them. These white men shot a baby out of its mother's arms, killed an old woman, and wounded some of the men. On their way to the Lava Beds, Hooker Jim and his men decided to avenge the deaths of their people. Stopping briefly at isolated ranch houses along the way, they had killed twelve settlers.

At first Jack thought Hooker Jim was merely boasting, but the others said it was true. When they named the dead white men, Jack could not believe it. Some of them were settlers he knew and trusted. "What did you kill those people for?" he demanded. "I never wanted you to kill my friends. You have done it on your own responsibility." [5]

Captain Jack knew for certain now that the soldiers would

be coming; even into the vastnesses of the Lava Beds they would come for revenge. And because he was chief of the Modocs he would have to answer for the crimes of Hooker Jim and the others.

Not until the Ice Moon did the soldiers come. On January 13, 1873, the Modocs guarding the outer defense ring sighted a Bluecoat reconnaissance party approaching a bluff overlooking the Lava Beds. The Modocs drove them away with a few long-distance shots. Three days later a force of 225 regular soldiers supported by 104 Oregon and California Volunteers came riding like ghosts through the fog of a wintry afternoon. They took positions along ridges facing Captain Jack's stronghold, and as darkness fell they began building sagebrush fires to keep warm. The military commanders were hopeful that if the Modocs saw the force arrayed against them, they might come in and surrender.

Captain Jack was in favor of surrendering. He knew that the soldiers most of all wanted the Modocs who had killed the settlers, and he was willing to put his life along with theirs in the hands of the soldier chiefs rather than sacrifice the lives of all his people in a bloody battle.

Hooker Jim, Curly Headed Doctor, and those who had killed the settlers were opposed to any surrender, and they forced Jack to call a council to vote on what action the tribe should take. Of the fifty-one warriors in the stronghold, only fourteen wanted to surrender. Thirty-seven voted to fight the soldiers to the death.

Before daylight on the seventeenth, they could hear the soldiers' bugles echoing across the fog-shrouded Lava Beds. Not long afterward, howitzers sounded the beginning of the Bluecoat attack. The Modocs were ready for them. Camouflaged with sagebrush head coverings, they moved in and out of crevices, picking off soldiers in the first skirmish line.

By midday the attackers were spread out for more than a mile, their communications badly broken because of fog and terrain. Keeping under cover, the Modoc warriors hurried back and forth along the front, creating an illusion of superiority of numbers. When one company of soldiers moved up close to the stronghold, the Modoc fire concentrated upon it, the women joining the warriors in the shooting. Late in the day, Jack and Ellen's Man led a charge that routed the soldiers, who left their casualties on the field.

Just before sunset the fog lifted, and the Modocs could see the soldiers retreating to their camp on the ridge. The warriors went out to where the dead Bluecoats were lying, and found nine carbines and six belts of cartridges. Farther on were more ammunition and some Army rations that had been thrown away by the fleeing soldiers.

When darkness came the Modocs built a big fire and celebrated. None had been killed in the fighting, and none was seriously wounded. They had captured enough rifles and ammunition to fight another day. Next morning they were ready for the soldiers, but when the soldiers came there were only a few of them, and they were carrying a white flag. They wanted to recover their dead. Before the end of that day all the soldiers were gone from the ridge.

Believing that the Bluecoats would return, Captain Jack kept scouts far out to watch for them. But the days passed one after the other, and the soldiers stayed far away. ("We fought the Indians through the Lava Beds to their stronghold," the commander of the attacking force reported, "which is the center of miles of rocky fissures, caves, crevices, gorges, and ravines. . . . One thousand men would be required to dislodge them from their almost impregnable position, and it must be done deliberately, with a free use of mortar batteries. . . . Please send me three hundred foot-troops at the earliest date." [6])

On February 28, Captain Jack's cousin, Winema, came to the Lava Beds. Winema was married to a white man named Frank Riddle, and he and three other white men accompanied her. These men had been friendly to the Modocs in the time when they visited freely in Yreka. Winema was a cheerful, energetic, round-faced young woman who now called herself Toby Riddle. She had adopted the ways of her husband, but Jack trusted her. She told him that she had brought the white men to have a talk with him, and that they intended to spend the night in the stronghold to prove their friendship. Jack assured her that they were welcome and that no harm would come to any of them.

In the council which followed, the white men explained that

the Great Father in Washington had sent out some commissioners who wanted to talk peace. The Great Father hoped to
avoid a war with the Modocs, and he wanted the Modocs to
come and talk with the commissioners so that they could find
a way to peace. The commissioners were waiting at Fairchild's
ranch not far from the Lava Beds.

When the Modocs raised the question of what would happen
to Hooker Jim's band for killing the Oregon settlers, they were
told that if they surrendered as prisoners of war they would not
be subject to trial by Oregon law. Instead they would be taken
far away and placed on a reservation in one of the warm places
—Indian Territory or Arizona.

"Go back and tell the commissioners," Jack replied, "that I
am willing to hear them in council and see what they have got
to offer me and my people. Tell them to come to see me, or
send for me. I will go and see them if they will protect me from
my enemies while I am holding these peace councils." [7]

Next morning the visitors departed, Winema promising that
she would inform Jack when the time and place for the council
was decided. On that same day Hooker Jim and his followers
slipped away to Fairchild's ranch, sought out the commissioners,
and declared that they wanted to surrender as prisoners of war.

The members of the peace commission were Alfred B.
Meacham, who had once been the Modocs' agent in Oregon;
Eleazar Thomas, a California clergyman; and L. S. Dyar, a sub-
agent from the Klamath reservation. Overseeing their activities
was the commander of the troops gathered outside the Lava
Beds, General Edward R. S. Canby—the same Canby who as
an Eagle Chief had fought and made peace with Manuelito's
Navahos twelve years earlier in New Mexico. (See Chapter 2.)

When Hooker Jim's Modocs came into Canby's headquarters
with their startling announcement of surrender, the general was
so delighted that he dispatched a hasty telegram to the Great
Warrior Sherman in Washington, informing him that the Modoc
war was ended and requesting instruction as to when and where
he should transport his prisoners of war.

In his excitement Canby failed to put Hooker Jim and his
eight followers under arrest. The Modocs wandered out into
the military camp to have a closer look at the soldiers who were

now supposed to protect them from the citizens of Oregon. During their rounds, they happened to meet an Oregon citizen who recognized them and threatened to have them arrested for murdering settlers on Lost River. The governor of Oregon had demanded their blood, he said, and as soon as the governor got his hands on them the law would hang them.

At the first opportunity, Hooker Jim and his band mounted their horses and rode as fast as they could back to the Lava Beds. They warned Captain Jack not to go to Fairchild's ranch to meet the commissioners; the proposed council was a trap to catch the Modocs and send them back to Oregon to be hanged.

During the next few days, as Winema and Frank Riddle came and went with messages, the suspicions of Hooker Jim's Modocs proved to be true insofar as they were concerned. Political pressure from Oregon forced General Canby and the commissioners to withdraw their offer of amnesty to Hooker Jim's band. Captain Jack and the remainder of the Modocs, however, were free to come in and surrender with a guarantee of protection.

Captain Jack was now caught in a classic dilemma. If he abandoned Hooker Jim's people, he could save his own. But Hooker Jim had come to him for protection under the chieftainship of the Modocs.

On March 6, with the help of his sister Mary, Jack wrote a letter to the commissioners, and she delivered it to Fairchild's ranch. "Let everything be wiped out, washed out, and let there be no more blood," he wrote. "I have got a bad heart about those murderers. I have got but a few men and I don't see how I can give them up. Will they give up their people who murdered my people while they were asleep? I never asked for the people who murdered my people. . . . I can see how I could give up my horse to be hanged; but I can't see how I could give up my men to be hanged. I could give up my horse to be hanged, and wouldn't cry about it, but if I gave up my men I would have to cry about it." [8]

Canby and the commissioners, however, still wanted to meet Captain Jack and persuade him that war for his people would be worse than surrendering the killers. Even though the Great Warrior Sherman advised Canby to use his soldiers against the

Modocs so "that no other reservation for them will be necessary except graves among their chosen Lava Beds," the general kept his patience.[9]

On March 21 Captain Jack and Scarfaced Charley sighted Canby and a small cavalry escort riding down from the ridge overlooking their stronghold. Jack did not know what to make of this bold approach. He deployed his warriors among the rocks, and watched a lone figure ride forward from the escort. The man was an Army surgeon, and he proposed an informal meeting between Captain Jack and General Canby. A few minutes later they were conversing. Canby assured Jack that if he would lead his people out of the Lava Beds they would be well treated; they would be given food, clothing, and many presents. Jack replied by asking Canby why he had not brought some of these things with him if he had so much to give the Modocs. He also asked Canby why he did not take the soldiers away; all that the Modocs wanted was to be left alone, he said.

During this short meeting neither Jack nor Canby made any mention of Hooker Jim's band and the killing of the settlers. Jack promised nothing; he wanted to wait and see what Canby would do next.

What Canby did next was to bring in additional troops and dispose them on opposite sides of the Modoc stronghold. Companies of the First Cavalry and Twenty-first Infantry, supported by the Fourth Artillery, were now in easy striking distance of the Indians.

On April 2 Captain Jack sent a message to the commissioners. He wanted to meet them halfway between the nearest soldier camp and his stronghold. That same day Canby, Meacham, Thomas, and Dyar, with Winema and Frank Riddle, rode out to a rocky basin below the soldier camp on the bluff. Jack, Hooker Jim, and several other Modocs were waiting for them there; they had brought along their women as an indication of peaceful intentions. Although Jack greeted Meacham as an old friend, he spoke somewhat bitterly to Canby, asking him why he had moved his soldiers so close and on both sides of the Modoc stronghold.

Canby tried to pass the question off lightly by replying that he had moved his headquarters closer to Jack's headquarters so they could meet more easily in councils, and that the soldiers were needed to make him feel safe. Jack did not accept Canby's explanation; he demanded that the soldiers be taken out of the Lava Beds and sent home. And then he brought up the sensitive subject of Hooker Jim's band. There could be no further talk of surrender, Jack said, unless Hooker Jim's people were treated the same as all the other Modocs. Canby replied that the Army would have to decide what would be done with them and where they would go; he could promise no amnesty for the killers of the settlers.

While they were talking, dark clouds overspread the Lava Beds, and a cold rain began falling. Canby said that further talk would not be possible in the rain. "You are better clothed than I," Jack replied mockingly, "and I won't melt like snow." [10] Canby ignored Jack's remark, but announced that he would have a tent shelter erected for the next meeting.

Next morning Canby sent some soldiers down to erect a council tent. They did not place it in the rocky basin, but instead chose a sagebrush flat that was in full view of the soldier camp and its formidable batteries of artillery.

Two days later Jack sent a message to Alfred Meacham, stating that he wanted to meet him and his old friend, John Fairchild, who owned the nearby ranch. Jack stipulated that they were not to bring General Canby or Reverend Thomas. Meacham and Fairchild were puzzled by the request, but they went out to the council tent with Winema and Frank Riddle. The Modocs were waiting, and Jack greeted the white men warmly. He explained that he did not trust Canby, because he wore a blue uniform and talked too much about his friendship for Indians; his talk did not ring with truth, because he kept bringing his soldiers closer to the Lava Beds. As for Reverend Thomas, he was a "Sunday doctor," and his holy medicine was opposed to the Modocs' beliefs. "Now we can talk," Jack said. "I know you and Fairchild. I know your hearts." He went on to explain how the soldiers had forced them to flee Lost River and take shelter in the Lava Beds. "Give me a home on Lost River," he pleaded. "I can take care of my people. I do not ask anybody to help me. We can make a living for ourselves. Let us have the same chance that other men have."

Meacham pointed out that Lost River was in Oregon, where the Modocs had shed the blood of white settlers. "The blood would always come up between you and the white men," the commissioner declared.

Jack sat in silence for some minutes. "I hear your words," he said. "Give me this Lava Bed for a home. I can live here; take away your soldiers, and we can settle everything. Nobody will ever want these rocks; give me a home here."

Meacham replied that the Modocs could not stay in peace in the Lava Beds unless they gave up the men who committed the killings on Lost River. They would be treated fairly, he promised, in a court of law.

"Who will try them?" Jack asked. "White men or Indians?"

"White men, of course," Meacham admitted.

"Then will you give up the men who killed the Indian women and children on Lost River, to be tried by the Modocs?"

Meacham shook his head. "The Modoc law is dead; the white man's law rules the country now; only one law lives at a time."

"Will you try the men who fired on my people?" Jack continued. "By your own law?"

Meacham knew and Captain Jack knew that this could not be done. "The white man's law rules the country," the commissioner repeated. "The Indian law is dead."

"The white man's laws are good for the white men," Jack said, "but they are made so as to leave the Indian out. No, my friend, I cannot give up the young men to be hung. I know they did wrong—their blood was bad. . . . *They* did not begin; the white man began first. . . . No, I cannot give up my young men; take away the soldiers, and all the trouble will stop."

"The soldiers cannot be taken away," Meacham replied, "while you stay in the Lava Beds."

Grasping Meacham's arm, Jack asked imploringly: "Tell me, my friend, what am I to do? I do not want to fight."

"The only way now to peace is to come out of the rocks," Meacham told him bluntly. "No peace can be made while you stay in the Lava Beds."

"You ask me to come out and put myself in your power," Jack cried. "I cannot do it. I am afraid—no, *I* am not afraid, but my people are. . . . I am the voice of my people. . . . I am a Modoc. I am not afraid to die. I can show him [Canby] how a Modoc can die."

Both men knew there was nothing more to be said. Meacham invited Jack to return with him to the soldier camp and continue their discussions with General Canby and the other commissioners, but Jack refused. He said he must first counsel with his people, and that he would let the commissioners know if there was to be any more talk.[11]

When Meacham reported to General Canby that Captain Jack would never give up Hooker Jim's band and therefore would not surrender the Lava Beds stronghold without a fight, Canby decided to give any Modocs who wished to leave one more opportunity to do so. Next day he sent Winema to inform Jack that any of his people who wanted to surrender could return with her.

While Winema waited, Captain Jack called a council. Only eleven Modocs voted to accept Canby's offer. Hooker Jim, Schonchin John, and Curly Headed Doctor all spoke strongly against surrender, accusing Canby and the commissioners of plotting treachery. The meeting ended with a threat from Hooker Jim's followers to kill any Modocs who tried to surrender.

That evening, as Winema was riding back to Canby's headquarters, a young Modoc named Weuim who was related to Winema halted her a short distance along the trail. He warned her not to come to the Modoc stronghold again, and to tell her white friends not to meet his people in council again. Hooker Jim's followers were planning to kill everyone who was against them, Weuim said. Winema rode back to the Army camp, but she was afraid to pass the warning on to anybody other than her husband. Frank Riddle, however, went immediately to headquarters and informed the commissioners of the warning. None of them believed it was anything more than angry talk.

In the Lava Beds, however, the angry talk against the white peacemakers grew stronger. On the night of April 7, Hooker Jim and his followers decided to have a showdown with their chief. Some of them suspected Jack of being on the verge of betraying them.

Schonchin John opened the council with a bitter speech: "I

have been trapped and fooled by the white people many times. I do not intend to be fooled again." He accused the peace commissioners of trickery, of playing for time while the Army brought in more soldiers and guns. "When they think there is enough men here, they will jump on us and kill the last soul of us."

Black Jim spoke next: "I for one am not going to be decoyed and shot like a dog by the soldiers. I am going to kill my man before they get me." He then spoke for killing the peace commissioners at the next council with them.

When Captain Jack saw how far the talk was going, he tried to convince the speakers they were wrong. He asked for time in which to bargain with the commissioners, to try to save Hooker Jim's band as well as to obtain a good piece of land for a reservation. "All I ask you to do is to behave yourselves and wait."

Black Jim accused Jack of being blind. "Can't you see soldiers arriving every two or three days? Don't you know the last soldiers that came brought big guns with them that shoot bullets as big as your head? The commissioners intend to make peace with you by blowing your head off with one of the big guns." Other speakers supported Black Jim's argument, and when Jack again tried to reason with them, they shouted him down: "Your talk is not good! We are doomed. Let us fight so we die sooner. We have to die anyway."

Believing it was useless to say more, Jack turned to leave the council, but Black Jim stopped him. "If you are our chief, promise us that you will kill Canby next time you meet him."

"I cannot do it and I will not do it."

Hooker Jim, who had been watching silently, now stepped up to his chief. "You will kill Canby or be killed yourself. You will kill or be killed by your own men."

Jack knew this was a challenge to his chieftaincy, but he held in his anger. "Why do you want to force me to do a coward's act?"

"It is not a coward's act," Hooker Jim retorted. "It will be brave to kill Canby in the presence of all those soldiers."

Refusing to promise anything, Jack again started to leave the council. Some of Hooker Jim's men threw a woman's shawl and headdress over his shoulders, taunting him: "You're a woman, a fish-hearted woman. You are not a Modoc. We disown you."

To save his power, to gain time, Jack knew he had to speak. "I will kill Canby," he said. He pushed the men aside and walked on alone to the cave.

Winema did not come with any messages the next day or the next, and so Boston Charley, who could speak and understand English, was sent to tell General Canby that the Modocs wanted to counsel with him and the commissioners on Friday morning, April 11. The Modocs would come unarmed to the council tent, Boston Charley told Canby, and they expected the commissioners to come unarmed.

On the morning of April 10, Jack called his men together outside the cave. The day was springlike, the sun quickly burning away the night fog. "My heart tells me I had just as well talk to the clouds and wind," he said, "but I want to say that life is sweet, love is strong; man fights to save his life; man also kills to win his heart's desire; that is love. Death is mighty bad. Death will come to us soon enough." He told his listeners that if they started fighting again, all would die, including their women and children. If they had to fight, let the soldiers start it. He reminded them that he had promised the commissioners to commit no acts of war as long as the peace councils continued. "Let me show the world that Captain Jack is a man of his word," he pleaded. Then he came to the promise he had made to kill General Canby. "Do not hold me to it. If you hold me to what I said in anger, we are doomed. Hooker Jim, you know that as well as I do."

"We hold you to the promise," Hooker Jim replied. "You have to kill Canby. Your talk is good, but now it is too late to put up such talk."

Jack looked at the fifty men seated around him on the rocks. The sunlight was bright on their dark faces. "All who want me to kill Canby," he said, "raise to your feet." Only about a dozen of his loyal followers remained seated.

"I see you do not love life nor anything else." His voice was somber as he grasped for an alternative. In the council with

Canby, he said, he would tell the general what the Modocs wanted. "I will ask him many times. If he comes to my terms I shall not kill him. Do you hear?"

"Yes," they all said.

"Will that do?"

"Yes," they agreed.

Now only the words of Canby could stop the killing.[12]

Good Friday, 1873, dawned clear, with a chill breeze fluttering the canvas of the council tent, which still stood between the soldier camp and the Lava Beds stronghold. Captain Jack, Hooker Jim, Schonchin John, Ellen's Man, Black Jim, and Shacknasty Jim reached the council ground early, and one of them built a fire of sagebrush to keep warm by while they waited for the commissioners to arrive. They had not brought their women this time. None had brought a rifle, either, but all had pistols concealed beneath their coats.

The commissioners were late in arriving (Winema kept warning them not to go), but soon after eleven o'clock General Canby and Reverend Thomas appeared on foot, and behind them on horseback were L. S. Dyar, Alfred Meacham, Winema, and Frank Riddle. Accompanying the commissioners and the interpreters were Boston Charley and Bogus Charley, who had gone into camp to meet them. Both Charleys carried rifles carelessly slung. None of the commissioners had any arms showing; Meacham and Dyar carried derringers in their coat pockets.

Canby brought along a box of cigars, and as soon as he reached the tent he gave a cigar to each man. Using brands from the sagebrush fire, they lighted up and sat on stones around the fire, smoking silently for a few minutes.

As Frank Riddle later remembered, Canby made the first speech. "He told them that he had been dealing with Indians for some thirty years, and he had come there to make peace with them and to talk good; and that whatever he promised to give them that he would see that they got; and if they would come and go out with him, that he would take them to a good country, and fix them up, so that they could live like white people." [13]

Meacham spoke next, opening with the usual preliminary remarks about the Great Father in Washington sending him there to wipe out all the blood that had been shed. He said that he hoped to take them to a better country, where they could have good houses and plenty of food, clothing, and blankets. When Meacham finished talking, Captain Jack told him that he did not want to leave the Modoc country, and asked for a reservation somewhere near Tule Lake and the Lava Beds. He also repeated his previous demand that the soldiers be taken away before they talked peace.

Apparently Meacham was irritated by Jack's repetitious demands. He raised his voice: "Let us talk like men and not like children." He then suggested that those Modocs who wished to do so could remain in the Lava Beds until a reservation was found where they might live in peace.

Schonchin John, who was seated about ten feet in front of Meacham, spoke angrily in Modoc, telling the commissioner to shut up. At this moment Hooker Jim arose and strolled over to Meacham's horse, which was standing to one side of the commissioner. Meacham's overcoat was draped over the saddle. Hooker Jim took the coat, put it on, and buttoned it up, clowning a bit as he walked in front of the fire. The others had stopped talking and were watching him. "You think I look like Meacham?" he asked in broken English.

Meacham tried to make a joke of the interruption. He offered Hooker Jim his hat. "Take it and put it on; then you will be Meacham."

Hooker Jim stopped his clowning. "You keep a while. Hat will be mine by and by."

Canby evidently understood the meaning in Hooker Jim's words. He quickly resumed the parley by saying that only the Great Father in Washington had authority to send the soldiers away. He asked Jack to trust him.

"I want to tell you, Canby," Jack replied, "we cannot make peace as long as these soldiers are crowding me. If you ever promise me a home, somewhere in this country, promise me today. Now, Canby, promise me. I want nothing else. Now is your chance. I am tired waiting for you to speak."

Meacham sensed the urgency in Captain Jack's voice. "General, for heaven's sake, promise him," he cried.

Before Canby could say anything, Jack sprang to his feet

and moved away from the fire. Schonchin John turned toward
the general. "You take away soldiers, you give us back our land,"
he shouted. "We tired talking. We talk no more!" [14]

Captain Jack swung around, speaking in Modoc: *"Ot-we-kau-*
tux-e (All ready!)." He drew his pistol from his coat, pointing
it directly at Canby. The hammer clicked, but the weapon failed
to fire. Canby stared at him in astonishment, and then the pistol
fired and Canby fell back dead. At about the same moment,
Boston Charley shot Reverend Thomas, killing him. Winema
saved Meacham's life by knocking Schonchin John's pistol aside.
During the confusion, Dyar and Riddle escaped.

After stripping Canby of his uniform, Jack led the Modocs
back to the stronghold to await the coming of the soldiers. The
main point of contention—the surrender of Hooker Jim's killers
—had not even been discussed in that last council.

Three days later the fighting began. Batteries of mortars
pounded the Lava Beds, and waves of infantrymen charged the
rock breastworks. When the soldiers finally overran the stronghold, they found it empty. The Modocs had slipped away
through the caves and crevices. Having no taste for searching
these hard-fighting Indians out of their hiding places, the Army
employed seventy-two mercenary Tenino Indians from the
Warm Springs Reservation in Oregon. These Warm Springs
scouts discovered the Modocs' hiding place, but when the soldiers were brought up to capture it, Captain Jack set an ambush
and came very near wiping out the advance patrol.

At last the overwhelming numbers and firepower of the soldiers forced the Modocs to scatter. They had to slaughter their
horses for food, and some days there was no water to drink. As
casualties mounted among the Indians, Hooker Jim began quar-
reling with Captain Jack over his strategy. After a few days of
running, hiding, and fighting, Hooker Jim and his band abandoned the chief who had given them sanctuary and then had
refused to surrender them to Canby. Jack was left with thirty-
seven warriors to fight off more than a thousand soldiers.

Not long afterward, Hooker Jim's band surrendered to the
soldiers and offered to help them track down Captain Jack in
exchange for amnesty. The new military commander, General
Jefferson C. Davis, gave them the protection of the Army, and

on May 27 Hooker Jim and three members of his band set out to betray the chief who had refused to betray them. They found Jack near Clear Lake, arranged to parley with him, and told him they had been sent to take his surrender. The soldiers would give the Modocs justice, they said, and plenty to eat.

"You are no better than coyotes that run in the valleys," Jack answered them. "You come here riding soldiers' horses, armed with government guns. You intend to buy your liberty and freedom by running me to earth and delivering me to the soldiers. You realize that life is sweet, but you did not think so when you forced me to promise that I would kill that man, Canby. I knew life was sweet all the time; that is the reason I did not want to fight the white people. I thought we would stand side by side if we did fight, and die fighting. I see now I am the only one to forfeit my life for killing Canby, perhaps one or two others. You and all the others that gave themselves up are getting along fine, and plenty to eat, you say. Oh, you bird-hearted men, you turned against me. . . ." [15]

What galled the Modoc chief most of all was that these turncoats had been the very ones who had thrown squaw's clothing over his head and called him a fish-hearted woman a few weeks before, thus forcing him to promise to kill Canby. They knew as well as he that it was too late for him to surrender; he would be hanged for murdering Canby. He told them he had made up his mind to die with a gun in his hand instead of a rope around his neck, and then ordered them to go back and live with the whites if they wanted to. But he swore to them that if they ever came within range of his gun again he would shoot them down like dirty dogs.

For a few more days the pursuit continued. It was "more of a chase after wild beasts than war," General Davis said, "each detachment vying with each other as to which should be the first in at the finish." [16]

After a grueling foot race across jagged rocks and through a thicket, a small party of troops surrounded Captain Jack and three warriors who stayed with him to the end. When Jack came out to surrender he was wearing General Canby's blue uniform; it was dirty and in tatters. He handed his rifle to an officer. "Jack's legs gave out," he said. "I am ready to die."

General Davis wanted him to die immediately by hanging, but the War Department in Washington ordered a trial. It was held at Fort Klamath in July, 1873. Captain Jack, Schonchin John, Boston Charley, and Black Jim were charged with murder. No lawyer represented the Modocs, and although they were given the right to cross-examine witnesses, most of them understood very little English, and all spoke it poorly. While the trial was in progress soldiers were constructing a gallows outside the prisoners' stockade, so there was no doubt as to what the verdict would be.

Among the witnesses against the doomed men were Hooker Jim and his followers. The Army had given them their freedom for betraying their own people.

After Hooker Jim was questioned by the prosecution, Captain Jack did not cross-examine him, but in his final courtroom speech, translated by Frank Riddle, Jack said: "Hooker Jim is the one that always wanted to fight, and commenced killing and murdering. . . . Life is mine only for a short time. You white people conquered me not; my own men did." [17]

Captain Jack was hanged on October 3. On the night following the execution, his body was secretly disinterred, carried off to Yreka, and embalmed. A short time later it appeared in eastern cities as a carnival attraction, admission price ten cents.

As for the surviving 153 men, women, and children, including Hooker Jim and his band, they were exiled to Indian Territory. Six years later Hooker Jim was dead, and most of the others died also before 1909, when the government decided to permit the remaining fifty-one Modocs to return to an Oregon reservation.

ELEVEN

The War to Save the Buffalo

1874—January 13, unemployed workmen battle police in New York City; hundreds injured. February 13, U.S. troops land at Honolulu to protect the king. February 21, Benjamin Disraeli becomes English Prime Minister, replacing William E. Gladstone. March 15, France assumes protectorate over Annam (Vietnam). May 29, Germany dissolves Social Democratic party. July, Alexander Graham Bell demonstrates his new invention, the electric telephone. July 7, Theodore Tilton accuses the Reverend Henry Ward Beecher of adultery. November 4, Samuel J. Tilden elected governor of New York after overthrow of Tweed Ring. December, the Whiskey Ring, involving distillers and U.S. government officials, is exposed.

I have heard that you intend to settle us on a reservation near the mountains. I don't want to settle. I love to roam over the prairies. There I feel free and happy, but when we settle down we grow pale and die. I have laid aside my lance, bow, and shield, and yet I feel safe in your presence. I have told you the truth. I have no little lies hid about me, but I don't know how it is with the commissioners. Are they as clear as I am? A long time ago this land belonged to our fathers; but when I go up to the river I see camps of soldiers on its banks. These soldiers cut down my timber; they kill my buffalo; and when I see that, my heart feels like bursting; I feel sorry. . . . Has the white man become a child that he should recklessly kill and not eat? When the red men slay game, they do so that they may live and not starve.

—Satanta, Chief of the Kiowas

My people have never first drawn a bow or fired a gun against the whites. There has been trouble on the line between us, and my young men have danced the war dance. But it was not begun by us. It was you who sent out the first soldier and we who sent out the second. Two years ago I came upon this road, following the buffalo, that my wives

and children might have their cheeks plump and their bodies warm.
But the soldiers fired on us, and since that time there has been a noise
like that of a thunderstorm, and we have not known which way to
go. So it was upon the Canadian. Nor have we been made to cry once
alone. The blue-dressed soldiers and the Utes came from out of the
night when it was dark and still, and for campfires they lit our lodges.
Instead of hunting game they killed my braves, and the warriors of
the tribe cut short their hair for the dead. So it was in Texas. They
made sorrow come in our camps, and we went out like buffalo bulls
when their cows are attacked. When we found them we killed them,
and their scalps hang in our lodges. The Comanches are not weak and
blind, like the pups of a dog when seven sleeps old. They are strong
and farsighted, like grown horses. We took their road and we went
on it. The white women cried and our women laughed.

But there are things which you have said to me which I do not like.
They are not sweet like sugar, but bitter like gourds. You said that
you wanted to put us upon a reservation, to build us houses and make
us medicine lodges. I do not want them. I was born upon the prairie,
where the wind blew free and there was nothing to break the light of
the sun. I was born where there were no enclosures and where
everything drew a free breath. I want to die there and not within
walls. I know every stream and every wood between the Rio Grande
and the Arkansas. I have hunted and lived over that country. I lived
like my fathers before me, and, like them, I lived happily.

When I was at Washington the Great White Father told me that all
the Comanche land was ours, and that no one should hinder us in
living upon it. So, why do you ask us to leave the rivers, and the sun,
and the wind, and live in houses? Do not ask us to give up the buffalo
for the sheep. The young men have heard talk of this, and it has made
them sad and angry. Do not speak of it more. . . .

If the Texans had kept out of my country, there might have been
peace. But that which you now say we must live on is too small. The
Texans have taken away the places where the grass grew the thickest
and the timber was the best. Had we kept that, we might have done
the things you ask. But it is too late. The white man has the country
which we loved, and we only wish to wander on the prairie until we
die.

—Parra-Wa-Samen (Ten Bears) of the Yamparika Comanches

A FTER the Battle of the Washita in December, 1868, General Sheridan ordered all Cheyennes, Arapahos, Kiowas, and Comanches to come in to Fort Cobb and surrender, or face extinction by being hunted down and killed by his Bluecoat soldiers. (See chapter seven.) Little Robe, who succeeded the dead Black Kettle as chief, brought in the Cheyennes. Yellow Bear brought in the Arapahos. A few Comanche leaders—notably Tosawi, who was told by Sheridan that the only good Indian was a dead Indian—also came to surrender. The proud and free Kiowas, however, gave no sign of cooperating, and Sheridan sent Hard Backsides Custer to force them to surrender or to destroy them.

The Kiowas could see no reason for going to Fort Cobb, giving up their arms, and living on the white man's handouts. The treaty of Medicine Lodge, which the chiefs had signed in 1867, gave them their own territory in which to live and the right to hunt on any lands south of the Arkansas "so long as the buffalo may range thereon in such numbers as to justify the chase." [1] Between the Arkansas and the western tributaries of the Red River, the Plains were black with thousands of buffalo driven down from the north by the white man's advancing civilization. The Kiowas were rich in fast-footed ponies, and when ammunition was scarce they could use their arrows to kill enough animals to supply all their needs for food, clothing, and shelter.

Nevertheless, long columns of Bluecoat pony soldiers came riding to the Kiowa winter camp on Rainy Mountain Creek. Not wanting a fight, Satanta and Lone Wolf, with an escort of warriors, went out to parley with Custer. Satanta was a burly giant, with jet black hair reaching to his enormous shoulders. His arms and legs were thickly muscled, his open face revealing strong confidence in his power. He wore brilliant red paint on his face and body, and carried red streamers on his lance. He liked to ride hard and fight hard. He was a hearty eater and drinker, and laughed with gusto. He enjoyed even his enemies. When he rode up to greet Custer he was grinning with pleasure. He offered his hand, but Custer disdained to touch it.

243

Having been around the Kansas forts enough to know the prejudices of white men, Satanta held his temper. He did not want his people destroyed as Black Kettle's had been. The parley began coldly, with two interpreters attempting to translate the exchange of conversation. Realizing the interpreters knew fewer words of Kiowa than he knew of English, Satanta called up one of his warriors, Walking Bird, who had acquired a considerable vocabulary from white teamsters. Walking Bird spoke proudly to Custer, but the soldier chief shook his head; he could not understand the Kiowa's accent. Determined to make himself understood, Walking Bird went closer to Custer and began stroking his arm as he had seen soldiers stroke their ponies. "Heap big nice sonabitch," he said. "Heap sonabitch." [2]

Nobody laughed. The interpreters finally made Satanta and Lone Wolf understand that they must bring their Kiowa bands into Fort Cobb or face destruction by Custer's soldiers. Then, in violation of the truce, Custer suddenly ordered the chiefs and their escort party put under arrest; they would be taken to Fort Cobb and held as prisoners until their people joined them there. Satanta accepted the pronouncement calmly, but said he would have to send a messenger to summon his people to the fort. He sent his son back to the Kiowa villages, but instead of ordering his people to follow him to Fort Cobb, he warned them to flee westward to the buffalo country.

Each night as Custer's military column was marching back to Fort Cobb, a few of the arrested Kiowas managed to slip away. Satanta and Lone Wolf were too closely guarded, however, to make their escapes. By the time the Bluecoats reached the fort, the two chiefs were the only prisoners left. Angered by this, General Sheridan declared that Satanta and Lone Wolf would be hanged unless all their people came into Fort Cobb and surrendered.

This was how by guile and treachery most of the Kiowas were forced to give up their freedom. Only one minor chief, Woman's Heart, fled with his people to the Staked Plains, where they joined their friends the Kwahadi Comanches.

To keep close watch upon the Kiowas and Comanches, the Army built a new soldier town a few miles north of the Red River boundary and called it Fort Sill. General Benjamin Grier-

18. *Satanta, or White Bear. From a photograph by William S. Soule, taken around 1870. Courtesy of the Smithsonian Institution.*

son, a hero of the white man's Civil War, was in command of the troops, most of them being black soldiers of the Tenth Cavalry. Buffalo soldiers, the Indians called them, because of their color and hair. Soon an agent with no hair on his head arrived from the East to teach them how to live by farming instead of hunting buffalo. His name was Lawrie Tatum, but the Indians called him Bald Head.

General Sheridan came to the new fort, released Satanta and Lone Wolf from arrest, and held a council in which he scolded the chiefs for their past misdeeds and warned them to obey their agent.

"Whatever you tell me," Satanta replied, "I mean to hold fast to. I will pick it up and hold it close to my breast. It don't alter my opinion a particle if you take me by the hand now, or take and hang me. My opinion will be just the same. What you have told me today has opened my eyes, and my heart is open also. All this ground is yours to make the road for us to travel on. After this, I am going to have the white man's road, to plant corn and raise corn. . . . You will not hear of the Kiowas killing any more whites. . . . I am not telling you a lie now. It is the truth." [3]

By corn-planting time, two thousand Kiowas and twenty-five hundred Comanches were settled on the new reservation. For the Comanches there was something ironic in the government's forcing them to turn away from buffalo hunting to farming. The Comanches had developed an agricultural economy in Texas, but the white men had come there and seized their farmlands, forcing them to hunt buffalo in order to survive. Now this kindly old man, Bald Head Tatum, was trying to tell them they should take the white man's road and go to farming, as if the Indians knew nothing of growing corn. Was it not the Indian who first taught the white man how to plant corn and make it grow?

For the Kiowas it was a different matter. The warriors looked upon digging in the ground as women's work, unworthy of mounted hunters. Besides, if they needed corn they could trade pemmican and robes to the Wichitas for corn, as they had always done. The Wichitas liked to grow corn, but were too fat and lazy to hunt buffalo. By midsummer the Kiowas were com-

19. *Lone Wolf, or Guipago. Photographed by William S. Soule sometime between 1867 and 1874. Courtesy of the Smithsonian Institution.*

plaining to Bald Head Tatum about the restrictions of farming. "I don't like corn," Satanta told him. "It hurts my teeth." He was also tired of eating stringy Longhorn beef, and he asked Tatum for an issue of arms and ammunition so the Kiowas could go on a buffalo hunt.[4]

That autumn the Kiowas and Comanches harvested about four thousand bushels of corn. It did not last long, distributed among 5,500 Indians and several thousand ponies. By spring-time of 1870 the tribes were starving, and Bald Head Tatum gave them permission to go on a buffalo hunt.

In the Summer Moon of 1870, the Kiowas held a big sun dance on the North Fork of Red River. They invited the Comanches and Southern Cheyennes to come as guests, and during the cere-monies many disillusioned warriors talked of staying out on the Plains and living in plenty with buffalo instead of returning to the reservation for meager handouts.

Ten Bears of the Comanches and Kicking Bird of the Kiowas spoke against this talk; they thought it best for the tribes to continue taking the white man's hand. The young Comanches did not condemn Ten Bears; after all, he was too old for hunt-ing and fighting. But the young Kiowas scorned Kicking Bird's counsel; he had been a great warrior before the white men penned him up on the reservation. Now he talked like a woman.

As soon as the dancing was finished, many of the young men rode off to Texas to hunt buffalo and raid the Texans who had taken their lands. They were especially angry against white hunters who were coming down from Kansas to kill thousands of buffalo; the hunters took only the skins, leaving the bloody car-casses to rot on the Plains. To the Kiowas and Comanches the white men seemed to hate everything in nature. "This country is old," Satanta had scolded Old Man of the Thunder Hancock when he met him at Fort Larned in 1867. "But you are cutting off the timber, and now the country is of no account at all." At Medicine Lodge Creek he complained again to the peace com-missioners: "A long time ago this land belonged to our fathers; but when I go up to the river I see camps of soldiers here on its banks. These soldiers cut down my timber; they kill my buffalo; and when I see that, my heart feels like bursting; I feel sorry."[5]

Through that Summer Moon of 1870, the warriors who stayed

on the reservation taunted Kicking Bird unmercifully for advo-
cating farming instead of hunting. At last Kicking Bird could
bear no more. He organized a war party and invited his worst
tormentors—Lone Wolf, White Horse, and old Satank—to accompany him on a raid into Texas. Kicking Bird did not have
the bulky, muscular body of Satanta. He was slight and sinewy
and light-skinned. He may have been sensitive because he was
not a full-blooded Kiowa; one of his grandfathers had been a
Crow Indian.

With a hundred warriors at his back, Kicking Bird crossed the
Red River boundary and deliberately captured a mail coach as
a challenge to the soldiers at Fort Richardson, Texas. When the
Bluecoats came out to fight, Kicking Bird displayed his skill in
military tactics by engaging the soldiers in a frontal skirmish
while he sent two pincer columns to strike his enemy's flanks
and rear. After mauling the troopers for eight hours under a
broiling sun, Kicking Bird broke off the fight and led his warriors triumphantly back to the reservation. He had proved his
right to his chieftaincy, but from that day he worked only for
peace with the white man.

By the coming of cold weather, many roving bands were back
in their camps near Fort Sill. Several hundred young Kiowas
and Comanches, however, remained on the Plains that winter.
General Grierson and Bald Head Tatum scolded the chiefs for
raiding in Texas, but they could say nothing against the dried
buffalo meat and robes which the hunters brought back to help
see their families through another season of scanty government
rations.

Around the Kiowa campfires that winter there was much talk
about the white men who were pressing in from all four directions. Old Satank was grieving for his son, who had been killed
that year by the Texans. Satank had brought back his son's
bones and placed them upon a raised platform inside a special
tepee, and now he always spoke of his son as sleeping, not as
dead, and every day he put food and water near the platforms
so that the boy might refresh himself on awakening. In the evenings the old man sat squinting into the campfires, his bony
fingers stroking the gray strands of his moustache. He seemed to
be waiting for something.

Satanta moved restlessly about, always talking, making proposals to the other chiefs as to what they should do. From
everywhere they heard rumors that steel tracks for an Iron
Horse were coming into their buffalo country. They knew that
railroads had driven the buffalo from the Platte and the Smoky
Hill; they could not permit a railroad through their buffalo
country. Satanta wanted to talk to the officers at the fort, convince them that they should take the soldiers away and let the
Kiowas live as they had always lived, without a railroad to
frighten the buffalo herds.

Big Tree was more direct. He wanted to go to the fort some
night, set the buildings on fire, and then kill all the soldiers as
they ran out. Old Satank spoke against such talk. It would be a
waste of words to talk to the officers, he said, and even if they
killed all the soldiers at the fort, more would come to take their
places. The white men were like coyotes; there were always more
of them, no matter how many were killed. If the Kiowas wanted
to drive the white men out of their country and save the buffalo,
they should start on the settlers, who kept fencing the grass and
building houses and making railroads and slaughtering all the
wild game.

When spring came in 1871, General Grierson sent out patrols
of his black soldiers to guard the fords along Red River, but the
warriors were eager to see the buffalo again, and they slipped
past the soldiers. Everywhere they went that summer on the
Texas plains they found more fences, more ranches, and more
white buffalo hunters with deadly long-range rifles slaughtering
the diminishing herds.

In the Leaf Moon of that spring, some Kiowa and Comanche
chiefs took a large hunting party up the North Fork of Red
River, hoping to find buffalo without leaving the reservation.
They found only a few, most of the herds being far out in Texas.
Around the evening campfires they began talking again of how
the white men, especially the Texans, were trying to drive all
the Indians into the ground. Soon they would have an Iron
Horse running across the prairie, and all the buffalo would disappear. Mamanti the Sky Walker, a great medicine man, suggested that it was time for them to go down to Texas and start
driving the Texans into the ground.

20. *Kicking Bird, chief of the Kiowas. Photographed by William S. Soule at Fort Dodge, Kansas, in 1868. Courtesy of the Smithsonian Institution.*

They made preparations, and in mid-May the war party eluded Grierson's patrols and splashed across Red River into Texas. Satanta, Satank, Big Tree, and many other war leaders were in the party, but the raid had been a vision of Mamanti, and therefore he was the leader. On May 17 Mamanti brought the warriors to a halt on a hill overlooking the Butterfield Trail between forts Richardson and Belknap. There they waited through the night and until noon of the following day, when they saw an Army ambulance escorted by mounted soldiers heading east along the trail. Some of the warriors wanted to attack, but Mamanti refused to give the signal. He assured them a much richer prize would soon follow, perhaps a wagon train filled with rifles and ammunition. (Unknown to the Indians, the passenger in the Army vehicle was none other than the Great Warrior Sherman on an inspection tour of southwestern military posts.)

As Mamanti had predicted, a train of ten freight wagons rolled into view a few hours later. At the proper moment he motioned to Satanta, who was holding a bugle ready. Satanta blasted a call on the instrument, and the warriors swarmed down the slope. The teamsters formed a corral and made a desperate stand, but the onrush of Kiowas and Comanches was too much for them. The warriors broke through the corral, killed seven teamsters, and then let the others escape in a nearby thicket while they plundered the wagons. They found no rifles or ammunition, nothing but corn. They took the mules from the wagons, fastened their wounded to horses, and rode north for Red River.

Five days later the Great Warrior Sherman arrived at Fort Sill. When General Grierson introduced him to Bald Head Tatum, Sherman asked the agent if any of his Kiowas or Comanches had been absent from the reservation during the past week. Tatum promised to inquire into the matter.

Shortly afterward several of the chiefs arrived from their camps to draw weekly rations. Kicking Bird, Satank, Big Tree, Lone Wolf, and Satanta were among them. Agent Tatum summoned them into his office. With his usual kindly solemnity, Tatum asked the chiefs if they had heard of an attack on a wagon train in Texas. If any of them knew anything about it, he said, he would like to hear them speak.

Disregarding the fact that Mamanti had led the raid, Satanta immediately arose and said that he was the leader. Various reasons have been given as to why he did this. Was it vanity? Was he merely boasting, or did he feel it his duty as principal chief to assume all responsibility? At any rate, he used the opportunity to rebuke Tatum for the way the Indians were being treated: "I have repeatedly asked you for arms and ammunition, which you have not furnished, and made many other requests which have not been granted. You do not listen to me talk. The white people are preparing to build a railroad through our country, which will not be permitted. Some years ago we were taken by the hair and pulled close to the Texans where we have to fight. . . . When General Custer was here two or three years ago, he arrested me and kept me in confinement several days. But arresting Indians is played out now and is never to be repeated. On account of these grievances, I took, a short time ago, about one hundred of my warriors, with the chiefs Satank, Eagle Heart, Big Tree, Big Bow, and Fast Bear. . . . We went to Texas where we captured a train not far from Fort Richardson. . . . If any other Indian comes here and claims the honor of leading the party he will be lying to you for I did it myself!" [6]

Tatum remained outwardly unperturbed by Satanta's surprising speech. He told Satanta that he had no authority to issue arms and ammunition, but that the Great Warrior Sherman was visiting Fort Sill, and if the chiefs wished to petition Sherman for arms and ammunition they were free to do so.

While the Kiowa chiefs were debating the advisability of a council with Sherman, Tatum sent a note to General Grierson, informing him that Satanta had admitted leading the raid on the wagon train and had named other chiefs who were present. Not long after Grierson received the message and passed it on to Sherman, Satanta arrived alone at the fort's headquarters, asking to see the great soldier chief from Washington. Sherman stepped out on the wide porch, shook hands with Satanta, and told him he was summoning all the chiefs for a council.

Most of the summoned chiefs came voluntarily, but soldiers had to force old Satank to attend. Big Tree tried to run away, but was caught. Eagle Heart fled when he saw soldiers arresting the others.

As soon as the chiefs were assembled on the porch, Sherman

told them he was arresting Satanta, Satank, and Big Tree for murdering civilian teamsters in Texas. Furthermore, his soldiers would return them to Texas for trial by a court of law.

Satanta flung his blanket back and reached for his pistol, shouting in Kiowa that he would rather die than be taken as a prisoner to Texas. Sherman calmly gave a command; the shutters on the porch windows flew open, and a dozen carbines were leveled at the chiefs. The headquarters office was filled with black troopers of the Tenth Cavalry.

Kicking Bird now arose to protest. "You have asked for these men to kill them," he said. "But they are my people, and I am not going to let you have them. You and I are going to die right here." [7]

About this time a troop of mounted cavalry arrived on the scene. As they took positions along a picket fence facing the porch, Lone Wolf rode up. Ignoring the soldiers, he dismounted casually, tied his pony to the fence, and placed his two repeating carbines on the ground. He stood there for a moment tightening his pistol belt, his eyes alert, an expression of amused contempt on his face. Then he picked up his weapons and strode toward the porch. When he reached the steps he handed his pistol to the nearest chief and said loudly in Kiowa: "Make it smoke if anything happens." [8] He tossed a carbine to another chief, and then sat down on the porch floor, cocking his remaining weapon and staring impudently at the Great Warrior Sherman.

An officer called an order, and the cavalrymen brought their carbines to firing positions, hammers drawn.

Satanta threw up his hands. "No, no, no!" he shouted. [9]

Sherman calmly ordered the soldiers to lower arms.

It was June 8, in the Summer Moon, when the soldiers loaded the three chiefs into wagons for the long ride to Fort Richardson. Handcuffed and hobbled with chains, Satanta and Big Tree were shoved into one wagon, and Satank into another.

As the wagons rolled out of the fort with their cavalry escorts, old Satank began singing the death song of his Kiowa soldier society:

> O sun, you remain forever, but we Kaitsenko must die.
> O earth, you remain forever, but we Kaitsenko must die. [10]

He pointed to a tree where the road turned to cross a stream. "I shall never go beyond that tree," he shouted in Kiowa, and pulled his blanket over his head. Beneath the blanket, he tore flesh from his hands as he freed them from the manacles. He drew a concealed knife from his clothing. With a cry of desperation he leaped for the nearest guard, stabbing him and throwing him from the wagon. An instant later he had seized a carbine from one of the other startled guards. Outside, a lieutenant shouted a command to fire. A volley cut the old Kiowa down. The wagons had to be halted for an hour while the soldiers waited for Satank to die. Then they tossed his body into a ditch beside the road and resumed the journey to Texas.

The trial of Satanta and Big Tree for murder began on July 5, 1871, in the courthouse at Jacksboro, Texas. A jury of ranchers and cowboys wearing pistols in their belts listened to three days of testimony, and promptly returned a verdict of guilty. The judge sentenced the prisoners to be hanged. The governor of Texas, however, took heed of warnings that their executions might arouse the Kiowas to war, and he commuted the sentence to life imprisonment in the Huntsville Penitentiary.

Now the Kiowas had lost their three strongest leaders. During the autumn many young men slipped away in small parties to join the Indians who lived the old free life by keeping to the Staked Plains. Avoiding white hunters and settlers, they followed buffalo herds between the Red and Canadian. With the coming of the Geese-Going Moon they made winter camps in Palo Duro Canyon. The Kwahadi Comanches dominated this group of Indians, but they welcomed the growing numbers of Kiowas who came to join them.

Lone Wolf had hunted with the Kwahadis and must have given some thought to joining them, but in the early months of 1872 he was engaged in a struggle with Kicking Bird over which direction the reservation Kiowas should take. Kicking Bird and Stumbling Bear advocated following the white man's way, even though it meant abandoning the buffalo hunts in Texas. Lone Wolf opposed such talk. The Kiowas could not live without their buffalo hunts. If the white men stubbornly insisted that the Indians must hunt within the reservation, he said, then the reservation must be extended to the Rio Grande on the south and the Missouri on the north!

That Lone Wolf's vigorous arguments gained him strong support was evidenced when the Kiowas chose him over Kicking Bird and Stumbling Bear to be their principal representative on a mission to Washington. In August the Indian Bureau invited delegations from all the dissident tribes in the territory to visit Washington for a discussion of treaty obligations.

When a special commissioner, Henry Alvord, arrived at Fort Sill to conduct the Kiowa delegation to Washington, Lone Wolf informed the commissioner that he could not go to Washington until he had consulted with Satanta and Big Tree. Even though they were in a Texas prison, Satanta and Big Tree were the tribe's leaders, and no decision could be made in Washington without their advice.

Alvord was dumbfounded, but after he realized that Lone Wolf meant what he said, he began the tedious arrangements for a meeting with the imprisoned chiefs. A somewhat reluctant governor of Texas finally agreed to release his famous prisoners to temporary control of the United States Army. An extremely apprehensive cavalry commander took possession of the manacled chiefs at Dallas, Texas, on September 9 (1872) and started overland for Fort Sill. The cavalry escort was trailed by bands of armed Texans, each man eager to win glory by killing Satanta and Big Tree.

As the caravan neared Fort Sill, the acting commander there grew so agitated that he sent a civilian scout to warn the cavalry officer to take his prisoners elsewhere: "Indians here and in or about the Fort Sill Reservation . . . are sullen, ugly and warlike. . . . To bring Satanta, their principal war chief, here in irons and expect to take him back to the State Penitentiary, without trouble, probably a desperate fight, would be almost impossible. . . . I beg therefore, in spite of your positive orders to the contrary, not to bring them here on the reservation, but to take them to the present terminal of the M. K. & T. Railroad." [11]

Commissioner Alvord now had to convince the Kiowas that a meeting with Satanta and Big Tree was being arranged in the great city of St. Louis. To get there, Alvord explained, they would have to travel by wagons to a railroad and ride the Iron Horse. With an escort of warriors, the suspicious Kiowa delegation journeyed for 165 miles eastward to Atoka, Indian Territory, the terminal of the Missouri, Kansas, and Texas Railroad.

At Atoka this comic-opera affair reached its climax. Almost as soon as Alvord arrived there with Lone Wolf's delegation, he received a message from the cavalry commander that he was bringing Satanta and Big Tree to the railroad station for transfer to the commissioner's custody. Alvord was alarmed by such a prospect. The railroad terminal was a lonely place, and the commissioner feared that if Satanta should suddenly appear there, the emotional reaction might bring on an uncontrollable situation. He rushed the messenger back to the cavalry commander, begging him to keep his prisoners hidden somewhere in the blackjack thickets until he could get the Kiowa delegation started to St. Louis.

At last, on September 29, in special rooms at the Everett. House in St. Louis, Satanta and Big Tree celebrated their temporary freedom with Lone Wolf, who had made it all possible. Commissioner Alvord described the reunion as "a most impressive and affecting occasion," but he apparently did not realize that the Kiowa chiefs were conducting important business. Before Satanta and Big Tree were started back to prison, Lone Wolf knew exactly what he must accomplish on his mission to Washington.[12]

Several other Indian delegations arrived in Washington at the same time as the Kiowas—some minor Apache chiefs, a group of Arapahos, and a few Comanches. The Kwahadi Comanches, who were the real power in the tribe, would not send anybody; Ten Bears represented the Yamparika band, and Tosawi the Penatekas.

Washington officials gave the Indians a grand tour, a display of the government's military might, a Sunday sermon complete with interpreters supplied by the Methodist Church, and a reception by Great Father Ulysses Grant in the East Room of the White House. After everyone had exchanged flowery speeches filled with the usual blandishments, the Commissioner of Indian Affairs, Francis Walker, arranged to address the Kiowas and Comanches together. He delivered a surprising ultimatum: "First, the Kiowas and Comanches here represented must, before the fifteenth of December next, camp every chief, head man, brave, and family complete within ten miles of Fort Sill and the agency; they must remain there until spring, without giving any trouble, and shall not then leave unless with the consent of their agent." [13] He went on to say that the Kwahadi Comanches and other bands who had declined to send representatives to Washington would soon hear that United States troops had been directed to operate against them. Furthermore, every Indian not camped within ten miles of Fort Sill by December 15 would be considered an enemy of the United States government, and soldiers would kill them wherever they were found.

Ten Bears and Tosawi replied that their Comanche bands would do what the Great Father wanted them to do, but Lone Wolf expressed doubt that he could enforce such an ultimatum on all the Kiowas. Satanta and Big Tree, he explained, were the war chiefs of the tribe, and as long as the Texans kept them in prison, many of the young warriors would be bound to carry on a war with the Texans. Peace could be obtained only if Satanta and Big Tree were given their freedom and returned to the reservation, where they could keep the young men from raiding in Texas.

This condition, of course, was what had been decided upon in that "most impressive and affecting occasion" of the Kiowa chieftains' reunion in St. Louis. Lone Wolf's maneuver was worthy of a trained diplomat, and although Commissioner Walker had no authority to order the governor of Texas to release Satanta and Big Tree, he finally had to promise to free the chiefs before Lone Wolf would agree to obey his ultimatum. Furthermore, Lone Wolf set a deadline for the release—no later than the end of the next Bud Moon and the beginning of the Leaf Moon, or about the end of March, 1873.

One effect of the Washington visit was the complete alienation of Ten Bears from the Comanches. While Lone Wolf returned to the reservation as a hero, Ten Bears was virtually ignored. Ailing and exhausted, the old poet of the Plains gave up and died on November 23, 1872. "With the exception of his son," said the agency schoolmaster, Thomas Battey, "his people had all left him." [14]

Meanwhile, on the Staked Plains, as Commissioner Walker

21. *Ten Bears of the Comanches. Photographed by Alexander Gardner in Washington, D.C., 1872. Courtesy of the Smithsonian Institution.*

had warned, the Army began searching out the free Kwahadi Comanches. From Fort Richardson, the Fourth Cavalry prowled through the upper forks of Red River. These pony soldiers were led by Ranald Mackenzie, a wiry, irascible, mutton-chopped Eagle Chief. The Comanches called him Mangoheute, Three Fingers. (He had lost his index finger in the Civil War.) On September 29, along McClellan's Creek, Three Fingers' scouts discovered a large Comanche village, Bull Bear's people. The Indians were busily drying meat in preparation for winter. Charging in at a gallop, the troopers overran the village, killed twenty-three Comanches, captured 120 women and children, and took almost the entire herd, more than a thousand ponies. After burning the 262 lodges, Mackenzie moved back downstream and made a night camp. In the meantime, the hundreds of warriors who had escaped the attack had walked to a neighboring Comanche village. With borrowed ponies and fresh reinforcements they made a surprise night attack on the cavalrymen. "We got all our horses back and some of the soldiers' too," one of the warriors said afterward.[15] But they could not rescue the captive women and children, and after Mackenzie took them to Fort Sill, Bull Bear and a number of other Kwahadis came to the reservation in order to be with their families. The main force of Kwahadis, however, still roamed free with the buffalo, continued to gain recruits from other southwestern tribes, and under the leadership of a twenty-seven-year-old half-breed, Quanah Parker, was more implacable than ever.

With the first signs of spring in 1873, the Kiowas began preparing for a big celebration to welcome back Satanta and Big Tree. All winter long, Bald Head Tatum had used his influence to block release of the chiefs, but the Commissioner of Indian Affairs overruled him. Tatum resigned, and James Haworth came to replace him. When the Bud Moon passed and the calendar was well into the Leaf Moon, Lone Wolf began to talk of a war with the Texans if they refused to free the chiefs. Kicking Bird urged the warriors to be patient; the governor of Texas was having trouble with the Indian-hating settlers. At last, in the Moon of Deer Horns Dropping Off (August), officials from Washington arranged for Satanta and Big Tree to be transferred

22. *White Horse, or Tsen-tainte. Photographed by William S. Soule in 1870. Courtesy of the Smithsonian Institution.*

to Fort Sill as prisoners. Not long afterward the governor of Texas himself arrived for a grand council.

On the day of the council Satanta and Big Tree were allowed to be present under a soldier guard. The governor opened the proceedings by telling the Kiowas they must settle down on farms near the agency. They must draw their rations and answer to a roll call every three days, they must stop their young men from raiding in Texas, they must give up their arms and ponies and raise corn like civilized Indians. "In the meantime," he continued, "Satanta and Big Tree are to remain in the guardhouse until the commanding officer at Fort Sill is satisfied that these conditions are carried out."

Lone Wolf was the first to speak: "You have already made our hearts good by bringing back these prisoners. Make them still better by releasing them today."

But the governor would not yield. "I will not change these conditions," he said, and the council ended.[16]

Lone Wolf was bitterly disappointed. The conditions were too harsh, and the chiefs were still prisoners. "I want peace," he told Thomas Battey, the schoolmaster. "I have worked hard for it. Washington has deceived me—has failed to keep faith with me and my people—has broken his promises; and now there is nothing left us but war. I know that war with Washington means the extinction of my people, but we are driven to it; we had rather die than live."

Even Kicking Bird was offended by the governor's demands. "My heart is as a stone; there is no soft spot in it. I have taken the white man by the hand, thinking him to be a friend, but he is not a friend; government has deceived us; Washington is rotten." [17]

Battey and the new agent, Haworth, both realized that bloodshed, possibly open war, was likely if the governor did not make a gesture of goodwill by releasing Satanta and Big Tree from the guardhouse. They went to the governor, explained the situation to him, and firmly persuaded him to relent. Late that night the governor sent a message to Lone Wolf and the other chiefs, asking them to meet with him the next morning. The Kiowas agreed, but they made up their minds before daybreak that they would listen to no more broken promises. They came to the meeting fully armed, with warriors placed near the guardhouse and fast horses ready for flight.

None of this was lost on the governor of Texas. He kept his speech short, saying that he was sure the Kiowas would keep their part of the bargain, and then announced that he was paroling Satanta and Big Tree over to their agent. They were free men. Lone Wolf had won another bloodless victory.

In the Moon When the Leaves Fall Off, Satanta moved into his red-painted tepee with its red streamers waving from the ends of the poles above the smoke holes. He gave his red medicine lance to his old friend White Cowbird, and said he had no desire to be a chief anymore. He wanted only to be free and happy, to roam over the prairies. But he kept his word and stayed close to the agency, and did not slip away that autumn to hunt buffalo with the young men on the Staked Plains.

In the Geese-Going Moon some white thieves from Texas raided the Kiowa and Comanche horse herds and stole two hundred of their finest ponies. A party of warriors went in pursuit, but recovered only a few animals before the Texan thieves crossed Red River.

A short time after that a group of nine young Kiowas and twenty-one Comanches decided to go south after horses to replace the stolen ones. Not wishing to cause trouble for Satanta and Big Tree by raiding Texan horses, they headed for Mexico. Keeping away from settlements, they rode swiftly for five hundred miles and crossed the Rio Grande between Eagle Pass and Laredo. In Mexico they raided ranches until they collected about the same number of horses the Texans had stolen from them. But they had to kill some Mexicans in order to take the horses, and on the way back they killed two Texans who tried to stop them. Then the Bluecoats came in hot pursuit, and during a running fight not far from Fort Clark nine of the young Indians were killed. Among them were Tauankia and Guitan, the son and nephew of Lone Wolf.

It was midwinter when the survivors returned to Fort Sill. The Kiowas and Comanches went into mourning over the loss of their bravest young men. In his grief for his son, Lone Wolf cut off his hair, burned his tepee, slew his horses, and swore revenge upon the Texans.

As soon as the grass greened on the prairies in the spring of 1874, Lone Wolf organized a party to go deep into Texas to recover the bodies of Tauankia and Guitan. Because they were watched so closely on the reservation, the Kiowas could not keep the expedition a secret, and they had scarcely crossed Red River before columns of Bluecoats were riding to intercept them—from forts Concho, McKavett, and Clark. Somehow Lone Wolf managed to elude all his pursuers. His party reached the burial place, recovered the bodies of his son and nephew, and swung northward toward the Staked Plains. A troop of cavalry, however, came so close upon them that Lone Wolf was forced to rebury the bodies on the side of a mountain. Breaking up into small parties, the Kiowas took flight across the Staked Plains. Most of them reached Red River in time to hear about a very special sun dance that was being held on Elk Creek.

For many years the Kiowas had been inviting their Comanche friends to attend their sun dances, but the Comanches had always come as spectators and had never held such a ceremony of their own. In that spring of 1874 they invited the Kiowas to come to their first sun dance and help them decide what should be done about the white buffalo hunters who were destroying the herds out on the Staked Plains. Kicking Bird refused to accept the invitation. He had heard that the Kwahadis had organized the sun dance, and as they were considered hostile to the government, Kicking Bird convinced his followers to stay in their camps and wait until July for their own sun dance. Lone Wolf, however, still grieving over the death of his son and angry at the white men for refusing to even let him bring the boy's bones back for a proper burial, decided to lead his followers to the Comanche sun dance. Satanta went along with him; the paroled chief could see no harm in attending a Comanche ceremony within the reservation boundary; it was the courteous thing to do.

The Kwahadis arrived on Elk Creek in force, riding in from the Staked Plains with bad news about the buffalo herds. White hunters and skinners were everywhere; the stench of rotting carcasses fouled the very winds of the Plains; like the Indians, the great herds were being driven into the ground.

(Of the 3,700,000 buffalo destroyed from 1872 through 1874, only 150,000 were killed by Indians. When a group of concerned Texans asked General Sheridan if something should not be done to stop the white hunters' wholesale slaughter, he replied: "Let them kill, skin, and sell until the buffalo is exterminated, as it is the only way to bring lasting peace and allow civilization to advance." [18])

The free Kwahadis wanted no part of a civilization that advanced by exterminating useful animals. At the Comanche sun dance, a Kwahadi prophet named Isatai spoke for a war to save the buffalo. Isatai was a man of great magic; it was said that he could vomit wagonloads of ammunition from his belly, and that he had the power to stop the white men's bullets in mid-flight.

Quanah Parker, the young war chief of the Kwahadis, also spoke for a war to drive the white hunters from the grazing grounds. He suggested that they strike first at the hunters' base, a trading post near the Canadian River known as Adobe Walls.

Before the sun dance ended, a party of Cheyennes and Arapahos arrived from their reservation in the north. They were very angry because some white horse thieves had stolen fifty of their best mustangs. They suspected the thieves might be buffalo hunters. When they heard about Quanah's plan to attack the white hunters at Adobe Walls, they decided to join the Kwahadis. Lone Wolf and Satanta and their Kiowa warriors also volunteered to fight. To their minds, the urgency to save the buffalo from extermination was a much more important matter than obeying petty reservation rules. After all, were not the hunters intruding upon buffalo ranges reserved by treaty for exclusive use of Indians? If the soldiers would not drive the hunters away as they were supposed to do, then the Indians must do it.

Altogether seven hundred warriors rode westward from Elk Creek in the waning Summer Moon. Along the way Isatai made medicine and reassured the warriors. "Those white men can't shoot you," he said. "With my medicine I will stop all their guns. When you charge, you will wipe them all out." [19]

Before sunrise on June 27, the warriors rode up close to Adobe
Walls and made preparations for one mighty charge that would
wipe out every buffalo hunter in the supply base. "We charged
pretty fast on our horses, throwing up dust high," Quanah
Parker said afterward. Prairie-dog holes dotted the ground, and
some of the ponies caught their hooves in them, falling and rolling with their painted riders. The Indians found two hunters
trying to escape in a wagon, and they killed and scalped both
of them. The gunfire and thundering hooves alerted the white
men inside the adobes, and they opened up with their long-range
buffalo rifles. The Indians pulled away and then began their
traditional circling attack, individual warriors darting in to hurl
lances or to fire through windows.

"I got up to the adobe houses with another Comanche,"
Quanah said. "We poked holes through roof to shoot." [20] Several
times the Indians withdrew to make new charges, hoping to
force the hunters to expend all their ammunition. In one of
these charges Quanah's horse was shot from under him, and as
he tried to take cover, a bullet creased his shoulder. He crawled
into a plum thicket and was later rescued.

"The buffalo hunters were too much for us," one of the Comanche warriors admitted. "They stood behind adobe walls.
They had telescopes on their guns. . . . One of our men was
knocked off his horse by a spent bullet fired at a range of about
a mile. It stunned but did not kill him." [21]

Early in the afternoon the attackers withdrew out of range
of the powerful buffalo rifles. Fifteen warriors were dead; many
more were badly wounded. They turned their rage and frustration against Isatai, who had promised them protection from
the white men's bullets and a great victory. An angry Cheyenne
lashed Isatai with his quirt, and several other braves came up
to join in, but Quanah stopped the flogging. Isatai's disgrace
was punishment enough, he said. From that day, Quanah Parker
never again put his trust in a medicine man.

After the chiefs gave up the useless siege of Adobe Walls,
Lone Wolf and Satanta took their warriors back to the North
Fork of Red River to attend the Kiowa sun dance. They of
course invited their Comanche and Cheyenne friends to come
along. That summer the main feature of the Kiowa ceremonies

23. *Quanah Parker of the Comanches. Photographed by Hutchins and/or Lanney on the Kiowa reservation (for Kiowas, Comanches, and Kiowa-Apaches) in Oklahoma between 1891 and 1893. Courtesy of the Smithsonian Institution.*

was a celebration of the return of Satanta and Big Tree to the reservation. The Kwahadis and the Cheyennes chided the reservation people for celebrating while their buffalo herds were being rubbed out by invading white hunters. They urged all the Kiowas to come and join them in a war to save the buffalo.

Kicking Bird would listen to none of their arguments. As soon as the sun dance ended, he started his followers hurrying back toward the agency. Lone Wolf and his followers, however, were convinced that their duty lay with the determined Kwahadis.

This time Satanta did not join Lone Wolf. Deciding that he had pushed his luck far enough, the gregarious, action-loving chief reluctantly turned back toward Fort Sill. On the way he took his family and a few friends down Rainy Mountain Creek to visit the Wichita reservation to do some trading with those corn-growing Indians. It was a pleasant summer, and he was in no hurry to return to Fort Sill to start answering roll calls and drawing rations.

Out on the Plains later that summer it seemed that everything had turned bad. Day after day the sun baked the dry earth drier, the streams stopped running, great whirlwinds of grasshoppers were flung out of the metallic sky to consume the parched grass. If such a season had come upon this land a few years earlier, a thunder of a million buffalo hooves would have shaken the prairie in frantic stampedes for water. But now the herds were gone, replaced by an endless desolation of bones and skulls and rotting hooves. Most of the white hunters departed. Bands of Comanches, Kiowas, Cheyennes, and Arapahos roamed restlessly, finding a few small herds, but many had to return to their reservations to keep from starving.

At the agencies everything was in turmoil. The Army and the Indian Bureau were at cross-purposes. Supplies failed to arrive. Some agents withheld rations to punish the Indians for roving without permission. Here and there outbreaks occurred; shots were exchanged between warriors and soldiers. By mid-July half the Kiowas and Comanches registered at the Fort Sill agency were gone. As though by some mystical power, these last tribes to live by the buffalo were drawn to the heart of the last buffalo range, the Place of Chinaberry Trees, Palo Duro Canyon.

The Palo Duro was invisible from the flat horizon, a curving chasm slashed into the Plains, an oasis of springs and waterfalls and streams that kept its willows and buffalo grass green and lush. The canyon could be entered only by a few trails beaten out by buffalo herds. Coronado had visited there in the sixteenth century, but only a few white men had seen it since or knew of its existence.

All through the late summer of 1874 Indians and buffalo sought sanctuary there. The Indians killed only enough animals to supply their needs for winter—stripping the meat carefully to dry in the sun, storing marrow and fat in skins, treating the sinews for bowstrings and thread, making spoons and cups of the horns, weaving the hair into ropes and belts, curing the hides for tepee covers, clothing, and moccasins.

Before the beginning of the Yellow Leaves Moon, the floor of the canyon along the creek was a forest of tepees—Kiowa, Comanche, and Cheyenne—all well stocked with food to last until spring. Almost two thousand horses shared the rich grass with the buffalo. Without fear, the women went about their tasks and the children played along the streams. For Quanah and the Kwahadis this was the way they had always lived; for Lone Wolf and the Kiowas and the other agency fugitives this was a beginning of life all over again.

Such defiance of the white man's way was of course intolerable to authorities on the emptying reservations. The implacable Kwahadis and their allies had scarcely settled into their hidden villages for winter when the Great Warrior Sherman began issuing military orders. In September five columns of Bluecoats were in motion. From Fort Dodge, Bear Coat Nelson Miles struck southward; from Fort Concho, Three Fingers Mackenzie marched northward. From Fort Bascom, New Mexico, Major William Price moved eastward; from forts Sill and Richardson came colonels John Davidson and George Buell. Thousands of Bluecoats armed with repeating rifles and artillery were in search of a few hundred Indians who wanted only to save their buffalo and live out their lives in freedom.

Using mercenary Tonkawa scouts, Mackenzie's pony soldiers found the great Palo Duro village on September 26. Lone Wolf's Kiowas bore the fury of the first assault. Although caught by surprise, the warriors held long enough for their women and children to escape, and they then retreated under a cloud of dense powder smoke. Mackenzie's troopers stormed up the creek, burning tepees and destroying the Indians' winter supplies. By the end of the day they rounded up more than a thousand ponies. Mackenzie ordered the animals driven into Tule Valley, and there the Bluecoats slaughtered them, a thousand dead horses left to the circling buzzards.

Across the Plains the Indians scattered on foot, without food, clothing, or shelter. And the thousands of Bluecoats marching from the four directions methodically hunted them down, the columns crossing and crisscrossing, picking up the wounded Indians first, then the aged, then the women and children.

Lone Wolf and 252 Kiowas managed to avoid capture, but at last they could run no more. On February 25, 1875, they came into Fort Sill and surrendered. Three months later Quanah brought in the Kwahadis.

In this turmoil of military action the paroled chiefs, Satanta and Big Tree, fled the reservation. When they reached the Cheyenne agency they surrendered voluntarily, but were shackled in irons and placed in the guardhouse.

At Fort Sill each surrendering band of Indians was herded into a corral, where soldiers disarmed them. What little property they carried was piled into a heap and burned. Their horses and mules were driven out upon the prairie and shot. Chiefs and warriors suspected of responsibility for leaving the reservation were locked in cells or were confined behind the high walls of an unroofed icehouse. Each day their captors threw chunks of raw meat to them as if they were animals in a cage.

From Washington, the Great Warrior Sherman ordered trials and punishments for the captives. Agent Haworth requested leniency for Satanta and Big Tree. Sherman had nothing in his heart against Big Tree, but he remembered the defiance of Satanta, and it was Satanta who had to return alone to the Texas penitentiary.

Because the military authorities could not decide which of their many prisoners to punish, they ordered Kicking Bird to select twenty-six Kiowas for exile to the dungeons of Fort Marion, Florida. Repugnant as the task was, Kicking Bird obeyed.

He knew that Lone Wolf would have to go, Woman's Heart and White Horse, and Mamanti the Sky Walker, because of their fighting in Texas. For the remainder of the quota, he chose obscure warriors and a few Mexican captives who had grown up with the tribe.

Even so, Kicking Bird's part in the judgment of his tribesmen lost him the support of his followers. "I am as a stone, broken and thrown away," he told Thomas Battey sadly. "One part thrown this way, and one part thrown that way." [22]

On the day the chained prisoners were being loaded into wagons for the start of their long journey to Florida, Kicking Bird rode out to say good-bye to them. "I am sorry for you," he said. "But because of your stubbornness, I have failed to keep you out of trouble. You will have to be punished by the government. Take your medicine. It will not be for long. I love you and will work for your release."

Mamanti the Sky Walker answered him scornfully: "You remain free, a big man with the whites. But you will not live long, Kicking Bird. I will see to that." [23]

Two days later, after drinking a cup of coffee in his lodge near the post, Kicking Bird died mysteriously. Three months later, at Fort Marion, after learning of the death of Kicking Bird, Mamanti also died suddenly, and the Kiowas said the medicine man had willed his own death because he had used his power to destroy a fellow tribesman. Three years later, wasting away in a prison hospital in Texas, Satanta threw himself from a high window to find release in death. That same year, Lone Wolf, racked by malarial fever, was permitted to return to Fort Sill, but he also was dead within a year.

The great leaders were gone; the mighty power of the Kiowas and Comanches was broken; the buffalo they had tried to save had vanished. It had all happened in less than ten years.

TWELVE

The War for the Black Hills

1875—May 1, indictments brought against 238 members of Whiskey Ring; charged with defrauding Treasury of Internal Revenue taxes; high government officials involved. December 6, 44th Congress convenes; Democrats control House of Representatives for first time since 1859.

1876—February 7, President Grant's private secretary, Orville Babcock, acquitted for complicity in Whiskey Ring frauds, but Grant dismisses him from office. March 4, U.S. Congress resolves to impeach Secretary of War Belknap for complicity in Indian Ring frauds. May 10, Centennial Exhibition opens in Philadelphia. June 11, Republicans nominate Rutherford B. Hayes for President. June 27, Democrats nominate Samuel J. Tilden for President. July 9, massacre of Negro militiamen in Hamburg, South Carolina. August 1, Colorado admitted to Union as thirty-eighth state. September, Thomas Edison establishes laboratory at Menlo Park, New Jersey. September 17, race war breaks out in South Carolina. November 7, both political parties claim victory in presidential election; Tilden is winner in popular vote. December 6, Electoral College meets and gives Hayes 185 electoral votes, Tilden 184.

No white person or persons shall be permitted to settle upon or occupy any portion of the territory, or without the consent of the Indians to pass through the same.
—TREATY OF 1868

We want no white men here. The Black Hills belong to me. If the whites try to take them, I will fight.
—TATANKA YOTANKA (SITTING BULL)

One does not sell the earth upon which the people walk.
—TASHUNKA WITKO (CRAZY HORSE)

The white man is in the Black Hills just like maggots, and I want you to get them out just as quick as you can. The chief of all thieves [General Custer] made a road into the Black Hills last summer, and I want the Great Father to pay the damages for what Custer has done.
—BAPTISTE GOOD

The land known as the Black Hills is considered by the Indians as the center of their land. The ten nations of Sioux are looking toward that as the center of their land.
—TATOKE INYANKE (RUNNING ANTELOPE)

The Great Father's young men are going to carry gold away from the hills. I expect they will fill a number of houses with it. In consideration of this I want my people to be provided for as long as they shall live.
—MATO NOUPA (TWO BEARS)

The Great Father told the commissioners that all the Indians had rights in the Black Hills, and that whatever conclusion the Indians themselves should come to would be respected. . . . I am an Indian and am looked on by the whites as a foolish man; but it must be because I follow the advice of the white man.
—SHUNKA WITKO (FOOL DOG)

Our Great Father has a big safe, and so have we. The hill is our safe. . . . We want seventy million dollars for the Black Hills. Put the money away some place at interest so we can buy livestock. That is the way the white people do.
—MATO GLESKA (SPOTTED BEAR)

You have put all our heads together and covered them with a blanket. That hill there is our wealth, but you have been asking it from us. . . . You white people, you have all come in our reservation and helped yourselves to our property, and you are not satisfied, you went beyond to take the whole of our safe.
—DEAD EYES

I never want to leave this country; all my relatives are lying here in the ground, and when I fall to pieces I am going to fall to pieces here.
—SHUNKAHA NAPIN (WOLF NECKLACE)

We have sat and watched them pass here to get gold out and have said nothing. . . . My friends, when I went to Washington I went into your money-house and I had some young men with me, but none of them took any money out of that house while I was with them. At the same time, when your Great Father's people come into my country, they go into my money-house [the Black Hills] and take money out.

—MAWATANI HANSKA (LONG MANDAN)

My friends, for many years we have been in this country; we never go to the Great Father's country and bother him about anything. It is his people who come to our country and bother us, do many bad things and teach our people to be bad. . . . Before you people ever crossed the ocean to come to this country, and from that time to this, you have never proposed to buy a country that was equal to this in riches. My friends, this country that you have come to buy is the best country that we have . . . this country is mine, I was raised in it; my forefathers lived and died in it; and I wish to remain in it.

—KANGI WIYAKA (CROW FEATHER)

You have driven away our game and our means of livelihood out of the country, until now we have nothing left that is valuable except the hills that you ask us to give up. . . . The earth is full of minerals of all kinds, and on the earth the ground is covered with forests of heavy pine, and when we give these up to the Great Father we know that we give up the last thing that is valuable either to us or the white people.

—WANIGI SKA (WHITE GHOST)

When the prairie is on fire you see animals surrounded by the fire; you see them run and try to hide themselves so that they will not burn. That is the way we are here.

—NAJINYANUPI (SURROUNDED)

NOT LONG after Red Cloud and Spotted Tail and their Teton peoples settled down on their reservations in northwestern Nebraska, rumors began to fly among the white settlements that immense amounts of gold were hidden in the Black Hills. *Paha Sapa,* the Black Hills, was the center of the world, the place of gods and holy mountains, where warriors went to speak with the Great Spirit and await visions. In 1868 the Great Father considered the hills worthless and gave them to the Indians forever by treaty. Four years later white miners were violating the treaty. They invaded *Paha Sapa,* searching the rocky passes and clear-running streams for the yellow metal which, drove white men crazy. When Indians found these crazy white men in their sacred hills, they killed them or chased them out. By 1874 there was such a mad clamor from gold-hungry Americans that the Army was ordered to make a reconnaissance into the Black Hills. The United States government did not bother to obtain consent from the Indians before starting on this armed invasion, although the treaty of 1868 prohibited entry of white men without the Indians' permission.

During the Moon of Red Cherries, more than a thousand pony soldiers marched across the Plains from Fort Abraham Lincoln to the Black Hills. They were the Seventh Cavalry, and at their head rode General George Armstrong Custer, the same Star Chief who in 1868 had slaughtered Black Kettle's Southern Cheyennes on the Washita. The Sioux called him Pahuska, the Long Hair, and because they had no warning of his coming, they could only watch from afar as the long columns of blue-uniformed cavalrymen and canvas-covered supply wagons invaded their sacred country.

When Red Cloud heard about the Long Hair's expedition, he protested: "I do not like General Custer and all his soldiers going into the Black Hills, as that is the country of the Oglala Sioux." It was also the country of the Cheyennes, Arapahos, and other Sioux tribes. The anger of the Indians was strong enough that the Great Father, Ulysses Grant, announced his determination "to prevent all invasion of this country by intruders so long as by law and treaty it is secured to the Indians."[1]

But when Custer reported that the hills were filled with gold "from the grass roots down," parties of white men began forming like summer locusts, crazy to begin panning and digging. The trail that Custer's supply wagons had cut into the heart of *Paha Sapa* soon became the Thieves' Road.

Red Cloud was having trouble that summer with his reservation agent, J. J. Saville, over the poor quality of rations and supplies being issued to the Oglalas. Preoccupied as he was, Red Cloud failed to assess the full impact upon the Sioux of Custer's intrusion into the Black Hills, especially upon those who left the reservations every spring to hunt and camp near the hills. Like many other aging leaders, Red Cloud was too much involved with petty details, and he was losing touch with the younger tribesmen.

In the autumn following Custer's expedition, the Sioux who had been hunting in the north began returning to the Red Cloud agency. They were angry as hornets over the invasion of *Paha Sapa*, and some talked of forming a war party to go back after the miners who were pouring into the hills. Red Cloud listened to the talk, but advised the young men to be patient; he was sure the Great Father would keep his promise and send soldiers to drive out the miners. In the Moon of Falling Leaves, however, something happened that made Red Cloud realize just how angry his young men were at the Long Hair's soldiers. On October 22 agent Saville sent some of his white workmen to cut a tall pine and bring the trunk back to the stockade. When the Indians saw the pine pole lying on the ground they asked Saville what it was to be used for. A flagpole, the agent told them; he was going to fly a flag over the stockade. The Indians protested. Long Hair Custer had flown flags in his camps across the Black Hills; they wanted no flags or anything else in their agency to remind them of soldiers.

Saville paid no attention to the protests, and next morning he put his men to work digging a hole for the flagpole. In a few minutes a band of young warriors came with axes and began chopping the pole to pieces. Saville ordered them to stop, but they paid no attention to him, and the agent strode across to Red

Cloud's office and begged him to stop the warriors. Red Cloud refused; he knew the warriors were only expressing their rancor over the Long Hair's invasion of the Black Hills.

Infuriated, Saville now ordered one of his workmen to ride to the Soldiers' Town (Fort Robinson) and request a company of cavalrymen to come to his aid. When the demonstrating warriors saw the man riding toward the fort, they guessed his mission. They rushed for their tepee camps, armed and painted themselves for battle, and went to intercept the cavalrymen. There were only twenty-six Bluecoats led by a lieutenant; the warriors encircled them, fired their guns into the air, and yelled a few war cries. The lieutenant (Emmet Crawford) betrayed no fear. Through the great cloud of dust thrown up by the milling warriors, he kept his men moving steadily toward the agency. Some of the younger warriors began riding in close, colliding their ponies with the troopers' mounts, determined to precipitate a fight.

This time it was not another troop of cavalry which came galloping to Lieutenant Crawford's rescue, but a band of agency Sioux led by Young-Man-Afraid-of-His-Horses, son of Old-Man-Afraid. The agency Indians broke through the ring of warriors, formed a protective wall around the Bluecoats, and escorted them on to the stockade. The belligerent warriors were still so angry, however, that they tried to burn down the stockade, and only the persuasive oratory of Red Dog and Old-Man-Afraid-of-His-Horses stopped the demonstration.

Again Red Cloud refused to interfere. He was not surprised when many of the protesters packed up, dismantled their tepees, and started back north to spend the winter off the reservation. They had proved to him that there were still Sioux warriors who would never take lightly any invasion of *Paha Sapa,* yet apparently Red Cloud did not realize that he was losing these young men forever. They had rejected his leadership for that of Sitting Bull and Crazy Horse, neither of whom had ever lived on a reservation or taken the white man's handouts.

By the spring of 1875, tales of Black Hills gold had brought hundreds of miners up the Missouri River and out upon the Thieves' Road. The Army sent soldiers to stop the flow of prospectors. A few were removed from the hills, but no legal action was taken against them, and they soon returned to prospect their claims. General Crook (the Plains Indians called him Three Stars instead of Gray Wolf) made a reconnaissance of the Black Hills, and found more than a thousand miners in the area. Three Stars politely informed them that they were violating the law and ordered them to leave, but he made no effort to enforce his orders.

Alarmed by the white men's gold craze and the Army's failure to protect their territory, Red Cloud and Spotted Tail made strong protests to Washington officials. The Great Father's response was to send out a commission "to treat with the Sioux Indians for the relinquishment of the Black Hills." In other words, the time had come to take away one more piece of territory that had been assigned to the Indians in perpetuity. As usual, the commission was made up of politicians, missionaries, traders, and military officers. Senator William B. Allison of Iowa was the chairman. Reverend Samuel D. Hinman, who had long endeavored to replace the Santees' religion and culture with Christianity, was the principal missionary. General Alfred Terry represented the military. John Collins, post trader at Fort Laramie, represented the commercial interests.

To ensure representation of nonagency as well as agency Indians, runners were sent to invite Sitting Bull, Crazy Horse, and other "wild" chiefs to the council. Half-breed Louis Richard took the government letter to Sitting Bull and read it to him. "I want you to go and tell the Great Father," Sitting Bull responded, "that I do not want to sell any land to the government." He picked up a pinch of dust and added: "Not even as much as this." [2] Crazy Horse was also opposed to the selling of Sioux land, especially the Black Hills. He refused to attend the council, but Little Big Man would go as an observer for the free Oglalas.

If the commissioners expected to meet quietly with a few compliant chiefs and arrange an inexpensive trade, they were in for a rude surprise. When they arrived at the meeting place—on White River between the Red Cloud and Spotted Tail agencies —the Plains for miles around were covered with Sioux camps and immense herds of grazing ponies. From the Missouri River on the east to the Bighorn country on the west, all the nations of the Sioux and many of their Cheyenne and Arapaho friends had gathered there—more than twenty thousand Indians.

Few of them had ever seen a copy of the treaty of 1868, but a goodly number knew the meaning of a certain clause in that sacred document: "No treaty for the cession of any part of the reservation herein described . . . shall be of any validity or force . . . unless executed and signed by at least *three-fourths of all the adult male Indians,* occupying or interested in the same." [3] Even if the commissioners had been able to intimidate or buy off every chief present, they could not have obtained more than a few dozen signatures from those thousands of angry, well-armed warriors who were determined to keep every pinch of dust and blade of grass within their territory.

On September 20, 1875, the commission assembled under the shade of a large tarpaulin which had been strung beside a lone cottonwood on the rolling plain. The commissioners seated themselves on chairs facing the thousands of Indians who were moving restlessly about in the distance. A troop of 120 cavalrymen on white horses filed in from Fort Robinson and drew up in a line behind the canvas shelter. Spotted Tail arrived in a wagon from his agency, but Red Cloud had announced that he would not be there. A few other chiefs drifted in, and then suddenly a cloud of dust boiled up from the crest of a distant rise. A band of Indians came galloping down upon the council shelter. The warriors were dressed for battle, and as they came nearer they swerved to encircle the commissioners, fired their rifles skyward, and gave out a few whoops before trotting off to form a line immediately in the rear of the cavalrymen. By this time a second band of Indians was approaching, and thus tribe by tribe the Sioux warriors came in, making their demonstrations of power, until a great circle of several thousand Indians enclosed the council. Now the chiefs came forward, well satisfied that they had given the commissioners something strong to think about. They sat in a semicircle facing the nervous white men, eager to hear what they would have to say about the Black Hills.

During the few days that the commissioners had been at Fort Robinson observing the mood of the Indians, they recognized the futility of trying to buy the hills and had decided instead to negotiate for the mineral rights. "We have now to ask you

24. *Sitting Bull.*
Photo from the U.S. Signal Corps.

if you are willing to give our people the right to mine in the
Black Hills," Senator Allison began, "as long as gold or other
valuable minerals are found, for a fair and just sum. If you are
so willing, we will make a bargain with you for this right. When
the gold or other valuable minerals are taken away, the country will again be yours to dispose of in any manner you may
wish."

Spotted Tail took this proposal as a ludicrous joke. Was the
commissioner asking the Indians to *lend* the Black Hills to the
white men for a while? His rejoinder was to ask Senator Allison
if he would lend him a team of mules on such terms.

"It will be hard for our government to keep the whites out
of the hills," Allison continued. "To try to do so will give you
and our government great trouble, because the whites that may
wish to go there are very numerous." The senator's ignorance
of the Plains Indians' feeling for the Powder River country was
displayed in his next proposal: "There is another country lying
far toward the setting sun, over which you roam and hunt, and
which territory is yet unceded, extending to the summit of the
Bighorn Mountains. . . . It does not seem to be of very great
value or use to you, and our people think they would like to
have the portion of it I have described." [4]

While Senator Allison's incredible demands were being translated, Red Dog rode up on a pony and announced that he had
a message from Red Cloud. The absent Oglala chief, probably
anticipating the greed of the commissioners, requested a week's
recess to give the tribes time to hold councils of their own in
which to consider all proposals concerning their lands. The commissioners considered the matter and agreed to give the Indians
three days for holding tribal councils. On September 23 they
would expect definite replies from the chiefs.

The idea of giving up their last great hunting ground was so
preposterous that none of the chiefs even discussed it during
their councils. They did debate very earnestly the question of
the Black Hills. Some reasoned that if the United States government had no intention of enforcing the treaty and keeping
the white miners out, then perhaps the Indians should demand
payment—a great deal of money—for the yellow metal taken

from the hills. Others were determined not to sell at any price. The Black Hills belonged to the Indians, they argued; if the Bluecoat soldiers would not drive out the miners, then the warriors must.

On September 23 the commissioners, riding in Army ambulances from Fort Robinson and escorted by a somewhat enlarged cavalry troop, again arrived at the council shelter. Red Cloud was there early, and he protested vigorously about the large number of soldiers. Just as he was preparing to give his preliminary speech to the commissioners, a sudden commotion broke out among the warriors far in the distance. About three hundred Oglalas who had come in from the Powder River country trotted their ponies down a slope, occasionally firing off rifles. Some were chanting a song in Sioux:

> The Black Hills is my land and I love it
> And whoever interferes
> Will hear this gun.[5]

An Indian mounted on a gray horse forced his way through the ranks of warriors gathered around the canvas shelter. He was Crazy Horse's envoy, Little Big Man, stripped for battle and wearing two revolvers belted to his waist. "I will kill the first chief who speaks for selling the Black Hills!" he shouted. He danced his horse across the open space between the commissioners and the chiefs.[6]

Young-Man-Afraid-of-His-Horses and a group of unofficial Sioux policemen immediately swarmed around Little Big Man and moved him away. The chiefs and the commissioners, however, must have guessed that Little Big Man voiced the feelings of most of the warriors present. General Terry suggested to his fellow commissioners that they board the Army ambulances and return to the safety of Fort Robinson.

After giving the Indians a few days to calm down, the commissioners quietly arranged a meeting with twenty chiefs in the headquarters building of the Red Cloud agency. During three days of speech making, the chiefs made it quite clear to the Great Father's representatives that the Black Hills could not be bought cheaply, if at any price. Spotted Tail finally grew impatient with the commissioners and asked them to submit a definite proposal in writing.

The offer was four hundred thousand dollars a year for the mineral rights; or if the Sioux wished to sell the hills outright the price would be six million dollars payable in fifteen annual installments. (This was a markdown price indeed, considering that one Black Hills mine alone yielded more than five hundred million dollars in gold.)

Red Cloud did not even appear for the final meeting, letting Spotted Tail speak for all the Sioux. Spotted Tail rejected both offers, firmly. The Black Hills were not for lease or for sale.

The commissioners packed up, returned to Washington, reported their failure to persuade the Sioux to relinquish the Black Hills, and recommended that Congress disregard the wishes of the Indians and appropriate a sum fixed "as a fair equivalent of the value of the hills." This forced purchase of the Black Hills should be "presented to the Indians as a finality," they said.[7]

Thus was set in motion a chain of actions which would bring the greatest defeat ever suffered by the United States Army in its wars with the Indians, and ultimately would destroy forever the freedom of the northern Plains Indians:

November 9, 1875: E. C. Watkins, special inspector for the Indian Bureau, reported to the Commissioner of Indian Affairs that Plains Indians living outside reservations were fed and well armed, were lofty and independent in their attitudes, and were therefore a threat to the reservation system. Inspector Watkins recommended that troops be sent against these uncivilized Indians "in the winter, the sooner the better, and *whip* them into subjection." [8]

November 22, 1875: Secretary of War W. W. Belknap warned of trouble in the Black Hills "unless something is done to obtain possession of that section for the white miners who have been strongly attracted there by reports of rich deposits of the precious metal." [9]

December 3, 1875: Commissioner of Indian Affairs Edward P. Smith ordered Sioux and Cheyenne agents to notify all Indians off reservations to come in and report to their agencies by

January 31, 1876, or a "military force would be sent to compel them."

February 1, 1876: The Secretary of the Interior notified the Secretary of War that the time given the "hostile Indians" to come in to their reservations had expired, and that he was turning them over to the military authorities for such action as the Army might deem proper under the circumstances.[10]

February 7, 1876: The War Department authorized General Sheridan, commanding the Military Division of the Missouri, to commence operations against the "hostile Sioux," including the bands under Sitting Bull and Crazy Horse.

February 8, 1876: General Sheridan ordered generals Crook and Terry to begin preparations for military operations in the direction of the headwaters of the Powder, Tongue, Rosebud, and Bighorn rivers, "where Crazy Horse and his allies frequented." [11]

Once this machinery of government began moving, it became an inexorable force, mindless and uncontrollable. When runners went out from the agencies late in December to warn the non-agency chiefs to come in, heavy snows blanketed the northern Plains. Blizzards and severe cold made it impossible for some couriers to return until weeks after the January 31 deadline; it would have been impossible to move women and children by ponies and travois. Had a few thousand "hostiles" somehow managed to reach the agencies, they would have starved there. On the reservations during the late winter, food supplies were so short that hundreds of Indians left in March to go north in search of game to supplement their meager government rations.

In January a courier found Sitting Bull camped near the mouth of the Powder. The Hunkpapa chief sent the messenger back to the agent, informing him that he would consider the order to come in, but could not do so until the Moon When the Green Grass Is Up.

Crazy Horse's Oglalas were in winter camp near Bear Butte, where the Thieves' Road came into the Black Hills from the north. During the spring it would be a good place to make up raiding parties to go against the miners violating *Paha Sapa*. When agency couriers made their way through the snow to Crazy Horse, he told them politely that he could not come until the cold went away. "It was very cold," a young Oglala remembered afterward, "and many of our people and ponies would have died in the snow. Also, we were in our own country and were doing no harm." [12]

The January 31 ultimatum was little short of a declaration of war against the independent Indians, and many of them accepted it as that. But they did not expect the Bluecoats to strike so soon. In the Moon of the Snowblind, Three Stars Crook came marching north from Fort Fetterman along the old Bozeman Road, where ten years before Red Cloud had begun his stubborn fight to keep the Powder River country inviolate.

About this same time, a mixed band of Northern Cheyennes and Oglala Sioux left Red Cloud agency to go to the Powder River country, where they hoped to find a few buffalo and antelope. About the middle of March they joined some nonagency Indians camped a few miles from where the Little Powder runs into the Powder. Two Moon, Little Wolf, Old Bear, Maple Tree, and White Bull were the Cheyenne leaders. Low Dog was the Oglala chief, and some of the warriors with him were from Crazy Horse's village farther north.

Without warning, at dawn on March 17, Crook's advance column under Colonel Joseph J. Reynolds attacked this peaceful camp. Fearing nothing in their own country, the Indians were asleep when Captain James Egan's white-horse troop, formed in a company front, dashed into the tepee village, firing pistols and carbines. At the same time, a second troop of cavalry came in on the left flank, and a third swept away the Indians' horse herd.

The first reaction from the warriors was to get as many women and children as possible out of the way of the soldiers, who were firing recklessly in all directions. "Old people tottered and hobbled away to get out of reach of the bullets singing among the lodges," Wooden Leg said afterward. "Braves seized whatever weapons they had and tried to meet the attack." As soon as the noncombatants were started up a rugged mountain slope, the warriors took positions on ledges or behind huge rocks. From these places they held the soldiers at bay until the women and children could escape across the Powder.

"From a distance we saw the destruction of our village,"

Wooden Leg said. "Our tepees were burned with everything in them. . . . I had nothing left but the clothing I had on." The Bluecoats destroyed all the pemmican and saddles in the camp, and drove away almost every pony the Indians owned, "between twelve and fifteen hundred head." [13] As soon as darkness fell, the warriors went back to where the Bluecoats were camped, determined to recover their stolen horses. Two Moon succinctly described what happened: "That night the soldiers slept, leaving the horses to one side; so we crept up and stole them back again, and then we went away." [14]

Three Stars Crook was so angry at Colonel Reynolds for allowing the Indians to escape from their village and recover their horses that he ordered him court-martialed. The Army reported this foray as "the attack on Crazy Horse's village," but Crazy Horse was camped miles away to the northeast. That was where Two Moon and the other chiefs led their homeless people in hopes of finding food and shelter. They were more than three days making the journey; the temperature was below zero at night; only a few had buffalo robes; and there was very little food.

Crazy Horse received the fugitives hospitably, gave them food and robes, and found room for them in the Oglala tepees. "I'm glad you are come," he said to Two Moon after listening to accounts of the Bluecoats plundering the village. "We are going to fight the white man again."

"All right," Two Moon replied. "I am ready to fight. I have fought already. My people have been killed, my horses stolen; I am satisfied to fight." [15]

In the Geese Laying Moon, when the grass was tall and the horses strong, Crazy Horse broke camp and led the Oglalas and Cheyennes north to the mouth of Tongue River, where Sitting Bull and the Hunkpapas had been living through the winter. Not long after that, Lame Deer arrived with a band of Minneconjous and asked permission to camp nearby. They had heard about all the Bluecoats marching through the Sioux hunting grounds and wanted to be near Sitting Bull's powerful band of Hunkpapas should there be any trouble.

As the weather warmed, the tribes began moving northward in search of wild game and fresh grass. Along the way they were joined by bands of Brulés, Sans Arcs, Blackfoot Sioux, and additional Cheyennes. Most of these Indians had left their reservations in accordance with their treaty rights as hunters, and those who had heard of the January 31 ultimatum either considered it as only another idle threat of the Great Father's agents or did not believe it applied to peaceful Indians. "Many young men were anxious to go for fighting the soldiers," said the Cheyenne warrior Wooden Leg. "But the chiefs and old men all urged us to keep away from the white men." [16]

While these several thousand Indians were camped on the Rosebud, many young warriors joined them from the reservations. They brought rumors of great forces of Bluecoats marching from three directions. Three Stars Crook was coming from the south. The One Who Limps (Colonel John Gibbon) was coming from the west. One Star Terry and Long Hair Custer were coming from the east.

Early in the Moon of Making Fat, the Hunkpapas had their annual sun dance. For three days Sitting Bull danced, bled himself, and stared at the sun until he fell into a trance. When he rose again, he spoke to his people. In his vision he had heard a voice crying: "I give you these because they have no ears." When he looked into the sky he saw soldiers falling like grasshoppers, with their heads down and their hats falling off. They were falling right into the Indian camp. Because the white men had no ears and would not listen, Wakantanka the Great Spirit was giving these soldiers to the Indians to be killed. [17]

A few days later a hunting party of Cheyennes sighted a column of Bluecoats camped for the night in the valley of the Rosebud. The hunters rode back to camp, sounding the wolf howl of danger. Three Stars was coming, and he had employed mercenary Crows and Shoshones to scout ahead of his troops.

The different chiefs sent criers through their villages and then held hasty councils. It was decided to leave about half the warriors to protect the villages while the others would travel through the night and attack Three Stars's soldiers the next morning. About a thousand Sioux and Cheyennes formed the party. A few women went along to help with the spare horses. Sitting Bull, Crazy Horse, and Two Moon were among the leaders. Just before daylight they unsaddled and rested for a while; then they turned away from the river and rode across the hills.

Three Stars's Crow scouts had told him of a great Sioux village down the Rosebud, and the general started these mercenaries out early that morning. As the Crows rode over the crest of a hill and started down, they ran into the Sioux and Cheyenne warriors. At first the Sioux and Cheyennes chased the Crows in all directions, but Bluecoats began coming up fast, and the warriors pulled back.

For a long time Crazy Horse had been waiting for a chance to test himself in battle with the Bluecoats. In all the years since the Fetterman fight at Fort Phil Kearny, he had studied the soldiers and their ways of fighting. Each time he went into the Black Hills to seek visions, he had asked Wakantanka to give him secret powers so that he would know how to lead the Oglalas to victory if the white men ever came again to make war upon his people. Since the time of his youth, Crazy Horse had known that the world men lived in was only a shadow of the real world. To get into the real world, he had to dream, and when he was in the real world everything seemed to float or dance. In this real world his horse danced as if it were wild or crazy, and this was why he called himself Crazy Horse. He had learned that if he dreamed himself into the real world before going into a fight, he could endure anything.

On this day, June 17, 1876, Crazy Horse dreamed himself into the real world, and he showed the Sioux how to do many things they had never done before while fighting the white man's soldiers. When Crook sent his pony soldiers in mounted charges, instead of rushing forward into the fire of their carbines, the Sioux faded off to their flanks and struck weak places in their lines. Crazy Horse kept his warriors mounted and always moving from one place to another. By the time the sun was in the top of the sky he had the soldiers all mixed up in three separate fights. The Bluecoats were accustomed to forming skirmish lines and strong fronts, and when Crazy Horse prevented them from fighting like that they were thrown into confusion. By making many darting charges on their swift ponies, the Sioux kept the soldiers apart and always on the defensive. When the Bluecoats' fire grew too hot, the Sioux would draw away, tantalize a few soldiers into pursuit, and then turn on them with a fury.

The Cheyennes also distinguished themselves that day, especially in the dangerous charges. Chief-Comes-in-Sight was the bravest of all, but as he was swinging his horse about after a charge into the soldiers' flank the animal was shot down in front of a Bluecoat infantry line. Suddenly another horse and rider galloped out from the Cheyennes' position and swerved to shield Chief-Comes-in-Sight from the soldiers' fire. In a moment Chief-Comes-in-Sight was up behind the rider. The rescuer was his sister Buffalo-Calf-Road-Woman, who had come along to help with the horse herds. That was why the Cheyennes always remembered this fight as the Battle Where the Girl Saved Her Brother. The white men called it the Battle of the Rosebud.

When the sun went down, the fighting ended. The Indians knew they had given Three Stars a good fight, but they did not know until the next morning that they had whipped him. At first daylight, Sioux and Cheyenne scouts went out along the ridges, and they could see the Bluecoat column retreating far away to the south. General Crook was returning to his base camp on Goose Creek to await reinforcements or a message from Gibbon, Terry, or Custer. The Indians on the Rosebud were too strong for one column of soldiers.

After the fight on the Rosebud, the chiefs decided to move west to the valley of the Greasy Grass (Little Bighorn). Scouts had come in with reports of great herds of antelope west of there, and they said grass for the horses was plentiful on the nearby benchlands. Soon the camp circles were spread along the west bank of the twisting Greasy Grass for almost three miles. No one knew for certain how many Indians were there, but the number could not have been smaller than ten thousand people, including three or four thousand warriors. "It was a very big village and you could hardly count the tepees," Black Elk said.[18]

Farthest upstream toward the south was the Hunkpapa camp, with the Blackfoot Sioux nearby. The Hunkpapas always camped at the entrance, or at the head end of the circle, which was the meaning of their name. Below them were the Sans Arcs,

Minneconjous, Oglalas, and Brulés. At the north end were the Cheyennes.

The time was early in the Moon When the Chokecherries Are Ripe, with days hot enough for boys to swim in the melted snow water of the Greasy Grass. Hunting parties were coming and going in the direction of the Bighorns, where they had found a few buffalo as well as antelope. The women were digging wild turnips out on the prairies. Every night one or more of the tribal circles held dances, and some nights the chiefs met in councils. "The chiefs of the different tribes met together as equals," Wooden Leg said. "There was only one who was considered as being above all the others. This was Sitting Bull. He was recognized as the one old man chief of all the camps combined." [19]

Sitting Bull did not believe the victory on the Rosebud had fulfilled his prophecy of soldiers falling into the Indian camp. Since the retreat of Three Stars, however, no hunting parties had sighted any Bluecoats between the Powder and the Bighorn.

They did not know until the morning of June 24 that Long Hair Custer was prowling along the Rosebud. Next morning scouts reported that the soldiers had crossed the last high ridge between the Rosebud and the Indian camp and were marching toward the Little Bighorn.

The news of Custer's approach came to the Indians in various ways:

"I and four women were a short distance from the camp digging wild turnips," said Red Horse, one of the Sioux council chiefs. "Suddenly one of the women attracted my attention to a cloud of dust rising a short distance from camp. I soon saw that the soldiers were charging the camp. To the camp I and the women ran. When I arrived a person told me to hurry to the council lodge. The soldiers charged so quickly that we could not talk. We came out of the council lodge and talked in all directions. The Sioux mount horses, take guns, and go fight the soldiers. Women and children mount horses and go, meaning to get out of the way." [20]

Pte-San-Waste-Win, a cousin of Sitting Bull, was one of the young women digging turnips that morning. She said the soldiers were six to eight miles distant when first sighted. "We could see the flashing of their sabers and saw that there were very many soldiers in the party." The soldiers first seen by Pte-San-Waste-Win and other Indians in the middle of the camp were those in Custer's battalion. These Indians were not aware of Major Marcus Reno's surprise attack against the south end of camp until they heard rifle fire from the direction of the Blackfoot Sioux lodges. "Like that the soldiers were upon us. Through the tepee poles their bullets rattled. . . . The women and children cried, fearing they would be killed, but the men, the Hunkpapa and Blackfeet, the Oglala and Minneconjou, mounted their horses and raced to the Blackfoot tepees. We could still see the soldiers of Long Hair marching along in the distance, and our men, taken by surprise, and from a point whence they had not expected to be attacked, went singing the song of battle into the fight behind the Blackfoot village." [21]

Black Elk, a thirteen-year-old Oglala boy, was swimming with his companions in the Little Bighorn. The sun was straight above and was getting very hot when he heard a crier shouting in the Hunkpapa camp: "The chargers are coming! They are charging! The chargers are coming!" The warning was repeated by an Oglala crier, and Black Elk could hear the cry going from camp to camp northward to the Cheyennes. [22]

Low Dog, an Oglala chief, heard this same warning cry. "I did not believe it. I thought it was a false alarm. I did not think it possible that any white man would attack us, so strong as we were. . . . Although I did not believe it was a true alarm, I lost no time getting ready. When I got my gun and came out of my lodge the attack had begun at the end of the camp where Sitting Bull and the Hunkpapas were."

Iron Thunder was in the Minneconjou camp. "I did not know anything about Reno's attack until his men were so close that the bullets went through the camp, and everything was in confusion. The horses were so frightened we could not catch them."

Crow King, who was in the Hunkpapa camp, said that Reno's pony soldiers commenced firing at about four hundred yards' distance. The Hunkpapas and Blackfoot Sioux retreated slowly on foot to give the women and children time to go to a place of safety. "Other Indians got our horses. By that time we had warriors enough to turn upon the whites." [23]

Near the Cheyenne camp, three miles to the north, Two Moon was watering his horses. "I washed them off with cool water, then took a swim myself. I came back to the camp afoot. When I got near my lodge, I looked up the Little Bighorn toward Sitting Bull's camp. I saw a great dust rising. It looked like a whirlwind. Soon a Sioux horseman came rushing into camp shouting: 'Soldiers come! Plenty white soldiers!' "

Two Moon ordered the Cheyenne warriors to get their horses, and then told the women to take cover away from the tepee village. "I rode swiftly toward Sitting Bull's camp. Then I saw the white soldiers fighting in a line [Reno's men]. Indians covered the flat. They began to drive the soldiers all mixed up —Sioux, then soldiers, then more Sioux, and all shooting. The air was full of smoke and dust. I saw the soldiers fall back and drop into the riverbed like buffalo fleeing." [24]

The war chief who rallied the Indians and turned back Reno's attack was a muscular, full-chested, thirty-six-year-old Hunkpapa named Pizi, or Gall. Gall had grown up in the tribe as an orphan. While still a young man he distinguished himself as a hunter and warrior, and Sitting Bull adopted him as a younger brother. Some years before, while the commissioners were attempting to persuade the Sioux to take up farming as a part of the treaty of 1868, Gall went to Fort Rice to speak for the Hunkpapas. "We were born naked," he said, "and have been taught to hunt and live on the game. You tell us that we must learn to farm, live in one house, and take on your ways. Suppose the people living beyond the great sea should come and tell you that you must stop farming and kill your cattle, and take your houses and lands, what would you do? Would you not fight them?" [25] In the decade following that speech, nothing changed Gall's opinion of the white man's self-righteous arrogance, and by the summer of 1876 he was generally accepted by the Hunkpapas as Sitting Bull's lieutenant, the war chief of the tribe.

Reno's first onrush caught several women and children in the open, and the cavalry's flying bullets virtually wiped out Gall's family. "It made my heart bad," he told a newspaperman some years later. "After that I killed all my enemies with the hatchet." His description of the tactics used to block Reno was equally terse: "Sitting Bull and I were at the point where Reno attacked. Sitting Bull was big medicine. The women and children were hastily moved downstream. . . . The women and children caught the horses for the bucks to mount them; the bucks mounted and charged back Reno and checked him, and drove him into the timber." [26]

In military terms, Gall turned Reno's flank and forced him into the woods. He then frightened Reno into making a hasty retreat which the Indians quickly turned into a rout. The result made it possible for Gall to divert hundreds of warriors for a frontal attack against Custer's column, while Crazy Horse and Two Moon struck the flank and rear.

Meanwhile Pte-San-Waste-Win and the other women had been anxiously watching the Long Hair's soldiers across the river. "I could hear the music of the bugle and could see the column of soldiers turn to the left to march down to the river where the attack was to be made. . . . Soon I saw a number of Cheyennes ride into the river, then some young men of my band, then others, until there were hundreds of warriors in the river and running up into the ravine. When some hundreds had passed the river and gone into the ravine, the others who were left, still a very great number, moved back from the river and waited for the attack. And I knew that the fighting men of the Sioux, many hundreds in number, were hidden in the ravine behind the hill upon which Long Hair was marching, and he would be attacked from both sides." [27]

Kill Eagle, a Blackfoot Sioux chief, later said that the movement of Indians toward Custer's column was "like a hurricane . . . like bees swarming out of a hive." Hump, the Minneconjou comrade of Gall and Crazy Horse during the old Powder River days, said the first massive charge by the Indians caused the long-haired chief and his men to become confused. "The first dash the Indians made my horse was shot from under me and I was wounded—shot above the knee, and the ball came out at the hip, and I fell and lay right there." Crow King, who was with the Hunkpapas, said: "The greater portion of our warriors

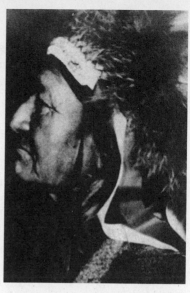

25. Gall. Photo from the
U.S. Signal Corps.

26. Two Moon, chief of the
Cheyennes. Courtesy of
Denver Public Library.

27. Hump, photographed at Fort
Bennett, South Dakota, in 1890.
Photo from the National
Archives.

28. Crow King of the Sioux.
Courtesy of Denver
Public Library.

came together in their front and we rushed our horses on them. At the same time warriors rode out on each side of them and circled around them until they were surrounded." [28] Thirteen-year-old Black Elk, watching from across the river, could see a big dust whirling on the hill, and then horses began coming out of it with empty saddles.

"The smoke of the shooting and the dust of the horses shut out the hill," Pte-San-Waste-Win said, "and the soldiers fired many shots, but the Sioux shot straight and the soldiers fell dead. The women crossed the river after the men of our village, and when we came to the hill there were no soldiers living and Long Hair lay dead among the rest. . . . The blood of the people was hot and their hearts bad, and they took no prisoners that day." [29]

Crow King said that all the soldiers dismounted when the Indians surrounded them. "They tried to hold on to their horses, but as we pressed closer they let go their horses. We crowded them toward our main camp and killed them all. They kept in order and fought like brave warriors as long as they had a man left." [30]

According to Red Horse, toward the end of the fighting with Custer, "these soldiers became foolish, many throwing away their guns and raising their hands, saying, 'Sioux, pity us; take us prisoners.' The Sioux did not take a single soldier prisoner, but killed all of them; none were alive for even a few minutes." [31]

Long after the battle, White Bull of the Minneconjous drew four pictographs showing himself grappling with and killing a soldier identified as Custer. Among others who claimed to have killed Custer were Rain-in-the-Face, Flat Hip, and Brave Bear. Red Horse said that an unidentified Santee warrior killed Custer. Most Indians who told of the battle said they never saw Custer and did not know who killed him. "We did not know till the fight was over that he was the white chief," Low Dog said. [32]

In an interview given in Canada a year after the battle, Sitting Bull said that he never saw Custer, but that other Indians had seen and recognized him just before he was killed. "He did not wear his long hair as he used to wear it," Sitting Bull said.

"It was short, but it was the color of the grass when the frost comes. . . . Where the last stand was made, the Long Hair stood like a sheaf of corn with all the ears fallen around him." [33] But Sitting Bull did not say who killed Custer.

An Arapaho warrior who was riding with the Cheyennes said that Custer was killed by several Indians. "He was dressed in buckskin, coat and pants, and was on his hands and knees. He had been shot through the side, and there was blood coming from his mouth. He seemed to be watching the Indians moving around him. Four soldiers were sitting up around him, but they were all badly wounded. All the other soldiers were down. Then the Indians closed in around him, and I did not see any more." [34]

Regardless of who had killed him, the Long Hair who made the Thieves' Road into the Black Hills was dead with all his men. Reno's soldiers, however, reinforced by those of Major Frederick Benteen, were dug in on a hill farther down the river. The Indians surrounded the hill completely and watched the soldiers through the night, and next morning started fighting them again. During the day, scouts sent out by the chiefs came back with warnings of many more soldiers marching in the direction of the Little Bighorn.

After a council it was decided to break camp. The warriors had expended most of their ammunition, and they knew it would be foolish to try to fight so many soldiers with bows and arrows. The women were told to begin packing, and before sunset they started up the valley toward the Bighorn Mountains, the tribes separating along the way and taking different directions.

When the white men in the East heard of the Long Hair's defeat, they called it a massacre and went crazy with anger. They wanted to punish all the Indians in the West. Because they could not punish Sitting Bull and the war chiefs, the Great Council in Washington decided to punish the Indians they could find—those who remained on the reservations and had taken no part in the fighting.

On July 22 the Great Warrior Sherman received authority to assume military control of all reservations in the Sioux country and to treat the Indians there as prisoners of war. On August 15 the Great Council made a new law requiring the Indians to give up all rights to the Powder River country and the Black Hills. They did this without regard to the treaty of 1868, maintaining that the Indians had violated the treaty by going to war with the United States. This was difficult for the reservation Indians to understand, because they had not attacked United States soldiers, nor had Sitting Bull's followers attacked them until Custer sent Reno charging through the Sioux villages.

To keep the reservation Indians peaceful, the Great Father sent out a new commission in September to cajole and threaten the chiefs and secure their signatures to legal documents transferring the immeasurable wealth of the Black Hills to white ownership. Several members of this commission were old hands at stealing Indian lands, notably Newton Edmunds, Bishop Henry Whipple, and the Reverend Samuel D. Hinman. At the Red Cloud agency, Bishop Whipple opened the proceedings with a prayer, and then Chairman George Manypenny read the conditions laid down by Congress. Because these conditions were stated in the usual obfuscated language of lawmakers, Bishop Whipple attempted to explain them in phrases which could be used by the interpreters.

"My heart has for many years been very warm toward the red man. We came here to bring a message to you from your Great Father, and there are certain things we have given to you in his exact words. We cannot alter them even to the scratch of a pen. . . . When the Great Council made the appropriation this year to continue your supplies they made certain provisions, three in number, and unless they were complied with no more appropriations would be made by Congress. Those three provisions are: First, that you shall give up the Black Hills country and the country to the north; second, that you shall receive your rations on the Missouri River; and third, that the Great Father shall be permitted to locate three roads from the Missouri River across the reservation to that new country where the Black Hills are. . . . The Great Father said that his heart was full of tenderness for his red children, and he selected this commission of friends of the Indians that they might devise a plan, as he directed them, in order that the Indian nations might be saved, and that instead of growing smaller and smaller until the last Indian looks upon his own grave, they might become as the white man has become, a great and powerful people." [35]

To Bishop Whipple's listeners, this seemed a strange way indeed to save the Indian nations, taking away their Black Hills and hunting grounds, and moving them far away to the Missouri River. Most of the chiefs knew that it was already too late to save the Black Hills, but they protested strongly against having their reservations moved to the Missouri. "I think if my people should move there," Red Cloud said, "they would all be destroyed. There are a great many bad men there and bad whiskey; therefore I don't want to go there." [36]

No Heart said that white men had already ruined the Missouri River country so that Indians could not live there. "You travel up and down the Missouri River and you do not see any timber," he declared. "You have probably seen where lots of it has been, and the Great Father's people have destroyed it."

"It is only six years since we came to live on this stream where we are living now," Red Dog said, "and nothing that has been promised us has been done." Another chief remembered that since the Great Father promised them that they would never be moved they had been moved five times. "I think you had better put the Indians on wheels," he said sardonically, "and you can run them about whenever you wish."

Spotted Tail accused the government and the commissioners of betraying the Indians, of broken promises and false words. "This war did not spring up here in our land; this war was brought upon us by the children of the Great Father who came to take our land from us without price, and who, in our land, do a great many evil things. . . . This war has come from robbery —from the stealing of our land." [37] As for moving to the Missouri, Spotted Tail was utterly opposed, and he told the commissioners he would not sign away the Black Hills until he could go to Washington and talk to the Great Father.

The commissioners gave the Indians a week to discuss the terms among themselves, and it soon became evident that they were not going to sign anything. The chiefs pointed out that the treaty of 1868 required the signatures of three-fourths of the male adults of the Sioux tribes to change anything in it, and

more than half of the warriors were in the north with Sitting
Bull and Crazy Horse. In reply to this the commissioners explained that the Indians off the reservations were hostiles; only
friendly Indians were covered by the treaty. Most of the chiefs
did not accept this. To break down their opposition, the commissioners dropped strong hints that unless they signed, the Great
Council in its anger would cut off all rations immediately, would
remove them to the Indian Territory in the south, and the Army
would take all their guns and horses.

There was no way out. The Black Hills were stolen; the
Powder River country and its herds of wild game were gone.
Without wild game or rations, the people would starve. The
thought of moving far away to a strange country in the south
was unbearable, and if the Army took their guns and ponies they
would no longer be men.

Red Cloud and his subchiefs signed first, and then Spotted
Tail and his people signed. After that the commissioners went
to agencies at Standing Rock, Cheyenne River, Crow Creek,
Lower Brulé, and Santee, and badgered the other Sioux tribes
into signing. Thus did *Paha Sapa*, its spirits and its mysteries, its
vast pine forests, and its billion dollars in gold pass forever from
the hands of the Indians into the domain of the United
States.

Four weeks after Red Cloud and Spotted Tail touched pens to
the paper, eight companies of United States cavalry under
Three Fingers Mackenzie (the Eagle Chief who destroyed the
Kiowas and Comanches in Palo Duro Canyon) marched out of
Fort Robinson into the agency camps. Under orders of the War
Department, Mackenzie had come to take the reservation Indians' ponies and guns. All males were placed under arrest, tepees were searched and dismantled, guns collected, and all ponies
were rounded up by the soldiers. Mackenzie gave the women
permission to use horses to haul their goods into Fort Robinson.
The males, including Red Cloud and the other chiefs, were
forced to walk to the fort. The tribe would have to live henceforth at Fort Robinson under the guns of the soldiers.

Next morning, to degrade his beaten prisoners even further,
Mackenzie presented a company of mercenary Pawnee scouts
(the same Pawnees the Sioux had once driven out of their

29. *Young-Man-Afraid-of-His-Horses. Courtesy of the
Nebraska State Historical Society.*

Powder River country) with the horses the soldiers had taken from the Sioux.

Meanwhile, the United States Army, thirsting for revenge, was prowling the country north and west of the Black Hills, killing Indians wherever they could be found. In late summer of 1876, Three Stars Crook's reinforced column ran out of rations in the Heart River country of Dakota, and started a forced march southward to obtain supplies in the Black Hills mining camps. On September 9, near Slim Buttes, a forward detachment under Captain Anson Mills stumbled upon American Horse's village of Oglalas and Minneconjous. These Indians had left Crazy Horse's camp on Grand River a few days before and were moving south to spend the winter on their reservation. Captain Mills attacked, but the Sioux drove him back, and while he was waiting for Three Stars to arrive, all the Indians escaped except American Horse, four warriors, and fifteen women and children, who were trapped in a cave at the end of a small canyon.

When Crook came up with the main column, he ordered soldiers to positions from which they could fire volleys into the mouth of the cave. American Horse and his four warriors returned the fire, and after some hours of continuous dueling, two Bluecoats were dead and nine wounded. Crook then sent a scout, Frank Grouard, to ask the Indians to surrender. Grouard, who had lived with the Sioux, spoke to them in their language. "They told me they would come out if we would not kill them, and upon receiving this promise, they came out." American Horse, two warriors, five women, and several children crawled out of the cave; the others were dead or too badly wounded to move. American Horse's groin had been ripped open by buckshot. "He was holding his entrails in his hands as he came out," Grouard said. "Holding out one of his bloodstained hands, he shook hands with me." [38]

Captain Mills had found a little girl, three or four years old, hiding in the village. "She sprang up and ran away like a young partridge," he said. "The soldiers caught her and brought her to me." Mills comforted her and gave her some food, and then he asked his orderly to bring her along when he went down to the cave where the soldiers were dragging out the Indian casualties.

Two of the dead were women, bloody with many wounds. "The little girl began to scream and fought the orderly until he placed her on the ground, when she ran and embraced one of these squaws, who was her mother. I told Adjutant Lemly I intended to adopt this little girl, as I had slain her mother."

A surgeon came to examine American Horse's wound. He pronounced it fatal, and the chief sat down before a fire, holding a blanket over his bullet-torn abdomen, until he lost consciousness and died.

Crook ordered Captain Mills to ready his men for a resumption of the march to the Black Hills. "Before starting," Mills said, "Adjutant Lemly asked me if I really intended to take the little girl. I told him I did, when he remarked, 'Well, how do you think Mrs. Mills will like it?' It was the first time I had given that side of the matter a thought, and I decided to leave the child where I found her." [39]

While Three Stars was destroying American Horse's village, some of the Sioux who had escaped made their way to Sitting Bull's camp and told him about the attack. Sitting Bull and Gall, with about six hundred warriors, immediately went to help American Horse, but they arrived too late. Although Sitting Bull launched an attack on Crook's soldiers, his warriors had so little ammunition that the Bluecoats held them off with rearguard actions while the main column marched on to the Black Hills.

When the soldiers were all gone, Sitting Bull and his warriors went into American Horse's devastated village, rescued the helpless survivors, and buried the dead. "What have we done that the white people want us to stop?" Sitting Bull asked. "We have been running up and down this country, but they follow us from one place to another." [40]

In an effort to get as far away from the soldiers as possible, Sitting Bull took his people north along the Yellowstone, where buffalo could be found. In the Moon of Falling Leaves, Gall went out with a hunting party and came upon an Army wagon train traveling through the Yellowstone country. The soldiers were taking supplies to a new fort they were building where Tongue River flowed into the Yellowstone (Fort Keogh, named for Captain Myles Keogh, who was killed at the Little Bighorn).

Gall's warriors ambushed the train near Glendive Creek and captured sixty mules. As soon as Sitting Bull heard about the wagon train and the new fort, he sent for Johnny Brughiere, a half-breed who had joined his camp. Brughiere knew how to write, and Sitting Bull told him to put down on a piece of paper some words he had to say to the commander of the soldiers:

> I want to know what you are doing on this road. You scare all the buffalo away. I want to hunt in this place. I want you to turn back from here. If you don't, I will fight you again. I want you to leave what you have got here, and turn back from here. I am your friend.
>
> —SITTING BULL [41]

When Lieutenant Colonel Elwell Otis, commanding the wagon train, received the message, he sent a scout with a reply to Sitting Bull. The soldiers were going to Fort Keogh, Otis said, and many more soldiers were coming to join them. If Sitting Bull wanted a fight, the soldiers would give him one.

Sitting Bull did not want a fight; he wanted only to be left alone to hunt buffalo. He sent a warrior out with a white flag, asking for a talk with the soldier chief. By this time Colonel Nelson Miles and more soldiers had overtaken the train. As Miles had been searching for Sitting Bull since the end of summer, he immediately agreed to a parley.

They met on October 22 between a line of soldiers and a line of warriors. Miles was escorted by an officer and five men, Sitting Bull by a subchief and five warriors. The day was very cold, and Miles was wearing a long coat trimmed with bear fur. From the first moment of his appearance, he was Bear Coat to the Indians.

There were no preliminary speeches, no friendly smokes of the pipe. With Johnny Brughiere interpreting, Bear Coat began the parley by accusing Sitting Bull of always being against the white man and his ways. Sitting Bull admitted that he was not for the whites, but neither was he an enemy to them as long as they left him alone. Bear Coat wanted to know what Sitting Bull was doing in the Yellowstone country. The question was a foolish one, but the Hunkpapa answered it politely; he was hunting buffalo to feed and clothe his people. Bear Coat then made passing mention of a reservation for the Hunkpapas, but Sitting Bull brushed it aside. He would spend the winter in the Black Hills, he said. The parley ended with nothing resolved, but the two men agreed to meet again the next day.

The second meeting quickly became a succession of disagreements. Sitting Bull began by saying that he had not fought the soldiers until they came to fight him, and promised that there would be no more fighting if the white men would take their soldiers and forts out of the Indians' country. Bear Coat replied that there could be no peace for the Sioux until they were all on reservations. At this, Sitting Bull became angry. He declared that the Great Spirit had made him an Indian but not an agency Indian, and he did not intend to become one. He ended the conference abruptly, and returned to his warriors, ordering them to scatter because he suspected that Bear Coat's soldiers would try to attack them. The soldiers did open fire, and once again the Hunkpapas had to start running up and down the country.

By springtime of 1877 Sitting Bull was tired of running. He decided there was no longer room enough for white men and the Sioux to live together in the Great Father's country. He would take his people to Canada, to the land of the Grandmother, Queen Victoria. Before he started, he searched for Crazy Horse, hoping to persuade him to bring the Oglalas to the Grandmother's land. But Crazy Horse's people were running up and down the country trying to escape the soldiers, and Sitting Bull could not find them.

In those same cold moons, General Crook was also looking for Crazy Horse. This time Crook had assembled an enormous army of infantry, cavalry, and artillery. This time he took along enough rations to fill 168 wagons and enough powder and ammunition to burden the backs of 400 pack mules. Three Stars's mighty column swept through the Powder River country like a swarm of grizzly bears, mauling and crushing all Indians in its path.

The soldiers were looking for Crazy Horse, but they found a Cheyenne village first, Dull Knife's village. Most of these Cheyennes had not been in the Little Bighorn battle, but had slipped away from Red Cloud agency in search of food after the Army took possession there and stopped their rations. General Crook sent Three Fingers Mackenzie against this village of 150 lodges.

It was in the Deer Rutting Moon, and very cold, with deep snow in the shaded places and ice-crusted snow in the open places. Mackenzie brought his troopers up to attacking positions during the night, and struck the Cheyennes at first daylight. The Pawnee mercenaries went in first, charging on the fast ponies Mackenzie had taken from the reservation Sioux. They caught the Cheyennes in their lodges, killing many of them as they came awake. Others ran out naked into the biting cold, the warriors trying to fight off the Pawnees and the onrushing soldiers long enough for their women and children to escape.

Some of the best warriors of the Northern Cheyennes sacrificed their lives in those first furious moments of fighting; one of them was Dull Knife's oldest son. Dull Knife and Little Wolf finally managed to form a rear guard along the upper ledges of a canyon, but their scanty supply of ammunition was soon exhausted. Little Wolf was shot seven times before he and Dull Knife broke away to join their women and children in full flight toward the Bighorns. Behind them Mackenzie was burning their lodges, and after that was done he herded their captured ponies against the canyon wall and ordered his men to shoot them down, just as he had done to the ponies of the Comanches and Kiowas in Palo Duro Canyon.

For Dull Knife's Cheyennes, their flight was a repetition of the flight of Two Moon's Cheyennes after the surprise attack in March by the Eagle Chief, Reynolds. But the weather was colder; they had only a few horses, and scarcely any blankets, robes, or even moccasins. Like Two Moon's people, they knew only one sanctuary—Crazy Horse's village on Box Elder Creek.

During the first night of flight, twelve infants and several old people froze to death. The next night, the men killed some of the ponies, disemboweled them, and thrust small children inside to keep them from freezing. The old people put their hands and feet in beside the children. For three days they tramped across the frozen snow, their bare feet leaving a trail of blood, and then they reached Crazy Horse's camp.

Crazy Horse shared food, blankets, and shelter with Dull Knife's people, but warned them to be ready to run. The Oglalas did not have enough ammunition left to stand and fight. Bear

Coat Miles was looking for them in the north, and now Three Stars Crook was coming from the south. To survive, they would have to keep running up and down the country.

In the Moon of Popping Trees, Crazy Horse moved the camp north along the Tongue to a hiding place not far from the new Fort Keogh, where Bear Coat was wintering his soldiers. Cold and hunger became so unbearable for the children and old people that some of the chiefs told Crazy Horse it was time to go and parley with Bear Coat and find out what he wanted them to do. Their women and children were crying for food, and they needed warm shelters they would not have to run away from. Crazy Horse knew that Bear Coat wanted to make prisoners of them on a reservation, but he agreed that the chiefs should go if they wished to do so. He went with the party, about thirty chiefs and warriors, to a hill not far from the fort. Eight chiefs and warriors volunteered to ride down to the fort, one of them carrying a large white cloth on a lance. As they neared the fort, some of Bear Coat's mercenary Crows came charging out. Ignoring the truce flag, the Crows fired point-blank into the Sioux. Only three of the eight escaped alive. Some of the Sioux watching from the hill wanted to ride out and seek revenge on the Crows, but Crazy Horse insisted that they hurry back to camp. They would have to pack up and run again. Now that Bear Coat knew there were Sioux nearby, he would come searching through the snow for them.

Bear Coat caught up with them on the morning of January 8 (1877) at Battle Butte, and sent his soldiers charging through foot-deep snow. Crazy Horse had but little ammunition left to defend his people, but he had some good warrior chiefs who knew enough tricks to mislead and punish the soldiers while the main body of Indians escaped through the Wolf Mountains toward the Bighorns. Working in concert, Little Big Man, Two Moon, and Hump decoyed the troops into a canyon. For four hours they kept the soldiers—who were encumbered with bulky winter uniforms—stumbling and falling over ice-covered cliffs. Snow began sifting down during the engagement, and by early afternoon a blizzard was raging. This was enough for Bear Coat. He took his men back to the warmth of Fort Keogh.

Through the screen of sleety snow, Crazy Horse and his peo-

ple made their way to the familiar country of the Little Powder.
They were camped there in February, living off what game they
could find, when runners brought news that Spotted Tail and a
party of Brulés were coming from the south. Some of the Indians
in the camp thought that perhaps Spotted Tail at last had tired of
being told what to do on his reservation and was running away
from the soldiers, but Crazy Horse knew better.

During the cold moons, Three Stars Crook had taken his men
out of the snow into Fort Fetterman. While he was waiting for
spring, he paid a visit to Spotted Tail and promised him that the
reservation Sioux would not have to move to the Missouri River
if the Brulé chief would go as a peace emissary to Crazy Horse
and persuade him to surrender. That was the purpose of Spotted
Tail's visit to Crazy Horse's camp.

Just before Spotted Tail arrived, Crazy Horse told his father
that he was going away. He asked his father to shake hands with
Spotted Tail and tell him the Oglalas would come in as soon as
the weather made it possible for women and children to travel.
Then he went off to the Bighorns alone. Crazy Horse had not
made up his mind yet whether he would surrender; perhaps he
would let his people go while he stayed in the Powder River
country alone—like an old buffalo bull cast out of the herd.

When Spotted Tail arrived, he guessed that Crazy Horse was
avoiding him. He sent messengers out to find the Oglala leader,
but Crazy Horse had vanished in the deep snows. Before Spotted
Tail returned to Nebraska, however, he convinced Big Foot that
he should surrender his Minneconjous, and he received promises
from Touch-the-Clouds and three other chiefs that they would
bring their people to the agency early in the spring.

On April 14 Touch-the-Clouds, with a large number of Minneconjous and Sans Arcs from Crazy Horse's village, arrived at the
Spotted Tail agency and surrendered. A few days before this
happened, Three Stars Crook had sent Red Cloud out to find
Crazy Horse and promise him that if he surrendered he could
have a reservation in the Powder River country. On April 27
Red Cloud met Crazy Horse and told him of Three Stars's promise. Crazy Horse's nine hundred Oglalas were starving, the warriors had no ammunition, and their horses were thin and bony.
The promise of a reservation in the Powder River country was all

30. *Little Big Man. Photo from the U.S. Signal Corps.*

that Crazy Horse needed to bring him in to Fort Robinson to surrender.

The last of the Sioux war chiefs now became a reservation Indian, disarmed, dismounted, with no authority over his people, a prisoner of the Army, which had never defeated him in battle. Yet he was still a hero to the young men, and their adulation caused jealousies to arise among the older agency chiefs. Crazy Horse remained aloof, he and his followers living only for the day when Three Stars would make good his promise of a reservation for them in the Powder River country.

Late in the summer, Crazy Horse heard that Three Stars wanted him to go to Washington for a council with the Great Father. Crazy Horse refused to go. He could see no point in talking about the promised reservation. He had seen what happened to chiefs who went to the Great Father's house in Washington; they came back fat from the white man's way of living and with all the hardness gone out of them. He could see the changes in Red Cloud and Spotted Tail, and they knew he saw and they did not like him for it.

In August news came that the Nez Percés, who lived beyond the Shining Mountains, were at war with the Bluecoats. At the agencies, soldier chiefs began enlisting warriors to do their scouting for them against the Nez Percés. Crazy Horse told the young men not to go against those other Indians far away, but some would not listen, and allowed themselves to be bought by the soldiers. On August 31, the day these former Sioux warriors put on their Bluecoat uniforms to march away, Crazy Horse was so sick with disgust that he said he was going to take his people and go back north to the Powder River country.

When Three Stars heard of this from his spies, he ordered eight companies of pony soldiers to march to Crazy Horse's camp outside Fort Robinson and arrest him. Before the soldiers arrived, however, Crazy Horse's friends warned him they were coming. Not knowing what the soldiers' purpose was, Crazy Horse told his people to scatter, and then he set out alone to Spotted Tail agency to seek refuge with his old friend Touch-the-Clouds.

The soldiers found him there, placed him under arrest, and informed him they were taking him back to Fort Robinson to

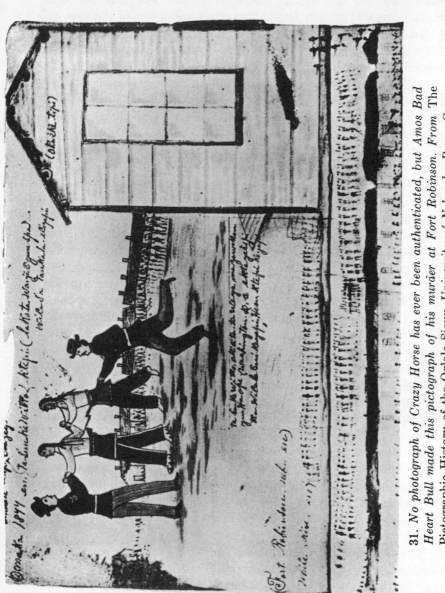

31. *No photograph of Crazy Horse has ever been authenticated, but Amos Bad Heart Bull made this pictograph of his murder at Fort Robinson. From The Pictographic History of the Oglala Sioux, University of Nebraska Press, Copyright © 1967. Used by special permission.*

see Three Stars. Upon arrival at the fort, Crazy Horse was told
that it was too late to talk with Three Stars that day. He was
turned over to Captain James Kennington and one of the agency
policemen. Crazy Horse stared hard at the agency policeman.
He was Little Big Man, who not so long ago had defied the
commissioners who came to steal *Paha Sapa,* the same Little
Big Man who had threatened to kill the first chief who spoke
for selling the Black Hills, the brave Little Big Man who had
last fought beside Crazy Horse on the icy slopes of the Wolf
Mountains against Bear Coat Miles. Now the white men had
bought Little Big Man and made him into an agency policeman.

As Crazy Horse walked between them, letting the soldier
chief and Little Big Man lead him to wherever they were taking
him, he must have tried to dream himself into the real world,
to escape the darkness of the shadow world in which all was
madness. They walked past a soldier with a bayoneted rifle on
his shoulder, and then they were standing in the doorway of a
building. The windows were barred with iron, and he could see
men behind the bars with chains on their legs. It was a trap for
an animal, and Crazy Horse lunged away like a trapped animal,
with Little Big Man holding on to his arm. The scuffling went
on for only a few seconds. Someone shouted a command, and
then the soldier guard, Private William Gentles, thrust his bayo-
net deep into Crazy Horse's abdomen.

Crazy Horse died that night, September 5, 1877, at the age
of thirty-five. At dawn the next day the soldiers presented the
dead chief to his father and mother. They put the body of Crazy
Horse into a wooden box, fastened it to a pony-drawn travois,
and carried it to Spotted Tail agency, where they mounted it
on a scaffold. All through the Drying Grass Moon, mourners
watched beside the burial place. And then in the Moon of Falling
Leaves came the heartbreaking news: the reservation Sioux must
leave Nebraska and go to a new reservation on the Missouri
River.

Through the crisp dry autumn of 1877, long lines of exiled
Indians driven by soldiers marched northeastward toward the
barren land. Along the way, several bands slipped away from
the column and turned northwestward, determined to escape to
Canada and join Sitting Bull. With them went the father and

mother of Crazy Horse, carrying the heart and bones of their son. At a place known only to them they buried Crazy Horse somewhere near Chankpe Opi Wakpala, the creek called Wounded Knee.

SONG OF SITTING BULL

I - ki - ći - ze wa - oŋ koŋ *he* wa - na he - na - la ye - lo

he i - yo - ti - ye ki - ya wa - oŋ

Courtesy of the Bureau of American Ethnology Collection

A warrior
I have been.
Now
it is all over.
A hard time
I have.

THIRTEEN

The Flight of the Nez Percés

1877—January 1, Queen Victoria proclaimed Empress of India. January 25, U.S. Congress passes Electoral Commission Bill requiring recount of electoral votes; Hayes-Tilden contest still in doubt. February 12, railroad workers begin strikes in protest over wage cuts. February 26, Southern Democrats meet secretly with Hayes's Republican representatives and conclude the Compromise of 1877, in which Southern Democrats agree to support Republicans in exchange for withdrawal of federal troops from the South and ending of Reconstruction. February 27, Electoral Commission declares recount in favor of Hayes. March 2, Congress confirms election of Hayes. March 5, Hayes inaugurated as President. April 10, President Hayes begins withdrawal of federal troops from Southern states, signaling end of Reconstruction era. April 15, first business telephone installed between Boston and Somerville, Massachusetts. July 14, general strike halts movement of railroad trains. July 20, strike riots spread across United States. July 21–27, troops battle railroad workers and force end to nationwide strike. October 17, contract between Pennsylvania Railroad and Standard Oil Company strengthens oil-transportation monopoly. December, Edison invents the phonograph. Tolstoy's *Anna Karenina* is published.

The whites told only one side. Told it to please themselves. Told much that is not true. Only his own best deeds, only the worst deeds of the Indians, has the white man told.

—YELLOW WOLF OF THE NEZ PERCÉS

The earth was created by the assistance of the sun, and it should be left as it was. . . . The country was made without lines of demarcation, and it is no man's business to divide it. . . . I see the whites all over the country gaining wealth, and see their desire to give us lands which are worthless. . . . The earth and myself are of one mind. The measure of the land and the measure of our bodies are the same. Say to us if you can say it, that you were sent by the Creative Power to talk to us. Perhaps you think the Creator sent you here to dispose of us as you see fit. If I thought you were sent by the Creator I might be induced to think you had a right to dispose of me. Do not misunderstand me, but understand me fully with reference to my affection for the land. I never said the land was mine to do with it as I chose. The one who has the right to dispose of it is the one who has created it. I claim a right to live on my land, and accord you the privilege to live on yours.

—HEINMOT TOOYALAKET (CHIEF JOSEPH) OF THE NEZ PERCÉS

———❖❖❖———

IN SEPTEMBER, 1805, when Lewis and Clark came down off the Rockies on their westward journey, the entire exploring party was half-famished and ill with dysentery—too weak to defend themselves. They were in the country of the Nez Percés, so named by French trappers, who observed some of these Indians wearing dentalium shells in their noses. Had the Nez Percés chosen to do so, they could have put an end to the Lewis and Clark expedition there on the banks of Clearwater River, and seized their wealth of horses. Instead the Nez Percés welcomed the white Americans, supplied them with food, and looked after the explorers' horses for several months while they continued by canoe to the Pacific shore.

Thus began a long friendship between the Nez Percés and white Americans. For seventy years the tribe boasted that no Nez Percé had ever killed a white man. But white men's greed for land and gold finally broke the friendship.

In 1855 Governor Isaac Stevens of Washington Territory invited the Nez Percés to a peace council. "He said there were a great many white people in the country, and many more would come; that he wanted the land marked out so that the Indians and white men could be separated. If they were to live in peace it was necessary, he said, that the Indians should have a country set apart for them, and in that country they must stay."

Tuekakas, a chief known as Old Joseph by the white men, told Governor Stevens that no man owned any part of the earth, and a man could not sell what he did not own.

The governor could not comprehend such an attitude. He urged Old Joseph to sign the treaty and receive presents of blankets. "Take away your paper," the chief replied. "I will not touch it with my hand."

Aleiya, who was called Lawyer by the white men, signed the treaty, and so did several other Nez Percés, but Old Joseph took his people back to their home in Wallowa Valley, a green country of winding waters, wide meadows, mountain forests, and a clear blue lake. Old Joseph's band of Nez Percés raised fine horses and cattle, lived in fine lodges, and when they needed anything from the white men they traded their livestock.

Only a few years after the first treaty signing, government men were swarming around the Nez Percés again, wanting more land. Old Joseph warned his people to take no presents from them, not even one blanket. "After a while," he said, "they will claim that you have accepted pay for your country." [1]

In 1863 a new treaty was presented to the Nez Percés. It took away the Wallowa Valley and three-fourths of the remainder of their land, leaving them only a small reservation in what is now Idaho. Old Joseph refused to attend the treaty signing, but Lawyer and several other chiefs—none of whom had ever lived in the Valley of Winding Waters—signed away their people's lands. The "thief treaty," Old Joseph called it, and he was so offended that he tore up the Bible a white missionary had given him to convert him to Christianity. To let the white men

know he still claimed the Wallowa Valley, he planted poles all
around the boundaries of the land where his people lived.

Not long after that, Old Joseph died (1871), and the chieftainship of the band passed to his son, Heinmot Tooyalaket
(Young Joseph), who was then about thirty years old. When
government officials came to order the Nez Percés to leave the
Wallowa Valley and go to Lapwai reservation, Young Joseph
refused to listen. "Neither Lawyer nor any other chief had authority to sell this land," he said. "It has always belonged to my
people. It came unclouded to them from our fathers, and we
will defend this land as long as a drop of Indian blood warms
the hearts of our men." [2] He petitioned the Great Father, Ulysses
Grant, to let his people stay where they had always lived, and
on June 16, 1873, the President issued an executive order withdrawing Wallowa Valley from settlement by white men.

In a short time a group of commissioners arrived to begin
organization of a new Indian agency in the valley. One of them
mentioned the advantages of schools for Joseph's people. Joseph
replied that the Nez Percés did not want the white man's
schools.

"Why do you not want schools?" the commissioner asked.

"They will teach us to have churches," Joseph answered.

"Do you not want churches?"

"No, we do not want churches."

"Why do you not want churches?"

"They will teach us to quarrel about God," Joseph said. "We
do not want to learn that. We may quarrel with men sometimes
about things on this earth, but we never quarrel about God.
We do not want to learn that." [3]

Meanwhile, white settlers were encroaching upon the valley,
with their eyes on the Nez Percé land. Gold was found in
nearby mountains. The goldseekers stole the Indians' horses,
and stockmen stole their cattle, branding them so the Indians
could not claim them back. White politicians journeyed to
Washington, telling lies about the Nez Percés. They charged
the Indians with being a threat to the peace and with stealing
the settlers' livestock. This was the reverse of the truth, but as
Joseph said, "We had no friend who would plead our cause before the law council." [4]

32. *Chief Joseph of the Nez Percés. Photo from the National Archives.*

Two years after the Great Father promised Wallowa Valley to Joseph's people forever, he issued a new proclamation, re-opening the valley to white settlement. The Nez Percés were given "a reasonable time" to move to the Lapwai reservation. Joseph had no intention of giving up the valley of his fathers, but in 1877 the government sent the One-Armed-Soldier-Chief, General Howard, to clear all Nez Percés out of the Wallowa area.

In the four years that had passed since Oliver Otis Howard treated Cochise and the Apaches with justice, he had learned that the Army was not tolerant of "Indian lovers." He came now to the Northwest country, determined to restore his standing with the military by carrying out his orders swiftly and to the letter. Privately he told trusted friends that "it is a great mistake to take from Joseph and his band of Nez Percé Indians that valley." But in May, 1877, he summoned Joseph to Lapwai for a council which was to set the date they must surrender their land.

To accompany him to Lapwai, Joseph chose White Bird, Looking Glass, his brother Ollokot, and the Wallowa prophet Toohoolhoolzote. The prophet was a tall, thick-necked, very ugly Indian with a gift for eloquent rebuttal. "A fugitive from hell," was the way one white man described him. At the opening of the council, which was held in a building across from the Fort Lapwai guardhouse, Joseph presented Toohoolhoolzote as spokesman for the Wallowa Nez Percés.

"Part of the Nez Percés gave up their land," the prophet said. "We never did. The earth is part of our body, and we never gave up the earth."

"You know very well that the government has set apart a reservation, and that the Indians must go on it," Howard declared.

"What person pretended to divide the land and put us on it?" Toohoolhoolzote demanded.

"I am the man. I stand here for the President." Howard was beginning to lose his temper. "My orders are plain and will be executed."

The prophet continued prodding the One-Armed-Soldier-Chief, asking him how the land could belong to white men if it had come down to the Nez Percés from their fathers. "We came from the earth, and our bodies must go back to the earth, our mother," he said.

"I don't want to offend your religion," Howard replied testily, "but you must talk about practicable things. Twenty times over I hear that the earth is your mother and about chieftainship from the earth. I want to hear it no more, but come to business at once."

"Who can tell me what I must do in my own country?" Toohoolhoolzote retorted.[5]

The argument continued until Howard felt he must demonstrate his power. He ordered the prophet arrested and taken to the guardhouse, and then he bluntly informed Joseph that the Nez Percés had thirty days in which to move from the Wallowa Valley to the Lapwai reservation.

"My people have always been the friends of white men," Joseph said. "Why are you in such a hurry? I cannot get ready to move in thirty days. Our stock is scattered, and Snake River is very high. Let us wait until fall, then the river will be low."

"If you let the time run over one day," Howard replied harshly, "the soldiers will be there to drive you onto the reservation, and all your cattle and horses outside of the reservation at that time will fall into the hands of the white men."

Joseph knew now that he had no alternative. To defend the valley with less than a hundred warriors was impossible. When he and his subchiefs returned home they found soldiers already there. They held a council and decided to gather their stock immediately for the move to Lapwai. "The white men were many and we could not hold our own with them. We were like deer. They were like grizzly bears. We had a small country. Their country was large. We were contented to let things remain as the Great Spirit made them. They were not, and would change the rivers and mountains if they did not suit them."[6]

Even before they started the long march, some of the warriors began talking of war rather than be driven like dogs from the land where they were born. Toohoolhoolzote, released from prison, declared that blood alone would wash out the disgrace the One-Armed-Soldier-Chief had put upon him. Joseph, however, continued to counsel peace.

To meet General Howard's deadline, they had to leave much

of their livestock in the valley, and when they came to Snake River the stream was swirling with melted snow from the mountains. Miraculously they got their women and children across on buffalo-hide rafts without serious accident, but while they were engaged in this task a party of white men came and stole some of their cattle from the waiting herd. Then, when they hurriedly tried to swim their livestock across the river, many animals were lost to the swift-flowing current.

More embittered than ever, the chiefs demanded that Joseph halt the march in Rocky Canyon and hold a council. Toohoolhoolzote, White Bird, and Ollokot spoke for war. Joseph told them it was "better to live at peace than to begin a war and lie dead." The others called him a coward, but he refused to back down.

While they were camped in the canyon, a small band of warriors slipped away one night, and when they returned the Nez Percés could no longer claim that they had never killed a white man. The warriors had killed eleven, in revenge for the theft of their stock and for being driven from their valley.

Like many another peace-loving Indian chief, Joseph was now trapped between the pressures of the white men and the fury of his desperate people. He chose to stay with his people. "I would have given my own life," he said, "if I could have undone the killing of white men by my people. I blame my young men and I blame the white men. . . . I would have taken my people to the buffalo country [Montana] without fighting, if possible. . . . We moved over to White Bird Creek, sixteen miles away, and there encamped, intending to collect our stock before leaving; but the soldiers attacked us, and the first battle was fought." [7]

Although outnumbered two to one, the Nez Percés drew Howard's soldiers into a trap at White Bird Canyon on June 17, turning the attackers' flank, killing a third of them, and routing the remainder. Ten days later the One-Armed-Soldier-Chief brought up heavy reinforcements to do battle again, but the Nez Percés slipped away across the mountains. In a succession of shrewd military actions, Joseph outmaneuvered the pursuing soldiers, severely punished an advance detachment, and then raced to the Clearwater, where Chief Looking Glass was waiting with more warriors.

The combined force of Nez Percés now numbered 250 warriors, with 450 noncombatants, their baggage, and two thousand horses. At White Bird Canyon they had captured several rifles and a good supply of ammunition.

After withdrawing beyond the Clearwater (where their fathers had welcomed Lewis and Clark as the forerunners of white civilization), Joseph called a council of chiefs. They all knew they could never return to the Valley of Winding Waters or go without punishment to Lapwai. Only one course was left to them —flight to Canada. Sitting Bull of the Sioux had fled to the Grandmother's land, and the American soldiers dared not go there to kill him. If the Nez Percés could reach the Lolo Trail and cross the Bitterroot Mountains, they might be able to escape to Canada.

Because they were accustomed to crossing the Bitterroots to hunt in Montana, the Nez Percés quickly outdistanced Howard's baggage-laden army. On July 25 they were filing down the canyon near the mouth of Lolo Creek when their scouts sighted soldiers ahead. The Bluecoats were constructing a log barricade at a narrow place in the pass.

Under a white flag, Joseph, Looking Glass, and White Bird rode down to the barricade, dismounted calmly, and shook hands with the commanding officer, Captain Charles Rawn. The chiefs noted that there were about two hundred soldiers in the camp.

"We are going by you without fighting, if you will let us," Joseph said to the captain, "but we are going by you anyhow." [8]

Rawn told Joseph that they could pass only if they gave up their arms. White Bird replied that their warriors would never do that.

Knowing that General Howard was approaching from the west and that another large force under Colonel John Gibbon was marching from the east, Captain Rawn decided to stall for time. He suggested that they meet again the next day to discuss arrangements for passage. To this the chiefs agreed, but after two more days of fruitless parleying, the Nez Percé leaders decided they could wait no longer.

Early on the morning of July 28, Looking Glass moved the warriors into a screening line among the trees on the upper slope of the canyon. At the same time, Joseph led the noncombatants and livestock up a gulch, climbed to the top of a mountain, and was well around the canyon barricade before Captain Rawn discovered what the Nez Percés were doing. The captain went in pursuit of the Indians, but after a few skirmishes with Joseph's rearguard warriors he decided not to risk a real fight and returned to his now useless barricade.

Believing that they had escaped from Howard, and unaware of Gibbon's approaching army, the chiefs decided to move south to the familiar hunting country of the Big Hole. There they could rest their ponies and hunt wild game. If the white men would leave them alone, perhaps they would not have to go to the Grandmother's land and join Sitting Bull.

On the night of August 9, the One Who Limps (Colonel Gibbon) brought up a mixed column of local volunteers and mounted infantrymen and concealed them on a hillside overlooking the Nez Percé camp on Big Hole River. As dawn approached, the volunteers asked Gibbon if they should take prisoners during the attack. Gibbon replied that he wanted no Indian prisoners, male or female. The night air was cold, and the men warmed themselves by drinking whiskey. At first daylight several were drunk when Gibbon gave the command to attack. The infantry line began firing volleys, and then charged the Nez Percé tepees.

Fifteen-year-old Kowtoliks was asleep when he heard the rattle of rifle fire. "I jumped from my blankets and ran about thirty feet and threw myself on hands and knees, and kept going. An old woman, Patsikonmi, came from the tepee and did the same thing—bent down on knees and hands. She was to my left and was shot in the breast. I heard the bullet strike. She said to me, 'You better not stay here. Be going. I'm shot.' Then she died. Of course I ran for my life and hid in the bushes. The soldiers seemed shooting everywhere. Through tepees and wherever they saw Indians. I saw little children killed and men fall before bullets coming like rain." [9]

Another teen-age boy, Black Eagle, was awakened by bullets passing through his family tepee. In his fright he ran and jumped into the river, but the water was too cold. He came out and helped save the horses by driving them up a hill and out of sight of the soldiers.

The Indians, meanwhile, had recovered from the shock of the surprise attack. While Joseph directed the rescue of the non-combatants, White Bird deployed the warriors for a counter-attack. "Fight! Shoot them down!" he shouted. "We can shoot as well as any of these soldiers." [10] The marksmanship of the Nez Percés, in fact, was superior to that of Gibbon's men. "We now mixed those soldiers badly," Yellow Wolf said. "Scared, they ran back across the river. They acted as if drinking. We thought some got killed by being drunk."

When the soldiers tried to set up a howitzer, the Nez Percés swarmed over the gun crew, seized the cannon, and wrecked it. A warrior fixed his rifle sights on Colonel Gibbon and made him the One Who Limps Twice.

By this time Joseph had the camp in motion, and while a handful of warriors kept Gibbon's soldiers pinned down behind a makeshift barricade of logs and boulders, the Nez Percés resumed flight. They turned southward and away from Canada, because they believed it was the only way left to shake off their pursuers. The warriors had killed thirty soldiers and wounded at least forty. But in Gibbon's merciless dawn attack, eighty Nez Percés had died, more than two-thirds of them women and children, their bodies riddled with bullets, their heads smashed in by bootheels and gunstocks. "The air was heavy with sorrow," Yellow Wolf said. "Some soldiers acted with crazy minds." [11]

The Nez Percé rear guard probably could have starved out Gibbon's barricaded soldiers and killed them all had not General Howard come to the rescue with a fresh force of cavalrymen. Withdrawing hurriedly, the warriors overtook Joseph to warn him that the One-Armed-Soldier-Chief was on their trail again.

"We retreated as rapidly as we could," Joseph said. "After six days General Howard came close to us, and we went out and attacked him, and captured nearly all his horses and mules." [12] Actually the captured livestock were mostly mules, but they were pack animals which had been carrying Howard's supplies and ammunition. Leaving the soldiers floundering in

their rear, the Indians crossed Targhee Pass into Yellowstone
Park on August 22.

Only five years earlier the Great Council in Washington had
made the Yellowstone area into the country's first national park,
and in that summer of 1877 the first adventuresome American
tourists were admiring its natural wonders. Among them was
none other than the Great Warrior Sherman, who had come out
West on an inspection tour to find out how fewer than three
hundred Nez Percé warriors, burdened with their women and
children, could make fools out of the entire Army of the Northwest.

When Sherman learned that the fleeing Indians were crossing
Yellowstone Park almost within view of his luxurious camp, he
began issuing urgent orders to fort commanders in all directions
to put a network of soldiers around these impudent warriors.
Nearest at hand was the Seventh Cavalry, which had been
brought back to strength during the year since Custer led it to
disaster on the Little Bighorn. Eager to vindicate the regiment's
honor by a victory over any Indians willing to fight, the Seventh
moved southwestward toward the Yellowstone. During the first
week in September Nez Percé scouts and Seventh Cavalry scouts
sighted each other's columns almost daily. By clever maneuvering, the Indians shook loose from the Seventh after a skirmish
at Canyon Creek, and headed north for Canada. They had no
way of knowing, of course, that the Great Warrior Sherman
had ordered Bear Coat Miles in a forced march from Fort
Keogh, on a course that would cut across their path.

On September 23, after fighting rearguard actions almost
daily, the Nez Percés forded the Missouri River at Cow Island
Landing. During the next three days scouts reported no sign
of soldiers anywhere. On the twenty-ninth, hunters located a
small buffalo herd. As they were short of food and ammunition
and their horses were badly worn from the fast pace, the chiefs
decided to camp in the Bear Paw Mountains. Next day, after
filling their empty stomachs on buffalo meat, they would try to
reach the Canadian border in one more long march.

"We knew General Howard was more than two suns back on
our trail," Yellow Wolf said. "It was nothing hard to keep ahead
of him." [13]

Next morning, however, two scouts came galloping from the south, shouting, "Soldiers! Soldiers!" While the camp was preparing to move out, another scout appeared on a distant bluff, waving a blanket signal—*Enemies right on us! Soon the attack!*

It was a cavalry charge ordered by Bear Coat Miles, whose Indian scouts a few hours earlier had picked up the trail of the Nez Percés. Riding with the charging cavalry were the thirty Sioux and Cheyenne scouts who had been bought by the Bluecoats at Fort Robinson, the young warriors who had turned their backs on their people by putting on soldier uniforms—an action which had precipitated the assassination of Crazy Horse.

The thunder of six hundred galloping horses made the earth tremble, but White Bird calmly posted his warriors in front of the camp. As the first wave of pony soldiers swept down upon them, the Nez Percé warriors opened with deadly accurate fire. In a matter of seconds they killed twenty-four soldiers, wounded forty-two others, and stopped the charge in a wild scramble of plunging horses and unsaddled troopers.

"We fought at close range," Chief Joseph said, "not more than twenty steps apart, and drove the soldiers back upon their main line, leaving their dead in our hands. We secured their arms and ammunition. We lost, the first day and night, eighteen men and three women." Among the dead were Joseph's brother Ollokot and the tough old prophet Toohoolhoolzote.

When darkness fell the Nez Percés tried to slip away to the north, but Bear Coat had put a cordon of soldiers completely around their camp. The warriors spent the night digging entrenchments, expecting another attack at daylight.

Instead of attacking, however, Bear Coat sent a messenger out with a white flag. The messenger brought a demand for Joseph to surrender and save the lives of his people. Joseph sent back a reply: he would think about it and let General Miles know his decision soon. Snow had begun to fall, and the warriors were hopeful that a blizzard might provide an escape screen to Canada.

Later in the day, some of Miles's Sioux scouts rode out under another truce flag. Joseph walked across the battlefield to meet them. "They said they believed that General Miles was sincere and really wanted peace. I walked on to General Miles's tent."

For the next two days Joseph was a prisoner, held by Bear Coat in violation of the flag of truce. During this time Miles brought up artillery and resumed the attack, but the Nez Percé warriors held their ground, and Joseph refused to surrender while he was a prisoner. On both days a bitter cold wind flung showers of snow over the battlefield.

On the third day, Joseph's warriors managed to get him free. They captured one of Miles's officers and threatened to kill him unless the general released their chief. That same day, however, General Howard and his lumbering army arrived to reinforce Miles, and Joseph knew that his dwindling band of warriors was doomed. When Miles sent truce messengers to arrange a battlefield council, Joseph went to hear the general's surrender terms. They were simple and direct: "If you will come out and give up your arms," Miles said, "I will spare your lives and send you to your reservation." [14]

Returning to his besieged camp, Joseph called his chiefs together for the last time. Looking Glass and White Bird wanted to fight on, to the death if necessary. They had struggled for thirteen hundred miles; they could not quit now. Joseph reluctantly agreed to postpone his decision. That afternoon in the final skirmish of the four-day siege, a sharpshooter's bullet struck Looking Glass in the left forehead and killed him instantly.

"On the fifth day," Joseph said, "I went to General Miles and gave up my gun." He also made an eloquent surrender speech, which was recorded in the English translation by Lieutenant Charles Erskine Scott Wood,* and in time it became the most quoted of all American Indian speeches:

> Tell General Howard I know his heart. What he told me before I have in my heart. I am tired of fighting. Our chiefs are killed. Looking Glass is dead. Toohoolhoolzote is dead. The old men are all dead. It is the young men who say yes or no. He who led on the young men [Ollokot] is dead. It is cold and we have no blankets. The little children are freezing to death. My people,

---

* Lieutenant Wood left the Army not long afterward to become a lawyer and an author of satirical poems and essays. His experiences with Chief Joseph and the Nez Percés influenced his later life; he became an ardent fighter for social justice and a defender of the dispossessed.

some of them, have run away to the hills, and have no blankets, no food; no one knows where they are—perhaps freezing to death. I want to have time to look for my children and see how many of them I can find. Maybe I shall find them among the dead. Hear me, my chiefs! I am tired; my heart is sick and sad. From where the sun now stands I will fight no more for-ever.[15]

After dark, while the surrender arrangements were under way, White Bird and a band of unyielding warriors crept through ravines in small groups and started running on foot for the Canadian border. On the second day they were across, and on the third day they saw mounted Indians in the distance. One of the approaching Indians made a sign: *What Indians are you?*

Nez Percé, they replied, and asked: *Who are you?*

Sioux, was the answer.

The next day Sitting Bull took the fugitive Nez Percés into his Canadian village.[16]

For Chief Joseph and the others, however, there was to be no freedom. Instead of conducting them to Lapwai, as Bear Coat Miles had promised, the Army shipped them like cattle to Fort Leavenworth, Kansas. There, on a swampy bottomland, they were confined as prisoners of war. After almost a hundred died, they were transferred to a barren plain in the Indian Territory. As had happened to the Modocs, the Nez Percés sickened and died—of malaria and heartbreak.

Bureaucrats and Christian gentlemen visited them frequently, uttering words of sympathy and writing endless reports to various organizations. Joseph was allowed to visit Washington, where he met all the great chiefs of government. "They all say they are my friends," he said, "and that I shall have justice, but while their mouths all talk right I do not understand why nothing is done for my people. . . . General Miles promised that we might return to our own country. I believed General Miles, or *I never would have surrendered.*"

He then made an impassioned appeal for justice: "I have heard talk and talk, but nothing is done. Good words do not last long unless they amount to something. Words do not pay for my dead people. They do not pay for my country, now overrun

by white men. . . . Good words will not give my people good
health and stop them from dying. Good words will not get my
people a home where they can live in peace and take care of
themselves. I am tired of talk that comes to nothing. It makes
my heart sick when I remember all the good words and broken
promises. . . . You might as well expect the rivers to run backward as that any man who was born a free man should be contented when penned up and denied liberty to go where he pleases.
. . . I have asked some of the great white chiefs where they get
their authority to say to the Indian that he shall stay in one
place, while he sees white men going where they please. They
cannot tell me.

"Let me be a free man—free to travel, free to stop, free to
work, free to trade where I choose, free to choose my own
teachers, free to follow the religion of my fathers, free to think
and talk and act for myself—and I will obey every law, or submit to the penalty." [17]

But no one listened. They sent Joseph back to Indian Territory, and there he remained until 1885. In that year, only 287
captive Nez Percés were still alive, most of them too young to
remember their previous life of freedom, or too old and sick and
broken in spirit to threaten the mighty power of the United
States. Some of the survivors were permitted to return to their
people's reservation at Lapwai. Chief Joseph and about 150
others were considered too dangerous to be penned up with other
Nez Percés, whom they might influence. The government shipped
them to Nespelem on the Colville Reservation in Washington,
and there they lived out their lives in exile. When Joseph died
on September 21, 1904, the agency physician reported the cause
of death as "a broken heart."

FOURTEEN

Cheyenne Exodus

1878—January 10, resolution introduced in U.S. Senate that women be given a hearing on suffrage. June 4, Britain takes Cyprus from Turkey. July 12, yellow-fever epidemic begins in New Orleans; 4,500 die. October 18, Edison succeeds in subdividing electric current, adapting it for household use; gas stocks fall on New York Exchange. December, in St. Petersburg, Russia, university students battle police and cossacks. In Austria, Ferdinand Mannlicher invents magazine repeating rifle. David Hughes invents the microphone. New York Symphony Society founded. Gilbert and Sullivan present *H.M.S. Pinafore*.

We have been south and suffered a great deal down there. Many have died of diseases which we have no name for. Our hearts looked and longed for this country where we were born. There are only a few of us left, and we only wanted a little ground, where we could live. We left our lodges standing, and ran away in the night. The troops followed us. I rode out and told the troops we did not want to fight; we only wanted to go north, and if they would let us alone we would kill no one. The only reply we got was a volley. After that we had to fight our way, but we killed none who did not fire at us first. My brother, Dull Knife, took one-half of the band and surrendered near Fort Robinson. . . . They gave up their guns, and then the whites killed them all.

—OHCUMGACHE (LITTLE WOLF) OF THE NORTHERN CHEYENNES

*All we ask is to be allowed to live, and live in peace. . . . We bowed
to the will of the Great Father and went south. There we found a
Cheyenne cannot live. So we came home. Better it was, we thought,
to die fighting than to perish of sickness. . . . You may kill me here;
but you cannot make me go back. We will not go. The only way to
get us there is to come in here with clubs and knock us on the head,
and drag us out and take us down there dead.*

—TAHMELAPASHME (DULL KNIFE) OF THE NORTHERN CHEYENNES

*I regard the Cheyenne tribe of Indians, after an acquaintance with
quite a number of bands, as the finest body of that race which I
have ever met.*

—THREE FINGERS (COLONEL RANALD S. MACKENZIE)

IN THE Moon of Greening Grass, 1877, when Crazy
Horse brought his Oglala Sioux to surrender at Fort Robinson,
various bands of Cheyennes who had joined him during the
winter also gave up their horses and arms, placing themselves
upon the mercy of the soldiers. Among the Cheyenne chiefs
were Little Wolf, Dull Knife, Standing Elk, and Wild Hog.
Together their people numbered about one thousand. Two Moon
and 350 Cheyennes, who had been separated from the others
after the Little Bighorn fight, went down the Tongue River to
Fort Keogh and surrendered to Bear Coat Miles.

The Cheyennes who came to Fort Robinson expected to live
on the reservation with the Sioux in accordance with the treaty
of 1868, which Little Wolf and Dull Knife had signed. Agents
from the Indian Bureau informed them, however, that the treaty
committed them to live either on the Sioux reservation *or on
a reservation set apart for the Southern Cheyennes*. The agents
recommended that the Northern Cheyennes be transferred to
Indian Territory to live with their kinsmen, the Southern Cheyennes.

"Our people did not like this talk," Wooden Leg said. "All of us wanted to stay in this country near the Black Hills. But we had one big chief, Standing Elk, who kept saying it would be better if we should go there. I think there were not as many as ten Cheyennes in our whole tribe who agreed with him. There was a feeling that he was talking this way only to make himself a big Indian among the white people." [1]

While the government authorities were deciding what to do with the Northern Cheyennes, the Bluecoat chiefs at Fort Robinson recruited some of the warriors to serve as scouts to help find scattered bands which were still out and were unwilling to accept the inevitability of surrender.

William P. Clark, a cavalry lieutenant, persuaded Little Wolf and a few of his warriors to work with him. Clark wore a white hat while in the field, and that was the name the Cheyennes gave him—White Hat. They soon discovered that White Hat genuinely liked Indians, was interested in their way of life, their culture, language, religion, and customs. (Clark later published a scholarly treatise on the Indian sign language.)

Little Wolf could have stayed on at Fort Robinson with White Hat, but when orders came from Washington for the Cheyennes to be marched overland to Indian Territory, he decided to go with his people. Before leaving, the apprehensive Cheyenne chiefs asked for a final council with Three Stars Crook. The general tried to reassure them, telling them to go down and have a look at the Indian Territory; if they did not like it they could come back north. (At least that was the way the interpreters translated Crook's words.)

The Cheyennes wanted White Hat to go south with them, but the Army assigned the escort duty to Lieutenant Henry W. Lawton. "He was a good man," Wooden Leg said, "always kind to the Indians." [2] They called Lawton the Tall White Man, and were pleased when he let the old and sick people ride in the soldier wagons during the day and gave them Army tents to sleep in at night. The Tall White Man also saw that everyone received enough bread and meat and coffee and sugar.

On the way south they followed familiar hunting trails, keeping away from towns, but they could see that the Plains were changing, filling up with railroads and fences and buildings

everywhere. They sighted a few small herds of buffalo and antelope, and the Tall White Man issued rifles to thirty warriors
chosen by the chiefs so they could go out and hunt.

There were 972 Cheyennes who started from Fort Robinson
in the Moon When the Ponies Shed. After traveling for almost
a hundred sleeps, 937 of them reached Fort Reno on the Cheyenne-Arapaho reservation, August 5, 1877. A few old people had
died along the way; a few young men had slipped away to turn
back north.

Three Fingers Mackenzie was at Fort Reno to meet them.
He took away their horses and what few weapons they had, but
this time he did not shoot their horses, promising that their
agent would return them after they had settled down to farming on their new land. Then he transferred the Cheyennes to
the care of the agent, John D. Miles.

After a day or so the Southern Cheyennes invited their northern relatives to a customary tribal feast for newcomers, and it
was there that Little Wolf and Dull Knife first discovered that
something was wrong. The feast consisted of little more than
a pot of watery soup; this was all that the southerners had to
offer. There was not enough to eat in this empty land—no wild
game, no clear water to drink, and the agent did not have enough
rations to feed them all. To make matters worse, the summer
heat was unbearable. and the air was filled with mosquitoes and
flying dust.

Little Wolf went to the agent and told him they had come
only to take a look at the reservation. Now, because they did
not like it, they were ready to go back north as Three Stars
Crook had promised they could do. The agent replied that only
the Great Father in Washington could decide when or whether
the Northern Cheyennes could go back to the Black Hills country. He promised to get more food; a beef herd was being driven
up from Texas for them.

The Texas Longhorns were scrawny, and their meat was as
tough as their hides, but at least the Northern Cheyennes could
now make soup as their relatives did. In late summer, the northerners began to fall sick with shaking chills, hot fevers, and an
aching of bones. The sufferers wasted away in their misery. "Our

people died, died, died, kept following one another out of this world." [3]

Little Wolf and Dull Knife complained to the agent and the soldier chief at Fort Reno until the Army at last sent Lieutenant Lawton, the Tall White Man, to make an inspection of the Northern Cheyenne camp. "They are not getting supplies enough to prevent starvation," Lawton reported. "Many of their women and children are sick for want of food. A few articles I saw given them they would not use themselves, but said they would take them to their children, who were crying for food. . . . The beef I saw given them was of very poor quality, and would not have been considered merchantable *for any use.*"

The post surgeon had no quinine to alleviate the epidemic of malaria which was decimating the northerners. "He frequently locked up his office because he had no medicines and went away, because he did not want to be called upon by the Indians when he could do nothing for them." [4]

The Tall White Man called the chiefs together, not to talk to them but to listen. "We came down on the word of General Crook," Dull Knife said. "We are still strangers in this country. We wish to get settled down where we are to live permanently and then we will send our children to school."

The other chiefs and head men indicated their impatience with Dull Knife's words. He was not talking strong enough. They held a short consultation and then chose Wild Hog to speak for them.

"Since we have been at this agency," Wild Hog said, "we have drawn from the agent no corn, hard bread, hominy, rice, beans, or salt; yeast powder and soap only once in a while. The sugar and coffee we get only lasts about three days, and is issued for seven; and beef about the same. The flour has been very bad, very black, and we cannot make it rise." As for the beef cattle, Wild Hog added, "a good many were lame, and looked as though they had been starved to death."

Other chiefs spoke up then and told of the sickness and death among the people. The Cheyennes had agreed to use the white man's medicine, but they could find no doctor who would give them any. If the Tall White Man would let them go hunting, they said, they could have buffalo meat to make them well again.

Only their agent could give them permission to hunt buffalo, Lawton replied, but he promised to ask Three Fingers Mackenzie (then commanding at Fort Sill) to intercede for them.

Mackenzie, who had made a career of killing Cheyennes and their horses, was able to afford compassion for the survivors now that they were defenseless. After receiving Lieutenant Lawton's reports, Three Fingers complained strongly to General Sheridan: "I am expected to see that Indians behave properly whom the government is starving—and not only that, but starving in flagrant violation of agreement." At the same time, he advised the commander at Fort Reno, Major John K. Mizner, to cooperate with the agent in obtaining rations for the Cheyennes. "If the Indians from hunger run off contrary to the wishes of the agent to get buffalo, do not attempt to cause their return, or the troops will be placed in the position of assisting in a great wrong." [5]

Not until the coming of the cold moons did agent Miles grant permission for the Northern Cheyennes to go out for a buffalo hunt, and then he put some of the southerners to spy on them to make certain they would not run away to the north on the horses he had returned to them. The buffalo hunt was so miserable a failure that the hunters would have joked about it had not everyone been starving for meat. Buffalo bones were everywhere on the southern Plains, ghostly heaps of bones left by white hunters, but the Cheyennes could find nothing to hunt but a few coyotes. They killed the coyotes and ate them, and before the winter was over they had to eat all their dogs to supplement the agency's meager rations of beef. Some talked of eating the horses given to them by the agent for hunting, but the chiefs would not hear of this. If they decided to go back north they would need every horse they could get.

All this while, Three Fingers and the Tall White Man had been trying to get more food for the Cheyennes, but no response came from Washington. When pressed for an explanation, the new Secretary of the Interior, Carl Schurz, said that "such details do not in the nature of things come to the knowledge of the Secretary. It is the business of the Indian Office." Yet Schurz

33. *Dull Knife. Courtesy of the Smithsonian Institution.*

had been appointed Secretary for the express purpose of bringing reforms to the Indian Office. He declared that the discontent among the Northern Cheyennes was traceable to chiefs
who wanted "to keep up the old traditions and to keep the other
Indians from work." He admitted that appropriations were not
sufficient to purchase enough rations to comply with treaty provisions, but hoped that through "utmost economy" and "careful management" the Indian Office would be able to get through
the year with only a small deficiency. (Some of the Indian Territory chiefs who went to Washington that year found Schurz
amazingly ignorant of Indian matters. The Cheyennes called
him Mah-hah Ich-hon, Big Eyes, and marveled that a man with
such enormous organs of vision could know so little.[6])

With the coming of the warm moons, mosquitoes began
swarming in the reservation bottomlands, and soon the Northern Cheyennes were again afflicted with fever and chills. To add
to the illnesses, a measles epidemic struck the children. In the
Moon of Red Cherries, there were so many burial ceremonies
that Little Wolf decided the chiefs must go and confront agent
Miles. He and Dull Knife were both getting old—well past the
half-century mark—and they knew it did not matter very much
what happened to them. But it was their duty to save the
young people, the tribe itself, from being blotted off the earth.

Miles agreed to meet them, and Little Wolf was spokesman.
"Since we have been in this country, we are dying every day,"
he said. "This is not a good country for us, and we wish to return to our home in the mountains. If you have not the power
to give us permission to go back there, let some of us go to
Washington, and tell them there how it is here, or do you write
to Washington and get permission for us to go back north."

"I cannot do this now," the agent replied. "Stay here for one
more year, and then we will see what we can do for you."

"No." Little Wolf spoke firmly. "We cannot stay another
year; we want to go now. Before another year has passed, we may
all be dead, and there will be none of us left to travel north."

Some of the young men then asked permission to add their
voices to the council. "We are sickly and dying here," one said,
"and no one will speak our names when we are gone."

"We will go north at all hazards," another said, "and if we.

34. *Little Wolf. Courtesy of the Smithsonian Institution.*

die in battle our names will be remembered and cherished by all our people." [7]

During August the chiefs counseled among themselves, and a division came among them. Standing Elk, Turkey Leg, and some others were fearful of starting back north. The soldiers would track them down and kill them all; it was better to die on the reservation. Early in September Little Wolf, Dull Knife, Wild Hog, and Left Hand moved their bands a few miles away from the others so as to be ready to travel quickly when they knew the time had come to start north. Every day they were making trades, giving up long-cherished belongings for ponies and what few old guns the Southern Cheyennes and Arapahos were willing to part with. But they did not try to fool the agent. In fact, when Little Wolf made up his mind to start north in the Drying Grass Moon, he went to see Miles and told him he was going back to his own country. "I do not want to see blood spilt about this agency. If you are going to send your soldiers after me, I wish that you would first let me get a little distance away from this agency. Then if you want to fight, I will fight you, and we can make the ground bloody at that place."

Miles apparently did not believe the dissident chiefs would actually attempt such an impossible journey; he reasoned that they knew as well as he that the Army would stop them. Yet he took the precaution of sending Edmond Guerrier (the half-breed Southern Cheyenne who had survived Sand Creek in 1864) out to Little Wolf's camp to warn him.

"If you go," Guerrier told Little Wolf, "you will have trouble."

"We do not want trouble," Little Wolf replied. "We are not looking for anything of that kind. All we want is to get back to where we came from." [8]

During the night of September 9, Little Wolf and Dull Knife told their people to pack and be ready to start at first daylight. They left their tepees standing empty behind them and headed northward across the sand hills—297 men, women, and children. Less than a third of them were warriors—the strongest of heart in a proud, doomed tribe. There were not enough horses for all, and they took turns at riding and walking. A few young men rode ahead, searching for more ponies wherever they could find them.

In the days when the Cheyennes numbered in the thousands, they had more horses than any of the Plains tribes. They were called the Beautiful People, but fate had turned against them both in the south and in the north. After twenty years of decimation they were closer to obliteration than the buffalo.

For three days they traveled as though driven by a common will, straining nerves and muscles, showing no mercy to their horses. On September 13 they crossed the Cimarron 150 miles north of Fort Reno, and chose a defensive position where four canyons crisscrossed. Cedar brakes gave the warriors excellent cover.

The soldiers caught up with them there, and sent an Arapaho guide into the canyons to parley. The Arapaho made blanket signs, warning the Cheyennes to turn around and go back to the reservation. When Little Wolf showed himself, the Arapaho moved closer and told him the soldier chief wanted no fight, but if the Cheyennes did not follow him back to Fort Reno, they would be attacked.

"We are going north," Little Wolf replied, "as it was promised we might, when we consented to come down to this country. We intend to go peaceably, if possible, without injuring or destroying any property of the white man on the way, and we will attack no one unless we are first molested. If the soldiers fight us we will fight them, and if white men, who are not soldiers, help to fight us, we will fight them also." [9]

Soon after the Arapaho took Little Wolf's reply back to the soldier chief (Captain Joseph Rendlebrock), the soldiers advanced into the canyons and began firing. This was a foolish thing for the soldiers to do, because the Cheyennes were hidden all around them in the cedar brakes. All day and all night they kept the soldiers trapped there without water. The following morning the Cheyennes began slipping away to the north in small parties, leaving the soldiers to retreat.

Now the fight became a running battle across Kansas and into Nebraska. Soldiers swarmed from all the forts—cavalrymen galloping from forts Wallace, Hays, Dodge, Riley, and Kearney, infantrymen riding in railroad cars back and forth along the three parallel iron tracks that ran between the Cimarron and the Platte. To keep moving swiftly, the Cheyennes exchanged their tired mounts for white men's horses. They tried to avoid fights, but the ranchers, cowboys, and settlers, even tradesmen in the little towns, joined in the pursuit. Ten thousand soldiers and three thousand white men who were not soldiers harried the fleeing Cheyennes unceasingly, thinning the defending warriors, picking off the old and young who fell behind. In the last two weeks of September, soldiers caught up with them five times, but each time they found their way out. By keeping to rough country, they made it impossible for the soldiers to use wagons or the big guns on wheels, yet as soon as they escaped from one pursuing column of Bluecoats, another was always there to take the place of the one left behind.

In the first days of the Moon of Falling Leaves, they crossed the Union Pacific Railroad, forded the Platte, and raced for the familiar sand hills of Nebraska. Three Stars Crook dispatched parallel columns across their path, but admitted that "to catch them would be as hard a task as to catch a flock of frightened crows." [10]

In the mornings now there was frost on the yellowing grass, but the crisp air was like a tonic after the long hot summer in Indian Territory. Six weeks of flight had left their clothing and blankets in tatters; there was never enough to eat; they were still so short of horses that half the men were taking turns riding and running.

At one night camp, the chiefs took a count. Thirty-four of those who had started from Indian Territory were missing. Some had scattered during the fights and were making their way north by other trails, but most had died from the white men's bullets. The older people had grown weak, the children were suffering from lack of food and sleep, and few of them could travel much farther. Dull Knife said that they should go to Red Cloud's agency and ask Red Cloud to give them food and shelter against the cold moons, which would soon be upon them. Many times they had helped Red Cloud when he was fighting for the Powder River country. Now it was his turn to help the Cheyennes.

Little Wolf scoffed at such talk. He was going to Cheyenne

country, to the Tongue river valley, where they could find plenty of meat and skins and live like Cheyennes again.

In the end the chiefs settled the matter amicably. Those who wished to go on to Tongue River could follow Little Wolf; those who were tired of running could follow Dull Knife to Red Cloud's agency. The next morning, 53 men, 43 women, and 38 children continued straight north with Little Wolf. About 150 turned northwestward with Dull Knife—a few warriors, and the old, the children, the wounded. After some deliberation, Wild Hog and Left Hand also went with Dull Knife so as to be with their children, the last strong seed of the Beautiful People.

On October 23 Dull Knife's column was only two sleeps from Fort Robinson when a driving snowstorm caught them on the open plain. The heavy wet flakes blinded the struggling marchers, turned the horses' coats white, and slowed their progress. Suddenly, out of the swirling blizzard, appeared a ghostly troop of cavalry. The Cheyennes were surrounded.

The soldier chief, Captain John B. Johnson, sent an interpreter forward and quickly arranged a parley. Dull Knife told the captain that he wanted no trouble; all he wanted was to reach Red Cloud or Spotted Tail so that his people could find food and shelter.

Red Cloud and Spotted Tail had been moved far north to Dakota, the captain informed him. No longer was there a reservation in the Nebraska country, but Fort Robinson had not yet been closed. The soldiers would take them to the fort.

At first Dull Knife objected, but as dusk came on there was an icy bite in the blizzard; the Cheyennes were freezing and starving. Dull Knife said he would follow the soldiers to the fort.

Darkness came down fast, and the soldiers made camp along a creek, posting guards around the Cheyennes. That night the chiefs talked uneasily among themselves, wondering what the soldiers would do with them. They decided to dismantle their best guns and pistols, leaving the broken ones to be turned in if the soldier chief ordered them to give up their arms. All through the hours of darkness they took the guns apart, giving the barrels to the women to conceal beneath their clothing, tying springs, locks, pins, cartridges, and other small pieces to beads and moccasins as though they were ornaments. Sure enough, the next morning Captain Johnson ordered his men to disarm the Cheyennes. They placed their broken rifles, pistols, and bows and arrows in a little pile, and the captain let the soldiers take them for souvenirs.

On October 25 they reached Fort Robinson and were assigned a log barracks that had been built to house a company of 75 soldiers. Although the 150 Cheyennes were crowded, they were glad for shelter. The soldiers gave them blankets, plenty of food and medicine, and there was friendliness and admiration in the eyes of the guards who kept watch over their barracks.

Each day Dull Knife asked the post commander, Major Caleb Carlton, when they could go on to Red Cloud's new agency. Carlton told him they would have to wait until he received orders from Washington. To show his sympathy for the Cheyennes, he gave permission for a few warriors at a time to go out after wild game, lending them hunting rifles and ponies. They found but few animals of any kind; the prairie around Fort Robinson was empty and lonely with all the tepees gone, but the Cheyennes enjoyed the freedom to roam without fear, even though it was only for a day at a time.

Early in the Moon When the Wolves Run Together, their friend Major Carlton left the fort and a new commander came. Captain Henry W. Wessells. The Cheyennes heard the enlisted men speak of him as the Flying Dutchman; Wessells was always darting about the fort, spying on the Cheyennes, entering their barracks unannounced, peering into corners, his eyes searching everywhere. It was during this moon the white men called December that Red Cloud was brought down from Dakota to counsel with them.

"Our hearts are sore for you," Red Cloud said. "Many of our blood are among your dead. This has made our hearts bad. But what can we do? The Great Father is all-powerful. His people fill the whole earth. We must do what he says. We have begged him to allow you to come to live among us. We hope he may let you come. What we have we will share with you. But remember, what he directs, that you must do. We cannot help you. The snows are thick on the hills. Our ponies are thin. The game is scarce. You cannot resist, nor can we. So listen to your old friend and do without complaint what the Great Father tells you."

So Red Cloud had grown old and cautious in his later years. Dull Knife had heard he was a prisoner on his own Dakota reservation. The Cheyenne chief arose, looking sadly on the seamed face of his old Sioux brother. "We know you for our friend, whose words we may believe," he said. "We thank you for asking us to share your lands. We hope the Great Father will let us come to you. All we ask is to be allowed to live, and to live in peace. I seek no war with anyone. An old man, my fighting days are done. We bowed to the will of the Great Father and went far into the south where he told us to go. There we found a Cheyenne cannot live. Sickness came among us that made mourning in every lodge. Then the treaty promises were broken, and our rations were short. Those not worn by diseases were wasted by hunger. To stay there meant that all of us would die. Our petitions to the Great Father were unheeded. We thought it better to die fighting to regain our old homes than to perish of sickness. Then our march was begun. The rest you know."

Dull Knife turned toward Captain Wessells: "Tell the Great Father that Dull Knife and his people ask only to end their days here in the north where they were born. Tell him we want no more war. We cannot live in the south; there is no game. Here, when rations are short, we can hunt. Tell him if he lets us stay here Dull Knife's people will hurt no one. Tell him if he tries to send us back we will butcher each other with our own knives." [11]

Wessells stammered out a few words. He promised to let the Great Father know what Dull Knife had spoken.

Less than a month later, January 3, 1879, a message came to Captain Wessells from the War Department. General Sheridan and Big Eyes Schurz had made up their minds about Dull Knife's Cheyennes. "Unless they are sent back to where they came from," Sheridan said, "the whole reservation system will receive a shock which will endanger its stability." Schurz concurred: "The Indians should be taken back to their reservation." [12]

In the fashion of the War Department the order was for immediate action, regardless of the winter weather. It was the Moon When the Snow Drifts into the Tepees, the season of bitter cold and raging blizzards.

"Does the Great Father desire us to die?" Dull Knife asked
Captain Wessells. "If so we will die right here. We will not go
back!" [13]

Wessells replied that he would give the Cheyennes five days to
change their minds. During that time they would be kept prisoners in the barracks and would receive no food, or wood for the
heating stove.

And so for five days the Cheyennes huddled together in the
barracks. Snow fell almost every night, and they scraped it off
the window ledges for water. But there was nothing to eat
except scraps and bones left from previous meals, and the frost
in the barracks bit at hands and faces.

On the ninth of January, Wessells summoned Dull Knife and
the other chiefs to his headquarters. Dull Knife refused to go,
but Wild Hog, Crow, and Left Hand went away with the soldiers. After a few minutes Left Hand came running out with his
wrists manacled, soldiers crowding upon him, but before he was
silenced he shouted so that the people in the barracks would
know what had happened. Wild Hog told Captain Wessells that
not one Cheyenne would go south again, and the captain had
ordered him put in irons. In an attempt to escape, Wild Hog tried
to kill the soldiers, but they had overcome him.

After a while Wessells came outside the barracks and talked
to them through the windows. "Let the women and children
out," he ordered, "so they will no longer suffer."

"We'll all die here together sooner than be sent south," they
answered.[14]

Wessells went away, and then soldiers came and put chains
and iron bars over the doors of the barracks. Night came, but
moonlight on the snow made everything outside as light as day;
it glittered on the steel bayonets of the six soldier guards who
stamped back and forth in their hooded greatcoats.

One of the warriors pushed the cold stove aside and lifted a
section of planking. Below on the dry earth were five gun barrels, hidden there since the first day. From ornaments and
moccasins, they began collecting triggers and hammers and
cartridges. Soon they had the rifles and a few pistols back
together again. The young men painted their faces and put on
their best clothing, while the women made little stacks of saddles

and bundles beneath each window so that everyone could leap out quickly. Then the best marksmen among the warriors took positions at assigned windows, each choosing one of the guards outside as his target.

At 9:45 P.M. the first shots were fired. At the same moment, every window sash burst outward, and the Cheyennes poured from the building. Seizing the rifles of the dead and wounded guards, they ran toward the line of bluffs beyond the bounds of the post. They had about ten minutes' start on foot before the first mounted troops galloped in pursuit, some riding in their winter underwear. The warriors quickly formed a defense line while the women and children crossed a creek. Because of their few weapons, the warriors kept firing and falling back, firing and falling back. More soldiers were coming all the time, fanning out into an enveloping arc, and they were shooting every Indian that moved across the snow. In the first hour of fighting, more than half the warriors died, and then the soldiers began overtaking scattered bands of women and children, killing many of them before they could surrender. Among the dead was Dull Knife's daughter.

When morning came, the soldiers herded 65 Cheyenne prisoners, 23 of them wounded, back into Fort Robinson. Most were women and children. Only 38 of those who had escaped were still alive and free; 32 were together, moving north through the hills and pursued by four companies of cavalry and a battery of mountain artillery. Six others were hidden among some rocks only a few miles from the fort. Among the latter was Dull Knife; the others were his wife and surviving son, his daughter-in-law and grandchild, and a young boy named Red Bird.

For several days the cavalrymen followed the 32 Cheyennes, until at last they trapped them near Hat Creek Bluffs in a deep buffalo wallow. Charging to the edge of the wallow, the cavalrymen emptied their carbines into it, withdrew, reloaded, and repeated the action until no fire was returned by the Indians. Only nine Cheyennes survived, most of them being women and children.

During the last days of January, traveling only by night, Dull Knife and his party made their way north to Pine Ridge. There they became prisoners on Red Cloud's reservation.

Little Wolf and his followers spent the winter in concealed pits which they dug along the frozen banks of Lost Chokecherry Creek, one of the tributaries of the Niobrara. When the weather warmed slightly in the Sore Eye Moon, they started northward for Tongue River country. On Box Elder Creek they met Two Moon and five other Northern Cheyennes, who were working as scouts for the Bluecoats at Fort Keogh.

Two Moon told Little Wolf that White Hat Clark was out looking for him, and wanted to hold a council with him. Little Wolf replied that he would be glad to see his old friend, White Hat. They met about half a mile from the Cheyenne camp, Lieutenant Clark disarming himself to show that he had confidence in their friendship. The lieutenant said that his orders were to bring the Cheyennes into Fort Keogh, where some of their relatives had surrendered and were now living. The price of peace, he added, was their guns and ponies; they could keep the ponies until they reached Fort Keogh, but they must surrender their guns now.

"Since I left you at Red Cloud agency," Little Wolf replied, "we have been down south, and have suffered a great deal down there. . . . My brother, Dull Knife, took one-half of the band and surrendered near Fort Robinson. He thought you were still there and would look out for him. They gave up their guns and then the whites killed them all. I am out in the prairie, and need my guns here. When I get to Keogh I will give you the guns and ponies, but I cannot give up the guns now. You are the only one who has offered to talk before fighting, and it looks as though the wind, which has made our hearts flutter for so long, would now go down." [15]

Little Wolf had to give up his guns, of course, but not until he was convinced that White Hat would not let the soldiers destroy his people. They went on to Fort Keogh, and there most of the young men enlisted as scouts. "For a long time we did not do much except to drill and work at getting out logs from the timber," Wooden Leg said. "I learned to drink whiskey at Fort Keogh. . . . I spent most of my scout pay for whiskey." [16] The Cheyennes drank whiskey from boredom and despair; it made the white traders rich, and it destroyed what was left of the leadership in the tribe. It destroyed Little Wolf.

After months and months of bureaucratic delay in Washington, the widows and orphans and the remnant of warriors at Fort Robinson were transferred to Red Cloud's agency at Pine Ridge, where they joined Dull Knife. And then after more months of waiting, the Cheyennes at Fort Keogh were given a reservation on Tongue River, and Dull Knife and the dwindling few at Pine Ridge were permitted to join their people.

For most of them it was too late. The force was gone out of the Cheyennes. In the years since Sand Creek, doom had stalked the Beautiful People. The seed of the tribe was scattered with the wind. "We will go north at all hazards," a young warrior had said, "and if we die in battle our names will be remembered and cherished by all our people." Soon there would be no one left who could care enough to remember, no one to speak their names now that they were gone.

FIFTEEN

Standing Bear Becomes a Person

1879—January 11, British-Zulu war begins in South Africa. February 17, in St. Petersburg, Russia, nihilists attempt to assassinate Czar Alexander. October 21, Edison exhibits his first incandescent lamp. Henry George's *Progress and Poverty* is published. First stage production of Henrik Ibsen's *A Doll's House.*

You have driven me from the East to this place, and I have been here two thousand years or more. . . . My friends, if you took me away from this land it would be very hard for me. I wish to die in this land. I wish to be an old man here. . . . I have not wished to give even a part of it to the Great Father. Though he were to give me a million dollars I would not give him this land. . . .

When people want to slaughter cattle they drive them along until they get them to a corral, and then they slaughter them. So it was with us. . . . My children have been exterminated; my brother has been killed.

—Standing Bear of the Poncas

The soldiers came to the borders of the village and forced us across the Niobrara to the other side, just as one would drive a herd of ponies; and the soldiers pushed us on until we came to the Platte River. They drove us on in advance just as if we were a herd of ponies. and I said, "If I have to go, I'll go to that land. Let the soldiers go away, our women are afraid of them." And so I reached the Warm Land [Indian Territory]. We found the land there was bad and we were dying one after another, and we said, "What man will take pity on us?" And our animals died. Oh, it was very hot. "This land is truly sickly, and we'll be apt to die here, and we hope the Great Father will take us back again." That is what we said. There were one hundred of us died there.

—White Eagle of the Poncas

I~N~ 1804, at the mouth of the Niobrara River on the right bank of the Missouri, Lewis and Clark met with a friendly tribe of Indians called the Poncas. The tribe then numbered only two or three hundred, the survivors of a massive epidemic of the white man's smallpox. Half a century later, the Poncas were still there, still friendly and eager to trade with white men, their sturdy tribe increased to about a thousand. Unlike most Plains Indians, the Poncas raised corn and kept vegetable gardens, and because they were prosperous and owned many horses, they frequently had to fight off raiders from Sioux tribes to the north.

In 1858, the year when government officials were traveling through the West setting up boundaries on the land for different tribes, the Poncas gave up part of their territory in exchange for promises made by the officials to guarantee them protection of their persons and property and a permanent home on the Niobrara. Ten years later, however—while the treaty makers were negotiating with the Sioux—through some bureaucratic blunder in Washington the Ponca lands were included with territory assigned the Sioux in the treaty of 1868.

Although the Poncas protested over and over again to Washington, officials took no action. Wild young men from the Sioux tribes came down demanding horses as tribute, threatening to drive the Poncas off land which they now claimed as their own. "The seven years that followed this treaty," said Peter Le Claire, a member of the tribe, "were years when the Poncas were obliged to work their gardens and cornfields as did the Pilgrims in New England . . . with hoe in one hand and rifle in the other." [1]

Congress at last acknowledged the treaty obligations of the United States "to protect" the Poncas, but instead of restoring their land, appropriated a small amount of money "to indemnify the tribe for losses by thefts and murders committed by the Sioux." [2] Then, in 1876, following the Custer defeat, Congress decided to include the Poncas in the list of northern tribes who were to be exiled to Indian Territory. The Poncas, of course, had nothing to do with the Custer fight, had never engaged in any warfare with the United States, yet someone in Washington arranged for Congress to appropriate twenty-five thousand dollars "for the removal of the Poncas to the Indian Territory, and providing them a home therein, with consent of said band." That last phrase was as conveniently overlooked as were the promises of the treaty which forbade white persons to settle on Ponca territory; for ten years white settlers had been intruding on Ponca lands, and their eyes were greedy for the rich alluvial fields on which grew the finest Indian corn on the Plains.

The first news the Poncas had of their impending removal was brought to them early in January, 1877, by a United States Indian inspector, Edward C. Kemble. "A white man came there suddenly after Christmas to see us," Chief White Eagle said. "We didn't get any news he was coming; he came suddenly. They called us all to the church and there they told us the purpose of his coming."

White Eagle's account of what followed:

> "The Great Father at Washington says you are to move, and for that reason I've come," said he.
>
> "My friend, you have caused us to hear these things very suddenly," I said. "When the Great Father has any business to transact with us he generally sends word to all the people, but you have come very suddenly."
>
> "No; the Great Father says you have to go," said he.
>
> "My friend, I want you to send a letter to the Great Father, and if he really says this I desire him to send for us," I said. "If it be so, and I hear of it the right way, I'll say the words are straight."
>
> "I'll send a letter to him," said he. He struck the wire. He sent the message by telegraph and it reached the Great Father very soon.
>
> "Your Great Father says you are to come with ten of your chiefs," said he. "You are to go and see the land, and after passing through a part you are to come to Washington. You are to look at the Warm Land [Indian Territory] and if you see any land that is good there you are to tell him about it," said he, "and also about any bad land there; tell him about both."
>
> And so we went there to the Warm Land. We went to the terminus of a railroad and passed through the land of the Osages and on to the land full of rocks, and next morning we came to the land of the Kaws; and leaving the Kansas reserva-

tion we came to Arkansas City, and so, having visited the lands of two of these Indian tribes and seen this land full of rocks and how low the trees were, I came to this town of the whites. We were sick twice and we saw how the people of that land were, and we saw those stones and rocks, and we thought those two tribes were not able to do much for themselves.

And he said to us the next morning, "We'll go to the Shicaska River and see that."

And I said, "My friend, I've seen these lands and I've been sick on the journey. From this on I'll stop on this journey, seeing these lands, and will go and see the Great Father. Run to the Great Father. Take me with you to see the Great Father. These two tribes are poor and sick, and these lands are poor; therefore, I've seen enough of them."

"No," said he, "come and see these other lands in the Indian Territory."

"My friend," said I, "take me, I beg, to see the Great Father. You said formerly we could tell him whatever we saw, good or bad, and I wish to tell him."

"No," said he, "I don't wish to take you to see him. If you take part of this land I'll take you to see him; if not, not."

"If you will not take me to see the Great Father," said I, "take me home to my own country."

"No," said he, "notwithstanding what you say, I'll not take you to see the Great Father. He did not say I should take you back to your own country."

"How in the world shall I act," said I. "You are unwilling to take me to the Great Father, and you don't want to take me back to my own country. You said formerly that the Great Father had called me, but now it is not so; you have not spoken the truth; you have not spoken the straight word."

"No," said he, "I'll not take you to your homes; walk there if you want to."

"It makes my heart feel sad," said I, "as I do not know this land." We thought we should die, and felt that I should cry, but I remembered that I was a man. After saying this, the white man, being in a bad humor, went upstairs. After he had gone upstairs, we chiefs sat considering what to do. We said, "He does not speak of taking us to see the Great Father or of taking us to our own country. We don't think the Great Father has caused this." We had one interpreter there with us, and we said, "As he will not take us back, we want him to give us a piece of

paper to show the whites, as we don't know the land." The
interpreter went upstairs to see the man and came back and
said, "He will not give you the paper. He does not wish to make
it for you." We sent the interpreter back again and said, "We
want some money from that due us from the Great Father, so
we can make our way home." When he came back, he said, "He
does not wish to give you the money." [3]

White Eagle, Standing Bear, Big Elk, and the other Ponca
chiefs who were left stranded in Indian Territory by Inspector
Kemble now started back home. It was the Moon When the
Ducks Come Back and Hide, and snow covered the Plains of
Kansas and Nebraska. As they had only a few dollars among
them, they walked the entire distance—more than five hundred
miles—each man with one blanket and no spare moccasins. Had
it not been for their old friends the Otoes and Omahas, on whose
reservations they stopped to rest and obtain food, few of the
older chiefs could have survived the winter journey.

Forty days later, when they reached the Niobrara, they found
Inspector Kemble there ahead of them.

White Eagle's narrative:

"Move ye," said he; "prepare to move."
We were unwilling. Said I, "I've come back weary. Every
one of us is unwilling to move."
"No," said he, "the Great Father wishes you to remove at
once, and you must move to the Indian Territory." [4]

The chiefs were united, however, in their determination to
hold the government to its treaty obligations, and Kemble decided to return to Washington to report to the Commissioner of
Indian Affairs. The commissioner took the problem to Secretary
of the Interior Schurz, who in turn passed it to the Great Warrior
Sherman. Sherman recommended the use of troops to force the
Poncas to move, and as usual Big Eyes Schurz concurred.

In April Kemble returned to the Niobrara, and by using the
threat of troops persuaded 170 members of the tribe to start with
him for Indian Territory. None of the leading chiefs would go
with him. Standing Bear protested so strongly that he was ordered arrested and taken to Fort Randall. "They fastened me

and made a prisoner of me and carried me to the fort," he said.[5] A few days later the government sent a new agent, E. A. Howard, to deal with the remaining three-fourths of the tribe, and Standing Bear was released.

White Eagle, Standing Bear, and the other chiefs continued to insist that the government had no right to move them from their land. Howard replied that he had nothing to do with the government's decision; he had been sent there to go with them to their new home. After a four-hour council on April 15, Howard ended it by demanding a final answer: "Will you go peaceably or by force?" [6]

The chiefs remained silent, but before they returned to their homes, a young Ponca hurried to warn them. "The soldiers have come to the lodges." The chiefs knew then that there would be no more councils. They would have to leave their homeland and go to Indian Territory. "The soldiers came with their guns and bayonets," Standing Bear said. "They aimed their guns at us, and our people and our children were crying."

They started on May 21, 1877. "The soldiers came to the borders of the village," White Eagle said, "and forced us across the Niobrara to the other side, just as one would drive a herd of ponies; and the soldiers pushed us on until we came to the Platte River." [7]

Agent Howard methodically kept a diary of that fifty-day overland journey. On the morning they started, a heavy thunderstorm caused a sudden flooding of the Niobrara, sweeping several of the soldiers off their horses; instead of watching them drown, the Poncas plunged in and rescued them. The next day a child died, and they had to stop for a burial on the prairie. On May 23 a two-hour thunderstorm caught them in the open, drenching everyone throughout the day. A second child died; several Poncas fell ill during the night. Next day they had to ford flooded streams because of washed-out bridges. The weather turned cold. On May 26 rain fell all day and there was no wood for fires.

On May 27 sickness from exposure was affecting most of the Poncas. Standing Bear's daughter, Prairie Flower, was very ill with pneumonia. Next day thunderstorms and heavy rain made progress almost impossible in the deep mud of the road.

Now it was the Hot Weather Begins Moon, with showers falling almost every day. On June 6 Prairie Flower died, and Standing Bear gave her a Christian burial in the cemetery at Milford, Nebraska. "The ladies of Milford prepared and decorated the body for burial in a style becoming the highest civilization," Howard noted proudly. "Standing Bear was led to say to those around him at the grave that he was desirous of leaving off the ways of the Indian and adopting those of the white man."

That night a tornado struck the Ponca camp, demolishing tents, overturning wagons, and hurling people hundreds of feet, seriously injuring several of them. Next day another child died.

On June 14 they reached the Otoe reservation. The Otoes, taking pity on the Poncas, gave them ten ponies to aid in the completion of their journey. For three days they waited for high waters to subside; illnesses continued to increase; the first male adult, Little Cottonwood, died. Howard had a coffin made for him and arranged a Christian burial near Bluewater, Kansas.

On June 24 illness was so prevalent that Howard employed a physician at Manhattan, Kansas, to attend the Poncas. Next day two women died on the march. Howard saw that they received Christian burials.

Now it was the Middle of the Summer Moon. A child of Buffalo Chief died and received a Christian burial at Burlington, Kansas. A Ponca named Buffalo Track went berserk and tried to kill Chief White Eagle, blaming him for the tribe's miseries. Agent Howard banished Buffalo Track from the caravan and sent him back north to the Omaha reservation. The Poncas envied him for his punishment.

Summer heat and biting flies plagued them for another week, and then at last, on July 9, after a severe drenching in a thunderstorm, they reached the Quapaw reservation, their new home, and found the small group of Poncas who had preceded them living wretchedly in tents.

"I am of the opinion that the removal of the Poncas from the northern climate of Dakota to the southern climate of the Indian Territory," agent Howard wrote his superiors, "will prove a mistake, and that a great mortality will surely follow among the people when they shall have been here for a time and become poisoned with the malaria of the climate." [8]

Howard's ominous prediction proved to be all too accurate. Like the Modocs, the Nez Percés, and the Northern Cheyennes, the Poncas died so rapidly that by the end of their first year in Indian Territory almost one-fourth of them had received Christian burials.

In the spring of 1878 Washington officials decided to give them a new reservation on the west bank of the Arkansas, but failed to allot funds for their transfer. The Poncas walked 150 miles to their new land, but for several weeks they had no agent to issue them provisions or medicines. "The land was good," White Eagle said, "but in the summer we were sick again. We were as grass that is trodden down; we and our stock. Then came the cold weather, and how many died we did not know." [9]

One of those who died was the oldest son of Standing Bear. "At last I had only one son left; then he sickened. When he was dying he asked me to promise him one thing. He begged me to take him, when he was dead, back to our old burying ground by the Swift Running Water, the Niobrara. I promised. When he died, I and those with me put his body into a box and then in a wagon and we started north." [10]

Sixty-six Poncas made up the burial party, all of Standing Bear's clan, following the old wagon drawn by two gaunt horses. It was the Snow Thaws Moon, January, 1879. (Ironically, far away to the north, Dull Knife's Cheyennes were making their last desperate fight for freedom at Fort Robinson.) For Standing Bear this was a second winter journey home. He led his people over trails away from settlements and soldiers, and they reached the Omaha reservation before the soldiers could find them.

Big Eyes Schurz meanwhile had made several attempts through his agents to arrange for the return of Standing Bear's Poncas to Indian Territory. Finally in March he asked the War Department to telegraph Three Stars Crook's headquarters in Omaha, Nebraska, ordering him to arrest the runaways without delay and return them to Indian Territory. In response, Crook sent a company of soldiers up to the Omaha reservation; they arrested Standing Bear and his Poncas and brought them back to Fort Omaha, where they were placed under guard, awaiting arrangements for shipment to Indian Territory.

For more than a decade Three Stars had been fighting Indians, meeting them in councils, making them promises which he could not keep. Grudgingly at first, he admitted admiration for Indian courage; since the surrenders of 1877 he was beginning to feel both respect and sympathy for his old enemies. The treatment of Cheyennes at Fort Robinson during the last few weeks had outraged him. "A very unnecessary act of power to insist upon this particular portion of the band going back to their former reservation," he bluntly stated in his official report.[11]

When Crook went to see the Poncas in the guardhouse at Fort Omaha, he was appalled by the pitiable conditions of the Indians. He was impressed by Standing Bear's simple statements of why he had come back north, his stoic acceptance of conditions over which he had lost control. "I thought God intended us to live," Standing Bear told Crook, "but I was mistaken. God intends to give the country to the white people, and we are to die. It may be well; it may be well." [12]

Crook was so moved by what he saw and heard that he promised Standing Bear he would do all he could to countermand the orders for the return of the Poncas to Indian Territory. At this time Crook took action to support his promise. He went to see an Omaha newspaper editor, Thomas Henry Tibbles, and enlisted the power of the press.

While Crook held up orders for transfer of the Poncas, Tibbles spread their story across the city, the state, and then by telegraph across the nation. The churches of Omaha sent an appeal to Secretary Schurz to order the Poncas released, but Mah-hah Ich-hon—Big Eyes—did not bother to reply. A young Omaha lawyer, John L. Webster, then volunteered his services without a fee, and he was soon supported by the chief attorney of the Union Pacific Railroad, Andrew Poppleton.

The lawyers had to work quickly to build a case for the Poncas; any day, General Crook could receive orders from Washington compelling him to start the Indians southward, and then nothing could be done for them. All efforts were bent toward obtaining the cooperation of Judge Elmer S. Dundy, a rugged frontiersman with four main interests in life—good literature, horses, hunting, and the administration of justice. It so happened that Dundy was away on a bear hunt, and the Ponca supporters spent several anxious hours before messengers could find and bring the judge back to Omaha.

With Crook's tacit agreement, Judge Dundy issued a writ of *habeas corpus* upon the general, requiring him to bring the Ponca prisoners into court and show by what authority he held them. Crook obeyed the writ by presenting his military orders from Washington, and the district attorney for the United States appeared before the judge to deny the Poncas' right to the writ on the ground that Indians were "not persons within the meaning of the law."

Thus began on April 18, 1879, the now almost forgotten civil-rights case of *Standing Bear v. Crook*. The Poncas' lawyers, Webster and Poppleton, argued that an Indian was as much a "person" as any white man and could avail himself of the rights of freedom guaranteed by the Constitution. When the United States attorney stated that Standing Bear and his people were subject to the rules and regulations which the government had made for tribal Indians, Webster and Poppleton replied that Standing Bear and any other Indian had the right to separate themselves from their tribes and live under protection of United States laws like any other citizens.

The climax of the case came when Standing Bear was given permission to speak for his people: "I am now with the soldiers and officers. I want to go back to my old place north. I want to save myself and my tribe. My brothers, it seems to me as if I stood in front of a great prairie fire. I would take up my children and run to save their lives; or if I stood on the bank of an overflowing river, I would take my people and fly to higher ground. Oh, my brothers, the Almighty looks down on me, and knows what I am, and hears my words. May the Almighty send a good spirit to brood over you, my brothers, to move you to help me. If a white man had land, and someone should swindle him, that man would try to get it back, and you would not blame him. Look on me. Take pity on me, and help me to save the lives of the women and children. My brothers, a power, which I cannot resist, crowds me down to the ground. I need help. I have done." [13]

Judge Dundy ruled that an Indian was a "person" within the meaning of the *habeas corpus* act, that the right of expatriation

35. *Chief Standing Bear of the Poncas. Courtesy of Nebraska State Historical Society.*

was a natural, inherent, and inalienable right of the Indian as
well as the white race, and that in time of peace no authority,
civil or military, existed for transporting Indians from one section of the country to another without the consent of the Indians or to confine them to any particular reservation against
their will.

"I have never been called upon to hear or decide a case that
appealed so strongly to my sympathy," he said. "The Poncas
are amongst the most peaceable and friendly of all the Indian
tribes. . . . If they could be removed to the Indian Territory by
force, and kept there in the same way, I can see no good reason
why they might not be taken and kept by force in the penitentiary at Lincoln, or Leavenworth, or Jefferson City, or any other
place which the commander of the forces might, in his judgment, see proper to designate. I cannot think that any such
arbitrary authority exists in this country." [14]

When Judge Dundy concluded the proceedings by ordering
Standing Bear and his Ponca band released from custody, the
audience in the courtroom rose to its feet and, according to a
newspaper reporter, "such a shout went up as was never heard in
a courtroom." General Crook was the first to reach Standing
Bear to congratulate him.[15]

At first the United States district attorney considered appeal-
ing the decision, but after studying Judge Dundy's written
opinion (a brilliant essay on human rights), he made no appeal
to the Supreme Court. The United States government assigned
Standing Bear and his band a few hundred acres of unclaimed
land near the mouth of the Niobrara, and they were back home
again.

As soon as the surviving 530 Poncas in Indian Territory
learned of this astonishing turn of events, most of them began
preparations to join their relatives in Nebraska. The Indian
Bureau, however, was not sympathetic. Through its agents the
bureau informed the Ponca chiefs that only the Great Council
in Washington could decide if and when the tribe might return.
The bureaucrats and politicians (the Indian Ring) recognized
Judge Dundy's decision as a strong threat to the reservation
system; it would endanger the small army of entrepreneurs who
were making fortunes funneling bad food, shoddy blankets, and

poisonous whiskey to the thousands of Indians trapped on reservations. If the Poncas were permitted to leave their new reservation in Indian Territory and walk away as free American citizens, this would set a precedent which might well destroy the entire military-political-reservation complex.

In his annual report, Big Eyes Schurz admitted that the Poncas in Indian Territory "had a serious grievance," but he strongly opposed permitting them to return to their homeland because it would make other Indians "restless with a desire to follow their example" and thereby cause a breakup of the territorial reservation system.[16]

At the same time, William H. Whiteman, who headed the lucrative Ponca agency, tried to discredit Standing Bear's band by describing them as "certain renegade members of the tribe," and then he wrote in glowing terms of his considerable expenditures for materials and tools to develop the reservation in Indian Territory. Whiteman made no mention of the discontent prevalent among the Poncas, their constant petitions to return to their homeland, or of his feud with Big Snake.

Big Snake was Standing Bear's brother, a giant with hands like hams and shoulders as big as a buffalo's. Like many huge men, Big Snake was quiet and gentle of manner (the Poncas called him the Peacemaker), but when he saw that White Eagle and the other head men were being intimidated by agent Whiteman, he decided to take action on his own. After all, he was the brother of Standing Bear, the Ponca who had won freedom for his people.

Determined to test the new law, Big Snake requested permission to leave the reservation and go north to join his brother. As he expected, permission to leave was refused by agent Whiteman. Big Snake's next move was not to leave Indian Territory, but to travel only a hundred miles to the Cheyenne reservation. With him went thirty other Poncas, making what they believed to be a gentle testing of the law which said that an Indian was a person and could not be confined to any particular reservation against his will.

Whiteman's reaction was that of any entrenched bureaucrat whose authority is threatened. On May 21, 1879, he telegraphed the Commissioner of Indian Affairs, reporting the defection of

Big Snake and his party to the Cheyenne reservation, and requesting that they be arrested and detained at Fort Reno "until the tribe has recovered from the demoralizing effects of the decision recently made by the United States district court in Nebraska, in the case of Standing Bear." [17]

Big Eyes Schurz agreed to the arrest, but evidently fearing another challenge in the courts, he asked the Great Warrior Sherman to transport Big Snake and his "renegades" back to the Ponca reservation as quickly and quietly as possible.

In his usual blunt manner, Sherman telegraphed General Sheridan on May 22: "The honorable Secretary of the Interior requests that the Poncas arrested and held at Fort Reno, in the Indian Territory . . . be sent to the agency of the Poncas. You may order this to be done." And then, as if anticipating Sheridan's apprehensions about flying in the face of Judge Dundy's recent decision, Sherman decreed: "The release under writ of *habeas corpus* of the Poncas in Nebraska *does not apply to any other than that specific case.*" [18] For the Great Warrior Sherman it was easier to unmake laws than it was for the courts of the land to interpret them.

And so Big Snake lost his first test of his brother's victory at law, and he never had a chance to try again. After being brought back to the Ponca agency in the Corn Is in Silk Moon, Big Snake was marked for destruction. Agent Whiteman reported to Washington that Big Snake had "a very demoralizing effect upon the other Indians . . . extremely sullen and morose." In one paragraph Whiteman charged that Big Snake had repeatedly threatened to kill him, and in another complained that the Ponca had never spoken to him since his return. The agent became so furious that he begged the Commissioner of Indian Affairs "to arrest Big Snake and convey him to Fort Reno and there confine him for the remainder of his natural life." [19]

Finally, on October 25, Whiteman obtained authorization from Sherman to arrest Big Snake and imprison him in the agency guardhouse. To make the arrest, Whiteman requested a detail of soldiers. Five days later, Lieutenant Stanton A. Mason and thirteen soldiers arrived at the agency. Whiteman told Mason that he would send out a notice to the Poncas, ordering those who had money coming to them for special work to report to his office the next day. Big Snake would be among them, and as soon as he entered the office, Mason was to make the arrest.

On October 31 Big Snake entered Whiteman's office about noon and was told to take a chair. Lieutenant Mason and eight armed men then surrounded him, Mason informing him that he was under arrest. Big Snake wanted to know why he was being arrested. Whiteman spoke up then and said one charge against him was threatening his (Whiteman's) life. Big Snake calmly denied this. According to the post trader, J. S. Sherburne, Big Snake then stood up and threw off his blanket to show he was not armed.

Hairy Bear's statement: "The officer told Big Snake to come along, to get up and come. Big Snake would not get up, and told the officer he wanted him to tell him what he had done. He said he had killed no one, stolen no horses, and that he had done nothing wrong. After Big Snake said that, the officer spoke to the agent, and then told Big Snake he had tried to kill two men, and had been pretty mean. Big Snake denied it. The agent then told him he had better go, and would then learn all about it down there. Big Snake said he had done nothing wrong, and that he would die before he would go. I then went up to Big Snake and told him this man [the officer] was not going to arrest him for nothing, and that he had better go along, and that perhaps he would come back all right; I coaxed all I could to get him to go; told him that he had a wife and children, and to remember them and not get killed. Big Snake then got up and told me that he did not want to go, and that if they wanted to kill him they could do it, right there. Big Snake was very cool. Then the officer told him to get up, and told him that if he did not go, there might something happen. He said there was no use in talking; I came to arrest you, and want you to go. The officer went for the handcuffs, which a soldier had, and brought them in. The officer and a soldier then tried to put them on, but Big Snake pushed them both away. Then the officer spoke to the soldiers, and four of them tried to put them on, but Big Snake pushed them all off. One soldier, who had stripes on his arms, also tried to put them on, but Big Snake pushed them all off. They tried several times, all of them, to get hold of Big Snake and hold him. Big Snake was sitting down, when six soldiers got hold of him. He raised up and threw them off. Just then one of the soldiers, who was in front of him, struck Big Snake in the face with his gun, another soldier struck him alongside the head with the barrel of his gun. It knocked him back to the wall. He straightened up again. The blood was running down his face. I saw the gun pointed at him, and was scared, and did not want to see him killed. So I turned away. Then the gun was fired and Big Snake fell down dead on the floor." [20]

The Interior Department first issued a statement that Standing Bear's brother "Big Snake, a bad man" had been "shot accidentally." [21] The American press, however, growing more sensitive to treatment of Indians since the Standing Bear case, demanded an investigation in Congress. This time the military-political-reservation complex was operating in the familiar climate of Washington, and nothing came of the investigation.

The Poncas of Indian Territory had learned a bitter lesson. The white man's law was an illusion; it did not apply to them. And so, like the Cheyennes, the diminishing Ponca tribe was split in two—Standing Bear's band free in the north, the others prisoners in the Indian Territory.

SIXTEEN

"The Utes Must Go!"

The Army conquered the Sioux. You can order them around. But we Utes have never disturbed you whites. So you must wait until we come to your ways of doing things.
—OURAY THE ARROW, CHIEF OF THE UTES

I told the officer that this was a very bad business; that it was very bad for the commissioner to give such an order. I said it was very bad; that we ought not to fight, because we were brothers, and the officer said that that didn't make any difference; that Americans would fight even though they were born of the same mother.
—NICAAGAT (JACK) OF THE WHITE RIVER UTES

THE UTES were Rocky Mountain Indians, and for a generation they had watched the invading white men move into their Colorado country like endless swarms of grasshoppers. They had seen the white men drive their old enemies, the Cheyennes, from the Colorado plains. Some Ute warriors had joined the Rope Thrower, Kit Carson, in the white men's war against the Navahos. In those times the Utes believed the white men were their allies, and they enjoyed visiting Denver to exchange buffalo hides for gaudy trade goods in the stores. But each year these strange men from the East became more numerous, invading the Utes' mountains to dig for yellow and white metal.

In 1863 the governor of Colorado Territory (John Evans) and other officials came to Conejos in the San Juan Mountains to meet with Ouray the Arrow and nine chiefs of the Utes. A treaty was signed there, giving the white men all the Colorado land east of the mountaintops (the Continental Divide), leaving the Utes all the land west of the divide. In exchange for ten

thousand dollars' worth of goods and ten thousand dollars' worth
of provisions to be distributed annually for ten years, the Utes
agreed to relinquish mineral rights to all parts of their territory,
and they promised not to molest any citizen of the United
States who might come into their mountains to dig.

Five years later, the white men of Colorado decided they had
let the Utes keep too much land. Through political pressures
they persuaded the Indian Bureau that the Utes were a constant nuisance—wandering everywhere, visiting towns and mining camps, and stealing livestock from settlers. They said they
wanted the Utes placed on a reservation with well-defined lines,
but what they truly wanted was more Ute land. Early in 1868,
with a great deal of fanfare, the Indian Bureau invited Ouray,
Nicaagat (Jack), and eight other chiefs to Washington. Rope
Thrower Carson accompanied them as trusted friend and ad-
viser. In Washington they were quartered in a fine hotel, served
excellent meals, and given an abundance of tobacco, candy, and
medals.

When the time came for treaty making, the officials insisted
that one of the visiting chiefs must accept responsibility for all
seven bands represented. Ouray the Arrow was the unanimous
choice for chief of all the Utes. He was half-Apache, half-Un-
compahgre Ute, a handsome, round-faced, sharp-eyed Indian
who could speak English and Spanish as fluently as the two
Indian tongues he knew. When the land-hungry politicians
tried to put him on the defensive, Ouray was sophisticated
enough to present the Utes' case to newspaper reporters. "The
agreement an Indian makes to a United States treaty," he said,
"is like the agreement a buffalo makes with his hunters when
pierced with arrows. All he can do is lie down and give in." [1]

The officials could not fool Ouray with their bright-tinted
maps and unctuous phraseology about boundary lines. Instead
of accepting a small corner of western Colorado, he held out for
sixteen million acres of western slope forests and meadows, considerably less territory than his people had claimed before, but
considerably more than the Colorado politicians wanted them
to have. Two agencies were to be established, one at Los Pinos
for the Uncompahgres and other southern bands, one on White
River for the northern bands. Ouray also demanded the inclu-

36. *Ouray. Courtesy of State Historical Society of Colorado.*

sion of certain protective clauses in the new treaty, words meant
to keep miners and settlers off the Ute reservation. According
to the treaty, no unauthorized white men would "ever be permitted to pass over, settle upon, or reside in" the territory assigned to the Utes.

In spite of this restriction, the miners continued to trespass.
Among them was Frederick W. Pitkin, a New England Yankee
who ventured into the San Juan Mountains and made a quick
fortune mining silver. In 1872 Pitkin became a leading advocate among owners of wealthy mining interests who wanted to
add the San Juan area—one-fourth of the Ute reservation—to
Colorado Territory. Bowing to the miners' wishes, the Indian
Bureau sent out a special commission headed by Felix R. Brunot
to negotiate with the Utes for cession of this land.

At Los Pinos agency in September, 1873, Brunot's commission met Ouray and representatives of the seven Ute nations.
Brunot told the chiefs that the Great Father had asked him to
come and talk to them about giving up some of their reservation
land. He assured them that he did not want the land for himself, and had not come to tell them what to do, but to hear what
they had to say about the matter. "It is much better sometimes
to do what does not please us just now," Brunot counseled, "if
we think it will be best for our children."

The chiefs wanted to know how it would benefit their children
if they gave up their land. Brunot explained that the government would set aside a large sum of money for the Utes, and
each year the tribe would be paid interest from it for the ceded
land.

"I do not like the interest part of the agreement," Ouray declared. "I would rather have the money in the bank." He then
complained because the government had not kept its treaty
promise to remove white men who were found trespassing on
the Ute reservation.

Brunot replied frankly that if the government tried to drive
the miners out, this would bring on a war, and the Utes would
lose their land without receiving any pay for it. "The best thing
that can be done," he said, "if you can spare these mountains,
is to sell them, and to have something coming in every year."

"The miners care very little about the government and do not obey the laws," Ouray agreed. "They say they do not care about the government. It is a long way off in the States, and they say the man who comes to make the treaty will go off to the States, and it will all be as they want it."

"Suppose you sell the mountains," Brunot continued, "and if there is no gold in them, then it would be a benefit to you. The Utes get the pay for them and the Americans would stay away. But suppose there are mines there, it will not stop the trouble. We could not keep the people away."

"Why cannot you stop them?" Ouray demanded. "Is not the government strong enough to keep its agreements with us?"

"I would like to stop them," Brunot said, "but Ouray knows it is hard to do."

Ouray said he was willing to sell the mountains, but not all the fine hunting land around them. "The whites can go and take the gold and come out again. We do not want them to build houses there."

Brunot replied that he did not believe this could be done. There was no way to force the miners to leave Ute territory once they had come and dug their mines there. "I will ask the Great Father to drive the miners away," he promised, "but a thousand other men will tell him to let them alone. Perhaps he will do as I say, perhaps not." [2]

After seven days of discussions, the chiefs agreed to accept the government's offer of twenty-five thousand dollars a year for the four million acres of treasure. As a bonus, Ouray was to receive a salary of one thousand dollars a year for ten years, "or so long as he shall remain head chief of the Utes and at peace with the United States." Thus did Ouray become a part of the establishment, motivated to preserve the status quo.

Living in a paradise of magnificent meadows and forests abundant with wild game, berries, and nuts, the Utes were self-supporting and could have existed entirely without the provisions doled out to them by their agents at Los Pinos and White River. In 1875 agent F. F. Bond at Los Pinos replied to a request for a census of his Utes: "A count is quite impossible. You might as well try to count a swarm of bees when on the wing. They travel all over the country like the deer which they hunt." Agent E. H. Danforth at White River estimated that about nine hundred Utes used his agency as a headquarters, but he admitted that he had had no luck in inducing them to settle down in the valley around the agency. At both places, the Utes humored their agents by keeping small beef herds and planting a few rows of corn, potatoes, and turnips, but there was no real need for any of these pursuits.

The beginning of the end of freedom upon their own reservation came in the spring of 1878, when a new agent reported for duty at White River. The agent's name was Nathan C. Meeker, former poet, novelist, newspaper correspondent, and organizer of cooperative agrarian colonies. Most of Meeker's ventures failed, and although he sought the agency position because he needed the money, he was possessed of a missionary fervor and sincerely believed that it was his duty as a member of a superior race to "elevate and enlighten" the Utes. As he phrased it, he was determined to bring them out of savagery through the pastoral stage to the barbaric, and finally to "the enlightened, scientific, and religious stage." Meeker was confident he could accomplish all this in "five, ten, or twenty years." [3]

In his humorless and overbearing way, Meeker set out systematically to destroy everything the Utes cherished, to make them over into his own image, as he believed he had been made in God's image. His first unpopular action was to move the agency fifteen miles down White River, where there was fine pastureland suitable for plowing. Here Meeker planned to build a cooperative agrarian colony for Ute Indians, but he overlooked the fact that the Utes had long been using the area as a hunting ground and for pasturing their horses. The site he chose to build agency buildings on was a traditional racing strip where the Utes enjoyed their favorite sport of betting on pony races.

Meeker found Quinkent (Douglas) to be the most amiable of the chiefs at White River. He was a Yampa Ute about sixty years old, his hair still dark, his pendant moustaches turning white. Douglas owned more than a hundred ponies, which made him rich by Ute standards, but he had lost most of his following among the younger men to Nicaagat (Jack).

Like Ouray, Jack was a half-blood Apache. As a boy he had

learned to speak a few words of English while living with a Mormon family, and he had served as a scout for General Crook during the Sioux wars. When he first met Meeker, Jack was wearing his scout uniform—frontier buckskins, Army boots, and a wide-brimmed hat. He always wore the silver medal given him by the Great Father when he went to Washington with Ouray in 1868.

Jack and his people were away on a buffalo hunt during the period that Meeker moved the agency, and when they came back to the original site they found everything gone. They made camp there, and after a few days Meeker came up to order Jack to move to the new site.

"I told him [Meeker] that the site of the old agency had been settled by treaty," Jack said afterward, "and that I knew of no law or treaty that made mention of the new site. Then the agent told me that we had better all move down below, and that if we did not we should be obliged to; that for that they had soldiers." [4] Meeker tried to placate Jack by promising to obtain milk cows for his band, but Jack replied that Utes had no need for either cows or milk.

Colorow was the third chief of importance, a Muache Ute in his sixties. For a few years after the treaty of 1868, Colorow and his people lived on a small temporary reservation adjoining Denver. When it pleased them they roamed freely through the town, dining in restaurants, attending theaters, and clowning for the white citizens. In 1875 the reservation was closed, and Colorow took his Muaches up to White River to join Jack's people. They missed the excitement of Denver, but enjoyed the fine hunting in the White River country. The Muaches were not interested in Meeker's agrarian society, and they visited the agency only when they wanted a few sacks of flour or some coffee and sugar.

Canalla (Johnson) was the chief medicine man, a brother-in-law of Ouray, and the operator of the pony-racing track where Meeker wanted to build the new agency houses. Johnson liked to wear a plugged hat which he had obtained in Denver. For some reason Meeker chose Johnson as the most likely man to help him lead the Utes out of savagery.

Also to assist him in his great crusade, Meeker brought his

wife, Arvilla, and his daughter, Josie, to the agency. He employed seven white workmen, including a surveyor, to lay out an irrigation canal, a lumberman, a bridge builder, a carpenter, and a mason. These men were expected to teach the Utes their trades while they were building the new agrarian paradise.

It was Meeker's fancy to have the Utes address him as Father Meeker (in their savage state he looked upon them as children), but most of them called him "Nick," much to his displeasure.

By the spring of 1879 Meeker had a few agency buildings under construction and forty acres of land plowed. Most of the work was done by his white employees, who were paid money for their efforts. Meeker could not understand why the Utes also expected money for building their very own cooperative agrarian community, but in order to get his irrigation ditches dug, he agreed to pay money to thirty Utes. They were willing workers until Meeker's funds were exhausted; then they went away to hunt or attend pony races. "Their needs are so few that they do not wish to adopt civilized habits," Meeker complained to the Commissioner of Indian Affairs. "What we call conveniences and comforts are not sufficiently valued by them to cause them to undertake to obtain them by their own efforts . . . the great majority look upon the white man's ways with indifference and contempt." He proposed a course of action to correct this barbaric condition: first, take away the Utes' hundreds of ponies so that they could not roam and hunt, replace the ponies with a few draft horses for plowing and hauling, and then as soon as the Utes were thus forced to abandon the hunt and remain near the agency, he would issue no more rations to those who would not work. "I shall cut every Indian down to the bare starvation point," he wrote Colorado's Senator Henry M. Teller, "if he will not work." [5]

Meeker's inveterate itch for writing down his ideas and observations, and then sending them off to be put into print, eventually brought him to a complete breaking point with the Utes. During the spring of 1879 he wrote an imaginary dialogue with one of the Ute women, attempting to show how the Indians could not comprehend the joys of work or the value of material goods. During the course of his dialogue, Meeker declared that the reservation land belonged to the government

37. *Nicaagat (Jack). From a group photograph taken around 1874. Courtesy of State Historical Society of Colorado.*

and was only assigned to the Utes for their use. "If you don't use it and won't work," he warned, "white men away off will come in and by and by you will have nothing." [6]

This little composition was first published in the *Greeley* (Colorado) *Tribune,* where it was seen by William B. Vickers, a Denver editor-politician who despised all Indians, especially Utes. Vickers at that time was serving as secretary to Frederick Pitkin, the wealthy miner who in 1873 had been the leader in separating the San Juan Mountains from Ute ownership. Pitkin had used his power to become governor of Colorado when it became a state in 1876. After the end of the Sioux wars in 1877, Pitkin and Vickers began drumming up a propaganda campaign to have all the Utes exiled to Indian Territory, thus leaving an immense amount of valuable land free for the taking. Vickers seized upon Nathan Meeker's newspaper essay as a fine argument for removing the Utes from Colorado, and he wrote an article about it for the *Denver Tribune:*

> The Utes are actual, practical Communists and the government should be ashamed to foster and encourage them in their idleness and wanton waste of property. Living off the bounty of a paternal but idiotic Indian Bureau, they actually become too lazy to draw their rations in the regular way but insist on taking what they want wherever they find it. Removed to Indian Territory, the Utes could be fed and clothed for about one half what it now costs the government.
>
> Honorable N. C. Meeker, the well-known Superintendent of the White River agency, was formerly a fast friend and ardent admirer of the Indians. He went to the agency in the firm belief that he could manage the Indians successfully by kind treatment, patient precept and good example. But utter failure marked his efforts and at last he reluctantly accepted the truth of the border truism that the only truly good Indians are dead ones. [7]

Vickers wrote considerably more, and his article was reprinted across Colorado under the title "The Utes Must Go!" By late summer of 1879, most of the white orators who abounded in frontier Colorado were uttering the applause-producing cry The Utes Must Go! whenever they were called upon to speak in public places.

In various ways the Utes learned that "Nick" Meeker had betrayed them in print. They were especially angry because their agent had said the reservation land did not belong to them, and they delivered a sort of official protest to him through the agency interpreter. Meeker reiterated his statement, and added that he had the right to plow any of the reservation he chose because it was government land and he was the agent of the government.

Meanwhile, William Vickers was accelerating his "Utes Must Go" campaign by manufacturing stories of Indian crimes and outrages. He even blamed the numerous forest fires of that unprecedented drought year on the Utes. On July 5 Vickers prepared a telegram to the Commissioner of Indian Affairs for Governor Pitkin's signature:

> Reports reach me daily that a band of White River Utes are off their reservation, destroying forests. . . . They have already burned millions of dollars of timber and are intimidating settlers and miners. . . . I am satisfied there is an organized effort on the part of Indians to destroy the timber of Colorado. These savages should be removed to Indian Territory where they can no longer destroy the finest forests in this state.[8]

The commissioner replied with a promise to the governor to take action, and then sent a warning to Meeker to keep his Utes on the reservation. When Meeker sent for the chiefs, he discovered they were holding an indignation meeting. They had already heard about the governor's false charges and his threats to send them to Indian Territory. A white friend named Peck who operated a supply store on Bear River north of the reservation had read the story in a Denver newspaper and told it to Nicaagat (Jack).

According to the news report, the Utes had set fires along Bear River and burned down a house belonging to James B. Thompson, a former Ute agent. Jack was much disturbed by the account, and Peck agreed to go with him to Denver to see Governor Pitkin to tell him that it was not true. They chose a route which would take them by the Thompson house. "We passed by there," Jack said afterward, "and we saw Thompson's house standing; it was not burned."

After a great deal of difficulty, Jack secured admittance to
Governor Pitkin's office. "The governor asked me how things
were in my country, on White River, saying that the papers
were saying a great deal about us. I told him I thought so myself, and for that reason I had come to Denver. I said I did not
understand why this business was in such a state. . . . He then
said, 'Here is a letter from your Indian agent.' I told him that,
as the Indian agent [Meeker] could write, he had written that
letter; but that I, not being able to write, had come to see him
in person and answer it. That much we talked; and then I told
him I did not wish him to believe what was written in that
letter. . . . He asked me if it was true that Thompson's house
was burned. I told him that I had seen the house—that it was
not burned. I then talked to the governor about the Indian
agent, and told him it would be well for him to write to Washington and recommend that some other agent be put in his place.
and he promised to write the next day." [9]

Pitkin, of course, had no intention of recommending a replace-
ment for Meeker. From the governor's viewpoint, everything
was moving in the right direction. All he had to do was wait for
a showdown between Meeker and the Utes, and then perhaps
—"The Utes Must Go!"

About this same time, Meeker was preparing his monthly report for the Commissioner of Indian Affairs. He wrote that he
was planning to establish a police force among the Utes. "They
are in a bad humor," he added, yet only a few days later he ini-
tiated actions which he surely must have known would make
the Utes even more belligerent. Although there is no direct evidence that Meeker sympathized with Governor Pitkin's "Utes
Must Go" program, almost every step he took seemed designed
to arouse the Indians to revolt.

Meeker may not have wanted the Utes to go, but he certainly
wanted their ponies banished. Early in September he ordered
one of his white workmen, Shadrach Price, to begin plowing a
section of grassland on which the Utes pastured their ponies.
Some of the Utes protested immediately, asking Meeker why
he did not plow somewhere else; they needed the grass for their
ponies. West of the pasture was a section of sageland, which
Quinkent (Douglas) offered to clear for plowing, but Meeker

stubbornly insisted upon plowing up the grass. The Utes' next move was to send out a few young men with rifles. They approached the plowman and ordered him to stop. Shadrach Price obeyed, but when he reported the threat to Meeker, the agent sent him back to finish his work. This time the Utes fired warning shots above Price's head, and the plowman hurriedly unhitched his horses and left the pasture.

Meeker was furious. He composed an indignant letter to the Commissioner of Indian Affairs. "This is a bad lot of Indians," he wrote; "they have had free rations so long, and have been flattered and petted so much, that they think themselves lords of all." [10]

That afternoon the medicine man, Canalla (Johnson), came to the agency office to see Meeker. He told Meeker that the land being plowed had been assigned to him for pasturing his ponies. Now that the plowing was stopped, he did not want it started again.

Meeker interrupted Johnson's impassioned speech. "The trouble is this, Johnson. You have too many ponies. You had better kill some of them." [11]

For a moment Johnson stared at Meeker in disbelief. Suddenly he moved toward the agent, caught him by the shoulders, pushed him out on the porch, and shoved him against the hitching rail. Without saying a word, Johnson then stalked away.

Johnson afterward related his version of the incident: "I told the agent that it was not right that he should order the men to plow my land. The agent told me I was always a troublesome man, and that it was likely I might come to the calaboose. I told him that I did not know why I should go to prison. I told the agent that it would be better for another agent to come, who was a good man, and was not talking such things. I then took the agent by the shoulder and told him it was better that he should go. Without doing anything else to him—striking him or anything else—I just took him by the shoulder. I was not mad at him. Then I went to my house." [12]

Before Meeker took further action, he summoned Nicaagat (Jack) to his office for a talk. Jack later recalled the meeting: "Meeker told me that Johnson had been mistreating him. I told Meeker that it was nothing, that it was a small matter and he

had better let it drop. Meeker said it didn't make any difference; that he would mind it and complain about it. I still told
him that it would be a very bad business to make so much fuss
about nothing. Meeker said he didn't like to have a young man
take hold of him, that he was an old man and had no strength
to retaliate, and he didn't want to have a young man take hold
of him in that way; he said that he was an old man and Johnson had mistreated him and he would not say any more to him;
that he was going to ask the commissioner for soldiers and that
he would drive the Utes from their lands. Then I told him it
would be very bad to do that. Meeker said that anyhow the land
did not belong to the Utes. I answered that the land did belong
to the Utes, and that was the reason why the government had
the agencies there, because it was the Utes' land, and I told
him again that the trouble between him and Johnson was a very
small matter and he had better let it drop and not make so much
fuss about it." [13]

For another day and night Meeker brooded over his deteriorat-
ing relations with the Utes, and then he finally made up his mind
that he must teach them a lesson. He dispatched two telegrams,
one to Governor Pitkin asking for military protection, another
to the Commissioner of Indian Affairs:

> I have been assaulted by a leading chief, Johnson, forced out
> of my own house, and injured badly. It is now revealed that
> Johnson originated all the trouble. . . . His son shot at the
> plowman, and the opposition to plowing is wide. Plowing stops;
> life of self, family, and employees not safe; want protection
> immediately; have asked Governor Pitkin to confer with
> General Pope.

During the following week, the ponderous machineries of the
Interior and War departments slowly moved into action. On
September 15 Meeker received notice that orders were being
transmitted to cavalry units to march to White River; the agent
was authorized to arrest "leaders in the late disturbance." [14]

The War Department dispatched orders to Major Thomas T.
Thornburgh, commanding at Fort Fred Steele, "to move with a
sufficient number of troops to the White River Ute agency,
Colorado, under special instructions." Because Thornburgh was

on an elk hunt, the orders were delayed in reaching him, and he did not move out until September 21. For the 150-mile march to White River, he outfitted about two hundred cavalrymen and mounted infantrymen.[15]

On September 25 Thornburgh reached Fortification Creek. The column was about halfway to the White River agency, and the major decided to send one of his guides ahead to notify Meeker that he could reach the agency in four more days; he asked Meeker to inform him of the current situation there. On that same day, Colorow and Nicaagat (Jack) learned of the approaching soldiers; the Ute chiefs were moving with their people toward Milk River for the customary autumn hunts.

Jack rode north to Bear River and met the troops there. "What is the matter?" he asked them. "What are you coming for? We do not want to fight with the soldiers. We have the same father over us. We do not want to fight them."

Thornburgh and his officers told Jack that they had received a telegram to go to the agency; that the Indians were burning up the forests around there and had burned Mr. Thompson's cabin. Jack replied that it was a lie; the Utes had not burned any forests or cabins. "You leave your soldiers here," he said to Thornburgh. "I am a good man. I am Nicaagat. Leave your soldiers here, and we will go down to the agency." Thornburgh replied that he had orders to march his soldiers to the agency. Unless he received word from agent Meeker to halt the column, he would have to take the soldiers on to White River.[16]

Jack again insisted that the Utes did not want to fight. He said it was not good that soldiers were coming into their reservation. Then he left Thornburgh and hurried back to the agency to warn "Nick" Meeker that bad things would happen if he let the soldiers come to White River.

On the way to Meeker's office, Jack stopped to see Quinkent (Douglas). They were rival chiefs, but now that all the White River Utes were in danger, Jack felt that the leaders must not be divided. The young Utes had heard too much talk about the white men sending them off to Indian Territory; some said they had heard Meeker boast that the soldiers were bringing a wagon-load of handcuffs and shackles and ropes and that several bad Utes would be hanged and others taken as prisoners. If they

believed the soldiers were coming to take them away from their
homeland, they would fight them to the death, and not even
the chiefs could stop them from fighting. Douglas said that he
wanted nothing to do with it. After Jack left, he put his American flag on a pole and mounted it above his lodge. (Perhaps
he had not heard that Black Kettle of the Cheyennes was flying
an American flag at Sand Creek in 1864.)

"I told the agent [Meeker] that the soldiers were coming,"
Jack said, "and that I hoped he would do something to stop
their coming to the agency. He said it was none of his business;
he would have nothing to do with it. I then said to the agent
I would like he and I to go where the soldiers were, to meet
them. The agent said that I was all the time molesting him; he
would not go. This he told me in his office; and after finally
speaking he got up and went into another room, and shut and
locked the door. That was the last time I ever saw him." [17]

Later in the day, Meeker evidently changed his mind and
decided to heed Jack's advice. He sent a message to Major
Thornburgh, suggesting that he halt his column and then come
to the agency with an escort of five soldiers. "The Indians seem
to consider the advance of the troops as a declaration of real
war," he wrote.[18]

On the following day (September 28), when the message
reached Thornburgh's camp on Deer Creek, Colorow also arrived
there to try to convince the major that he should proceed no
farther. "I told him I did not know at all why the troops had
come," Colorow said afterward, "or why there should be war." [19]
The column was then only thirty-five miles from White River
agency.

After reading Meeker's message, Thornburgh told Colorow
that he would move his troops down to the Milk River boundary of the Ute reservation; there he would camp his soldiers,
and then he and five men would go on to the agency to confer
with Meeker.

Not long after Colorow and his braves left Thornburgh's
camp, the major held an officers' meeting, during which he decided to change his plans. Instead of halting on the edge of the
reservation, the column would march on through Coal Creek
Canyon. This was a military necessity, Thornburgh explained,

38. *Quinkent, or Douglas. Courtesy of State Historical Society of Colorado.*

because Colorow's and Jack's camps were just below it. If the troops halted on Milk River, and the Utes decided to block the canyon, they could keep the soldiers from reaching the agency. From the south end of the canyon, however, only a few miles of open country would lie between them and White River.

Riding ahead of the column, Colorow arrived at his camp about nine o'clock on the morning of the twenty-ninth. He found his people very much excited over the approach of the soldiers. "I saw several start out in the direction toward the road where the soldiers were," he said. "Afterward I left also and came up to where the first ones who went out had gathered." There he met Jack and about sixty of his warriors. The two chiefs exchanged information, Jack telling Colorow about his unsatisfactory meeting with Meeker, and Colorow telling Jack that Major Thornburgh had promised to halt his soldiers at Milk River. "I then told Jack I thought it would be well for him to advise the young men not to make any warlike demonstrations at all, and he said it would be better to move them a piece off from the road. As yet we saw no soldiers from where we were, and we retired some distance from the road. Jack then said that when the soldiers should have arrived at Milk River [the line of the reservation] he would go down and see them." [20]

Neither Colorow nor Jack knew that Thornburgh's column had already passed Milk River. After watering his horses there, Thornburgh decided to send the wagons along the canyon road with one escort troop while he took the remainder of the cavalry over a more direct route across a high ridge. By an irony of chance this would bring them directly upon the angry Utes that Jack had drawn away from the road in order to avoid any possible encounter.

About this time, a young Ute who had gone ahead to reconnoiter came galloping back. "The troops are not stopping where they promised to stop yesterday, but are coming on," he told Jack.

Very much concerned now, Jack started up the ridge with his small band of warriors. In a few minutes he could see the soldiers' wagons strung out along the road that twisted through the sagebrush toward the canyon. "I stood up on the hill with twenty or thirty of my men, and all at once I saw thirty or

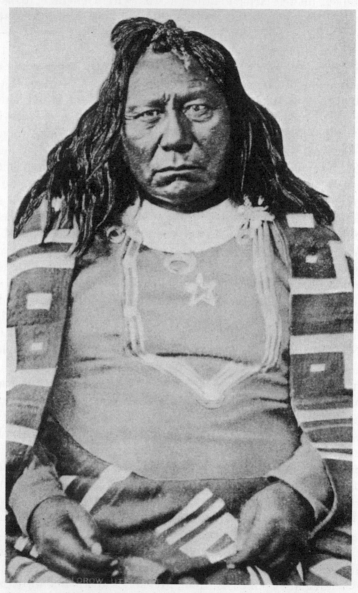

39. *Colorow. Possibly a William H. Jackson photograph. Courtesy of State Historical Society of Colorado.*

forty soldiers in my front, and just as soon as they saw me they deployed off one after another. I was with General Crook the year before, fighting the Sioux, and I knew in a minute that as soon as this officer deployed his men out in that way it meant fight; so I told my men to deploy also."

The officer commanding the advance cavalry troop was Lieutenant Samuel Cherry. After ordering his men to deploy, Cherry halted them at the base of the ridge and waited for Major Thornburgh to come forward. Thornburgh rode out a few yards and waved his hat to the Indians watching from the ridge. Several waved back.

For four or five minutes Jack waited for one of the officers to signal for a council, but they held their positions as though expecting the Utes to make the first move. "Then," Jack said afterward, "I and another Indian went out to meet them." Lieutenant Cherry dismounted and started walking toward the Utes. After taking a few steps, he waved his hat. A second later a single rifle shot broke the silence. "While we were still some distance apart, between the skirmish lines," Jack said, "a shot was fired. I don't know from which side, and in a second so many shots were fired, that I knew I could not stop the fight, although I swung my hat to my men and shouted, 'Don't fire; we only want to talk'; but they understood me to be encouraging them to fight." [21]

While the fighting grew in intensity, spreading to the wagon train, which went into a corral defense, news of the encounter reached Quinkent (Douglas) on the agency. He immediately went to "Nick" Meeker's office and told him that soldiers had come inside the reservation. Douglas was sure the Ute warriors would fight them. Meeker replied that he did not believe there would be any trouble, and then he asked Douglas to go with him the following morning to meet the soldiers.

By early afternoon all the Utes at White River had heard that the soldiers were fighting their people at Milk River. About a dozen of them took their rifles and went out among the agency buildings shooting at every white workman in sight. Before the day ended they killed Nathan Meeker and all his white male employees. They made captives of the three white women, and then fled toward an old Ute camp on Piceance Creek. Along the way each of the three white women was raped.

For almost a week the fighting continued at Milk River, with three hundred Ute warriors virtually surrounding the two hundred soldiers. Major Thornburgh was killed in the first skirmishing. When the fighting ended, his column had lost twelve killed, forty-three wounded. Thirty-seven Utes died in what they believed was a desperate stand to save their reservation from military seizure and to keep themselves from being taken as prisoners to Indian Territory.

At the Los Pinos agency, 150 miles to the south, Chief Ouray heard of the fighting with dismay. He knew that only immediate action could save his chieftainship and the entire Ute reservation. He dispatched a message by runner on October 2:

> To the chief captains, headmen, and Utes at the White River agency:
>
> You are hereby requested and commanded to cease hostilities against the whites, injuring no innocent persons or any others farther than to protect your own lives and property from unlawful and unauthorized combinations of horse thieves and desperados, as anything farther will ultimately end in disaster to all parties.[22]

Ouray's message and the arrival of cavalry reinforcements ended the fighting, but it was already too late to save the Utes from disaster. Governor Pitkin and William Vickers had been flooding Colorado with wild atrocity stories, many of them aimed at the innocent Uncompahgres at Los Pinos, most of whom were going peacefully about their business with no knowledge of what was happening at White River. Vickers called upon the white citizens of Colorado to rise up and "wipe out the red devils," inspiring the frantic organization of militia units in towns and villages across the state. So many newspaper reporters arrived from the East to report this exciting new "Indian War" that Governor Pitkin decided to give them a special statement for publication:

"I think the conclusion of this affair will end the depredations in Colorado. It will be impossible for the Indians and whites to live in peace hereafter. This attack had no provocation and the whites now understand that they are liable to be attacked in any part of the state where the Indians happen to be in sufficient force.

"My idea is that, unless removed by the government, they must necessarily be exterminated. I could raise 25,000 men to protect the settlers in twenty-four hours. The state would be willing to settle the Indian trouble at its own expense. The advantages that would accrue from the throwing open of 12,000,000 acres of land to miners and settlers would more than compensate all the expenses incurred." [23]

The White River Utes surrendered their three women captives, and then the inevitable investigating commission was formed to sift the causes, fix the blame, and set the punishments. The fight at Milk River was called an ambush, which it was not, and the affair at White River agency was called a massacre, which it was. Jack and Colorow and their followers were eventually excused from punishment on the grounds that they were warriors engaged in a fair fight. Douglas and the men at the agency were judged as murderers, but there was no one who could identify the Utes who had fired the shots that killed Nathan Meeker and his employees.

Douglas testified that he was in the agency storeroom when he heard the first gunshot. "I left the storeroom and went out a little way. Then I went to my house directly from where I was. When I started and got to my house it made me cry to think into what a state my friends had fallen." [24] But because Arvilla Meeker swore in secret hearings that Douglas had forced sexual union with her, the sixty-year-old chief was sent off to Leavenworth prison. He was not charged with or tried for any crime; a public accusation of rape would have caused embarrassment to Mrs. Meeker, and in that age of sexual reticence, the fact that the act involved an Indian made it doubly abhorrent.

Individual punishments, however, were of little interest to the miners and politicians. They wanted to punish the entire seven nations of Utes, to push them off those twelve million acres of land waiting to be dug up, dammed up, and properly deforested so that fortunes could be made in the process.

Ouray was a dying man in 1880 when the Indian Bureau brought him to Washington to defend the future of his people. Ill with nephritis, he bowed to the wishes of Big Eyes Schurz and other officials who decided "the Utes must go" to a new reservation in Utah—on land the Mormons did not want. Ouray died before the Army herded his people together in August, 1881, for the 350-mile march out of Colorado into Utah. Except for a small strip of territory along the southwest corner—where a small band of Southern Utes was allowed to live—Colorado was swept clean of Indians. Cheyenne and Arapaho, Kiowa and Comanche, Jicarilla and Ute—they had all known its mountains and plains, but now no trace of them remained but their names on the white man's land.

SEVENTEEN

The Last of the Apache Chiefs

1880—June 1, population of United States is 50,155,783.

1881—March 4, James A. Garfield inaugurated as President.
March 13, in Russia, nihilists assassinate Czar Alexander.
July 2, Garfield shot by assassin; dies September 19; Chester
A. Arthur becomes President.

1882—April 3, Jesse James shot and killed at St. Joseph, Missouri.
September 4, Edison switches on first commercial electric
lights in New York Central Station. Mark Twain's *Huckleberry
Finn* published.

1883—March 24, first telephone connection between New York and
Chicago. November 3, U.S. Supreme Court decides that an
American Indian is by birth an alien and a dependent.
Robert Louis Stevenson's *Treasure Island* published.

1884—January, Russia abolishes poll tax, last relic of serfdom.
March 13, in the Sudan, Siege of Khartoum begins.

1885—January 26, Khartoum falls to the Mahdi; Governor General
Charles George Gordon killed. March 4, Grover Cleveland
becomes first Democratic President since Civil War.

1886—May 1, general strikes spread across United States in
demand for eight-hour day. May 4, anarchists bomb police
in Haymarket Square, Chicago, killing seven, wounding sixty.
October 28, Statue of Liberty erected on Bedloe's Island.
December 8, American Federation of Labor founded.

I was living peacefully with my family, having plenty to eat, sleeping well, taking care of my people, and perfectly contented. I don't know where those bad stories first came from. There we were doing well and my people well. I was behaving well. I hadn't killed a horse or man, American or Indian. I don't know what was the matter with the people in charge of us. They knew this to be so, and yet they said I was a bad man and the worst man there; but what had I done? I was living peacefully there with my family under the shade of the trees, doing just what General Crook had told me I must do and trying to follow his advice. I want to know now who it was ordered me to be arrested. I was praying to the light and to the darkness, to God and to the sun, to let me live quietly there with my family. I don't know what the reason was that people should speak badly of me. Very often there are stories put in the newspapers that I am to be hanged. I don't want that anymore. When a man tries to do right, such stories ought not to be put in the newspapers. There are very few of my men left now. They have done some bad things but I want them all rubbed out now and let us never speak of them again. There are very few of us left.

—GOYATHLAY (GERONIMO)

A⸢FTER⸣ the death of Cochise in 1874, his oldest son, Taza, became chief of the Chiricahuas, and Taglito (Tom Jeffords) continued as agent on the Apache Pass reservation. Unlike his father, Taza was not able to secure the steadfast allegiance of all the Chiricahuas. Within a few months these Apaches were split into factions, and in spite of earnest efforts by both Taza and Jeffords, the raiding which Cochise had strictly forbidden was resumed. Because of the Chiricahua reservation's proximity to Mexico, it became a way station and sanctuary for Apache raiding parties moving in and out of Arizona and Mexico. Land-hungry settlers, miners, and politicians wasted no time in demanding removal of all Chiricahuas to some other location.

By 1875 the United States government's Indian policy was turning toward concentration of tribes either in Indian Territory or on large regional reservations. White Mountain, with its 2.5 million acres in eastern Arizona, was larger than all the other Apache reservations in the Southwest combined. Its agency, San Carlos, was already the administration point for seven Apache bands, and when Washington officials began receiving reports of trouble on the Chiricahua reservation, they saw this as an excellent excuse to move the Chiricahuas to San Carlos.

The agency, located at the junction of the San Carlos and Gila rivers, was considered by Army officers as a most undesirable hardship post. "A gravelly flat," wrote one, "rose some thirty feet or so above the river bottoms and was dotted here and there by the drab adobe buildings of the agency. Scrawny, dejected lines of scattered cottonwoods, shrunken, almost leafless, marked the course of the streams. Rain was so infrequent that it took on the semblance of a phenomenon when it came at all. Almost continuously dry, hot, dust-and-gravel-laden winds swept the plain, denuding it of every vestige of vegetation. In summer a temperature of 110° in the shade was cool weather. At all other times of the year flies, gnats, unnamable bugs . . . swarmed in the millions." [1]

The agent at this post in 1875 was John Clum, who a few months earlier had rescued Eskiminzin and his Aravaipas from Camp Grant and helped them become virtually self-sufficient on irrigated land along the Gila River. In his stubborn way, Clum forced the military to withdraw from the vast White Mountain reservation, and he replaced the troops with a company of Apaches to police their own agency, as well as establishing an Apache courts system to try offenders. Although his superiors were suspicious of Clum's unorthodox method of permitting Indians to make their own decisions, they could not quarrel with his success in keeping peace at San Carlos.

On May 3, 1876, agent Clum received a telegram from the Commissioner of Indian Affairs, ordering him to proceed to the

Chiricahua reservation to take charge of the Indians there, suspend agent Jeffords, and remove the Chiricahuas to San Carlos.
Clum had no enthusiasm for this distasteful assignment; he
doubted that the freedom-loving Chiricahuas would adjust to
the regulated life on White Mountain reservation. Insisting
that the Army keep its cavalrymen at a distance, Clum took
his Indian police to Apache Pass to inform the Chiricahuas of
their forced removal. He was surprised to find Jeffords and
Taza cooperative. Taza, like his father, Cochise, wanted to keep
peace. If the Chiricahuas must leave their homeland and go to
White Mountain in order to keep the peace, they would do so.
Only about half the Chiricahuas, however, marched overland to
San Carlos. When the Army moved into the abandoned reservation to round up the recalcitrants, most of them fled across the
border into Mexico. Among their leaders was a forty-six-year-
old Bedonkohe Apache who had allied himself as a youth with
Mangas Colorado, and then afterward followed Cochise, and
now considered himself a Chiricahua. He was Goyathlay, better
known to the white men as Geronimo.

Although the Chiricahuas who went voluntarily to San Carlos
did not have the same warmth of feeling for agent Clum that
some of the other Apache bands did, they caused him no trouble.
Later in the summer of 1876, when Clum secured permission
from the Indian Bureau to take twenty-two Apaches on a tour
of the East, he invited Taza to go along. Unfortunately, while
the party was visiting Washington, Taza died suddenly of
pneumonia and was buried in the Congressional Cemetery.
Upon Clum's return to San Carlos, he was confronted by Naiche,
a younger brother of Taza. "You took my brother away," Naiche
said. "He was well and strong, but you come back without him,
and you say he is dead. I do not know. I think maybe you not
take good care of him. You let him be killed by evil spirits of
paleface. I have great pain in my heart." [2]

Clum attempted to reassure Naiche by asking Eskiminzin to
give an account of Taza's death and burial, but the Chiricahuas
remained suspicious. Without Taglito Jeffords to advise them,
they were not sure how far they could trust John Clum or any
other white man.

During the winter of 1876–77, their relatives from Mexico

40. *Geronimo. From a photograph taken by A. Frank Randall in 1886. Courtesy of the Smithsonian Institution.*

occasionally slipped into the reservation with news of events below the border. They heard that Geronimo and his band were raiding their old enemies, the Mexicans, and were accumulating large herds of cattle and horses. In the spring Geronimo brought these stolen livestock up to New Mexico, sold them to white ranchers, and bought new guns, hats, boots, and much whiskey. These Chiricahuas settled down in a hideout near their Mimbres cousins at the Ojo Caliente agency, where Victorio was chief.

In March, 1877, John Clum received orders from Washington to take his Apache police to Ojo Caliente and transfer the Indians there to San Carlos. In addition, he was to arrest Geronimo and any other "renegade" Chiricahuas found in the vicinity.

Geronimo told about it afterward: "Two companies of scouts were sent from San Carlos. They sent word for me and Victorio to come to town. The messengers did not say what they wanted with us, but as they seemed friendly we thought they wanted a council and rode in to meet the officers. As soon as we arrived in town soldiers met us, disarmed us, and took us both to headquarters where we were tried by court-martial. They asked us only a few questions and then Victorio was released and I was sentenced to the guardhouse. Scouts conducted me to the guardhouse and put me in chains. When I asked them why they did this they said it was because I had left Apache Pass.

"I do not think that I ever belonged to those soldiers at Apache Pass, or that I should have asked them where I might go. . . . I was kept a prisoner for four months, during which time I was transferred to San Carlos. Then I think I had another trial, although I was not present. In fact I do not know that I had another trial, but I was told that I had, and at any rate I was released." [3]

Although Victorio was not put under arrest, he and most of the Warm Springs Apaches were transferred to San Carlos in the spring of 1877. Clum made an effort to win Victorio's confidence by assigning him more authority than the chief had ever had at Ojo Caliente. For a few weeks it seemed as if peaceable Apache communities might be developed on the White Mountain reservation, but then suddenly the Army moved a company of soldiers to the Gila River (Fort Thomas). The Army announced this as a precautionary move because of the concentra-

41. *Naiche and his wife. Courtesy of Arizona Historical Society.*

tion at San Carlos of "nearly all of the most refractory Indians in the Territory." [4]

Clum was furious. He telegraphed the Commissioner of Indian Affairs, requesting authority to equip an additional company of Apache police to replace the soldiers, and asking that the mili-tary be removed. In Washington, newspapers learned of Clum's bold demand and published it. The story aroused the ire of the War Department. In Arizona and New Mexico, civilian Army contractors, fearing a wholesale departure of soldiers and a loss of lucrative business, condemned the "brass and impudence" of the twenty-six-year-old upstart who thought he could do alone what several thousand soldiers had been unable to do since the Apache wars began.

The Army stayed at San Carlos, and John Clum resigned. Although *simpático,* Clum had never learned to think as an Apache, to make himself into an Apache, as Tom Jeffords had done. He could not understand the chiefs who resisted to the bitter end. He could not see them as heroic figures who preferred death to the loss of their heritage. In John Clum's eyes, Geron-imo, Victorio, Nana, Loco, Naiche, and the other fighters were outlaws, thieves, murderers, and drunkards—too reactionary to take the white man's road. And so John Clum left the Apaches at San Carlos. He went to Tombstone, Arizona, and founded a crusading newspaper, the *Epitaph.*

Before summer's end of 1877, conditions at San Carlos became chaotic. Although the number of Indians had increased by sev-eral hundred, additional supplies were slow in arriving. To make matters worse, instead of distributing rations at various camps, the new agent required that all the bands come to the main agency building. Some of the Apaches had to walk twenty miles, and if old people and children were unable to come, they re-ceived no rations. Miners also encroached upon the northeastern portion of the reservation and refused to leave. The self-policing system established by Clum began to break down.

On the night of September 2, Victorio led his Warm Springs band off the reservation and started back to Ojo Caliente. Apache police went in pursuit, recaptured most of the horses and mules that the Warm Springs Indians had taken from the

White Mountain corrals, but let the people go. After engaging in several fights with ranchers and soldiers along the way, Victorio reached Ojo Caliente. For a year the Army let him and his people stay there under guard of soldiers from Fort Wingate, and then late in 1878 orders came to take them back to San Carlos.

Victorio begged the Army officers to let his people live in the country where they had been born, but when he realized that this was not to be, he shouted: "You can take our women and children in your wagons, but my men will not go!" [5]

Victorio and about eighty of his warriors fled into the Mimbres Mountains to spend a hard winter away from their families. In February, 1878, Victorio and a few men came into the post at Ojo Caliente and offered to surrender if the Army would return their families from San Carlos. For weeks the Army delayed its decision, then finally announced that it would compromise. The Warm Springs Apaches could make their homes in New Mexico, but they would have to live with the Mescaleros at Tularosa. Victorio agreed, and for the third time in two years he and his people had to begin life over again.

In the summer of 1879 an old charge of horse stealing and murder was brought up against Victorio, and lawmen entered the reservation to put him under arrest. Victorio escaped, and this time he resolved that never again would he put himself upon the mercy of white men by living on a reservation. He was convinced that he had been marked for death, and that all Apaches were doomed unless they fought back as they had been doing in Mexico since the coming of the Spaniards.

Establishing a stronghold in Mexico, Victorio began recruiting a guerrilla army "to make war forever" against the United States. Before the end of 1879 he had a warrior band of two hundred Mescaleros and Chiricahuas. To obtain horses and supplies they raided Mexican ranches, and then made daring thrusts into New Mexico and Texas, killing settlers where they could find them, ambushing pursuing cavalry forces, and then dashing back across the border.

As the constant fighting continued, Victorio's hatred deepened. He became a ruthless killer, torturing and mutilating his victims. Some of his followers considered him a madman and left

42. *Victorio. Courtesy of Arizona Historical Society.*

him. A price of three thousand dollars was placed on his head. At last the United States and Mexican armies decided to cooperate in a concentrated effort to track him down. On October 14, 1880, Mexican soldiers trapped Victorio's band in the Tres Castillos Hills between Chihuahua and El Paso. They slaughtered seventy-eight Apaches, including Victorio, and captured sixty-eight women and children. About thirty warriors escaped.

Among those who escaped was a Mimbres warrior who had already passed his seventieth birthday. His name was Nana. He had been fighting Spanish-speaking white men and English-speaking white men as long as he could remember. In Nana's mind there was no doubt that the resistance must continue. He would recruit another guerrilla army, and the best source for warriors was the reservations, where hundreds of young men were penned up with nothing to do. In the summer of 1881 this scarred and wrinkled little Apache crossed the Rio Grande with his handful of followers. In less than a month they fought eight battles, captured two hundred horses, and escaped back into Mexico with a thousand cavalrymen on their heels. Nana's raids were nowhere near White Mountain, but the Apaches there heard of his daring exploits, and the Army reacted by dispatching hundreds of troops to guard the reservation.

In September the Chiricahuas at San Carlos were alarmed by a cavalry demonstration near their camp. Rumors were flying everywhere; it was said that the Army was preparing to arrest all leaders who had ever been hostile. One night late in the month, Geronimo, Juh, Naiche, and about seventy Chiricahuas slipped out of White Mountain and raced southward for their old Sierra Madre stronghold in Mexico.

Six months later (April, 1882), well armed and equipped, the Chiricahuas returned to White Mountain. They were determined to free all their people and any other Apaches who wanted to return to Mexico with them. It was an audacious enterprise. They galloped into Chief Loco's camp and persuaded most of the remaining Chiricahuas and Warm Springs Apaches to leave for Mexico.

In swift pursuit came six companies of cavalry commanded by Colonel George A. Forsyth. (He had survived the Battle When Roman Nose Was Killed; see chapter seven.) At Horse

Shoe Canyon, Forsyth caught up with the fleeing Apaches, but in a brilliant rearguard action the Indians held off the troopers long enough for the main body to cross into Mexico. Here disaster struck from an unexpected source. A Mexican infantry regiment stumbled upon the Apache column, slaughtering most of the women and children who were riding in front.

Among the chiefs and warriors who escaped were Loco, Naiche, Chato, and Geronimo. Embittered, their ranks depleted, they soon joined forces with old Nana and his guerrillas. For all of them, it was now a war of survival.

Each recent outbreak at White Mountain had brought an increase in the number of soldiers. They swarmed everywhere—at Fort Thomas, Fort Apache, Fort Bowie—and each increase brought more unrest among the Apaches on the reservation, more flights to Mexico, with the inevitable raiding against ranchers along the escape routes.

To bring order out of chaos, the Army again called on General George Crook—quite a different man from the one who had left Arizona ten years earlier to go north to fight the Sioux and Cheyennes. He had learned from them and from the Poncas during the trial of Standing Bear that Indians were human beings, a viewpoint that most of his fellow officers had not yet accepted.

On September 4, 1882, Crook assumed command of the Department of Arizona at Whipple Barracks, and then hurried on to the White Mountain reservation. He held councils with the Apaches at San Carlos and Fort Apache; he searched out individual Indians and talked privately with them. "I discovered immediately that a general feeling of distrust of our people existed among all the bands of the Apaches," he reported. "It was with much difficulty that I got them to talk, but after breaking down their suspicions they conversed freely with me. They told me . . . that they had lost confidence in everybody, and did not know whom or what to believe; that they were constantly told, by irresponsible parties, that they were to be disarmed, that they were to be attacked by troops on the reservation, and removed from their country; and that they were fast arriving at the conclusion that it would be more manly to die fighting than to be

43. *Nana. Courtesy of Arizona Historical Society.*

thus destroyed." Crook was convinced that the reservation
Apaches "had not only the best reasons for complaining, but had
displayed remarkable forbearance in remaining at peace."

Early in his investigations he discovered that the Indians had
been plundered "of their rations and of the goods purchased by
the government for their subsistence and support, by rascally
agents and other unscrupulous white men." He found plenty of evidence that white men were trying to arouse the Apaches to
violent action so that they could be driven from the reservation,
leaving it open for land-grabbing.[6]

Crook ordered immediate removal of all white squatters and
miners from the reservation, and then demanded complete cooperation from the Indian Bureau in introducing reforms. Instead of being forced to live near San Carlos or Fort Apache, the
different bands were given the right to choose any part of the
reservation to build their homes and ranches. Hay contracts
would be given to Apaches instead of to white suppliers; the
Army would buy all the excess corn and vegetables the Indians
could raise, paying for it in cash. They would be expected to
govern themselves, to reorganize their police and hold their own
courts, as they had done under John Clum. Crook promised that
they would see no soldiers on their reservation unless they found
it impossible to control themselves.

At first the Apaches were skeptical. They remembered Crook's
harsh ways in the old days when he was the Gray Wolf hunting
down Cochise and the Chiricahuas, but they soon discovered
that he meant what he said. Rations became more plentiful, the
agents and traders no longer cheated them, there were no soldiers
to bully them, and the Gray Wolf encouraged them to build up
their herds and seek out better places to grow corn and beans.
They were free again, so long as they remained within the reservation.

But they could not forget their relatives who were truly free
in Mexico, and there were always a few young men slipping
southward, a few returning with exciting news of adventures
and good times.

Crook also gave much thought to the Chiricahuas and Warm
Springs Apaches in Mexico. He knew it was only a matter of
time before they would raid once again across the border, and

he knew he must be ready for them. The United States government had recently signed an agreement with the Mexican government permitting soldiers of each country to cross the border in pursuit of hostile Apaches. He was preparing to take advantage of this agreement, hoping that by doing so he could keep the Arizona and New Mexico civilians from forcing him to start a war.

"It is too often the case," Crook said, "that border newspapers . . . disseminate all sorts of exaggerations and falsehoods about the Indians, which are copied in papers of high character and wide circulation, in other parts of the country, while the Indians' side of the case is rarely ever heard. In this way the people at large get false ideas with reference to the matter. Then when the outbreak does come public attention is turned to the Indians, their crimes and atrocities are alone condemned, while the persons whose injustice has driven them to this course escape scot-free and are the loudest in their denunciations. No one knows this fact better than the Indian, therefore he is excusable in seeing no justice in a government which only punishes him, while it allows the white man to plunder him as he pleases."

The thought of another guerrilla war with the Apaches aroused the utmost abhorrence in Crook. He knew that it was practically impossible to subdue them in the rugged country where the fighting would have to be done. "With all the interests at stake we cannot afford to fight them," he admitted frankly. "We are too culpable, as a nation, for the existing condition of affairs. It follows that we must satisfy them that hereafter they shall be treated with justice, and protected from inroads of white men." [7]

Crook believed that he could convince Geronimo and the other guerrilla leaders of his good intentions—not by fighting them but by talking with them. The best place for this would be in one of their own Mexican strongholds, where there would be no unscrupulous promoters of Indian wars or rumor-spreading newspapers to stir up a profit-making, land-grabbing war.

While he waited for a border raid to give him an excuse to enter Mexico, Crook quietly put together his "expeditionary force." It consisted of about fifty carefully chosen soldiers and civilian interpreters, and about two hundred young Apaches from the reservation, many of whom at one time or another had been raiders in Mexico. In the early weeks of 1883 he moved part of this force down to the tracks of the new Southern Pacific Railroad, which streaked across Arizona to within about fifty miles of the border. On March 21 three minor chiefs—Chato, Chihuahua, and Bonito—raided a mining camp near Tombstone. As soon as Crook learned of the incident he began final preparations for his Mexican entry. Not until after weeks of searching, however, did his scouts find the location of the Chiricahuas' base camp in the Sierra Madres of Mexico.

In that Season When the Leaves Are Dark Green (May), Geronimo led a raid against Mexican ranchers to obtain cattle. Mexican soldiers pursued them, but Geronimo ambushed the soldiers, punished them severely, and escaped. As the Apaches were returning to their base, one of the men who had been left behind as a guard met Geronimo and told him that the Gray Wolf (Crook) had captured the camp and all the women and children.

Jason Betzinez, one of Geronimo's cousins who was riding with the Apache party, afterward told of how Geronimo chose two of his older warriors to go down with a truce flag and find out what the Gray Wolf had come for. "Instead of returning to where Geronimo stood," Betzinez said, "the two men came back halfway up the mountain and called for us all to come down. . . . Our warriors descended the mountainside, went up to General Crook's tent, where, after a lengthy conference between the leaders, we all surrendered to the general." [8]

Actually Geronimo had three long parleys with Crook before they came to an agreement. The Apache leader declared that he had always wanted peace but that he had been ill-treated at San Carlos by bad white men. Crook agreed that this was probably true, but if Geronimo wanted to return to the reservation the Gray Wolf would see that he was treated fairly. All Chiricahuas who returned, however, would have to work at farming and stock-raising to make their own livings. "I am not taking your arms from you," Crook added, "because I am not afraid of you." [9]

Geronimo liked Crook's blunt manner, but when the general

announced that he must start his column back to Arizona in a day or so, Geronimo decided to test him, to make certain that Crook truly trusted him. The Apache leader said it would require several months to round up all his people. "I will remain here," he said, "until I have gathered up the last man, woman, and child of the Chiricahuas." Chato would also remain to assist him. Together they would bring all the people to San Carlos.[10]

To Geronimo's surprise, Crook agreed to the proposition. On May 30 the column started northward. With it went 251 women and children and 123 warriors, including Loco, Mangas (Mangas Colorado's son), Chihuahua, Bonito, even wrinkled old Nana— all the war leaders except Geronimo and Chato.

Eight months passed, and then it was Crook's turn to be surprised. True to their word, Geronimo and Chato crossed the border in February, 1884, and were escorted to San Carlos. "Unfortunately, Geronimo made the mistake of driving along with him a large herd of cattle which he had stolen from the Mexicans," Jason Betzinez said. "This seemed quite proper to Geronimo, who felt that he was only providing a good supply of food for his people. The authorities, taking a different view, pried the cattle loose from the chief." [11] The honest Gray Wolf ordered the cattle sold, and then he returned the proceeds of $1,762.50 to the Mexican government for distribution to the original owners if they could be found.

For more than a year General Crook could boast that "not an outrage or depredation of any kind" was committed by the Indians of Arizona and New Mexico. Geronimo and Chato vied with each other in the development of their *ranchos,* and Crook kept a watchful eye on their agent to see that he issued adequate supplies. Outside the reservation and the Army posts, however, there was much criticism of Crook for being too easy on the Apaches; the newspapers that he had condemned for disseminating "all sorts of exaggerations and falsehoods about the Indians" now turned on him. Some of the rumor mongers went so far as to claim that Crook had surrendered to Geronimo in Mexico and had made a deal with the Chiricahua leader in order to escape alive. As for Geronimo, they made a special demon of him, inventing atrocity stories by the dozens and calling on vigilantes to hang him if the government would not. Mickey Free, the Chiricahuas' official interpreter, told Geronimo about these newspaper stories. "When a man tried to do right," Geronimo commented, "such stories ought not to be put in the newspapers." [12]

After the Corn Planting Time (spring of 1885), the Chiricahuas grew discontented. There was little for the men to do except draw rations, gamble, quarrel, loaf, and drink tiswin beer. Tiswin was forbidden on the reservation, but the Chiricahuas had plenty of corn for brewing it, and drinking was one of the few pleasures of the old days that was left to them.

On the night of May 17, Geronimo, Mangas, Chihuahua, and old Nana got fairly well drunk on tiswin and decided to go to Mexico. They went to see Chato to invite him to go along, but Chato was sober and refused to join the party. He and Geronimo had a bitter quarrel, which very nearly ended in violence before Geronimo and the others departed. In the group were ninety-two women and children, eight boys, and thirty-four men. As they left San Carlos, Geronimo cut the telegraph wire.

Many reasons were given by both white men and Apaches for this sudden exodus from a reservation where everything apparently had been running smoothly. Some said it was because of the tiswin spree; others said that the bad stories going around about the Chiricahuas made them fearful of being arrested. "Having been placed in irons once before when the band was shipped to San Carlos," Jason Betzinez said, "some of the leaders determined not to undergo such treatment again."

Geronimo later explained it this way: "Sometime before I left, an Indian named Wadiskay had a talk with me. He said, 'They are going to arrest you,' but I paid no attention to him, knowing that I had done no wrong; and the wife of Mangas, Huera, told me that they were going to seize me and put me and Mangas in the guardhouse, and I learned from the American and Apache soldiers, from Chato, and Mickey Free, that the Americans were going to arrest me and hang me, and so I left." [13]

The flight of Geronimo's party across Arizona was a signal for an outpouring of wild rumors. Newspapers featured big headlines: THE APACHES ARE OUT! The very word "Geronimo" became a cry for blood. The "Tucson Ring" of contractors, seeing a chance for a profitable military campaign, called on General Crook to rush troops to protect defenseless white citizens from murderous Apaches. Geronimo, however, was desperately trying to avoid any confrontation with white citizens; all he wanted to do was speed his people across the border to the old Sierra Madre sanctuary. For two days and nights the Chiricahuas rode without making camp. Along the way, Chihuahua changed his mind about going to Mexico; he turned his band off the trail, intending to return to the reservation. Pursuing soldiers caught up with Chihuahua, forced him into a fight, and started him on a bloody trail of plundering before he could cross into Mexico. Every assault he committed was blamed on Geronimo, because few Arizonans had ever heard of Chihuahua.

Crook meanwhile was trying to avoid the vast military operation that the Tucson Ring and their political friends in Washington were demanding of him. He knew that personal negotiation was the only way to deal with three dozen Apache warriors. For the benefit of local citizens, however, he ordered a few cavalrymen to march out of each fort under his command, but he depended entirely on his trusted Apache scouts to find the resistant Chiricahuas. He was gratified that Chato and Cochise's younger son, Alchise, both volunteered to search for Geronimo.

As autumn approached, it was clear that Crook once again would have to cross the border into Mexico. His orders from Washington were explicit: kill the fugitives or take their unconditional surrenders.

By this time the Chiricahuas had discovered that units of the Mexican Army were waiting for them in the Sierra Madres. Caught between Mexicans who wanted only to kill them and Americans who were willing to make prisoners of them, Geronimo and the other leaders finally decided to listen to Chato and Alchise.

On March 25, 1886, the "hostile" Apache chiefs met with Crook a few miles south of the border at Cañon de los Embudos. After three days of emotional speech making, the Chiricahuas agreed to surrender. Crook then told them they must surrender without conditions, and when they asked what that meant, he told them frankly that they would probably be taken far away to the East, to Florida, to become prisoners. They replied that they would not surrender unless the Gray Wolf would promise that they would be returned to their reservation after two years of imprisonment. Crook thought the proposition over; it seemed fair to him. Believing that he could convince Washington that such a surrender was better than no surrender, he agreed.

"I give myself up to you," Geronimo said. "Do with me what you please. I surrender. Once I moved about like the wind. Now I surrender to you and that is all."

Alchise closed the council with a plea to Crook to have pity on his erring Chiricahua brothers. "They are all good friends now and I am glad they have surrendered, because they are all the same people—all one family with me; just like when you kill a deer, all its parts are of the one body; so with the Chiricahuas. . . . Now we want to travel along the open road and drink the waters of the Americans, and not hide in the mountains; we want to live without danger or discomfort. I am very glad that the Chiricahuas surrendered, and that I have been able to talk for them. . . . I have never told you a lie, nor have you ever told me a lie, and now I tell you that these Chiricahuas really want to do what is right and live at peace. If they don't then I lie, and you must not believe me anymore. It's all right; you are going ahead to Fort Bowie; I want you to carry away in your pocket all that has been said here today." [14]

Convinced that the Chiricahuas would come into Fort Bowie with his scouting troop, Crook hurried on there to telegraph the War Department in Washington the terms he had given the Chiricahua chiefs. To his dismay a reply came back: "Cannot assent to the surrender of the hostiles on the terms of their imprisonment East for two years with their understanding of their return to the reservation." [15] The Gray Wolf had made another promise he could not keep. As a crowning blow, he heard the next day that Geronimo and Naiche had broken away from the column a few miles below Fort Bowie and were fleeing back into Mexico. A trader from the Tucson Ring had filled them full of whiskey and lies about how the white citizens of Arizona would surely hang them if they returned. According to Jason Betzinez, Naiche got drunk and fired his gun in the air. "Geronimo thought that fighting had broken out with the troops. He and

Naiche stampeded, taking with them some thirty followers." Perhaps there was more to it than that. "I feared treachery," Geronimo said afterward, "and when we became suspicious, we turned back." Naiche later told Crook: "I was afraid I was going to be taken off somewhere I didn't like; to some place I didn't know. I thought all who were taken away would die. . . . I worked it out in my own mind. . . . We talked to each other about it. We were drunk . . . because there was a lot of whiskey there and we wanted a drink, and took it." [16]

As a result of Geronimo's flight, the War Department severely reprimanded Crook for his negligence, for granting unauthorized surrender terms, and for his tolerant attitude toward Indians. He immediately resigned and was replaced by Nelson Miles (Bear Coat), a brigadier general eager for promotion.

Bear Coat took command on April 12, 1886. With full support from the War Department, he quickly put five thousand soldiers into the field (about one-third of the combat strength of the Army). He also had five hundred Apache scouts, and thousands of irregular civilian militia. He organized a flying column of cavalrymen and an expensive system of heliographs to flash messages back and forth across Arizona and New Mexico. The enemy to be subdued by this powerful military force was Geronimo and his "army" of twenty-four warriors, who throughout the summer of 1886 were also under constant pursuit by thousands of soldiers of the Mexican Army.

In the end it was the Big Nose Captain (Lieutenant Charles Gatewood) and two Apache scouts, Martine and Kayitah, who found Geronimo and Naiche hiding out in a canyon of the Sierra Madres. Geronimo laid his rifle down and shook hands with the Big Nose Captain, inquiring calmly about his health. He then asked about matters back in the United States. How were the Chiricahuas faring? Gatewood told him that the Chiricahuas who surrendered had already been shipped to Florida. If Geronimo would surrender to General Miles, he also would probably be sent to Florida to join them.

Geronimo wanted to know all about Bear Coat Miles. Was his voice harsh or agreeable to the ear? Was he cruel or kindhearted? Did he look you in the eyes or down at the ground when he talked? Would he keep his promises? Then he said to

Gatewood: "We want your advice. Consider yourself one of us
and not a white man. Remember all that has been said today,
and as an Apache, what would you advise us to do under the
circumstances?"

"I would trust General Miles and take him at his word,"
Gatewood replied.[17]

And so Geronimo surrendered for the last time. The Great
Father in Washington (Grover Cleveland), who believed all the
lurid newspaper tales of Geronimo's evil deeds, recommended
that he be hanged. The counsel of men who knew better pre-
vailed, and Geronimo and his surviving warriors were shipped
to Fort Marion, Florida. He found most of his friends dying
there in that warm and humid land so unlike the high, dry country of their birth. More than a hundred died of a disease diag-
nosed as consumption. The government took all their children
away from them and sent them to the Indian school at Carlisle,
Pennsylvania, and more than fifty of their children died there.

Not only were the "hostiles" moved to Florida, but so were
many of the "friendlies," including the scouts who had worked
for Crook. Martine and Kayitah, who led Lieutenant Gatewood
to Geronimo's hiding place, did not receive the ten ponies promised them for their mission; instead they were shipped to imprisonment in Florida. Chato, who had tried to dissuade Geronimo from leaving the reservation and then had helped Crook find
him, was suddenly removed from his *rancho* and sent to Florida.
He lost his land allotment and all his livestock; two of his children were taken to Carlisle, and both died there. The Chiricahuas were marked for extinction; they had fought too hard to
keep their freedom.

But they were not alone. Eskiminzin of the Aravaipas, who
had become economically independent on his Gila ranch, was
arrested on the charge of communicating with an outlaw known
as the Apache Kid. Eskiminzin and the forty surviving Aravaipas were sent to live with the Chiricahuas in Florida. Later, all
these exiles were transferred to Mount Vernon Barracks,
Alabama.

Had it not been for the efforts of a few white friends such as
George Crook, John Clum, and Hugh Scott, the Apaches soon
would have been driven into the ground at that fever-ridden

post on the Mobile River. Over the objections of Bear Coat Miles and the War Department, they succeeded in having Eskiminzin and the Aravaipas returned to San Carlos. The citizens of Arizona, however, refused to admit Geronimo's Chiricahuas within the state. When the Kiowas and Comanches learned of the Chiricahuas' plight from Lieutenant Hugh Scott, they offered their old Apache enemies a part of their reservation. In 1894 Geronimo brought the surviving exiles to Fort Sill. When he died there in 1909, still a prisoner of war, he was buried in the Apache cemetery. A legend still persists that not long afterward his bones were secretly removed and taken somewhere to the Southwest—perhaps to the Mogollons, or the Chiricahua Mountains, or deep into the Sierra Madres of Mexico. He was the last of the Apache chiefs.

"THE BUFFALO ARE COMING"

Courtesy of the Bureau of American Ethnology Collection

Listen, he said, yonder the buffalo are coming,
These are his sayings, yonder the buffalo are coming,
They walk, they stand, they are coming,
Yonder the buffalo are coming.

EIGHTEEN

Dance of the Ghosts

1887—February 4, U.S. Congress creates Interstate Commerce Commission to regulate railroads. June 21, Britain celebrates Golden Jubilee of Queen Victoria. July 2–4, Union and Confederate veterans hold reunion at Gettysburg.

1888—May 14, Brazil abolishes slavery. November 6, Grover Cleveland receives more popular votes than Benjamin Harrison, but Harrison wins Presidency by electoral votes.

1889—March 4, Benjamin Harrison inaugurated as President. March 23, President Harrison opens Oklahoma (former Indian Territory) to white settlement. March 31, Eiffel Tower is completed in Paris. May 31, five thousand lose lives in Johnstown Flood. November 2–11, North and South Dakota, Montana, and Washington become states of the Union.

1890—January 25, Nellie Bly wins race around the world in 72 days, 6 hours, and 11 minutes. June 1, population of United States reaches 62,622,250. July 3–10, Idaho and Wyoming become forty-third and forty-fourth states of the Union.

If a man loses anything and goes back and looks carefully for it he will find it, and that is what the Indians are doing now when they ask you to give them the things that were promised them in the past; and I do not consider that they should be treated like beasts, and that is the reason I have grown up with the feelings I have. . . . I feel that my country has gotten a bad name, and I want it to have a good name; it used to have a good name; and I sit sometimes and wonder who it is that has given it a bad name.

—Tatanka Yotanka (Sitting Bull)

Our land here is the dearest thing on earth to us. Men take up land and get rich on it, and it is very important for us Indians to keep it.

—White Thunder

All Indians must dance, everywhere, keep on dancing. Pretty soon in next spring Great Spirit come. He bring back all game of every kind. The game be thick everywhere. All dead Indians come back and live again. They all be strong just like young men, be young again. Old blind Indian see again and get young and have fine time. When Great Spirit comes this way, then all the Indians go to mountains, high up away from whites. Whites can't hurt Indians then. Then while Indians way up high, big flood comes like water and all white people die, get drowned. After that, water go way and then nobody but Indians everywhere and game all kinds thick. Then medicine man tell Indians to send word to all Indians to keep up dancing and the good time will come. Indians who don't dance, who don't believe in this word, will grow little, just about a foot high, and stay that way. Some of them will be turned into wood and be burned in fire.

—WOVOKA, THE PAIUTE MESSIAH

WHEN the Teton Sioux tribes surrendered after the wars of 1876–77, they had lost the Powder River country and the Black Hills. The government's next move was to change the western boundary of the Great Sioux Reservation from the 104th to the 103rd meridian, thus slicing off another fifty-mile strip adjoining the Black Hills, and taking an additional triangle of valuable land between the forks of the Cheyenne River. In 1877, after the government drove the Sioux out of Nebraska, all that was left to them was an anvil-shaped block between the 103rd meridian and the Missouri River—35,000 square miles of Dakota land which was believed to be virtually worthless by the surveyors who marked off the boundaries.

Some government officials wanted to transfer all the Tetons to Indian Territory; others wanted to establish agencies for them along the Missouri River. After strong protests by Red Cloud and Spotted Tail, a compromise was eventually reached. Red Cloud's Oglalas were settled in the southwest corner of the reservation at Wazi Ahanhan, Pine Ridge. Here the various bands of Oglalas made permanent camps along creeks flowing north to White River—the Yellow Medicine, Porcupine Tail, and Wounded Knee. East of Pine Ridge, Spotted Tail and his Brulés settled along the Little White River; their agency was called the Rosebud. For the remaining Sioux tribes four other agencies were established—Lower Brulé, Crow Creek, Cheyenne River, and Standing Rock. The agencies would remain there for almost a century, but most of the 35,000 square miles of the Great Sioux Reservation would gradually be taken from the Indians.

As the Tetons were settling into their new villages, a great wave of emigration from northern Europe poured into eastern Dakota, pressing against the Missouri River boundary of the Great Sioux Reservation. At Bismarck, on the Missouri, a west-ward-pushing railroad was blocked by the reservation. Settlers bound for Montana and the Northwest clamored for roads to be built across the reservation. Promoters eager for cheap land to be sold at high profits to immigrants hatched schemes to break up the Great Sioux Reservation.

In the old days the Sioux would have fought to keep all these interlopers out of their territory, but now they were disarmed, dismounted, unable even to feed and clothe themselves. Their greatest surviving war leader, Sitting Bull, was an exile in Canada. He and his three thousand followers were free, armed, and mounted. Someday they might return.

Like Geronimo free in Mexico, Sitting Bull free in Canada was an abomination to the United States government, a dangerous symbol of subversion. The Army became frenetic in its attempts to force the Hunkpapa leader and his followers to return to its control. At last, in September, 1877, the War Department arranged with the Canadian government for General Alfred Terry and a special commission to cross the border under escort of the Royal Canadian Mounted Police and proceed to Fort Walsh. There Terry was to meet with Sitting Bull and promise him a complete pardon, provided he would surrender all firearms and horses and bring his people back to the Hunkpapa agency at Standing Rock on the Great Sioux Reservation.

Sitting Bull was at first reluctant to meet with One Star Terry. "There is no use in talking to these Americans," he told Commissioner James MacLeod of the Mounted Police. "They are all liars, you cannot believe anything they say." Only the urging of Commissioner MacLeod, who was hopeful of getting Sitting Bull out of Canada, finally persuaded the Hunkpapa to come into Fort Walsh on October 17 for a council.[1]

One Star Terry made a short opening speech. "This band of yours," he said to Sitting Bull, "is the only one which has not surrendered. . . . We have come many hundred miles to bring you this message from the Great Father, who, as we have told you before, desires to live in peace with all his people. Too much white and Indian blood has already been shed. It is time that bloodshed should cease."

"What have we done that you should want us to stop?" Sitting Bull retorted. "We have done nothing. It is all the people on your side that have started us to do all these depredations. We could not go anywhere else, and so we took refuge in this country. . . . I would like to know why you came here. . . . You come here to tell us lies, but we don't want to hear them. I don't wish any such language used to me; that is, to tell me such lies in my Great Mother's [Queen Victoria's] house. Don't you say two more words. Go back home where you came from. . . . The part of the country you gave me you ran me out of. I have now come here to stay with these people, and I intend to stay here."

Sitting Bull let several of his followers speak, including a Santee and a Yankton who had joined his band. Their statements reinforced his previous remarks. Then he did a most unusual thing; he introduced a woman into the council, The-One-Who-Speaks-Once. Some Indians afterward said that it was a deliberate insult to Terry, permitting a woman to speak in council with a visitor. "I was over to your country," she said to Terry. "I wanted to raise my children over there, but you did not give me any time. I came over to this country to raise my children and have a little peace. That is all I have to say to you. I want you to go back where you came from. These are the people that I am going to stay with, and raise my children with."[2]

After the meeting ended, One Star Terry knew that it was useless to make any further pleas to Sitting Bull. His last hope was Commissioner MacLeod, who agreed to explain the Canadian government's position toward the Hunkpapas. MacLeod informed Sitting Bull that the Queen's government considered him an American Indian who had taken refuge in Canada, and that he could not claim to be a British Indian. "You can expect nothing whatsoever from the Queen's government," he said, "except protection so long as you behave yourselves. Your only hope are the buffalo, and it will not be many years before that source of supply will cease. You must not cross the border with hostile intent. If you do you will not only have the Americans for your enemies, but also the Mounted Police and the British government."

Nothing MacLeod said changed Sitting Bull's decision. He would remain in the Grandmother's land.

Next morning, One Star Terry started back to the United States. "The presence of this large body of Indians, bitterly hostile to us, in close proximity to the frontier," he warned the War Department, "is a standing menace to the peace of our Indian territories." [3]

Sitting Bull's exiles stayed in Canada four years, and had the government of that country been more cooperative, they probably would have lived out their lives on the plains of Saskatchewan. From the beginning, however, the Queen's government viewed Sitting Bull as a potential troublemaker, as well as an expensive guest, because additional Mounted Police had to be assigned to watch him. Sometimes he was the butt of parliamentary jokes. On February 18, 1878, a member of the Canadian House of Commons raised a question as to how much added expense the government had incurred as "the result of the crossing of our frontier by Sitting Bull."

> Sir John McDonald: I do not see how a Sitting Bull can cross the frontier.
> Mr. McKenzie: Not unless he rises.
> Sir John: Then he is not a Sitting Bull. [4]

This was the usual level of discussion reached in the Canadian Parliament whenever the problem of the exiled Sioux arose. No aid of any kind was offered—not even food or clothing; and in the bitter winters, the Indians suffered for lack of shelter and blankets. Wild game was sparse, and there was never enough meat, or skins to make clothes and tepee covers. Nostalgia seemed to affect the young more than the old. "We began to feel homesick for our own country where we used to be happy," said one of the young Oglalas.[5] As the seasons passed, a few hungry and ragged families drifted south across the border to surrender at the Sioux agencies in Dakota.

Sitting Bull begged the Canadians to give his people a reservation where they could support themselves, but he was repeatedly told that he was not a British subject and therefore was not entitled to a land reserve. During the bad winter of 1880, many Sioux horses froze to death in a blizzard, and when spring came more of the exiles began trekking southward on foot. Several of Sitting Bull's most loyal lieutenants, including Gall and Crow King, gave up and headed for the Great Sioux Reservation.

At last, on July 19, 1881, Sitting Bull and 186 of his remaining followers crossed the border and rode into Fort Buford. He was wearing a tattered calico shirt, a pair of shabby leggings, and a dirty blanket. He looked old and beaten when he surrendered his Winchester rifle to the commanding officer. Instead of sending him to the Hunkpapa agency at Standing Rock, the Army broke its promise to give him a pardon and held him at Fort Randall as a military prisoner.

During the late summer of 1881, the return of Sitting Bull was overshadowed by the assassination of Spotted Tail. The murderer was not a white man, but was one of Spotted Tail's own people, Crow Dog. Without giving any warning, Crow Dog shot the famed Brulé chief as he rode horseback along a trail on the Rosebud reservation.

White officials at the agency dismissed the killing as the culmination of a quarrel over a woman, but Spotted Tail's friends said that it was the result of a plot to break the power of the chiefs and transfer it to men who would bow to the will of the Indian Bureau's agents. Red Cloud believed that a cowardly assassin was found to remove Spotted Tail because he stood strong for the improvement of his people. "This was charged upon the Indians because an Indian did it," he said, "but who set on the Indian?" [6]

After the furor over Spotted Tail's death had subsided, the Sioux everywhere on the Great Reservation turned their attention toward Sitting Bull's presence at Fort Randall. Many chiefs and subchiefs came to visit him, wish him well, and do him honor. Newspapermen came to interview him. Instead of being beaten and forgotten as he had thought, Sitting Bull was famous. In 1882 representatives from the different Sioux agencies came to ask his advice concerning a new government proposal to break up the Great Reservation into smaller areas and sell about half the land for white settlement. Sitting Bull advised them not to sell; the Sioux had no land to spare.

In spite of their resistance, the Sioux in 1882 came very near losing 14,000 square miles of territory to a commission headed by Newton Edmunds, an expert at negotiating lands away from Indians. His colleagues were Peter Shannon, a frontier lawyer, and James Teller, a brother of the new Secretary of the Interior. Accompanying them was a "special interpreter," none other than the Reverend Samuel D. Hinman, who had been a missionary to the Sioux since the days of Little Crow. Hinman believed that what the Indians needed was less land and more Christianity.

As the commission traveled from one agency to the other, Hinman told the chiefs that he was there to lay out different parts of the reservation for the six agencies. This was necessary, he said, so that the different Sioux tribes could claim the areas as their own and have them as long as they lived. "After we have laid out the reservations," Hinman told Red Cloud, "the Great Father will give you 25,000 cows and 1,000 bulls." [7] To obtain the livestock, however, the Sioux had to sign some papers which the commissioners had brought along. As none of the Sioux chiefs could read, they did not know that they were signing away 14,000 square miles of land in exchange for the promised cows and bulls.

At agencies where the Sioux were reluctant to sign anything, Hinman alternately wheedled and bullied them. In order to obtain an abundance of signatures, he persuaded boys as young as seven years old to sign the papers. (According to the treaty, only adult male Indians could sign.) In a meeting at Wounded Knee Creek on Pine Ridge reservation, Hinman told the Indians that if they did not sign they would not receive any more rations or annuities, and furthermore they would be sent to Indian Territory.

Many of the older Sioux, who had seen the limits of their land shrink after "touching the pen" to similar documents, suspected that Hinman was trying to steal their reservation. Yellow Hair, a minor chief at Pine Ridge, stood strong against signing but then was frightened into doing so by Hinman's threats. After the ceremony of signing was completed and the commissioners departed, Yellow Hair took a round ball of earth and mockingly presented it to the Pine Ridge agent, Dr. Valentine McGillycuddy. "We have given up nearly all of our land," Yellow Hair said, "and you had better take the balance now, and here I hand it to you." [8]

Early in 1883 Edmunds and Hinman journeyed to Washington with their bundle of signatures and succeeded in getting a bill introduced in Congress ceding about half the lands of the Great Reservation to the United States. Fortunately for the Sioux, they had enough friends in Washington to question the bill and to point out that even if all the signatures were legal, Edmunds and Hinman still had not obtained the names of the required three-fourths of all adult male Sioux.

Another commission, headed by Senator Henry L. Dawes, was immediately dispatched to Dakota to inquire into the methods used by Edmunds and Hinman. Its members soon discovered the chicanery of their predecessors.

During the inquiry Dawes asked Red Cloud if he believed Mr. Hinman was an honest man. "Mr. Hinman fools you big men," Red Cloud replied. "He told you a lot of stuff, and you have to come out here and ask us about it."

Red Dog testified that Hinman had talked about giving them cows and bulls, but had said nothing about the Sioux giving up any land in exchange for them. Little Wound said: "Mr. Hinman told us that the way the reservation was now no Indian could tell his own ground, and the Great Father and his council thought it best to lay out different reservations and that is the reason we signed the paper."

"Did he say anything about the Great Father having what was left?" asked Senator Dawes.

"No, sir; he did not say anything about that."

When White Thunder told Dawes that the paper they had signed was a piece of rascality, the senator asked him what he meant by rascality.

"The rascality was that they came to take the land so cheap; that is what I call rascality."

"Do you mean that the Indians here would be willing to let the land go if they could be paid more for it?" Dawes asked.

"No, sir; they would not be willing to do that," White Thunder replied. "Our land here is the dearest thing on earth to us. Men take up land and get rich on it, and it is very important for us Indians to keep it." [9]

Shortly before the Dawes commission came to Dakota, Sitting Bull was released from imprisonment at Fort Randall and transferred to the Hunkpapa agency at Standing Rock. On August 22, when the commissioners arrived there to hear testimony, he came up to the agency headquarters from his assigned camp on Grand River to attend the council. The commissioners deliberately ignored the presence of the most famous living Sioux chief, inviting testimony first from Running Antelope and then from young John Grass, son of Old Grass, the chief of the Blackfoot Sioux.

At last Senator Dawes turned to the interpreter and said: "Ask Sitting Bull if he has anything to say to the committee."

"Of course I will speak to you if you desire me to do so," Sitting Bull responded. "I suppose it is only such men as you desire to speak who must say anything."

"We supposed the Indians would select men to speak for them," Dawes said, "but any man who desires to speak, or any man the Indians here desire shall talk for them, we will be glad to hear if he has anything to say."

"Do you know who I am, that you speak as you do?"

"I know that you are Sitting Bull, and if you have anything to say we will be glad to hear you."

"Do you recognize me; do you know who I am?"

"I know you are Sitting Bull."

"You say you know I am Sitting Bull, but do you know what position I hold?"

"I do not know any difference between you and the other Indians at this agency."

"I am here by the will of the Great Spirit, and by his will I am a chief. My heart is red and sweet, and I know it is sweet, because whatever passes near me puts out its tongue to me; and yet you men have come here to talk with us, and you say you do not know who I am. I want to tell you that if the Great Spirit has chosen anyone to be the chief of this country it is myself."

"In whatever capacity you may be here today, if you desire to say anything to us we will listen to you; otherwise we will dismiss this council."

"Yes; that is all right," Sitting Bull said. "You have conducted yourselves like men who have been drinking whiskey, and I came here to give you some advice." He made a sweeping motion with his hand, and every Indian in the council room arose and followed him out.[10]

Nothing could have dismayed the commissioners more than the thought of the Sioux rallying around a strong leader like Sitting Bull. Such a development endangered the entire Indian policy of the government, which aimed to eradicate everything *Indian* among the tribes and make them over into white men. In less than two minutes, right before their very eyes, they had let Sitting Bull demonstrate his power to block that policy.

Later that day the other Hunkpapa leaders talked with Sitting Bull; they assured him of their loyalty, but told him he should not have offended the commissioners. These men were not like the land thieves who had come there the previous year; these representatives of the Great Father had come to help them keep their land, not to take it away from them.

Sitting Bull was not so sure about the trustworthiness of any white men, but he said that if he had made a mistake he was willing to apologize for it. He sent word to the commissioners that he would like another council.

"I am here to apologize to you for my bad conduct," he began, "and to take back what I said. I will take it back because I consider I have made your hearts bad. . . . What I take back is what I said to cause the people to leave the council, and want to apologize for leaving myself. . . . Now I will tell you my mind and I will tell everything straight. I know the Great Spirit is looking down upon me from above and will hear what I say,

therefore I will do my best to talk straight; and I am in hopes
that someone will listen to my wishes and help me to carry
them out."

He then reviewed the history of the Sioux during his lifetime,
listing the government's broken promises, but said that he had
promised to travel the white man's path and would keep his
promises. "If a man loses anything and goes back and looks
carefully for it he will find it, and that is what the Indians are
doing now when they ask you to give them the things that were
promised them in the past; and I do not consider that they
should be treated like beasts, and that is the reason I have
grown up with the feelings I have. . . . The Great Father sent
me word that whatever he had against me in the past had been
forgiven and thrown aside, and he would have nothing against
me in the future, and I accepted his promises and came in; and
he told me not to step aside from the white man's path, and
I told him I would not, and I am doing my best to travel in
that path. I feel that my country has gotten a bad name, and
I want it to have a good name; it used to have a good name;
and I sit sometimes and wonder who it is that has given it a
bad name."

Sitting Bull went on to describe the condition of the Indians.
They had none of the things that white men had. If they were
to become like white men they must have tools, livestock, and
wagons, "because that is the way white people make a living."

Instead of accepting Sitting Bull's apology graciously and
listening to what he had to say, the commissioners immediately
launched an attack. Senator John Logan scolded him for breaking up the previous council and then for accusing the committee
members of being drunk. "I want to say further that you are
not a great chief of this country," Logan continued, "that you
have no following, no power, no control, and no right to any
control. You are on an Indian reservation merely at the suf-
france of the government. You are fed by the government,
clothed by the government, your children are educated by the
government, and all you have and are today is because of the
government. If it were not for the government you would be
freezing and starving today in the mountains. I merely say these
things to you to notify you that you cannot insult the people

of the United States of America or its committees. . . . The
government feeds and clothes and educates your children now,
and desires to teach you to become farmers, and to civilize you,
and *make you as white men.*" [11]

To speed the process of making the Sioux as white men, the
Indian Bureau assigned James McLaughlin to head the agency
at Standing Rock. McLaughlin, or White Hair, as the Indians
called him, was a veteran of the Indian Service, was married to
a half-breed Santee woman, and his superiors were confident
that he could efficiently destroy the culture of the Sioux and
replace it with the white man's civilization. After the departure
of the Dawes commission, White Hair McLaughlin attempted
to diminish Sitting Bull's influence by dealing with Gall in matters involving the Hunkpapas and with John Grass for the
Blackfoot Sioux. Every move that White Hair made was cal-
culated to keep Sitting Bull in the background, to demonstrate
to the Standing Rock Sioux that their old hero was powerless
to lead or help them.

White Hair's maneuvers had no effect whatsoever on Sitting
Bull's popularity with the Sioux. All visitors to the reservation,
Indian or white, wanted to meet Sitting Bull. In the summer
of 1883, when the Northern Pacific Railroad celebrated the driving of the last spike in its transcontinental track, one of the
officials in charge of ceremonies decided it would be fitting for
an Indian chief to be present to make a speech of welcome to
the Great Father and other notables. Sitting Bull was the choice
—no other Indian was even considered—and a young Army
officer who understood the Sioux language was assigned to work
with the chief in preparation of a speech. It was to be delivered
in Sioux and then translated by the officer.

On September 8 Sitting Bull and the young Bluecoat arrived
at Bismarck for the big celebration. They rode at the head of
a parade and then sat on the speakers' platform. When Sitting
Bull was introduced, he arose and began delivering his speech
in Sioux. The young officer listened in dismay. Sitting Bull had
changed the flowery text of welcome. "I hate all the white people," he was saying. "You are thieves and liars. You have taken
away our land and made us outcasts." [12] Knowing that only the
Army officer could understand what he was saying, Sitting Bull

paused occasionally for applause; he bowed, smiled, and then uttered a few more insults. At last he sat down, and the bewildered interpreter took his place. The officer had only a short translation written out, a few friendly phrases, but by adding several well-worn Indian metaphors, he brought the audience to its feet with a standing ovation for Sitting Bull. The Hunkpapa chief was so popular that the railroad officials took him to St. Paul for another ceremony.

During the following summer the Secretary of the Interior authorized a tour of fifteen American cities for Sitting Bull, and his appearances created such a sensation that William F. (Buffalo Bill) Cody decided he must add the famous chief to his Wild West Show. The Indian Bureau offered some resistance to the proposal at first but when White Hair McLaughlin was queried, he was enthusiastic. By all means, he said, let Sitting Bull go with the Wild West Show. At Standing Rock, Sitting Bull was a constant symbol of Indian resistance, a continual defender of the Indian culture that McLaughlin was determined to eradicate. White Hair would have liked to see Sitting Bull go on tour forever.

And so, in the summer of 1885, Sitting Bull joined Buffalo Bill's Wild West Show, traveling throughout the United States and into Canada. He drew tremendous crowds. Boos and catcalls sometimes sounded for the "Killer of Custer," but after each show these same people pressed coins upon him for copies of his signed photograph. Sitting Bull gave most of the money away to the band of ragged, hungry boys who seemed to surround him wherever he went. He once told Annie Oakley, another one of the Wild West Show's stars, that he could not understand how white men could be so unmindful of their own poor. "The white man knows how to make everything," he said, "but he does not know how to distribute it."

After the season ended, he returned to Standing Rock with two farewell presents from Buffalo Bill—a huge white sombrero and a performing horse. The horse had been trained to sit down and raise one hoof at the crack of a gunshot.

In 1887 Buffalo Bill invited Sitting Bull to accompany his show on a tour of Europe, but the chief declined. "I am needed here," he said. "There is more talk of taking our lands." [13]

The land-grab attempt did not come until the following year, when a commission arrived from Washington with a proposal to carve the Great Sioux Reservation into six smaller reservations, leaving nine million acres open for settlement. The commissioners offered the Indians fifty cents an acre for this land. Sitting Bull immediately went to work to convince Gall and John Grass that the Sioux would not stand for such a swindle; they had no more land to spare. For about a month the commissioners tried to persuade the Standing Rock Indians that Sitting Bull was misleading them, that the land cession was for their benefit, and that if they failed to sign they might lose the land anyhow. Only twenty-two Sioux signed at Standing Rock. After failing to obtain the required three-fourths of signatures at Crow Creek and Lower Brulé agencies, the commissioners gave up. Without even venturing into Pine Ridge or Rosebud, they returned to Washington and recommended that the government ignore the treaty of 1868 and take the land without consent of the Indians.

In 1888 the United States government was not quite ready to abrogate a treaty, but the following year Congress took the first step toward such action—if it became necessary. What the politicians preferred was to force the Indians into selling a large portion of their reservation out of fear that it would be taken away from them if they refused to sell. Should this scheme work, the government would not have to break the treaty.

Knowing that the Indians trusted General George Crook, officials in Washington first convinced him the Sioux would lose everything unless they voluntarily agreed to break up their reservation. Crook agreed to serve as chairman of a new commission, and was authorized to offer the Indians $1.50 per acre instead of the fifty cents offered by the previous commission.

With two earnest politicians, Charles Foster of Ohio and William Warner of Missouri, Crook journeyed to the Great Sioux Reservation in May, 1889. He was fully determined to obtain the required three-fourths of adult male signatures. Three Stars left his blue uniform in Chicago, and prepared to meet his former enemies in rumpled gray flannels. He deliberately chose the Rosebud agency for his first council. Since the assassination of Spotted Tail, the Brulés were split into factions, and Crook believed they were unlikely to offer a united front against signing their land away.

He reckoned without Hollow Horn Bear, who insisted that the commissioners call all the chiefs of the six agencies together for one council instead of traveling from one to the other. "You want to make everything safe here," Hollow Horn Bear said accusingly, "and then go on to the other agencies and tell them we have signed."

Crook replied that the Great Father had ordered the commissioners to consult with the Indians at the different agencies "because it is spring now and if you all come together at one place your crops will all suffer." Hollow Horn Bear refused to cooperate, however, and so did High Hawk. "The land you have now surveyed out for us is but a very small piece," High Hawk said. "And I expect my children to have children and grandchildren, and get all over the country, and now you want me to cut off my 'tool' and not make any more children."

Yellow Hair said: "Whenever we give you any land we never take it back, so this time we want to consider well before we give up this land."

"The white men in the East are like birds," Crook told them. "They are hatching out their eggs every year, and there is not room enough in the East and they must go elsewhere; and they come west, as you have seen them coming for the last few years. And they are still coming, and will come until they overrun all of this country; and you can't prevent it. . . . Everything is decided in Washington by the majority, and these people come out west and see that the Indians have a big body of land they are not using, and they say 'we want the land.' "[14]

After nine days of discussion, a majority of the Brulés followed Crook's advice and signed. The first signature on the agreement was that of Crow Dog, the assassin of Spotted Tail.

At Pine Ridge in June, the commissioners had to deal with Red Cloud, who demonstrated his power by surrounding the council with several hundred of his mounted warriors. Although Red Cloud and his loyal lieutenants stood firm, the commissioners managed to secure about half of the Oglalas' signatures. To make up the difference they moved on to the smaller agencies, obtaining signatures at Lower Brulé, Crow Creek, and

Cheyenne River. On July 27 they arrived at Standing Rock. Here the decision would be made. If a majority of the Hunkpapas and Blackfoot Sioux refused to sign, the agreement would fail.

Sitting Bull attended the first councils but remained silent. His presence was all that was needed to maintain a solid wall of opposition. "The Indians gave close attention," Crook said, "but gave no indication of favor. Their demeanor was rather that of men who had made up their minds and listened from curiosity as to what new arguments could be advanced."

John Grass was chief spokesman for the Standing Rock Sioux. "When we had plenty of land," he said, "we could give it to you at your own prices, whatever you had in mind to give, but now we have come down to the small portion there is to spare, and you wish to buy the balance. We are not the ones who are offering our lands for sale. It is the Great Father that is after us to sell the land. That is the reason that the price that is put on the land here we think is not enough, therefore we don't want to sell the land at that price." [15]

Sitting Bull and his followers, of course, did not want to sell at any price. As White Thunder had told the Dawes commission six years earlier, their land was "the dearest thing on earth" to them.

After several days of fruitless discussion, Crook realized that he could win no converts in general councils. He enlisted agent James McLaughlin in a concerted effort to convince individual Indians that the government would take their land away if they refused to sell. Sitting Bull remained unyielding. Why should the Indians sell their land in order to save the United States government the embarrassment of breaking a treaty to get it?

White Hair McLaughlin arranged secret meetings with John Grass. "I talked with him until he agreed that he would speak for its ratification and work for it," McLaughlin said afterward. "Finally we fixed up the speech he was to make receding from his former position gracefully, thus to bring him the active support of the other chiefs and settle the matter." [16]

Without informing Sitting Bull, McLaughlin arranged for a final meeting with the commissioners on August 3. The agent stationed his Indian police in a four-column formation around the council grounds to prevent any interruptions by Sitting Bull or any of his ardent supporters. John Grass had already delivered the speech, which McLaughlin had helped him write, before Sitting Bull forced his way through the police and entered the council circle.

For the first time he spoke: "I would like to say something unless you object to my speaking, and if you do I will not speak. No one told us of the council, and we just got here."

Crook glanced at McLaughlin. "Did Sitting Bull know that we were going to hold a council?" he asked.

"Yes, sir," McLaughlin lied. "Yes, sir, everybody knew it." [17]

At this moment John Grass and the chiefs moved forward to sign the agreement. It was all over. The Great Sioux Reservation was broken into small islands around which would rise the flood of white immigration. Before Sitting Bull could get away from the grounds, a newspaperman asked him how the Indians felt about giving up their lands.

"Indians!" Sitting Bull shouted. "There are no Indians left but me!"

In the Drying Grass Moon (October 9, 1890), about a year after the breaking up of the Great Reservation, a Minneconjou from the Cheyenne River agency came to Standing Rock to visit Sitting Bull. His name was Kicking Bear, and he brought news of the Paiute Messiah, Wovoka, who had founded the religion of the Ghost Dance. Kicking Bear and his brother-in-law, Short Bull, had returned from a long journey beyond the Shining Mountains in search of the Messiah. Hearing of this pilgrimage, Sitting Bull had sent for Kicking Bear in order to learn more about the Ghost Dance.

Kicking Bear told Sitting Bull of how a voice had commanded him to go forth and meet the ghosts of Indians who were to return and inhabit the earth. On the cars of the Iron Horse he and Short Bull and nine other Sioux had traveled far toward the place where the sun sets, traveled until the railroad stopped. There they were met by two Indians they had never seen before, but who greeted them as brothers and gave them meat and bread. They supplied the pilgrims with horses and they rode for four suns until they came to a camp of Fish Eaters (Paiutes) near Pyramid Lake in Nevada.

The Fish Eaters told the visitors that Christ had returned to earth again. Christ must have sent for them to come there, Kicking Bear said; it was foreordained. To see the Messiah they had to make another journey to the agency at Walker Lake.

For two days Kicking Bear and his friends waited at Walker Lake with hundreds of other Indians speaking in dozens of different tongues. These Indians had come from many reservations to see the Messiah.

Just before sundown on the third day the Christ appeared, and the Indians made a big fire to throw light on him. Kicking Bear had always thought that Christ was a white man like the missionaries, but this man looked like an Indian. After a while he rose and spoke to the waiting crowd. "I have sent for you and am glad to see you," he said. "I am going to talk to you after a while about your relatives who are dead and gone. My children, I want you to listen to all I have to say to you. I will teach you how to dance a dance, and I want you to dance it. Get ready for your dance, and when the dance is over, I will talk to you." Then he commenced to dance, everybody joining in, the Christ singing while they danced. They danced the Dance of the Ghosts until late at night, when the Messiah told them they had danced enough.[18]

Next morning, Kicking Bear and the others went up close to the Messiah to see if he had the scars of crucifixion which the missionaries on the reservations had told them about. There was a scar on his wrist and one on his face, but they could not see his feet, because he was wearing moccasins. Throughout the day he talked to them. In the beginning, he said, God made the earth, and then sent the Christ to earth to teach the people, but white men had treated him badly, leaving scars on his body, and so he had gone back to heaven. Now he had returned to earth as an Indian, and he was to renew everything as it used to be and make it better.

In the next springtime, when the grass was knee high, the earth would be covered with new soil which would bury all the white men, and the new land would be covered with sweet grass

44. *Wovoka, the Paiute Messiah.*
Courtesy of the Smithsonian
Institution.

45. *Kicking Bear. Photo by David*
F. Barry, from the Denver Public
Library Western Collection.

46. *Short Bull of the Sioux. Photo*
by David F. Barry, from the
Denver Public Library

47. *John Grass. Photo by David F.*
Barry, from the Denver Public
Library Western Collection.

and running water and trees. Great herds of buffalo and wild horses would come back. The Indians who danced the Ghost Dance would be taken up in the air and suspended there while a wave of new earth was passing, and then they would be set down among the ghosts of their ancestors on the new earth, where only Indians would live.

After a few days at Walker Lake, Kicking Bear and his friends learned how to dance the Ghost Dance, and then they mounted their horses to return to the railroad. As they rode along, the Messiah flew above them in the air, teaching them songs for the new dance. At the railroad, he left them, telling them to return to their people and teach what they had learned. When the next winter was passed, he would bring the ghosts of their fathers to meet them in the new resurrection.

After returning to Dakota, Kicking Bear had started the new dance at Cheyenne River, Short Bull had brought it to Rosebud, and others were introducing it at Pine Ridge. Big Foot's band of Minneconjous, Kicking Bear said, was made up mostly of women who had lost husbands or other male relatives in fights with Long Hair and Three Stars and Bear Coat; they danced until they fainted, because they wanted to bring their dead warriors back.

Sitting Bull listened to all that Kicking Bear had to relate about the Messiah and the Ghost Dance. He did not believe it was possible for dead men to return and live again, but his people had heard of the Messiah and were fearful he would pass them by and let them disappear when the new resurrection came, unless they joined in the dancing. Sitting Bull had no objections to his people dancing the Ghost Dance, but he had heard that agents at some reservations were bringing soldiers in to stop the ceremonies. He did not want soldiers coming in to frighten and perhaps shoot their guns at his people. Kicking Bear replied that if the Indians wore the sacred garments of the Messiah—Ghost Shirts painted with magic symbols—no harm could come to them. Not even the bullets of the Bluecoats' guns could penetrate a Ghost Shirt.

With some skepticism, Sitting Bull invited Kicking Bear to remain with his band at Standing Rock and teach them the Dance of the Ghosts. This was in the Moon of Falling Leaves,

and across the West on almost every Indian reservation the
Ghost Dance was spreading like a prairie fire under a high wind.
Agitated Indian Bureau inspectors and Army officers from
Dakota to Arizona, from Indian Territory to Nevada, were try-
ing to fathom the meaning of it. By early autumn the official
word was: Stop the Ghost Dancing.

"A more pernicious system of religion could not have been
offered to a people who stood on the threshold of civilization,"
White Hair McLaughlin said. Although he was a practicing
Catholic, McLaughlin, like most other agents, failed to recognize the Ghost Dance as being entirely Christian. Except for a
difference in rituals, its tenets were the same as those of any
Christian church.

"You must not hurt anybody or do harm to anyone. You must
not fight. Do right always," the Messiah commanded. Preach-
ing nonviolence and brotherly love, the doctrine called for no
action by the Indians except to dance and sing. The Messiah
would bring the resurrection.

But because the Indians were dancing, the agents became
alarmed and notified the soldiers, and the soldiers began to
march.

A week after Kicking Bear came to Standing Rock to teach
Sitting Bull's people the Ghost Dance, White Hair McLaughlin
sent a dozen Indian police to remove him from the reservation.
Awed by Kicking Bear's aura of holiness, the policemen referred McLaughlin's order to Sitting Bull, but the chief refused
to take action. On October 16 McLaughlin sent a larger force
of police, and this time Kicking Bear was escorted off the reservation.

The following day McLaughlin notified the Commissioner of
Indian Affairs that the real power behind the "pernicious system
of religion" at Standing Rock was Sitting Bull. He recommended
that the chief be arrested, removed from the reservation, and
confined to a military prison. The commissioner conferred with
the Secretary of War, and they decided that such action would
create more trouble than it would prevent.

By mid-November Ghost Dancing was so prevalent on the
Sioux reservations that almost all other activities came to a halt.
No pupils appeared at the schoolhouses, the trading stores were

empty, no work was done on the little farms. At Pine Ridge
the frightened agent telegraphed Washington: "Indians are
dancing in the snow and are wild and crazy. . . . We need protection and we need it now. The leaders should be arrested and
confined at some military post until the matter is quieted, and
this should be done at once." [19]

Short Bull led his band of believers down White River into
the Badlands, and in a few days their numbers swelled to more
than three thousand. Disregarding the wintry weather, they
donned their Ghost Shirts and danced from each dawn far into
the nights. Short Bull told the dancers not to fear the soldiers
if they came to stop the ceremonies. "Their horses will sink into
the earth," he said. "The riders will jump from their horses, but
they will sink into the earth also." [20]

At Cheyenne River, Big Foot's band increased to six hundred,
mostly widows. When the agent tried to interfere, Big Foot took
the dancers off the reservation to a sacred place on Deep Creek.

On November 20 the Indian Bureau in Washington ordered
agents in the field to telegraph the names of all "fomenters of
disturbances" among the Ghost Dancers. A list was quickly
assembled in Washington, and transmitted to Bear Coat Miles's
Army headquarters in Chicago. Miles saw Sitting Bull's name
among the "fomenters" and immediately assumed that he was
to blame for all the disturbances.

Miles knew that a forced arrest by soldiers would create trouble; he wanted Sitting Bull removed quietly. To accomplish
this, Bear Coat called on one of the few white men that Sitting
Bull ever liked or trusted—Buffalo Bill Cody. Buffalo Bill agreed
to visit Sitting Bull and try to persuade him to come to Chicago
for a conference with Miles. (The record is unclear as to whether
or not Cody knew that if he succeeded in his mission he would
be taking Sitting Bull to a military prison.)

When Buffalo Bill arrived at Standing Rock he met with an
uncooperative agent. Fearful that Cody would botch the arrest
attempt and only arouse Sitting Bull's anger, McLaughlin
quickly arranged for Washington to rescind the showman's authority. Without even seeing Sitting Bull, Cody left Standing
Rock in a bad humor and returned to Chicago.

Meanwhile, at Pine Ridge, the Army had already brought in

troops, creating a tense situation between the Indians and the military. A former agent, Dr. Valentine McGillycuddy, was sent there to make recommendations for a resolution of the difficulties. "I should let the dance continue," McGillycuddy said. "The coming of the troops has frightened the Indians. If the Seventh-Day Adventists prepare their ascension robes for the second coming of the Savior, the United States Army is not put in motion to prevent them. Why should not the Indians have the same privilege? If the troops remain, trouble is sure to come." This viewpoint, however, was not to prevail. On December 12 Lieutenant Colonel William F. Drum, commanding troops at Fort Yates, received orders from General Miles "to secure the person of Sitting Bull. Call on Indian agent [McLaughlin] to cooperate and render such assistance as will best promote the purpose in view." [21]

Just before daybreak on December 15, 1890, forty-three Indian police surrounded Sitting Bull's log cabin. Three miles away a squadron of cavalry waited as a support force if needed. Lieutenant Bull Head, the Indian policeman in charge of the party, found Sitting Bull asleep on the floor. When he was awakened, the chief stared incredulously at Bull Head. "What do you want here?" he asked.

"You are my prisoner," said Bull Head. "You must go to the agency."

Sitting Bull yawned and sat up. "All right," he replied, "let me put on my clothes and I'll go with you." He asked the policeman to have his horse saddled.

When Bull Head emerged from the cabin with Sitting Bull he found a crowd of Ghost Dancers gathering outside. They outnumbered the police four to one. Catch-the-Bear, one of the dancers, moved toward Bull Head. "You think you are going to take him," Catch-the-Bear shouted. "You shall not do it!"

"Come now," Bull Head said quietly to his prisoner, "do not listen to anyone." But Sitting Bull held back, making it necessary for Bull Head and Sergeant Red Tomahawk to force him toward his horse.

At this moment, Catch-the-Bear threw off his blanket and brought up a rifle. He fired at Bull Head, wounding him in the side. As Bull Head fell, he tried to shoot his assailant, but the bullet struck Sitting Bull instead. Almost simultaneously, Red Tomahawk shot Sitting Bull through the head and killed him.

During the firing, the old show horse that Buffalo Bill had presented to Sitting Bull began to go through his tricks. He sat upright, raised one hoof, and it seemed to those who watched that he was performing the Dance of the Ghosts. But as soon as the horse ceased his dancing and wandered away, the wild fighting resumed, and only the arrival of the cavalry detachment saved the Indian police from extinction.[22]

NINETEEN

Wounded Knee

There was no hope on earth, and God seemed to have forgotten us. Some said they saw the Son of God; others did not see Him. If He had come, He would do some great things as He had done before. We doubted it because we had seen neither Him nor His works.

The people did not know; they did not care. They snatched at the hope. They screamed like crazy men to Him for mercy. They caught at the promise they heard He had made.

The white men were frightened and called for soldiers. We had begged for life, and the white men thought we wanted theirs. We heard that soldiers were coming. We did not fear. We hoped that we could tell them our troubles and get help. A white man said the soldiers meant to kill us. We did not believe it, but some were frightened and ran away to the Badlands.

—Red Cloud

Had it not been for the sustaining force of the Ghost Dance religion, the Sioux in their grief and anger over the assassination of Sitting Bull might have risen up against the guns of the soldiers. So prevalent was their belief that the white men would soon disappear and that with the next greening of the grass their dead relatives and friends would return, they made no retaliations. By the hundreds, however, the leaderless Hunkpapas fled from Standing Rock, seeking refuge in one of the Ghost Dance camps or with the last of the great chiefs, Red Cloud, at Pine Ridge. In the Moon When the Deer Shed Their Horns (December 17) about a hundred of these fleeing Hunkpapas reached Big Foot's Minneconjou camp near Cherry Creek. That same day the War Department issued orders for the arrest and imprisonment of Big Foot. He was on the list of "fomenters of disturbances."

As soon as Big Foot learned that Sitting Bull had been killed, he started his people toward Pine Ridge, hoping that Red Cloud could protect them from the soldiers. En route, he fell ill of pneumonia, and when hemorrhaging began, he had to travel in a wagon. On December 28, as they neared Porcupine Creek, the Minneconjous sighted four troops of cavalry approaching. Big Foot immediately ordered a white flag run up over his wagon. About two o'clock in the afternoon he raised up from his blankets to greet Major Samuel Whitside, Seventh U.S. Cavalry. Big Foot's blankets were stained with blood from his lungs, and as he talked in a hoarse whisper with Whitside, red drops fell from his nose and froze in the bitter cold.

Whitside told Big Foot that he had orders to take him to a cavalry camp on Wounded Knee Creek. The Minneconjou chief replied that he was going in that direction; he was taking his people to Pine Ridge for safety.

Turning to his half-breed scout, John Shangreau, Major Whitside ordered him to begin disarming Big Foot's band.

"Look here, Major," Shangreau replied, "if you do that, there is liable to be a fight here; and if there is, you will kill all those women and children and the men will get away from you."

Whitside insisted that his orders were to capture Big Foot's Indians and disarm and dismount them.

"We better take them to camp and then take their horses from them and their guns," Shangreau declared.

"All right," Whitside agreed. "You tell Big Foot to move down to camp at Wounded Knee." [1]

The major glanced at the ailing chief, and then gave an order for his Army ambulance to be brought forward. The ambulance would be warmer and would give Big Foot an easier ride than the jolting springless wagon. After the chief was transferred to the ambulance, Whitside formed a column for the march to Wounded Knee Creek. Two troops of cavalry took the lead, the ambulance and wagons following, the Indians herded into a compact group behind them, with the other two cavalry troops and a battery of two Hotchkiss guns bringing up the rear.

Twilight was falling when the column crawled over the last

rise in the land and began descending the slope toward Chankpe Opi Wakpala, the creek called Wounded Knee. The wintry dusk and the tiny crystals of ice dancing in the dying light added a supernatural quality to the somber landscape. Somewhere along this frozen stream the heart of Crazy Horse lay in a secret place, and the Ghost Dancers believed that his disembodied spirit was waiting impatiently for the new earth that would surely come with the first green grass of spring.

At the cavalry tent camp on Wounded Knee Creek, the Indians were halted and carefully counted. There were 120 men and 230 women and children. Because of the gathering darkness, Major Whitside decided to wait until morning before disarming his prisoners. He assigned them a camping area immediately to the south of the military camp, issued them rations, and as there was a shortage of tepee covers, he furnished them several tents. Whitside ordered a stove placed in Big Foot's tent and sent a regimental surgeon to administer to the sick chief. To make certain that none of his prisoners escaped, the major stationed two troops of cavalry as sentinels around the Sioux tepees, and then posted his two Hotchkiss guns on top of a rise overlooking the camp. The barrels of these rifled guns, which could hurl explosive charges for more than two miles, were positioned to rake the length of the Indian lodges.

Later in the darkness of that December night the remainder of the Seventh Regiment marched in from the east and quietly bivouacked north of Major Whitside's troops. Colonel James W. Forsyth, commanding Custer's former regiment, now took charge of operations. He informed Whitside that he had received orders to take Big Foot's band to the Union Pacific Railroad for shipment to a military prison in Omaha.

After placing two more Hotchkiss guns on the slope beside the others, Forsyth and his officers settled down for the evening with a keg of whiskey to celebrate the capture of Big Foot.

The chief lay in his tent, too ill to sleep, barely able to breathe. Even with their protective Ghost Shirts and their belief in the prophecies of the new Messiah, his people were fearful of the pony soldiers camped all around them. Fourteen years before, on the Little Bighorn, some of these warriors had helped defeat some of these soldier chiefs—Moylan, Varnum, Wallace,

Godfrey, Edgerly—and the Indians wondered if revenge could still be in their hearts.

"The following morning there was a bugle call," said Wasumaza, one of Big Foot's warriors who years afterward was to change his name to Dewey Beard. "Then I saw the soldiers mounting their horses and surrounding us. It was announced that all men should come to the center for a talk and that after the talk they were to move on to Pine Ridge agency. Big Foot was brought out of his tepee and sat in front of his tent and the older men were gathered around him and sitting right near him in the center."

After issuing hardtack for breakfast rations, Colonel Forsyth informed the Indians that they were now to be disarmed. "They called for guns and arms," White Lance said, "so all of us gave the guns and they were stacked up in the center." The soldier chiefs were not satisfied with the number of weapons surrendered, and so they sent details of troopers to search the tepees. "They would go right into the tents and come out with bundles and tear them open," Dog Chief said. "They brought our axes, knives, and tent stakes and piled them near the guns." [2]

Still not satisfied, the soldier chiefs ordered the warriors to remove their blankets and submit to searches for weapons. The Indians' faces showed their anger, but only the medicine man, Yellow Bird, made any overt protest. He danced a few Ghost Dance steps, and chanted one of the holy songs, assuring the warriors that the soldiers' bullets could not penetrate their sacred garments. "The bullets will not go toward you," he chanted in Sioux. "The prairie is large and the bullets will not go toward you." [3]

The troopers found only two rifles, one of them a new Winchester belonging to a young Minneconjou named Black Coyote. Black Coyote raised the Winchester above his head, shouting that he paid much money for the rifle and that it belonged to him. Some years afterward Dewey Beard recalled that Black Coyote was deaf. "If they had left him alone he was going to put his gun down where he should. They grabbed him and spinned him in the east direction. He was still unconcerned even then. He hadn't his gun pointed at anyone. His intention was to put that gun down. They came on and grabbed the gun that he was

48. *Big Foot in death. Photographed at the Wounded Knee battlefield.
Courtesy of the Smithsonian Institution.*

going to put down. Right after they spun him around there was the report of a gun, was quite loud. I couldn't say that anybody was shot, but following that was a crash."

"It sounded much like the sound of tearing canvas, that was the crash," Rough Feather said. Afraid-of-the-Enemy described it as a "lightning crash." [4]

Turning Hawk said that Black Coyote "was a crazy man, a young man of very bad influence and in fact a nobody." He said that Black Coyote fired his gun and that "immediately the soldiers returned fire and indiscriminate killing followed." [5]

In the first seconds of violence, the firing of carbines was deafening, filling the air with powder smoke. Among the dying who lay sprawled on the frozen ground was Big Foot. Then there was a brief lull in the rattle of arms, with small groups of Indians and soldiers grappling at close quarters, using knives, clubs, and pistols. As few of the Indians had arms, they soon had to flee, and then the big Hotchkiss guns on the hill opened up on them, firing almost a shell a second, raking the Indian camp, shredding the tepees with flying shrapnel, killing men, women, and children.

"We tried to run," Louise Weasel Bear said, "but they shot us like we were a buffalo. I know there are some good white people, but the soldiers must be mean to shoot children and women. Indian soldiers would not do that to white children."

"I was running away from the place and followed those who were running away," said Hakiktawin, another of the young women. "My grandfather and grandmother and brother were killed as we crossed the ravine, and then I was shot on the right hip clear through and on my right wrist where I did not go any further as I was not able to walk, and after the soldier picked me up where a little girl came to me and crawled into the blanket." [6]

When the madness ended, Big Foot and more than half of his people were dead or seriously wounded; 153 were known dead, but many of the wounded crawled away to die afterward. One estimate placed the final total of dead at very nearly three hundred of the original 350 men, women, and children. The soldiers lost twenty-five dead and thirty-nine wounded, most of them struck by their own bullets or shrapnel.

After the wounded cavalrymen were started for the agency at

Pine Ridge, a detail of soldiers went over the Wounded Knee battlefield, gathering up Indians who were still alive and loading them into wagons. As it was apparent by the end of the day that a blizzard was approaching, the dead Indians were left lying where they had fallen. (After the blizzard, when a burial party returned to Wounded Knee, they found the bodies, including Big Foot's, frozen into grotesque shapes.)

The wagonloads of wounded Sioux (four men and forty-seven women and children) reached Pine Ridge after dark. Because all available barracks were filled with soldiers, they were left lying in the open wagons in the bitter cold while an inept Army officer searched for shelter. Finally the Episcopal mission was opened, the benches taken out, and hay scattered over the rough flooring.

It was the fourth day after Christmas in the Year of Our Lord 1890. When the first torn and bleeding bodies were carried into the candlelit church, those who were conscious could see Christmas greenery hanging from the open rafters. Across the chancel front above the pulpit was strung a crudely lettered banner: PEACE ON EARTH, GOOD WILL TO MEN.

I did not know then how much was ended. When I look back now from this high hill of my old age, I can still see the butchered women and children lying heaped and scattered all along the crooked gulch as plain as when I saw them with eyes still young. And I can see that something else died there in the bloody mud, and was buried in the blizzard. A people's dream died there. It was a beautiful dream . . . the nation's hoop is broken and scattered. There is no center any longer, and the sacred tree is dead.

—Black Elk

THE EARTH ONLY ENDURES

Courtesy of the Bureau of American Ethnology Collection

The old men
say
the earth
only
endures.
You spoke
truly.
You are right.

49. "*They made us many promises, more than I can remember, but they never kept but one; they promised to take our land, and they took it.*" *Reproduced from the collections of the Library of Congress. Photograph by E. S. Curtis.*

NOTES

CHAPTER TWO: THE LONG WALK OF THE NAVAHOS

1. U.S. Congress. 49th. 1st session. House of Representatives Executive Document 263, p. 14.
2. U.S. Congress. 39th. 2nd session. Senate Report 156, p. 314.
3. Official record. *The War of the Rebellion.* Series I, Vol. 15, p. 580.
4. U.S. Interior Dept., Report, 1863, pp. 544–45; Document published in Kelly, Lawrence C. *Navajo Roundup.* Boulder, Pruett, 1970; Cremony, John C. *Life Among the Apaches.* San Francisco, 1868, p. 201.
5. U.S. Congress. 39th. 2nd session. Senate Report 156, p. 103.
6. *Ibid.*, pp. 108, 116.
7. *Ibid.*, pp. 136, 139.
8. Document in Kelly, *Navajo Roundup;* Bailey, Lynn R. *Long Walk.* Los Angeles, Westernlore, 1964, p. 157; Senate Report 156, p. 141.
9. Senate Report 156, pp. 153–54, 255; Document in Kelly, *Navajo Roundup.*
10. U.S. Congress. 49th. 1st session. House of Representatives Executive Document 263, p. 15.
11. Senate Report 156, pp. 144, 157, 162–67, 174, 179, 183–84, 259–60; Bailey, *Long Walk,* pp. 164–66; Document in Kelly, *Navajo Roundup;* Kelleher, William A. *Turmoil in New Mexico, 1846–1868.* Santa Fe, Rydal Press, 1952, p. 441.
12. *Ibid.*, pp. 221–22.
13. *Ibid.*, p. 223.
14. U.S. Office of Indian Affairs. Report, 1867, p. 190.
15. U.S. Congress. 49th. 1st session. House of Representatives Executive Document 263, p. 15.

CHAPTER THREE: LITTLE CROW'S WAR

1. "Big Eagle's Story of the Sioux Outbreak of 1862." Minnesota Historical Society, *Collections.* Vol. VI, 1894, p. 385.
2. Folwell, William W. *A History of Minnesota.* St. Paul, Minnesota Historical Society, 1924. Vol. II, p. 232.
3. *Ibid.*, p. 233. Meyer, Roy W. *History of the Santee Sioux.* Lincoln, University of Nebraska Press, 1967, p. 114.
4. "Big Eagle's Story," p. 389.
5. "Ta-oya-te-duta Is Not a Coward." *Minnesota History,* Vol. 38, 1962, p. 115.
6. "Big Eagle's Story," p. 390.
7. Carley, Kenneth, ed. "As Red Men Viewed It; Three Indian Accounts of the Uprising." *Minnesota History,* Vol. 38, 1962, p. 144.
8. *Ibid.*, pp. 144–45.
9. *Ibid.*, pp. 145–46.
10. *Ibid.*, p. 148.

11. *Ibid.*, p. 146.
12. "Big Eagle's Story," pp. 394–97.
13. Heard, Isaac V. D. *History of the Sioux War.* New York, Harper & Brothers, 1864, p. 147.
14. Carley, Kenneth. *The Sioux Uprising of 1862.* St. Paul, Minnesota Historical Society, 1961, p. 54.
15. Heard, pp. 147–48.
16. Riggs, S. R. "Narrative of Paul Mazakootemane." Minnesota Historical Society, *Collections*, Vol. III, 1880, pp. 84–85.
17. Heard, pp. 151–52.
18. *Ibid.*, p. 150.
19. "Big Eagle's Story," pp. 398–99. Sibley Order Book 35. Folwell, p. 182.
20. Oehler, C. M. *The Great Sioux Uprising.* New York, Oxford University Press, 1959, p. 197.
21. Riggs, p. 8.
22. Folwell, pp. 202–05. Oehler, p. 208.
23. Lincoln to Sibley, December 6, 1963.
24. Folwell, p. 211.
25. Heard, p. 284.
26. "Big Eagle's Story," pp. 399–400.
27. Heard, p. 311.
28. *Ibid.*, p. 312. Trenerry, Walter N. "The Shooting of Little Crow: Heroism or Murder?" *Minnesota History*, Vol. 38, 1962, pp. 152–53.
29. Winks, Robin W. "The British North American West and the Civil War." *North Dakota History*, Vol. 24, 1957, pp. 148–51. Folwell, pp. 443–50.

CHAPTER FOUR: WAR COMES TO THE CHEYENNES

1. Grinnell, George Bird. *The Fighting Cheyennes.* Norman, University of Oklahoma Press, 1956, pp. 145–46. Hyde, George E. *Life of George Bent.* Norman, University of Oklahoma Press, 1968, pp. 131–32.
2. U.S. Congress. 39th. 2nd session. Senate Report 156, pp. 93–94.
3. Berthrong, Donald J. *The Southern Cheyennes.* Norman, University of Oklahoma Press, 1963, p. 185.
4. U.S. Congress. 39th. 2nd session. Senate Report 156, p. 94.
5. *Ibid.*, pp. 55–56.
6. U.S. Secretary of the Interior. Report, 1864, pp. 374–75.
7. *Ibid.*, pp. 374, 377.
8. Hoig, Stan. *The Sand Creek Massacre.* Norman, University of Oklahoma Press, 1961, p. 99.

9. Hyde, p. 142.
10. U.S. Congress. 39th. 2nd session. Senate Executive Document 26, p. 44.
11. Official record. *The War of the Rebellion.* Series I, Vol. 41, Pt. 3, p. 462.
12. U.S. Congress. 39th. 2nd session. Senate Report 156, p. 77.
13. *Ibid.,* pp. 87–90.
14. Hyde, p. 146.
15. Berthrong, p. 213.
16. U.S. Congress. 39th. 2nd session. Senate Executive Document 26, p. 226.
17. U.S. Congress. 38th. 2nd session. Senate Report 142, p. 18.
18. U.S. Congress. 39th. 2nd session. Senate Executive Document 26, p. 25.
19. *Ibid.,* p. 47. U.S. Congress. 39th. 2nd session. Senate Report 156, pp. 53, 74.
20. *Ibid.,* p. 66.
21. George Bent to George E. Hyde, April 14, 1906 (Coe Collection, Yale University).
22. U.S. Congress. 39th. 2nd session. Senate Report 156, pp. 66, 73.
23. U.S. Congress. 39th. 2nd session. Senate Executive Document 26, p. 70.
24. U.S. Congress. 39th. 2nd session. Senate Report 156, pp. 73, 96.
25. *Ibid.,* p. 53. Berthrong, p. 220.
26. Bent, George. "Forty Years with the Cheyennes." *The Frontier,* Vol. IV, No. 6, December, 1905, p. 3. Hyde, pp. 152, 158–59.
27. U.S. Congress. 39th. 2nd session. Senate Executive Document 26, pp. 73–74.
28. Hyde, p. 177.
29. U.S. Commissioner of Indian Affairs. Report, 1871, p. 439.
30. U.S. Secretary of the Interior. Report, 1865, pp. 701–11.
31. Kappler, Charles J. *Indian Affairs, Laws and Treaties.* Vol. 2, pp. 887–88.

CHAPTER FIVE: POWDER RIVER INVASION

1. Official record. *The War of the Rebellion.* Series I, Vol. 48, Pt. 2, pp. 1048–49.
2. Bent, George. "Forty Years with the Cheyennes." *The Frontier,* Vol. IV, No. 7, January, 1906, p. 4.
3. Holman, Albert M. *Pioneering in the Northwest.* Sioux City, Iowa, 1924.
4. Bent, p. 5.

5. *Ibid.*
6. Grinnell, George Bird. *The Fighting Cheyennes.* Norman, University of Oklahoma Press, 1956, pp. 210–11.
7. Humfreville, J. Lee. *Twenty Years Among Our Hostile Indians.* New York, Hunter and Co., 1903, p. 356.
8. Palmer, H. E. "History of the Powder River Indian Expedition of 1865." Nebraska State Historical Society, *Transactions and Reports,* Vol. II, p. 216.
9. Grinnell, George Bird. *Two Great Scouts and Their Pawnee Battalion.* Cleveland, Arthur H. Clark Co., 1928, p. 117.
10. Hyde, George E. *Life of George Bent.* Norman, University of Oklahoma Press, 1968, pp. 239–40.
11. Hafen, L. R. and Ann W. *Powder River Campaign and Sawyers' Expedition of 1865.* Glendale, Calif., A. H. Clark Co., 1961, p. 97.

CHAPTER SIX: RED CLOUD'S WAR

1. U.S. Congress. 40th. 2nd session. House Executive Document 97, p. 9.
2. U.S. Department of the Interior. Report, 1866, pp. 206–07.
3. Olson, James C. *Red Cloud and the Sioux Problem.* Lincoln, University of Nebraska Press, 1965, p. 31.
4. U.S. Congress. 50th. 1st session. Senate Executive Document 33, p. 5.
5. *Ibid.,* p. 18.
6. Carrington, Frances C. *My Army Life and the Fort Phil Kearny Massacre.* Philadelphia, Lippincott, 1911, pp. 291–92. Carrington, Margaret I. *Ab-sa-ra-ka, Land of Massacre.* Philadelphia, Lippincott, 1878, pp. 79–80.
7. Carrington, H. B. *The Indian Question.* Boston, 1909, p. 9.
8. U.S. Congress. 50th. 1st session. Senate Executive Document 33, pp. 20–21.
9. John Stands in Timber and Margot Liberty. *Cheyenne Memories.* New Haven, Yale University Press, 1967, p. 172.
10. *Ibid.,* pp. 174–76. Hyde, George E. *Life of George Bent.* Norman, University of Oklahoma Press, 1968, pp. 276–77.
11. Lockwood, James D. *Life and Adventures of a Drummer Boy; or Seven Years a Soldier.* Albany, N.Y., 1893, pp. 188–89.
12. Neihardt, John G. *Black Elk Speaks.* Lincoln, University of Nebraska Press, 1961, p. 17.
13. Stanley, Henry M. *My Early Travels and Adventures.* New York, Scribner's, 1895, Vol. I, pp. 201–16.

14. Simonin, Louis L. *The Rocky Mountain West in 1867*. Lincoln, University of Nebraska Press, 1966, p. 107.
15. U.S. Congress. 40th. 2nd session. House Executive Document 97, p. 5. U.S. Congress. 41st. 3rd session. Senate Executive Document 39, pp. 63–66.
16. *Omaha Weekly Herald,* June 10, 1868.
17. U.S. Congress. 44th. 2nd session. Senate Executive Document 9, p. 38.

CHAPTER SEVEN: "THE ONLY GOOD INDIAN IS A DEAD INDIAN"

1. Hyde, George E. *Life of George Bent*. Norman, University of Oklahoma Press, 1968, p. 253.
2. Hancock, Winfield Scott. *Reports of . . . upon Indian Affairs*. 1867, pp. 45–46, 77.
3. *Ibid.,* p. 47.
4. U.S. Secretary of the Interior. Report, 1867, p. 311.
5. Hyde, p. 259.
6. U.S. Secretary of the Interior. Report, 1867, p. 312.
7. Stanley, Henry M. *My Early Travels and Adventures*. New York, Scribner's, 1895, Vol. I, pp. 37–38. Grinnell, George B. *The Fighting Cheyennes*. Norman, University of Oklahoma Press, 1956, pp. 250–52.
8. U.S. Congress. 40th. 2nd session. House Executive Document 97, p. 12.
9. U.S. Congress. 40th. 1st session. Senate Executive Document 13, pp. 11–12, 95, 121.
10. Berthrong, Donald J. *The Southern Cheyennes*. Norman, University of Oklahoma Press, 1963, p. 294.
11. *Chicago Tribune,* November 4, 1867. Jones, Douglas C. *The Treaty of Medicine Lodge*. Norman, University of Oklahoma Press, 1966, pp. 165–69.
12. Brill, Charles J. *Conquest of the Southern Plains*. Oklahoma City, 1938, p. 107.
13. Grinnell, p. 286.
14. Keim, De Benneville Randolph. *Sheridan's Troopers on the Borders*. Philadelphia, McKay, 1885, p. 103.
15. U.S. War Department. Report, 1869, pp. 47–48.
16. *Ibid.,* p. 48. Berthrong, p. 332.
17. Sheridan Papers, January 1, 1869, as quoted in Berthrong, pp. 333–34.

18. Ellis, Edward S. *The History of Our Country.* Indianapolis, 1900, Vol. 6, p. 1483.

CHAPTER EIGHT: THE RISE AND FALL OF DONEHOGAWA

1. U.S. Department of the Interior. Report, 1870, pp. 672–82. U.S. Congress. 41st. 3rd session. Senate Executive Document 39, p. 2.
2. Parker, Arthur C. *The Life of General Ely S. Parker.* Buffalo, N.Y., Buffalo Historical Society, 1919, pp. 102–03.
3. U.S. Congress. 41st. 3rd session. Senate Executive Document 39, pp. 38–39.
4. *Ibid.,* p. 39.
5. *Ibid.,* pp. 40–41.
6. *Ibid.,* pp. 42–44.
7. *The New York Times,* June 17, 1870.
8. Olson, James C. *Red Cloud and the Sioux Problem.* Lincoln, University of Nebraska Press, 1965, p. 127.
9. *Cheyenne* (Wyoming) *Daily Leader,* March 3, 1870.
10. U.S. Congress. 41st. 3rd session. House of Representatives Report 39, p. 284.

CHAPTER NINE: COCHISE AND THE APACHE GUERRILLAS

1. Conner, Daniel E. *Joseph Reddeford Walker and the Arizona Adventure.* Norman, University of Oklahoma Press, 1956, p. 37.
2. McClintock, James H. *Arizona.* Chicago, 1916, Vol. I, pp. 176–78.
3. Conner, pp. 38–42.
4. U.S. Congress. 39th. 2nd session. Senate Report 156, pp. 305–06.
5. U.S. Secretary of the Interior. Report, 1871, p. 485.
6. *Ibid.,* p. 486.
7. *Ibid.,* p. 488.
8. U.S. Secretary of the Interior. Report, 1871, p. 470.
9. *Ibid.,* pp. 475–79.
10. Ellis, A. N. "Recollections of an Interview with Cochise, Chief of the Apaches." Kansas State Historical Society, *Collections,* Vol. 13, 1915, pp. 391–92.
11. Howard, O. O. *My Life and Experiences Among Our Hostile Indians.* Hartford, Conn., 1907, pp. 204–19.
12. Schmitt, Martin F., ed. *General George Crook.* Norman, University of Oklahoma Press, 1946, p. 182.
13. Clum, Woodworth. *Apache Agent, the Story of John P. Clum.* Boston, Houghton Mifflin, 1936, pp. 99–100, 129.

14. Lockwood, Frank C. *Pioneer Days in Arizona.* New York, Macmillan, 1932, pp. 171–72.

CHAPTER TEN: THE ORDEAL OF CAPTAIN JACK

1. U.S. Congress. 43rd. 1st session. House Executive Document 122, p. 173.
2. Riddle, Jeff C. *The Indian History of the Modoc War.* 1914, p. 44.
3. *Ibid.,* pp. 45–46.
4. U.S. Congress. 43rd. 1st session. House Executive Document 122, p. 173.
5. *Ibid.,* p. 174.
6. *Ibid.,* pp. 50–51.
7. Riddle, p. 61.
8. Britt, Albert. *Great Indian Chiefs.* New York, Whittlesey House, 1938, pp. 235–36.
9. Sherman to Canby, March 12, 1873, as quoted in Murray, Keith A. *The Modocs and Their War.* Norman, University of Oklahoma Press, 1959, pp. 156–57.
10. Meacham, A. B. *Wigwam and Warpath,* Boston, 1875, p. 441.
11. *Ibid.,* pp. 444–52.
12. Riddle, pp. 69–77.
13. U.S. Congress. 43rd. 1st session. House Executive Document 122, pp. 140–41.
14. Riddle, pp. 90–91.
15. *Ibid.,* pp. 143–44.
16. U.S. Congress. 43rd. 1st session. House Executive Document 122, p. 111.
17. *Ibid.,* pp. 140–41.

CHAPTER ELEVEN: THE WAR TO SAVE THE BUFFALO

1. Kappler, Charles J. *Indian Affairs, Laws and Treaties.* Vol. 2, p. 980.
2. Nye, W. S. *Carbine and Lance.* Norman, University of Oklahoma Press, 1937, p. 95.
3. Leckie, William H. *Military Conquest of the Southern Plains.* Norman, University of Oklahoma Press, 1963, p. 113.
4. Tatum, Lawrie. *Our Red Brothers.* Philadelphia, Winston, 1899, p. 29.
5. U.S. Bureau of American Ethnology. Annual Report, 17th, 1895–96, p. 208.

6. L. Tatum to E. Hoag, as quoted in Nye, pp. 173–74.
7. Nye, p. 179.
8. *Ibid.*, p. 182.
9. Leckie, p. 151.
10. U.S. Bureau of American Ethnology. Annual Report, 17th, 1895–96, p. 329.
11. Carter, Captain R. G. *On the Border with Mackenzie.* New York, Antiquarian Press, 1961, pp. 355–56.
12. U.S. Department of the Interior. Report, 1872, p. 516.
13. *Army and Navy Journal,* Vol. 10, October 26, 1872, p. 165.
14. Battey, Thomas C. *Life and Adventures of a Quaker Among the Indians.* Boston, Lee and Shepard, 1891, p. 90.
15. Nye, p. 209.
16. *Ibid.*, p. 219.
17. Battey, pp. 202–03.
18. Garretson, Martin S. *The American Bison.* New York Zoological Society, 1938, p. 128. Hornaday, W. T. *The Extermination of the American Bison.* Washington, Smithsonian Institution, 1889, pp. 496–501.
19. Nye, W. S. *Bad Medicine and Good.* Norman, University of Oklahoma Press, 1962, pp. 179–80.
20. *Ibid.*, p. 182.
21. Nye, *Carbine and Lance,* p. 246.
22. Battey, p. 296.
23. Nye, *Carbine and Lance,* p. 300.

CHAPTER TWELVE: THE WAR FOR THE BLACK HILLS

1. New York *Herald,* August 27 and September 25, 1874.
2. Gilbert, Hila. *"Big Bat" Pourier.* Sheridan, Wyoming, Mills Company, 1968, p. 43.
3. Kappler, Charles J. *Indian Affairs, Laws and Treaties.* Vol. 2, p. 1002.
4. U.S. Commissioner of Indian Affairs. Report, 1875, p. 187.
5. Gilbert, p. 43.
6. Mills, Anson. *My Story.* Washington, D.C., 1918, p. 168.
7. U.S. Commissioner of Indian Affairs. Report, 1875, p. 199.
8. U.S. Congress. 44th. 1st session. House Executive Document 184, pp. 8–9.
9. U.S. Secretary of War. Report, 1875, p. 21.
10. U.S. Congress. 44th. 1st session. House Executive Document 184, pp. 10, 17–18.

11. U.S. Secretary of War. Report, 1876, p. 441.
12. Neihardt, John G. *Black Elk Speaks.* Lincoln, University of Nebraska Press, 1961, p. 90.
13. Marquis, Thomas B. *Wooden Leg, a Warrior Who Fought Custer.* Lincoln, University of Nebraska Press, 1957, pp. 165, 168. De Barthe, Joe. *Life and Adventures of Frank Grouard.* Norman, University of Oklahoma Press, 1958, p. 98.
14. Garland, Hamlin. "General Custer's Last Fight as Seen by Two Moon." *McClure's Magazine,* Vol. 11, 1898, p. 444.
15. *Ibid.,* p. 445.
16. Marquis, p. 185.
17. Vestal, Stanley. *Sitting Bull, Champion of the Sioux.* Norman, University of Oklahoma Press, 1957, pp. 150–51.
18. Neihardt, p. 106.
19. Marquis, p. 205.
20. U.S. Bureau of American Ethnology. Annual Report, 19th, 1888–89, p. 564.
21. McLaughlin, James. *My Friend the Indian.* Boston, Houghton Mifflin Co., 1910, pp. 168–69.
22. Neihardt, pp. 108–09.
23. *Leavenworth* (Kansas) *Weekly Times,* August 18, 1881.
24. Garland, p. 446.
25. Robinson, D. W. "Editorial Notes on Historical Sketch of North and South Dakota." *South Dakota Historical Collections,* Vol. I, 1902, p. 151.
26. *St. Paul* (Minnesota) *Pioneer Press,* July 18, 1886.
27. McLaughlin, pp. 172–73.
28. New York *Herald,* September 24, 1876. Easterwood, T. J. *Memories of Seventy-Six.* Dundee, Oregon, 1880, p. 15.
29. McLaughlin, p. 175.
30. *Leavenworth* (Kansas) *Weekly Times,* August 18, 1881.
31. U.S. Bureau of American Ethnology. Annual Report, 10th, 1888–89, p. 565.
32. *Leavenworth* (Kansas) *Weekly Times,* August 18, 1881.
33. New York *Herald,* November 16, 1877.
34. Graham, W. A. *The Custer Myth.* Harrisburg, Pa., Stackpole Co., 1953, p. 110.
35. U.S. Congress. 44th. 2nd session. Senate Executive Document 9, pp. 5, 31.
36. New York *Herald,* September 23, 1876.
37. U.S. Congress. 44th. 2nd session. Senate Executive Document 9, pp. 8, 38–40, 66.

38. De Barthe, pp. 157–58.
39. Mills, pp. 171–72.
40. U.S. Secretary of the Interior. Report, 1877, p. 724.
41. U.S. War Department. Military Division of the Missouri. Record of Engagements with Hostile Indians. 1882, p. 62.

CHAPTER THIRTEEN: THE FLIGHT OF THE NEZ PERCÉS

1. Chief Joseph. "An Indian's Views of Indian Affairs." *North American Review*, Vol. 128, 1879, p. 417.
2. *Ibid.*, p. 418.
3. U.S. Commissioner of Indian Affairs. Annual Report, 1873, p. 527.
4. Chief Joseph, p. 419.
5. U.S. Secretary of War. Annual Report, 1877, p. 594. McWhorter, Lucullus V. *Yellow Wolf: His Own Story*. Caldwell, Idaho, 1940, p. 39.
6. Chief Joseph, pp. 420, 423.
7. *Ibid.*, p. 425.
8. *Ibid.*, p. 426.
9. McWhorter, p. 144.
10. Shields, G. D. *Battle of the Big Hole*. Chicago, 1889, pp. 51–52.
11. McWhorter, pp. 120, 132.
12. Chief Joseph, p. 427.
13. McWhorter, p. 204.
14. Chief Joseph, pp. 425, 428.
15. U.S. Secretary of War. Report, 1877, p. 630.
16. Chief Joseph, p. 432.
17. *Ibid.*

CHAPTER FOURTEEN: CHEYENNE EXODUS

1. Marquis, Thomas B. *Wooden Leg, a Warrior Who Fought Custer*. Lincoln, University of Nebraska Press, 1957, p. 308.
2. *Ibid.*, p. 310.
3. *Ibid.*, p. 320.
4. U.S. Congress. 46th. 2nd session. Senate Report 708, pp. 153, 266, 269.
5. *Ibid.*, pp. 267–68, 271–72.
6. *Ibid.*, pp. 146–47, 217–19.
7. *Ibid.*, p. 278. Grinnell, George B. *The Fighting Cheyennes*. Norman, University of Oklahoma Press, 1956, p. 401.

8. Grinnell, p. 403.
9. Campbell, C. E. "Down Among the Red Men." Kansas State Historical Society, *Collections,* Vol. 17, pp. 677–78.
10. U.S. Congress. 46th. 2nd session. Senate Report 708, p. 241.
11. Bronson, Edgar B. *Reminiscences of a Ranchman.* New York, McClure Company, 1908, pp. 167–69.
12. U.S. Congress. 46th. 2nd session. Senate Report 708, pp. 244, 251.
13. "Liquidation of Dull Knife." *Nebraska History,* Vol. 22, 1941, pp. 109–10.
14. U.S. Congress. 46th. 2nd session. Senate Report 708, p. 242.
15. *Ibid.,* p. 249.
16. Marquis, p. 333.

CHAPTER FIFTEEN: STANDING BEAR BECOMES A PERSON

1. Howard, James H. *The Ponca Tribe.* (U.S. Bureau of American Ethnology, Bulletin 195.) Washington, D.C., 1965, p. 21.
2. U.S. Congress. 46th. 3rd session. Senate Executive Document 30, p. 7.
3. *Ibid.,* pp. 14–15.
4. *Ibid.,* p. 15.
5. *Ibid.,* p. 31.
6. U.S. Secretary of the Interior. Report, 1877, p. 493.
7. U.S. Congress. 46th. 3rd session. Senate Executive Document 30, pp. 15, 31.
8. U.S. Secretary of the Interior. Report, 1877, pp. 493–96.
9. U.S. Congress. 46th. 3rd session. Senate Executive Document 30, p. 16.
10. Tibbles, Thomas H. *Buckskin and Blanket Days.* New York, Doubleday, 1957, p. 197.
11. U.S. Secretary of War. Report, 1879, p. 78.
12. Tibbles, p. 198.
13. Sheldon, Addison E. *Nebraska, the Land and the People.* Chicago, Lewis, 1931, Vol. I, p. 117.
14. *U.S. v. Crook,* 5 Dillon, 453.
15. Foreman, Grant. *The Last Trek of the Indians.* Chicago, University of Chicago Press, 1946, p. 253.
16. U.S. Secretary of the Interior. Report, 1880, pp. 22–25.
17. U.S. Congress. 46th. 3rd session. Senate Executive Document 14, p. 4.
18. *Ibid.,* p. 5.

19. *Ibid.*, pp. 5–6.
20. *Ibid.*, p. 13.
21. Tibbles, p. 15.

CHAPTER SIXTEEN: "THE UTES MUST GO!"

1. Sprague, Marshall. *Massacre; the Tragedy at White River*. Boston, Little, Brown, 1957, p. 92.
2. U.S. Secretary of the Interior. Report, 1873, pp. 465–79.
3. U.S. Secretary of the Interior. Report, 1879, p. 124.
4. U.S. Congress. 46th. 2nd session. House Executive Document 83. p. 66.
5. U.S. Secretary of the Interior. Report, 1879, pp. 124–25. Wellman, Paul. *Death on Horseback*. Philadelphia, Lippincott, 1947, p. 217.
6. Sprague, p. 157.
7. *Ibid.*, p. 163.
8. U.S. Secretary of the Interior. Report, 1879, p. 84.
9. U.S. Congress. 46th. 2nd session. House Executive Document 84, p. 68.
10. *Ibid.*, pp. 53–54.
11. Sprague, p. 176.
12. U.S. Congress. 46th. 2nd session. House Executive Document 84, pp. 7–8.
13. U.S. Congress. 46th. 2nd session. House Miscellaneous Document 38, p. 199.
14. U.S. Secretary of the Interior. Report, 1879, pp. 91–92.
15. U.S. Secretary of War. Report, 1879, p. 9.
16. U.S. Congress. 46th. 2nd session. House Miscellaneous Document 38, p. 193.
17. U.S. Congress. 46th. 2nd session. House Executive Document 83, p. 72.
18. U.S. Secretary of the Interior. Report, 1879, pp. 92–93.
19. U.S. Congress. 46th. 2nd session. House Executive Document 83, p. 62.
20. *Ibid.*, p. 63.
21. U.S. Congress. 46th. 2nd session. House Miscellaneous Document 38, p. 14.
22. U.S. Secretary of the Interior. Report, 1879, p. 94.
23. Emmitt, Robert. *The Last War Trail; the Utes and the Settlement of Colorado*. Norman, University of Oklahoma Press, 1954, pp. 234–35.
24. U.S. Congress. 46th. 2nd session. House Executive Report 83, p. 3.

CHAPTER SEVENTEEN: THE LAST OF THE APACHE CHIEFS

1. Davis, Britton. *The Truth About Geronimo*. Chicago, Lakeside Press, 1951, p. 48.
2. Clum, Woodworth. *Apache Agent; the Story of John P. Clum*. Boston, Houghton Mifflin, 1936, p. 198.
3. Barrètt, S. M. *Geronimo's Story of His Life*. New York, Duffield & Company, 1907, pp. 131–32.
4. U.S. Secretary of War. Report, 1877, p. 134.
5. Thrapp, Dan L. *The Conquest of Apacheria*. Norman, University of Oklahoma Press, 1967, p. 179.
6. U.S. Secretary of War. Report, 1883, pp. 159–65.
7. *Ibid.*, p. 167.
8. Betzinez, Jason, with W. S. Nye. *I Fought with Geronimo*. Harrisburg, Pa., Stackpole Company, 1959, p. 116.
9. Thrapp, p. 290.
10. Bourke, John G. *An Apache Campaign in the Sierra Madre*. New York, Charles Scribner's Sons, 1958, p. 114.
11. Betzinez and Nye, p. 122.
12. U.S. Congress. 51st. 1st session. Senate Executive Document 88, p. 12.
13. *Ibid.*, p. 11. Betzinez and Nye, p. 129.
14. U.S. Congress. 51st. 1st session. Senate Executive Document 88, pp. 16–17.
15. Crook, George. *Résumé of Operations Against Apache Indians, 1882 to 1886*. Omaha, Nebraska, 1886, p. 12.
16. Betzinez and Nye, p. 135. Barrett, p. 139. U.S. Congress. 51st. 1st session. Senate Executive Document 83, p. 33.
17. Faulk, Odie B. *The Geronimo Campaign*. New York, Oxford University Press, 1969, pp. 125–26.

CHAPTER EIGHTEEN: DANCE OF THE GHOSTS

1. Vestal, Stanley. *Sitting Bull, Champion of the Sioux*. Norman, University of Oklahoma Press, 1957, p. 215.
2. U.S. Secretary of the Interior. Report, 1877, pp. 723–25.
3. *Ibid.*, pp. 726–27.
4. Canada. House of Commons Debates, Session 1878, pp. 353–54.
5. Neihardt, John G. *Black Elk Speaks*. Lincoln, University of Nebraska Press, 1961, p. 159.
6. DeBarthe, Joe. *Life and Adventures of Frank Grouard*. Norman, University of Oklahoma Press, 1958, p. 248.

7. U.S. Congress. 48th. 1st session. Senate Report 283, p. 137.
8. *Ibid.,* pp. 135–36, 149.
9. *Ibid.,* pp. 139, 143, 158.
10. *Ibid.,* pp. 71–72.
11. *Ibid.,* pp. 79–81.
12. Glaspell, Kate E. "Incidents in the Life of a Pioneer." *North Dakota Historical Quarterly,* Vol. 8, 1941, pp. 187–88.
13. Vestal, pp. 251, 255.
14. U.S. Congress. 51st. 1st session. Senate Executive Document 51, pp. 52, 58, 65.
15. *Ibid.,* pp. 21, 203.
16. McLaughlin, James. *My Friend the Indian.* Boston, Houghton Mifflin Co., 1910, p. 285.
17. U.S. Congress. 51st. 1st session. Senate Executive Document 51, p. 213.
18. U.S. Bureau of Ethnology. Report, 14th, 1892–93, Part 2, p. 795.
19. Olson, James C. *Red Cloud and the Sioux Problem.* Lincoln, University of Nebraska Press, 1965, p. 326.
20. U.S. Bureau of Ethnology. Report, 14th, 1892–93, Part 2, p. 789.
21. U.S. Commissioner of Indian Affairs. Report, 1891, p. 333.
22. Schmitt, Martin F., and Dee Brown. *Fighting Indians of the West.* New York, Scribner's, 1948, p. 335. Utley, Robert M. *The Last Days of the Sioux Nation,* New Haven, Yale University Press, 1963, p. 159.

CHAPTER NINETEEN: WOUNDED KNEE

1. Utley, Robert M. *The Last Days of the Sioux Nation.* New Haven, Yale University Press, 1963, p. 195.
2. McGregor, James H. *The Wounded Knee Massacre from the Viewpoint of the Survivors.* Baltimore, Maryland, Wirth Brothers, 1940, pp. 105, 118, 134.
3. Utley, p. 210.
4. McGregor, pp. 106, 109, 126.
5. U.S. Bureau of Ethnology. Report, 14th, 1892–93, Part 2, p. 885.
6. McGregor, pp. 111, 140.

Bibliography

"The Affair at Slim Buttes." *South Dakota Historical Collections*, Vol. VI, 1912, pp. 493–590.

Allen, Charles W. "Red Cloud and the U.S. Flag." *Nebraska History*, Vol. 22, 1941, pp. 77–88.

Allison, E. H. "Surrender of Sitting Bull." *South Dakota Historical Collections*, Vol. VI, 1912, pp. 231–70.

Anderson, Harry H. "Cheyennes at the Little Big Horn—a Study of Statistics." *North Dakota History*, Vol. 27, 1960, pp. 81–93.

Andrist, Ralph K. *The Long Death; the Last Days of the Plains Indian*. New York, Macmillan, 1964.

Army and Navy Journal, Vol. 10, 1872–73.

Bailey, Lynn R. *Long Walk*. Los Angeles, Westernlore, 1964.

Barrett, S. M. *Geronimo's Story of His Life*. New York, Duffield & Co., 1907.

Battey, Thomas C. *Life and Adventures of a Quaker Among the Indians*. Boston, Lee and Shepard, 1891.

Beal, Merrill D. *"I Will Fight No More Forever"; Chief Joseph and the Nez Percé War*. Seattle, University of Washington Press, 1963.

Bent, George. "Forty Years with the Cheyennes." *The Frontier*, Vol. IV, 1905–06.

Berthrong, Donald J. *The Southern Cheyennes*. Norman, University of Oklahoma Press, 1963.

Betzinez, Jason, and W. S. Nye. *I Fought with Geronimo*. Harrisburg, Pa., Stackpole, 1960.

"Big Eagle's Story of the Sioux Outbreak of 1862." Minnesota Historical Society, *Collections*, Vol. VI, 1894, pp. 382–400.

Blankenburg, William B. "The Role of the Press in an Indian Massacre, 1871." *Journalism Quarterly*, Vol. 45, 1968, pp. 61–70.

Bourke, John G. *An Apache Campaign in the Sierra Madre*. New York, Scribner's, 1958.

————. *Mackenzie's Last Fight with the Cheyennes*. New York, Argonaut Press, 1966.

————. *On the Border with Crook*. New York, Scribner's, 1891.

Brandes, Ray. *Frontier Military Posts of Arizona*. Globe, Arizona, 1960.

Brill, Charles J. *Conquest of the Southern Plains*. Oklahoma City, 1938.

Britt, Albert. *Great Indian Chiefs*. New York, Whittlesey House, 1938.

Bronson, Edgar Beecher. *Reminiscences of a Ranchman.* New York, McClure Company, 1908.

Brown, Dee. *Fort Phil Kearney; an American Saga.* New York, Putnam's, 1962.

———. *The Galvanized Yankees.* Urbana, University of Illinois Press, 1963.

Brown, Mark H. *The Plainsmen of the Yellowstone.* New York, Putnam's, 1961.

Bryant, Charles S., and A. B. Murch. *A History of the Great Massacre by the Sioux Indians in Minnesota.* Cincinnati, 1864.

Campbell, C. E. "Down Among the Red Men." Kansas State Historical Society, *Collections,* Vol. XVII, 1928, pp. 623–91.

Carley, Kenneth, ed. "As Red Men Viewed It; Three Indian Accounts of the Uprising." *Minnesota History,* Vol. 38, 1962, pp. 126–49.

———. *The Sioux Uprising of 1862.* St. Paul, Minnesota Historical Society, 1961.

Carrington, Frances C. *My Army Life and the Fort Phil Kearny Massacre.* Philadelphia, Lippincott, 1911.

Carrington, H. B. *The Indian Question.* Boston, 1909.

Carrington, Margaret I. *Ab-sa-ra-ka, Land of Massacre.* Philadelphia, Lippincott, 1878.

Carter, R. G. *On the Border with Mackenzie.* New York, Antiquarian Press, 1961.

Chicago Tribune, 1867 and 1872.

Chief Joseph. "An Indian's Views of Indian Affairs." *North American Review,* Vol. 128, 1879, pp. 412–33.

Clum, John P. "Eskiminzin." *New Mexico Historical Review,* Vol. 4, 1929, pp. 1–27.

Clum, Woodworth. *Apache Agent, the Story of John P. Clum.* Boston, Houghton Mifflin, 1936.

Collins, John C. *Across the Plains in '64.* Omaha, Nebraska, 1904.

Conner, Daniel Ellis. *Joseph Reddeford Walker and the Arizona Adventure.* Norman, University of Oklahoma Press, 1956.

Cook, James H. *Fifty Years on the Old Frontier.* New Haven, Yale University Press, 1923.

Cook, John R. *The Border and the Buffalo.* New York, Citadel Press, 1967.

Cremony, John C. *Life Among the Apaches.* San Francisco, 1868.

Crook, George. *Autobiography,* edited by Martin F. Schmitt. Norman, University of Oklahoma Press, 1946.

———. *Résumé of Operations Against Apache Indians, 1882 to 1886.* Omaha, Nebraska, 1886.

Davis, Britton. *The Truth About Geronimo.* Chicago, Lakeside Press, 1951.

DeBarthe, Joe. *Life and Adventures of Frank Grouard.* Norman, University of Oklahoma Press, 1958.

Densmore, Frances. *Teton Sioux Music* (Bureau of American Ethnology Bulletin 61). Washington, D.C., 1918.

Easterwood, Thomas J. *Memories of Seventy-Six.* Dundee, Oregon, 1880.

Ellis, A. N. "Recollections of an Interview with Cochise, Chief of the Apaches." Kansas State Historical Society, *Collections,* Vol. 13, 1915, pp. 387–92.

Emmitt, Robert. *The Last War Trail; the Utes and the Settlement of Colorado.* Norman, University of Oklahoma Press, 1954.

Ewers, John C. *Indian Life on the Upper Missouri.* Norman, University of Oklahoma Press, 1968.

Falk, Odie B. *The Geronimo Campaign.* New York, Oxford University Press, 1969.

Fechet, E. G. "The True Story of the Death of Sitting Bull." Nebraska State Historical Society, *Proceedings and Collections,* Second Series, Vol. II, 1898, pp. 179–90.

Finerty, John F. *Warpath and Bivouac.* Chicago, Lakeside Press, 1955.

Folwell, William W. *A History of Minnesota,* Vol. II. St. Paul, Minnesota Historical Society, 1924.

Foreman, Grant. *The Last Trek of the Indians.* Chicago, University of Chicago Press, 1946.

Fritz, Henry E. *The Movement for Indian Assimilation, 1860–1890.* Philadelphia, University of Pennsylvania Press, 1963.

Garland, Hamlin. "General Custer's Last Fight as Seen by Two Moon." *McClure's Magazine,* Vol. 11, 1898, pp. 443–48.

Garretson, Martin S. *The American Bison.* New York Zoological Society, 1938.

Gilbert, Hila. *"Big Bat" Pourier.* Sheridan, Wyoming, Mills Company, 1968.

Gilles, Albert S., Sr. "Wer-que-yah, Jesus-Man Comanche." *Southwest Review,* Vol. 53, 1968, pp. 277–91.

Glaspell, Kate E. "Incidents in the Life of a Pioneer." *North Dakota Historical Quarterly,* Vol. 8, 1941, pp. 184–90.

Graham, W. A. *The Custer Myth.* Harrisburg, Pa., Stackpole, 1953.

Grange, Roger T., Jr. "Treating the Wounded at Fort Robinson." *Nebraska History,* Vol. 45, 1964, pp. 273–94.

Grinnell, George B. *The Fighting Cheyennes.* Norman, University of Oklahoma Press, 1956.

————. *Two Great Scouts and Their Pawnee Battalion.* Cleveland, A. H. Clark, 1928.

Hafen, Le Roy R. and Ann W. *Powder River Campaigns and Sawyers' Expedition of 1865.* Glendale, Calif., A. H. Clark, 1961.

Hancock, Winfield Scott. *Reports of . . . upon Indian Affairs, with Accompanying Exhibits,* 1867.

Heard, Isaac V. D. *History of the Sioux War.* New York, Harper, 1864.

Hoig, Stan. *The Sand Creek Massacre.* Norman, University of Oklahoma Press, 1961.

Holman, Albert M. *Pioneering in the Northwest.* Sioux City, Iowa, 1924.

Hornaday, William T. "The Extermination of the American Bison." U.S. National Museum, *Annual Report,* 1887, pp. 496–501.

Howard, Helen A., and D. L. McGrath. *War Chief Joseph.* Caldwell, Idaho, Caxton Printers, 1941.

Howard, James H. *The Ponca Tribe* (Bureau of American Ethnology Bulletin 195). Washington, D.C., 1965.

Howard, O. O. *My Life and Experiences Among Our Hostile Indians.* Hartford, Connecticut, 1907.

Hyde, George E. *Life of George Bent;* written from his letters. Edited by Savoie Lottinville. Norman, University of Oklahoma Press, 1967.

————. *Red Cloud's Folk; a History of the Oglala Sioux Indians.* Norman, University of Oklahoma Press, 1937.

————. *A Sioux Chronicle.* Norman, University of Oklahoma Press, 1956.

————. *Spotted Tail's Folk, a History of the Brulé Sioux.* Norman, University of Oklahoma Press, 1961.

Jackson, Donald. *Custer's Gold, the United States Cavalry Expedition of 1874.* New Haven, Yale University Press, 1966.

John Stands in Timber and Margot Liberty. *Cheyenne Memories.* New Haven, Yale University Press, 1967.

Jones, Douglas C. *The Treaty of Medicine Lodge.* Norman, University of Oklahoma Press, 1966.

Josephy, Alvin M., Jr. *The Nez Percé Indians and the Opening of the Northwest.* New Haven, Yale University Press, 1965.

————. *The Patriot Chiefs.* New York, Viking, 1961.

Kappler, Charles J. *Indian Affairs, Laws and Treaties.* 4 Vols. Washington, D.C., 1904–1927.

Lavender, David. *Bent's Fort.* New York, Doubleday, 1954.

Leckie, William H. *The Military Conquest of the Southern Plains.* Norman, University of Oklahoma Press, 1963.

"The Liquidation of Dull Knife." *Nebraska History*, Vol. 22, 1941, pp. 109–10.

Lockwood, Frank C. *Pioneer Days in Arizona*. New York, Macmillan, 1932.

McCreight, M. L. *Firewater and Forked Tongues; a Sioux Chief Interprets U.S. History*. Pasadena, Calif., Trail's End Pub. Co., 1947.

McGillycuddy, Julia B. *McGillycuddy Agent*. Palo Alto, Stanford University Press, 1941.

McGregor, James H. *The Wounded Knee Massacre from the Viewpoint of the Survivors*. Baltimore, Wirth Bros., 1940.

McLaughlin, James. *My Friend the Indian*. Boston, Houghton Mifflin, 1910.

McWhorter, Lucullus V. *Yellow Wolf: His Own Story*. Caldwell, Idaho, 1940.

Marquis, Thomas B. *Wooden Leg, a Warrior Who Fought Custer*. Lincoln, University of Nebraska Press, 1957.

Marriott, Alice. *The Ten Grandmothers*. Norman, University of Oklahoma Press, 1945.

Mayhall, Mildred P. *The Kiowas*. Norman, University of Oklahoma Press, 1962.

Meacham, A. B. *Wigwam and Warpath*. Boston, 1875.

Meyer, Roy W. *History of the Santee Sioux*. Lincoln, University of Nebraska Press, 1967.

Murray, Keith A. *The Modocs and Their War*. Norman, University of Oklahoma Press, 1959.

Neihardt, John G. *Black Elk Speaks*. Lincoln, University of Nebraska Press, 1961.

New York *Herald*, 1872.

Nye, W. S. *Bad Medicine and Good; Tales of the Kiowas*. Norman, University of Oklahoma Press, 1962.

———. *Carbine and Lance; the Story of Old Fort Sill*. Norman, University of Oklahoma Press, 1937.

———. *Plains Indian Raiders*. Norman, University of Oklahoma Press, 1968.

Oehler, C. M. *The Great Sioux Uprising*. New York, Oxford University Press, 1959.

Olson, James C. *Red Cloud and the Sioux Problem*. Lincoln, University of Nebraska Press, 1965.

Omaha Weekly Herald, 1868.

Palmer, H. E. "History of the Powder River Indian Expedition of 1865." Nebraska State Historical Society, *Transactions and Reports*, Vol. II, 1887, pp. 197–229.

Parker, Arthur C. *The Life of General Ely S. Parker*. Buffalo, N.Y.,
  Buffalo Historical Society, 1919.
A Pictographic History of the Oglala Sioux, drawings by Amos Bad
  Heart Bull, text by Helen H. Blish. Lincoln, University of Ne-
  braska Press, 1967.
Praus, Alexis A. *A New Pictographic Autobiography of Sitting Bull*
  (Smithsonian Miscellaneous Collections, Vol. 123, No. 6). Wash-
  ington, D.C., 1955.
Riddle, Jeff C. *The Indian History of the Modoc War*. 1914.
Riggs, S. R. "Narrative of Paul Mazakootemane." Minnesota Histori-
  cal Society, *Collections*, Vol. 3, 1880, pp. 82–90.
Robinson, D. W. "Editorial Notes on Historical Sketch of North and
  South Dakota." *South Dakota Historical Collections*, Vol. I,
  1902, pp. 85–162.
Robinson, Doane. "Crazy Horse's Story of Custer Battle." *South
  Dakota Historical Collections*, Vol. VI, 1912, pp. 224–28.
———. *A History of the Dakota or Sioux Indians*. Minneapolis, Ross
  & Haines, 1967.
Sacks, Benjamin H. "New Evidence on the Bascom Affair." *Arizona
  and the West*, Vol. 4, 1962, pp. 261–78.
Salzman, M., Jr. "Geronimo the Napoleon of Indians." *Journal of
  Arizona History*, Vol. 8, 1967, pp. 215–47.
Sandoz, Mari. *Cheyenne Autumn*. New York, Hastings House, 1953.
———. *Crazy Horse, the Strange Man of the Oglalas*. New York,
  Knopf, 1945.
———. *Hostiles and Friendlies*. Lincoln, University of Nebraska
  Press, 1959.
Schellie, Don. *Vast Domain of Blood; the Camp Grant Massacre*.
  Los Angeles, Westernlore, 1968.
Schmeckebier, Lawrence F. *The Office of Indian Affairs; Its History,
  Activities, and Organization*. Baltimore, Johns Hopkins Press,
  1927.
Schmitt, Martin F., and Dee Brown. *Fighting Indians of the West*.
  New York, Scribner's, 1948.
Scott, Hugh L. *Some Memories of a Soldier*. New York, Century Co.,
  1928.
Seymour, Flora W. *Indian Agents of the Old Frontier*. New York,
  Appleton-Century, 1941.
Sheldon, Addison E. *Nebraska, the Land and the People*. Vol. I. Chi-
  cago, Lewis Publishing Co., 1931.
Shields, G. O. *Battle of the Big Hole*. Chicago, 1889.
Sonnichsen, C. L. *The Mescalero Apaches*. Norman, University of
  Oklahoma Press, 1958.

Sprague, Marshall. *Massacre; the Tragedy at White River.* Boston, Little, Brown, 1957.

Stanley, F. *Satanta and the Kiowas.* Borger, Texas, 1968.

Stanley, Henry M. *My Early Travels and Adventures.* Vol. I. New York, Scribner's, 1895.

Stewart, Edgar I. *Custer's Luck.* Norman, University of Oklahoma Press, 1955.

Stirling, M. W. *Three Pictographic Autobiographies of Sitting Bull* (Smithsonian Miscellaneous Collections, Vol. 97, No. 5). Washington, D.C., 1938.

Swanton, John R. *The Indian Tribes of North America.* Washington, D.C., 1952.

"Ta-oya-te-duta Is Not a Coward." *Minnesota History,* Vol. 38, 1962, p. 115.

Tatum, Lawrie. *Our Red Brothers and the Peace Policy of President Ulysses Grant.* Philadelphia, Winston, 1899.

Taylor, Alfred A. "Medicine Lodge Peace Council." *Chronicles of Oklahoma,* Vol. 2, 1924, pp. 98–118.

Thrapp, Dan L. *The Conquest of Apacheria.* Norman, University of Oklahoma Press, 1967.

Tibbles, Thomas Henry. *Buckskin and Blanket Days.* New York, Doubleday, 1957.

Towl, Edwin S. "Judge Elmer S. Dundy." Nebraska State Historical Society, *Proceedings and Collections,* Second Series, Vol. V, 1902, pp. 83–95.

Trenerry, Walter N. "The Shooting of Little Crow: Heroism or Murder?" *Minnesota History,* Vol. 38, 1962, pp. 150–53.

Turner, Katherine C. *Red Men Calling on the Great White Father.* Norman, University of Oklahoma Press, 1951.

Tyler, Barbara Ann. "Cochise: Apache War Leader, 1858–1861." *Journal of Arizona History,* Vol. 6, 1965, pp. 1–10.

U.S. Board of Indian Commissioners. *Reports,* 1869–1891.

U.S. Bureau of American Ethnology. *Annual Reports,* 10th, 14th, 17th, and 46th.

U.S. Census Office. *Report on Indians Taxed and Indians Not Taxed in the United States.* Washington, D.C., 1894.

U.S. Commission to Investigate the Affair of the Red Cloud Indian Agency. *Report,* July, 1875. Washington, D.C., 1875.

U.S. Commissioner of Indian Affairs. *Annual Reports,* 1860–1891.

U.S. Congress. 38th. 2nd session. Senate Report 142.

U.S. Congress. 39th. 2nd session. House Miscellaneous Document 37.

U.S. Congress. 39th. 2nd session. Senate Executive Document 26.

U.S. Congress. 39th. 2nd session. Senate Report 156.

U.S. Congress. 40th. 1st session. Senate Executive Document 13.
U.S. Congress. 40th. 2nd session. House Executive Document 97.
U.S. Congress. 41st. 3rd session. House Report 39.
U.S. Congress. 41st. 3rd session. Senate Executive Document 39.
U.S. Congress. 43rd. 1st session. House Executive Document 122.
U.S. Congress. 44th. 1st session. House Executive Document 184.
U.S. Congress. 44th. 2nd session. Senate Executive Document 9.
U.S. Congress. 46th. 2nd session. House Executive Document 83.
U.S. Congress. 46th. 2nd session. House Miscellaneous Document 38.
U.S. Congress. 46th. 2nd session. Senate Report 708.
U.S. Congress. 46th. 3rd session. Senate Executive Document 14.
U.S. Congress. 46th. 3rd session. Senate Executive Document 30.
U.S. Congress. 48th. 1st session. Senate Report 283.
U.S. Congress. 49th. 1st session. House Executive Document 356.
U.S. Congress. 49th. 2nd session. Senate Executive Document 117.
U.S. Congress. 50th. 1st session. Senate Executive Document 33.
U.S. Congress. 50th. 2nd session. Senate Executive Document 17.
U.S. Congress. 51st. 1st session. Senate Executive Document 51.
U.S. Interior Department. *Annual Reports,* 1860–1891.
U.S. National Park Service. *Soldier and Brave.* New York, Harper & Row, 1963.
U.S. War Department. *Annual Reports,* 1860–1891.
U.S. War Department. Military Division of the Missouri. *Record of Engagements with Hostile Indians . . . 1868–1882.* Washington, D.C., 1882.
Urquhart, Lena M. *Colorow, the Angry Chieftain.* Denver, Golden Bell Press, 1968.
Utley, Robert M. "The Bascom Affair; a Reconstruction." *Arizona and the West,* Vol. 3, 1961, pp. 59–68.
———. *Custer and the Great Controversy.* Los Angeles, Westernlore, 1962.
———. *Frontiersmen in Blue; the U.S. Army and the Indian, 1848–1865.* New York, Macmillan, 1967.
———. *The Last Days of the Sioux Nation.* New Haven, Yale University Press, 1963.
Vaughn, J. W. *The Battle of Platte Bridge.* Norman, University of Oklahoma Press, 1964.
———. *Indian Fights; New Facts on Seven Encounters.* Norman, University of Oklahoma Press, 1966.
———. *The Reynolds Campaign on Powder River.* Norman, University of Oklahoma Press, 1961.
———. *With Crook at the Rosebud.* Harrisburg, Pa., Stackpole, 1956.

Vestal, Stanley. *Sitting Bull, Champion of the Sioux.* Norman, University of Oklahoma Press, 1957.

———. *Warpath and Council Fire.* New York, Random House, 1948.

Wallace, Ernest, and E. Adamson Hoebel. *The Comanches, Lords of the South Plains.* Norman, University of Oklahoma Press, 1952.

Ware, Eugene F. *The Indian War of 1864.* New York, St. Martin's Press, 1960.

Welsh, William. *Report and Supplementary Report, of a Visit to Spotted Tail's Tribe of Brulé Sioux Indians.* Philadelphia, 1870.

West, G. Derek. "The Battle of Adobe Walls (1874)." *Panhandle-Plains Historical Review,* Vol. 36, 1963, pp. 1–36.

The Westerners. Potomac Corral, Washington, D.C. *Great Western Indian Fights.* New York, Doubleday, 1960.

White Bull, Joseph. *The Warrior Who Killed Custer . . .* Translated and edited by James H. Howard. Lincoln, University of Nebraska Press, 1968.

Winks, Robin W. "The British North American West and the Civil War." *North Dakota History,* Vol. 24, 1957, pp. 139–52.

Wright, Peter M. "The Pursuit of Dull Knife from Fort Reno in 1878–1879." *Chronicles of Oklahoma,* Vol. 46, 1968, pp. 141–54.

INDEX

C

G

H

M

484

Index